Maker Innovations Series

Jump start your path to discovery with the Apress Maker Innovations series! From the basics of electricity and components through to the most advanced options in robotics and Machine Learning, you'll forge a path to building ingenious hardware and controlling it with cutting-edge software. All while gaining new skills and experience with common toolsets you can take to new projects or even into a whole new career.

The Apress Maker Innovations series offers projects-based learning, while keeping theory and best processes front and center. So you get hands-on experience while also learning the terms of the trade and how entrepreneurs, inventors, and engineers think through creating and executing hardware projects. You can learn to design circuits, program AI, create IoT systems for your home or even city, and so much more!

Whether you're a beginning hobbyist or a seasoned entrepreneur working out of your basement or garage, you'll scale up your skillset to become a hardware design and engineering pro. And often using low-cost and open-source software such as the Raspberry Pi, Arduino, PIC microcontroller, and Robot Operating System (ROS). Programmers and software engineers have great opportunities to learn, too, as many projects and control environments are based in popular languages and operating systems, such as Python and Linux.

If you want to build a robot, set up a smart home, tackle assembling a weather-ready meteorology system, or create a brand-new circuit using breadboards and circuit design software, this series has all that and more! Written by creative and seasoned Makers, every book in the series tackles both tested and leading-edge approaches and technologies for bringing your visions and projects to life.

More information about this series at https://link.springer.com/bookseries/17311

Simulation of Power Electronics Circuits with MATLAB®/ Simulink®

Design, Analyze, and Prototype Power Electronics

Farzin Asadi
Maltepe University
Istanbul, Turkey

Apress®

Simulation of Power Electronics Circuits with MATLAB®/Simulink®: Design, Analyze, and Prototype Power Electronics

Farzin Asadi
Maltepe University
Istanbul, Turkey

ISBN-13 (pbk): 978-1-4842-8219-9 ISBN-13 (electronic): 978-1-4842-8220-5
https://doi.org/10.1007/978-1-4842-8220-5

Managing Director, Apress Media LLC: Welmoed Spahr
Acquisitions Editor: Aaron Black
Development Editor: James Markham
Coordinating Editor: Jessica Vakili

Distributed to the book trade worldwide by Springer Science+Business Media New York, 233 Spring Street, 6th Floor, New York, NY 10013. Phone 1-800-SPRINGER, fax (201) 348-4505, e-mail orders-ny@springer-sbm.com, or visit www.springeronline.com. Apress Media, LLC is a California LLC and the sole member (owner) is Springer Science + Business Media Finance Inc (SSBM Finance Inc). SSBM Finance Inc is a **Delaware** corporation.

For information on translations, please e-mail booktranslations@springernature.com; for reprint, paperback, or audio rights, please e-mail bookpermissions@springernature.com.

Apress titles may be purchased in bulk for academic, corporate, or promotional use. eBook versions and licenses are also available for most titles. For more information, reference our Print and eBook Bulk Sales web page at http://www.apress.com/bulk-sales.

Any source code or other supplementary material referenced by the author in this book is available to readers on the Github repository: https://github.com/Apress/Simulation-of-Power-Electronics-Circuits-with-MATLAB®/Simulink®. For more detailed information, please visit http://www.apress.com/source-code.

Printed on acid-free paper

Dedicated to my lovely brother, Farzad, and my lovely sisters, Farnaz and Farzaneh.

Table of Contents

About the Author

Farzin Asadi received his BSc in electronics engineering, MSc in control engineering, and PhD in mechatronics engineering.

Currently, he is with the Department of Electrical and Electronics Engineering at the Maltepe University, Istanbul, Turkey.

Dr. Asadi has published more than 40 international papers and 16 books. He is on the editorial board of seven scientific journals as well. His research interests include switching converters, control theory, robust control of power electronic converters, and robotics.

About the Technical Reviewers

Vishwesh Ravi Shrimali graduated from BITS Pilani, where he studied mechanical engineering, in 2018. Since then, he has worked with Big Vision LLC on deep learning and computer vision and was involved in creating official OpenCV AI courses. Currently, he is working at Mercedes-Benz Research & Development India Pvt. Ltd. He has a keen interest in programming and AI and has applied that interest in mechanical engineering projects. He has also written multiple blogs on OpenCV and deep learning on LearnOpenCV, a leading blog on computer vision. He has also authored *Machine Learning for OpenCV 4* (second edition) by Packt. When he is not writing blogs or working on projects, he likes to go on long walks or play his acoustic guitar.

Sawai Pongswatd received his B.Sc. in Instrumentation Engineering, M.Sc. in Electrical Engineering and Ph.D. in Electrical Engineering. Currently he is with the Department of Instrumentation and Control Engineering, King Mongkut's Institute of Technology Ladkrabang (KMITL), Bangkok, Thailand.

Dr. Pongswatd is a chairman of technical committee of Thai Industrial Standards Institute and instructor of Fieldbus Certified Training Program (FCTP). His research interests include power electronics, energy conversion, and industrial applications.

Preface

A computer simulation is an attempt to model a real-life or hypothetical situation on a computer so that it can be studied to see how the system works. By changing variables in the simulation, predictions may be made about the behavior of the system. So computer simulation is a tool to virtually investigate the behavior of the system under study.

Computer simulation has many applications in science, engineering, education, and even entertainment. For instance, pilots use computer simulations to practice what they learned without any danger and loss of life.

This book shows you how you can simulate a power electronic circuit in a MATLAB®/Simulink® environment. This book can accompany any standard textbook on power electronics. Students who take/took power electronics/industrial electronics/electrical drive courses can use this book as a reference to learn how to simulate a power electronic circuit with the aid of Simulink. This book will be useful for engineers who want to simulate a power electronic circuit in a MATLAB/Simulink environment as well.

This book is composed of 11 chapters. A brief summary of the book chapters is as follows:

Chapters 1 and 2 introduce the Simulink environment. These chapters have 14 sample simulations.

Chapters 3, 4, 5, 6, and 7 show how you can simulate a power electronic circuit in a Simulink environment. These chapters have 40 sample simulations.

The original version of this book was revised. A correction to this book is available at https://doi.org/10.1007/978-1-4842-8220-5_12

Chapters 8, 9 and 10 show how you can obtain the small-signal transfer functions of a DC-DC converter and its input/output impedance with the aid of MATLAB programming. Three examples are studied in these chapters.

Chapter 11 reviews some of the important theoretical concepts used in the book.

I hope that this book will be useful to the readers, and I welcome comments on the book.

CHAPTER 1

Introduction to Simulink®

Simulink is a software package for modeling, simulating, and analyzing dynamic systems. It supports linear and nonlinear systems, modeled in continuous time, sampled time, or a hybrid of the two.

This chapter shows the basics of simulation with Simulink. It contains five examples, and they aim to make you familiar with the Simulink environment and how to do a simulation there. You can start from the next chapter if you are familiar with the Simulink environment.

Power Electronic Circuits and Simulation

Power electronics is the application of solid-state electronics to the control and conversion of electric power with high efficiency. Power electronic converters can be divided into four groups: AC-DC converters (rectifiers), DC-AC converters (inverters), DC-DC converters, and AC-AC converters.

Computer simulation is a tool to virtually investigate the behavior of the system under study. Computer simulation of power electronic converters is an easy, safe, and cheap way to observe the behavior of the converter (i.e., voltage of nodes and current of branches) and ensure that the converter does what we exactly need. Computer simulation permits

© Farzin Asadi 2022
F. Asadi, *Simulation of Power Electronics Circuits with MATLAB*/Simulink*,
Maker Innovations Series, https://doi.org/10.1007/978-1-4842-8220-5_1

us to test our ideas before we go wasting all that time building it with a breadboard or printed circuit board (PCB), just to find out it doesn't really work.

MATLAB®/Simulink® is one of the most powerful software for simulation of power electronic circuits. MATLAB/Simulink simulation results are accurate and quite close to laboratory measurements. When you want to simulate a power electronic converter with MATLAB/Simulink, you can use all of the ready-to-use blocks available in the Simulink environment. This is a very interesting property. For instance, assume that you want to simulate a DC-DC converter, which is controlled with a Fuzzy Logic controller. In this case you can simply use the ready-to-use Fuzzy Logic Toolbox® blocks. If you try to do the same simulation in other software, you need to consume a considerable amount of time to model the Fuzzy Logic controller from the ground up.

Example 1: Step Response of a Transfer Function Model

In this example a transfer function is stimulated with a unit step signal, and its response is observed.

Enter the Simulink environment with the aid of the simulink command (see Figures 1-1 and 1-2).

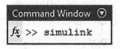

Figure 1-1. *simulink command*

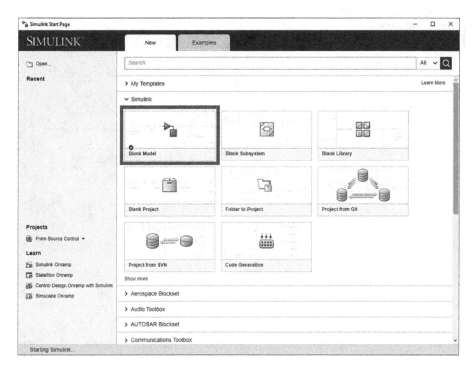

Figure 1-2. *Simulink Start Page*

The Simulink Start Page window appears. Click the Blank Model.

Now the Simulink environment with a blank project is ready (Figure 1-3).

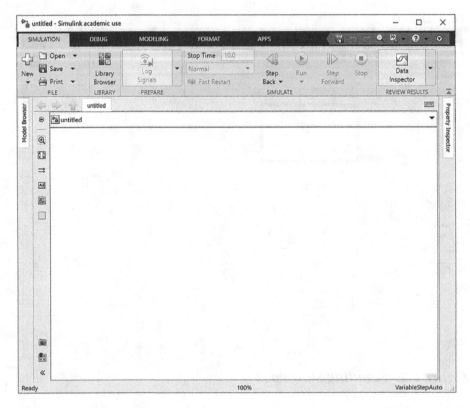

Figure 1-3. *Simulink environment*

Click the Library Browser button (Figure 1-4).

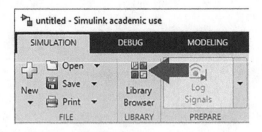

Figure 1-4. *Library Browser button*

After clicking the Library Browser icon, the Simulink Library Browser window (see Figure 1-5) will be opened, and you can add required components to the model.

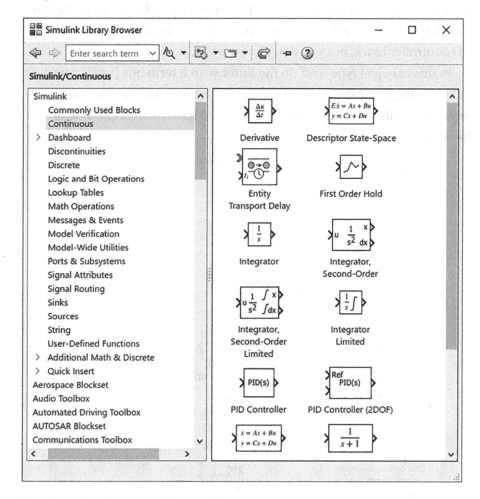

Figure 1-5. *Simulink Library Browser*

Locating Blocks

Simulink Library Browser contains many blocks, and it is impossible to memorize each block location. The Enter search term box is useful to find a block when you forgot its location. For instance, assume that you need a PID controller block, but you don't know where it is.

In this case just type "pid" in the Enter search term box (see Figure 1-6) and press the Enter key of your keyboard. After pressing the Enter key, Simulink will list blocks related to the entered term on the right side of the window.

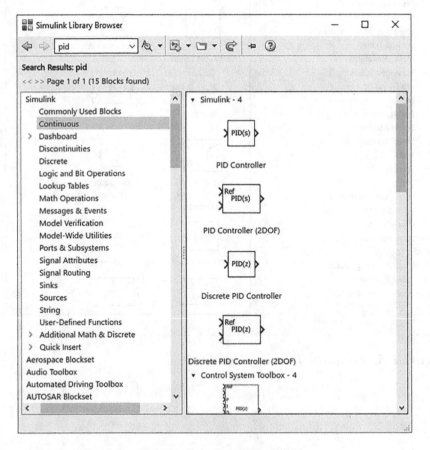

Figure 1-6. *Searching for blocks related to "pid"*

The Transfer Fcn block can be found in the Continuous section of Simulink Library Browser (see Figure 1-7). Click the Transfer Fcn block to select it. Then drag and drop it to the model (see Figure 1-8).

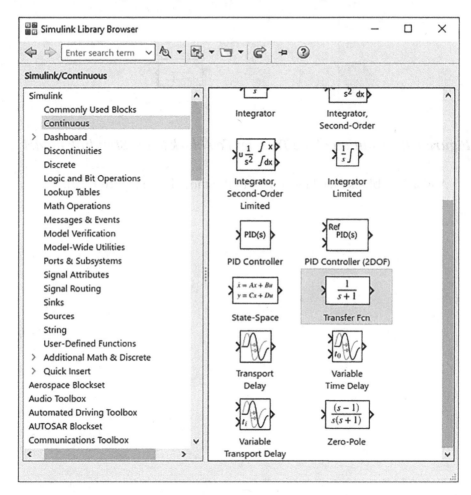

Figure 1-7. *Transfer Fcn block*

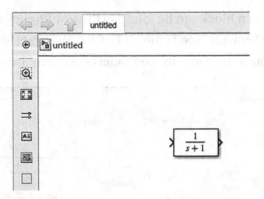

Figure 1-8. *Addition of the Transfer Fcn block to the Simulink model*

Add a Step block (see Figure 1-9) to the model (see Figure 1-10).

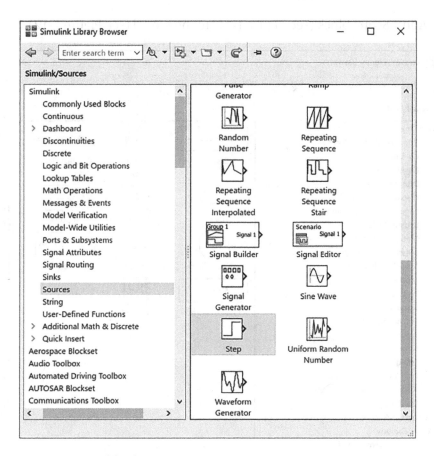

Figure 1-9. *Step block*

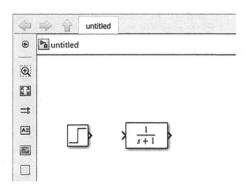

Figure 1-10. *Addition of the Step block to the Simulink model*

Add a Scope block (see Figure 1-11) to the model (see Figure 1-12).

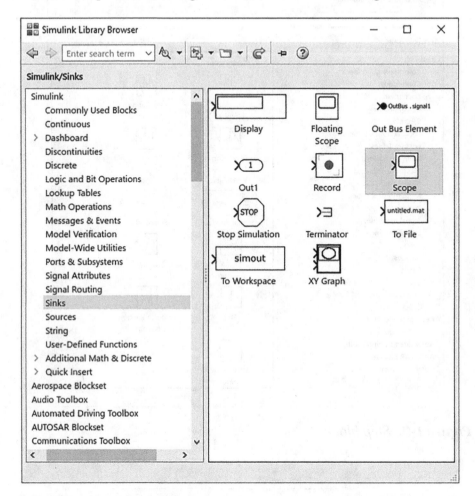

Figure 1-11. *Scope block*

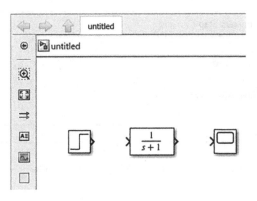

Figure 1-12. *Addition of the Scope block to the Simulink model*

When you bring the mouse pointer close to the block terminals, it will be changed to crosshair and permits you to start connecting them. After seeing the crosshair, hold down the left button on the mouse and drag the connection toward the destination terminal and release the button on the destination terminal. Use this method to connect the blocks together (Figure 1-13).

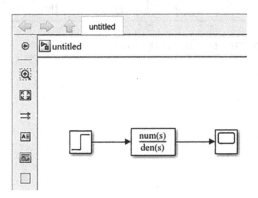

Figure 1-13. *Connecting the blocks together*

Double-click the blocks and configure their settings as shown in Figures 1-14 and 1-15. Settings of Figure 1-14 generate a pulse, which jumps from 0 to 1 at t=0. Settings of Figure 1-15 simulate the $\dfrac{100}{s^2 + 8s + 100}$ transfer function.

11

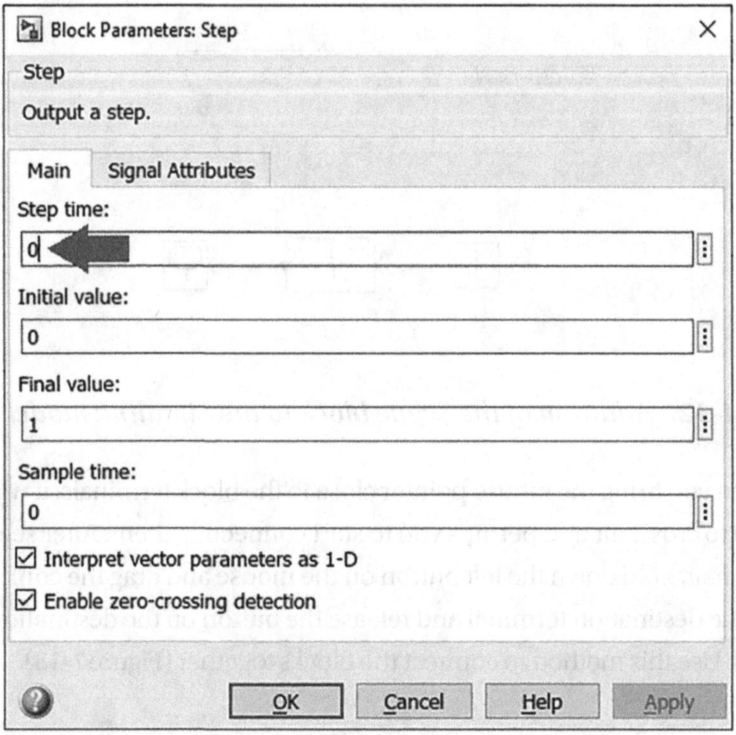

Figure 1-14. *Settings of the Step block*

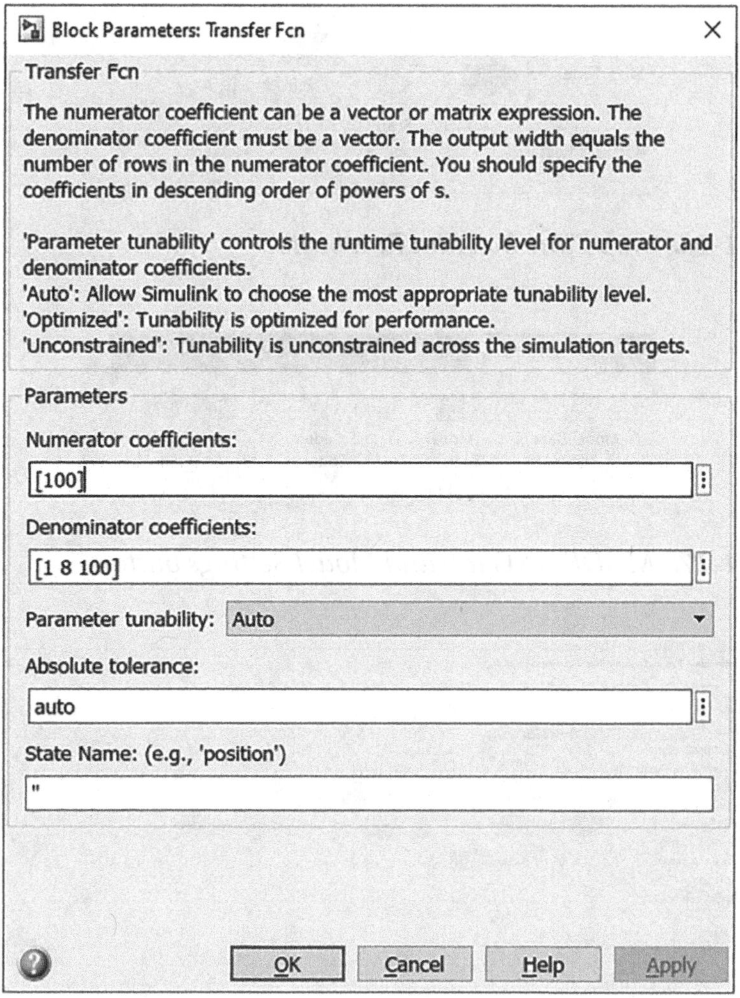

Figure 1-15. *Settings of the Transfer Fcn block*

Assume that you want to simulate the behavior of the system for time length of 2 s. Enter 2 in the Stop Time box and click the Run button (or press Ctrl+T) to simulate the behavior of the system (see Figure 1-16). Sometimes you need to do the simulation with a specific solver. In these cases, use Model Settings (see Figure 1-17) to select the desired solver. After clicking the Model Settings icon (or pressing Ctrl+E), the window shown in Figure 1-18 appears, and you can select the desired type of solver.

13

Figure 1-16. *Stop Time box and Run button*

Figure 1-17. *MODELING tab and Model Settings button*

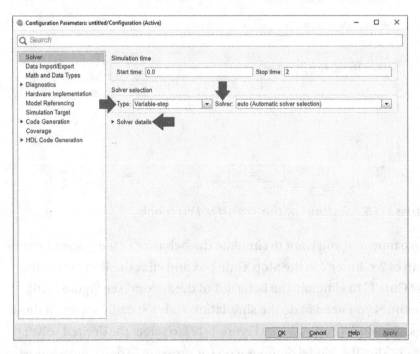

Figure 1-18. *Solver section of the Configuration Parameters window*

The simulation result is shown in Figure 1-19. It can be copied into the clipboard by pressing Ctrl+C. You can paste the copied waveform in other software by pressing Ctrl+V. This is very useful when you want to prepare a presentation or report.

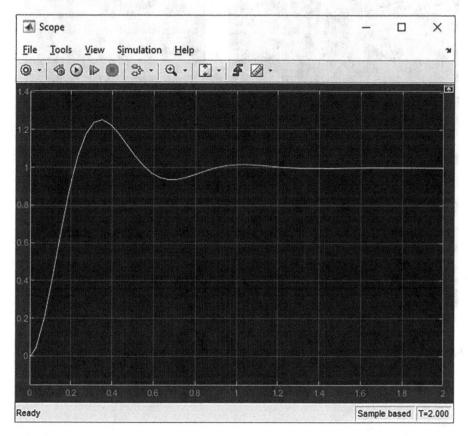

Figure 1-19. *Simulation result*

You can use Cursor Measurement (see Figure 1-20) to read the coordinates of different points on the graph. After clicking Cursor Measurement, two vertical lines will be added to the graph (see Figure 1-21). You can move them to read the coordinates of different points on the graph.

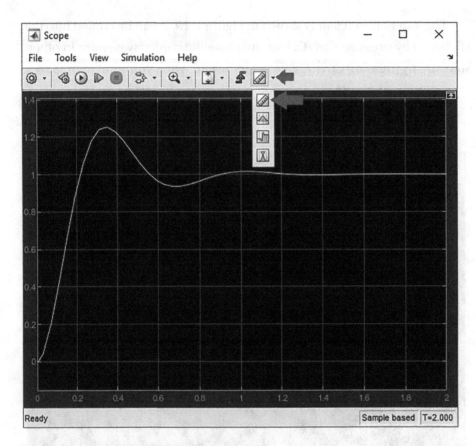

Figure 1-20. *Cursor Measurement icon*

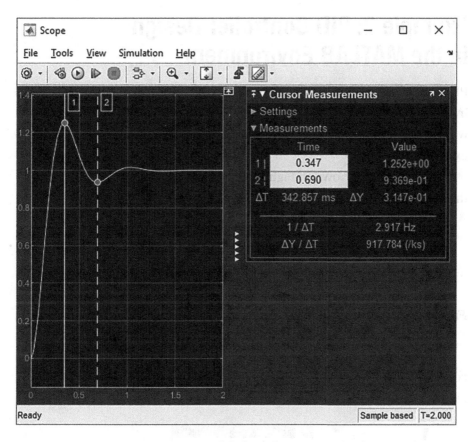

Figure 1-21. *Two cursors are added to the Scope block*

In this example you learned how to do a simple simulation in the Simulink environment. In the next example, we will learn how to tune a PID controller in MATLAB. PID controllers can be tuned in the Simulink environment as well. Tuning of PID controllers in the Simulink environment is studied in Example 4.

Example 2: PID Controller Design in the MATLAB Environment

PID controllers are the most widely used type of controllers used in industry. MATLAB can be used to tune the PID controllers. In this example we want to design a PID controller for the transfer function of the previous example.

The command shown in Figure 1-22 enters the transfer function into the MATLAB environment.

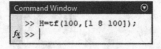

Figure 1-22. *Entering the* $H(s) = \dfrac{100}{s^2 + 8s + 100}$ *into MATLAB*

The pidTuner command (see Figure 1-23) helps you tune the PID controller. After running the pidTuner command, the window shown in Figure 1-24 appears.

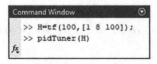

Figure 1-23. *pidTuner command*

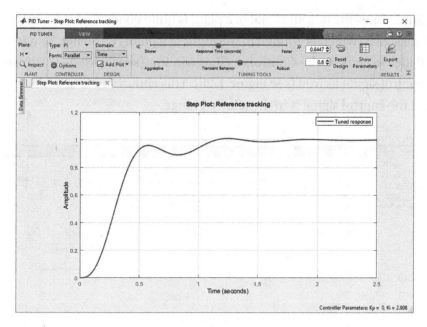

Figure 1-24. *PID Tuner window*

Move the sliders until you obtain a good response. By default, the PID Tuner does the tuning in the time domain (see Figure 1-25). You can do it in the frequency domain, as well (see Figure 1-26).

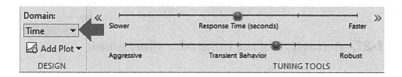

Figure 1-25. *Tuning is done in the time domain*

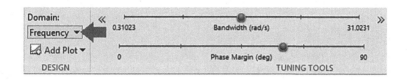

Figure 1-26. *Tuning is done in the frequency domain*

Sometimes the output signal of a plant is quite good; however, the control signal (which is applied to the input of a plant) is too big. So it is a good idea to activate the Controller effort window (see Figure 1-27) to see the control signal as well (see Figure 1-28). This allows you to see whether or not the control signal is in the allowed range.

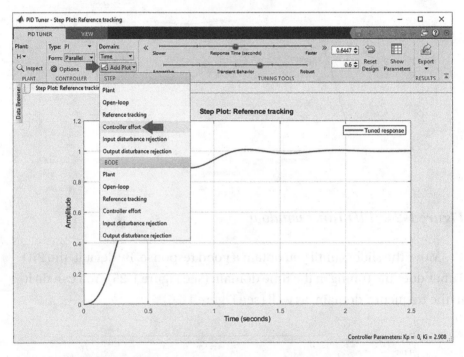

Figure 1-27. *Activation of the Controller effort graph*

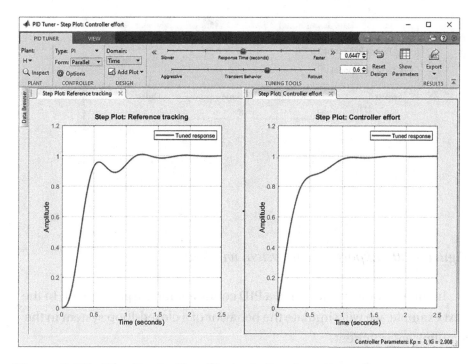

Figure 1-28. *The Controller effort window is activated*

After designing a suitable controller, you can export the designed controller to the MATLAB environment by clicking the Export button (see Figure 1-29). After clicking the Export button, the window shown in Figure 1-30 appears. Enter the desired name in the Export PID controller box and click the OK button.

Figure 1-29. *Export button*

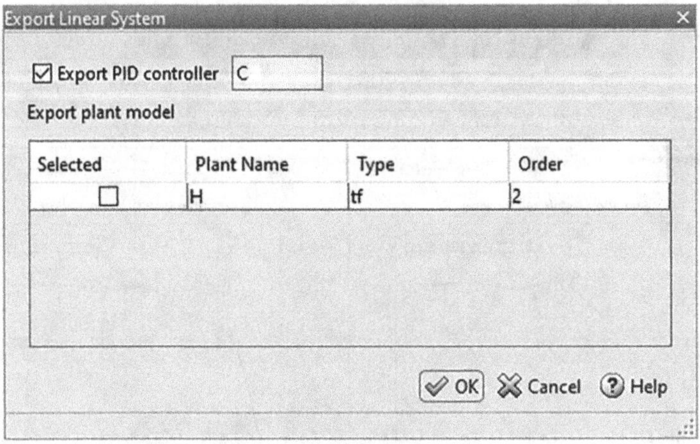

Figure 1-30. *Export Linear System window*

In this example we designed a PID controller for the given plant. In the next example, we will simulate the behavior of a closed-loop system in the Simulink environment.

Example 3: Feedback Control System

A feedback control system uses one or more than one sensor to measure the output of the system, compare the measured output with a reference signal, and give a suitable input to the system under control based on the difference between the reference signal and output of the system. MATLAB/Simulink has many tools for analysis and design of feedback control systems. In this example we will simulate a feedback control system in Simulink.

Consider the feedback control system shown in Figure 1-31.

$$\frac{100}{s^2 + 8s + 100}$$

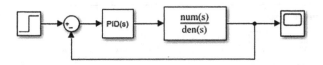

Figure 1-31. *Simulink model of Example 3*

The plant transfer function is $\dfrac{100}{s^2 + 8s + 100}$. This simulation uses the Sum (see Figure 1-32) and PID Controller (see Figure 1-33) blocks. Settings of the Sum and PID Controller blocks are shown in Figures 1-34 and 1-35, respectively.

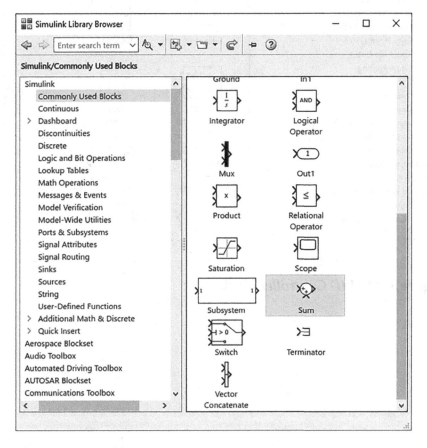

Figure 1-32. *Sum block*

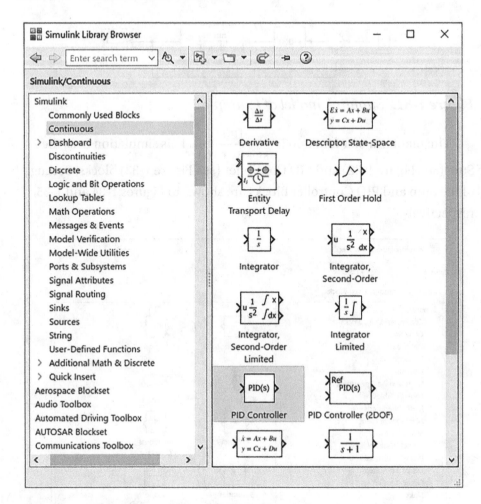

Figure 1-33. *PID Controller block*

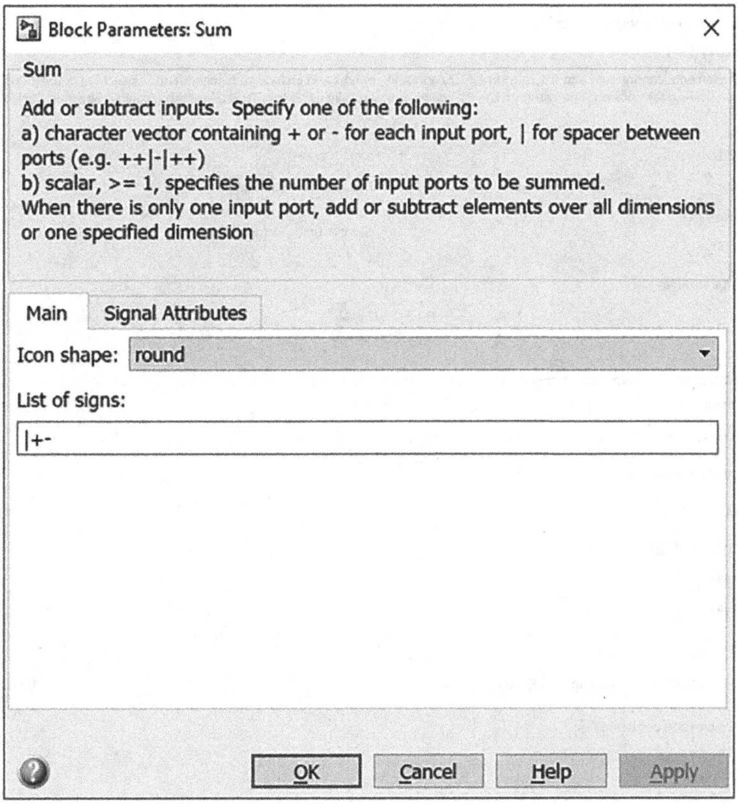

Figure 1-34. *Settings of the Sum block*

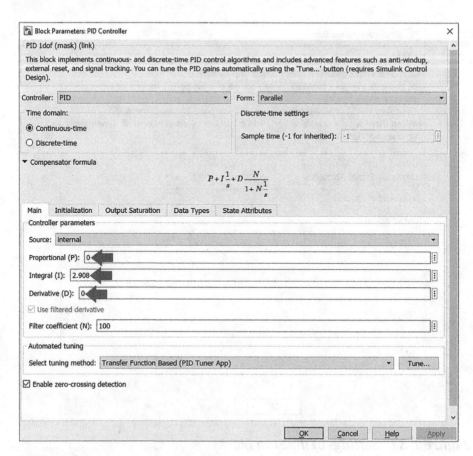

Figure 1-35. *Settings of the PID Controller block*

Run the simulation. The result shown in Figure 1-36 is obtained.

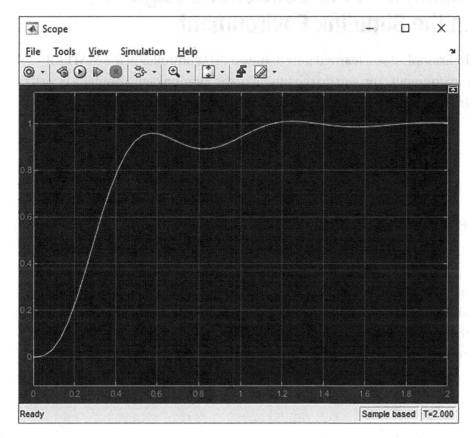

Figure 1-36. *Simulation result*

In Example 2 you learned how to design a PID controller in the MATLAB environment. In the next example, we will learn how to design the PID controller in the Simulink environment.

Example 4: PID Controller Design in the Simulink Environment

In Example 2 you learned how to tune a PID controller in the MATLAB environment. You can do the tuning in the Simulink environment as well. In this example we will tune a PID controller in the Simulink environment.

Consider the Simulink model shown in Figure 1-37.

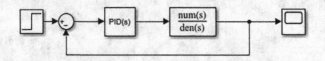

Figure 1-37. *Simulink model of Example 4*

The plant transfer function is $\dfrac{100}{s^2+8s+100}$. The PID Controller block has the default parameter values. Double-click the PID Controller block and click the Tune button (see Figure 1-38). After clicking the Tune button, the window shown in Figure 1-39 appears and permits you to tune the controller.

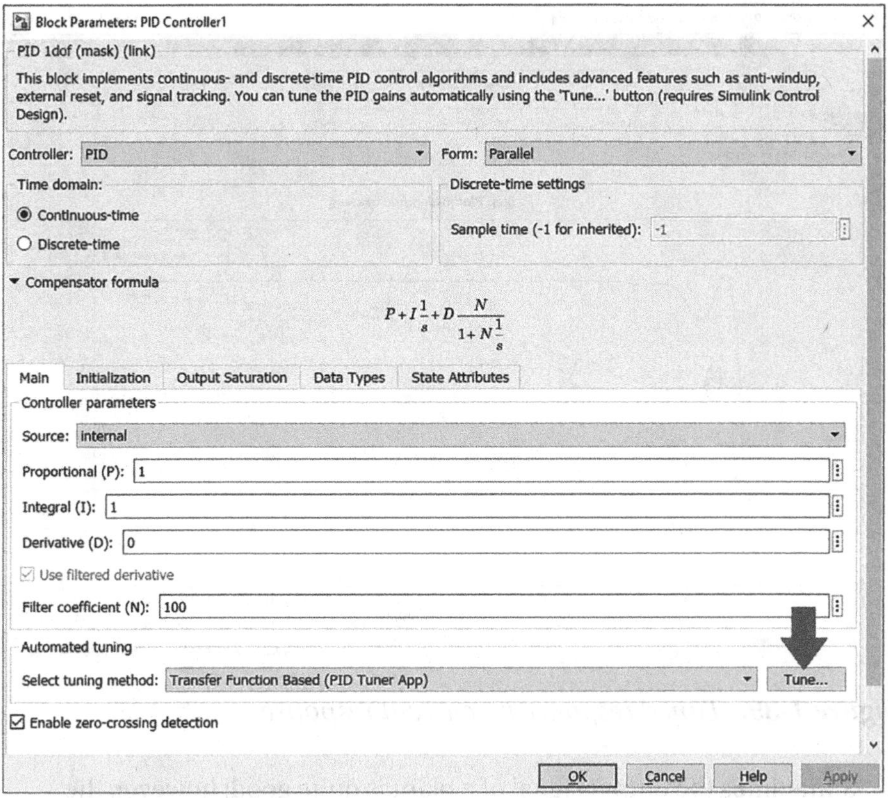

Figure 1-38. *PID Controller block settings*

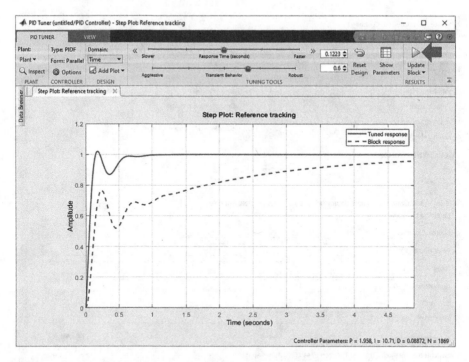

Figure 1-39. *Tuned response vs. current response*

Sometimes the output signal of a plant is quite good; however, the control signal (which is applied to the input of a plant) is too big. So it is a good idea to activate the Controller effort window (see Figure 1-40) to see the control signal as well (see Figure 1-41). This allows you to see whether or not the control signal is in the allowed range. After tuning the controller, click the Update Block button to apply the changes to the block.

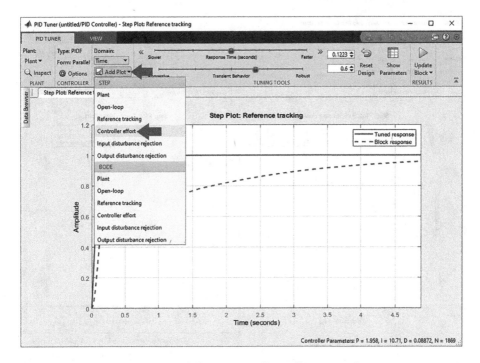

Figure 1-40. *Activation of the Controller effort graph*

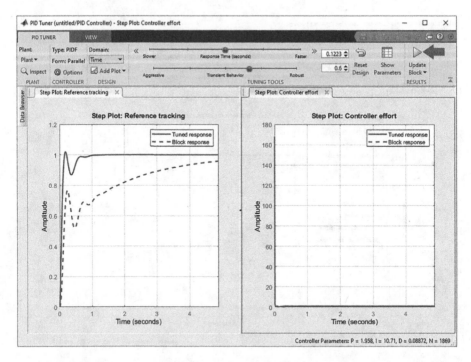

Figure 1-41. *The Controller effort window is activated*

Up to this point, the Scope blocks showed a graph of one signal only. Sometimes you need to view two or more signals simultaneously. We will learn how to do this in the next example.

Example 5: Plot Two or More Waveforms on One Scope Block

In this example we'll review a couple ways to view two or more signals simultaneously. Viewing two or more signals simultaneously permits you to clearly see the relationship between them. For instance, you can view the input and output simultaneously on a Scope block. This helps you observe the effect of the input on the output.

Option 1: Increasing the Number of Inputs on the Scope Block

Consider the model shown in Figure 1-42. The plant transfer function is $\dfrac{100}{s^2 + 8s + 100}$. Settings of the PID Controller block are shown in Figure 1-43.

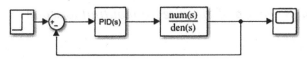

Figure 1-42. *Simulink model of Example 5*

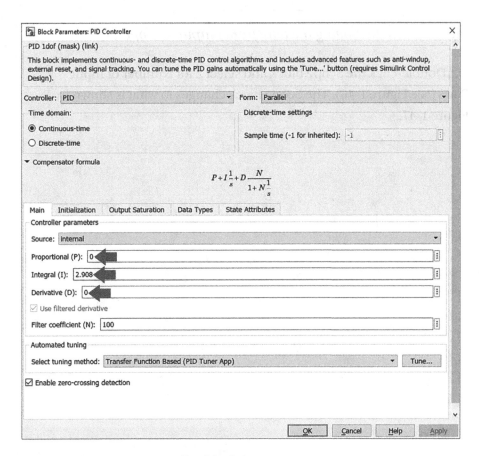

Figure 1-43. *PID Controller block settings*

Click the connection between the scope and output of the system (see Figure 1-44) and press the Delete key to remove it (see Figure 1-45).

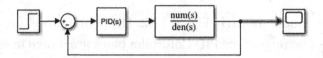

Figure 1-44. *Selection of the wire from output to scope*

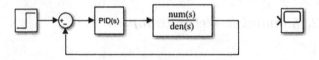

Figure 1-45. *Removing the wire from output to scope*

Double-click the Scope block and select 2 for Number of Input Ports (see Figure 1-46). The Scope block changes to what is shown in Figure 1-47.

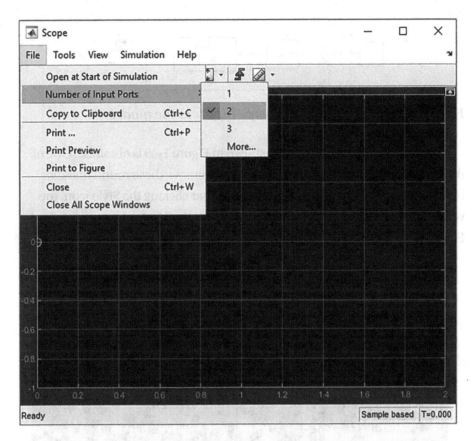

Figure 1-46. Determining the number of inputs

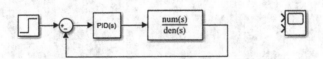

Figure 1-47. The Scope block has two inputs

Connect the inputs of the Scope block to the desired nodes of the system (Figure 1-48).

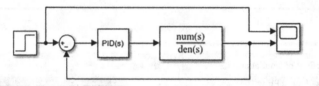

Figure 1-48. *Connecting the scope inputs to the model*

Run the simulation. The result shown in Figure 1-49 is obtained. One of the signals has round markers on it. You can remove these round markers by clicking the Style icon (see Figure 1-50). After clicking the Style icon, the window shown in Figure 1-51 appears. Convert the Marker box to none (see Figure 1-52). Now the waveform has no round markers on it (see Figure 1-53).

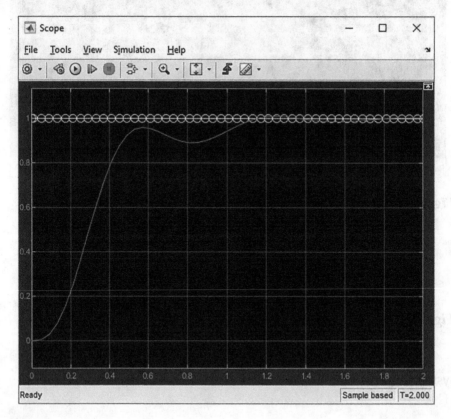

Figure 1-49. *Simulation result*

Figure 1-50. *Style icon*

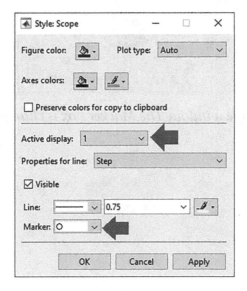

Figure 1-51. *Scope window. The round marker is selected*

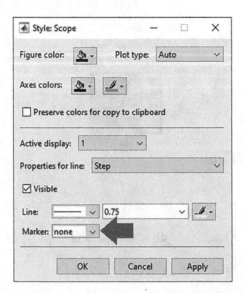

Figure 1-52. *Scope window. The Marker box is changed to none*

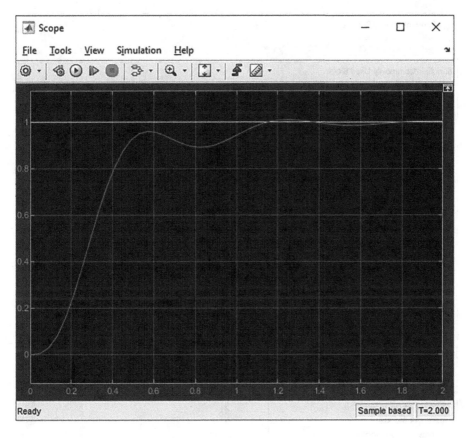

Figure 1-53. *Simulation result*

Option 2: Using the Multiplexer (Mux) Block

There is another way to see two or more signals simultaneously: using the multiplexer (Mux) block (see Figure 1-54). If you double-click the Mux block, the window shown in Figure 1-55 appears and permits you to determine the desired number of inputs for the Mux block.

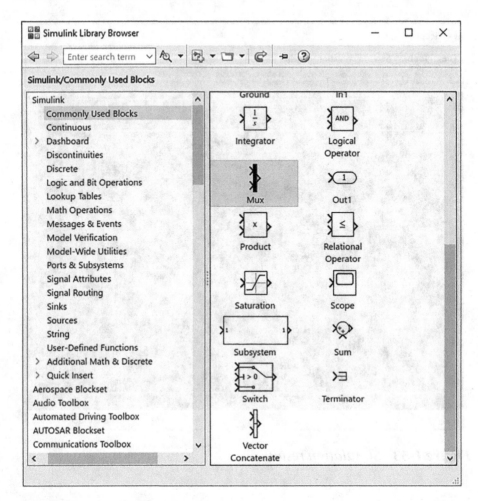

Figure 1-54. Multiplexer block

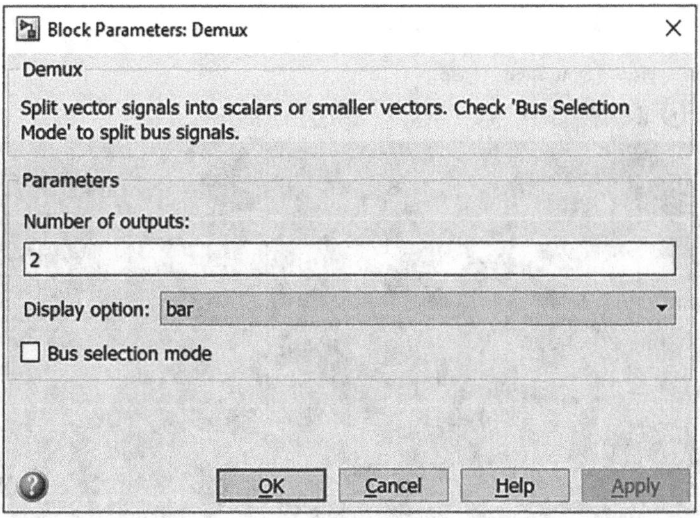

Block Parameters: Demux   ✕

Demux

Split vector signals into scalars or smaller vectors. Check 'Bus Selection Mode' to split bus signals.

Parameters

Number of outputs:

2

Display option: bar   ▾

☐ Bus selection mode

OK   Cancel   Help   Apply

Figure 1-55. Settings of the multiplexer block

The block diagram shown in Figure 1-56 shows the output of the system and control input simultaneously (see Figure 1-57).

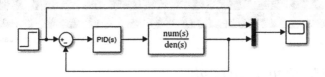

Figure 1-56. Showing two signals on the scope with the multiplexer block

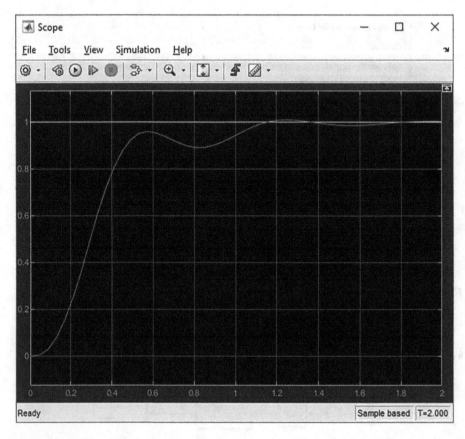

Figure 1-57. Simulation result

Summary

In this chapter you learned the basics of simulation with Simulink. You learned how to observe the step response of a system, how to tune a PID controller with MATLAB and Simulink, how to simulate a closed-loop feedback control system, and how to observe two or more signals simultaneously.

Power electronic converters are dynamic systems. In the next chapter, we will learn how to simulate a dynamic system in the Simulink environment.

CHAPTER 2

Simulation of Dynamic Systems in Simulink®

Basics of Simulink were studied in the previous chapter. In this chapter we will focus on the modeling of dynamic equations in the Simulink environment. Dynamic equations can be divided into two categories: continuous time dynamic equations (differential equations) and discrete time dynamic equations (difference equations). Modeling of both of these equations is studied in this chapter.

Differential equations can be divided into two groups: time domain equations and state space equations. In order to simulate a differential equation in the Simulink environment, you need to convert it into state space.

In this chapter we will learn how to convert a time domain differential equation into a state space equation, how to decrease the number of Integrator blocks used in the Simulink model, how to simulate a state space equation with the aid of State-Space and MATLAB Function blocks, how to transfer the simulation result from Simulink to the MATLAB environment, how to simulate a DC-DC boost converter, and how to simulate difference equations.

© Farzin Asadi 2022

F. Asadi, *Simulation of Power Electronics Circuits with MATLAB®/Simulink®*, Maker Innovations Series, https://doi.org/10.1007/978-1-4842-8220-5_2

Example 1: Simulation of Differential Equations

In this example we want to simulate the following system:

$$\ddot{y} + 5\dot{y} - 10y = 7\sin\left(3t + \frac{\pi}{3}\right), y(0) = 1, \dot{y}(0) = 4 \qquad (2.1)$$

Let's define two new variables and convert the given equation into the state space system:

$$x_1 = y, x_2 = \dot{y} = \frac{dy}{dt} \qquad (2.2)$$

The state space representation of the system is

$$\dot{x}_1 = x_2, \dot{x}_2 = 10x_1 - 5x_2 + 7\sin\left(3t + \frac{\pi}{3}\right), x_0 = [14] \qquad (2.3)$$

where x_0 indicates the initial condition of the system. This state space representation is suitable for drawing the Simulink model. Add two Integrator blocks (see Figure 2-1) to the Simulink model (see Figure 2-2).

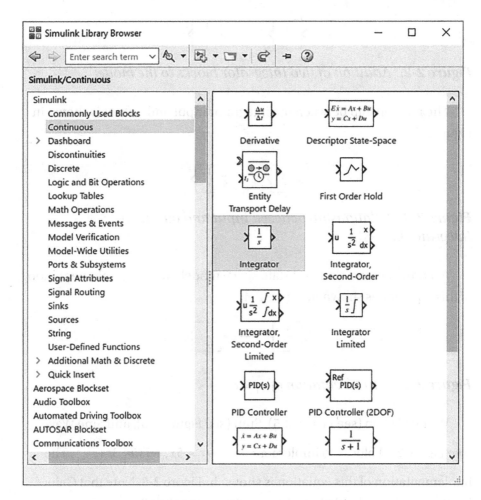

Figure 2-1. *Integrator block*

Figure 2-2. *Addition of two Integrator blocks to the model*

The relationship between the integrator input and output is shown in Figure 2-3.

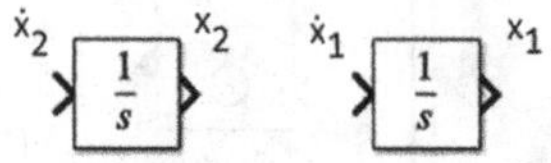

Figure 2-3. *Relationship between input and output of Integrator blocks*

According to the obtained state space model, $\dot{x}_1 = x_2$. Implementation of this equation is shown in Figure 2-4.

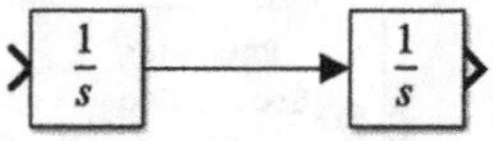

Figure 2-4. *Implementation of* $\dot{x}_1 = x_2$

We need Gain (see Figure 2-5), Sum (see Figure 2-6), and Sine Wave (see Figure 2-7) blocks to implement $\dot{x}_2 = 10x_1 - 5x_2 + 7sin\left(3t + \dfrac{\pi}{3}\right)$. The implementation of this equation is shown in Figure 2-8. Note that Gain blocks are rotated by clicking them and pressing Ctrl+R.

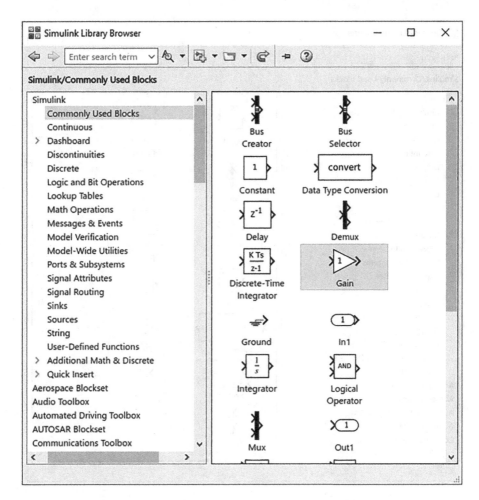

Figure 2-5. *Gain block*

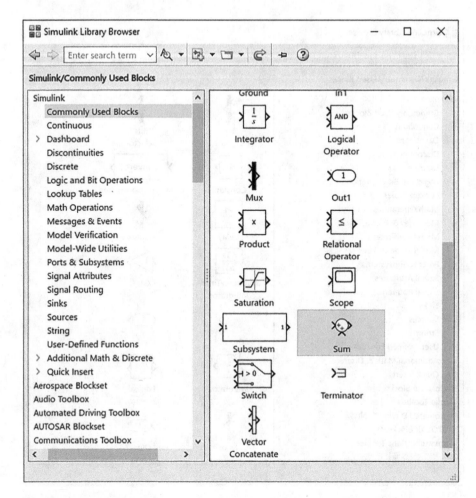

Figure 2-6. *Sum block*

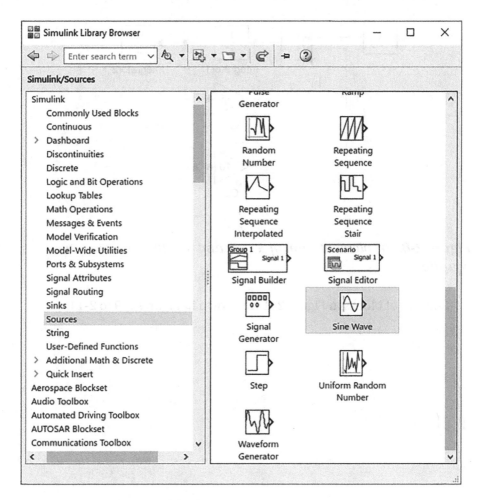

Figure 2-7. *Sine Wave block*

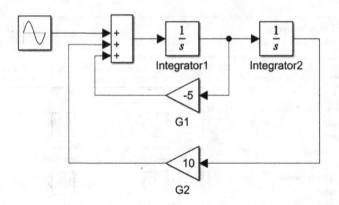

Figure 2-8. *Implementation of* $\dot{x}_1 = x_2$ *and* $\dot{x}_2 = 10x_1 - 5x_2 + 7sin\left(3t + \dfrac{\pi}{3}\right)$ *equations*

Settings of blocks in Figure 2-8 are shown in Figures 2-9 to 2-14.

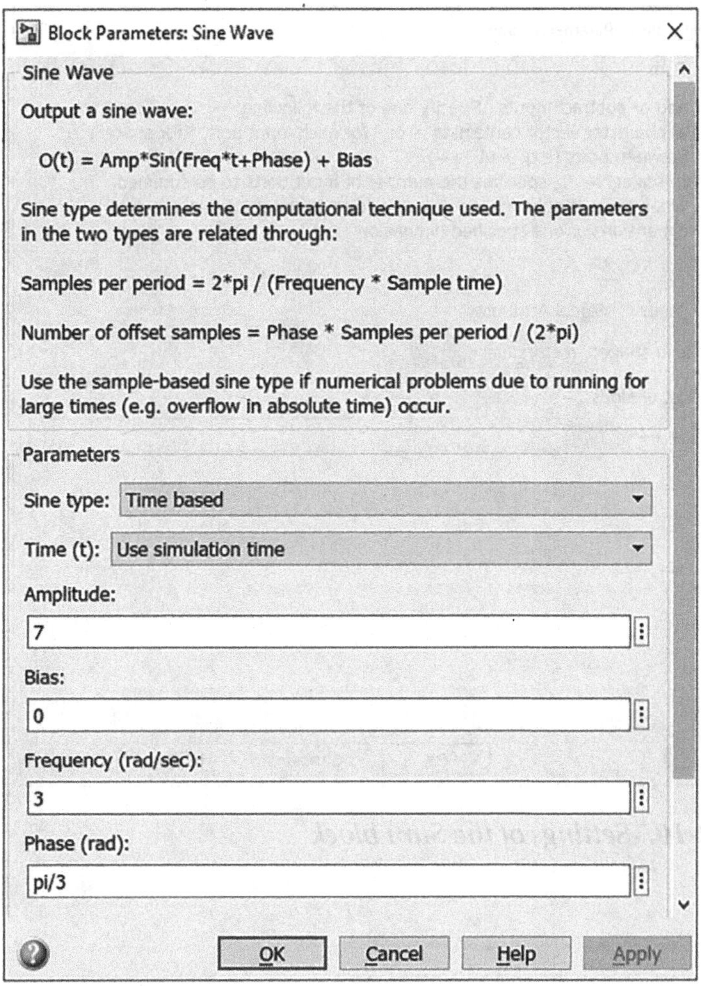

Block Parameters: Sine Wave ✕

Sine Wave

Output a sine wave:

O(t) = Amp*Sin(Freq*t+Phase) + Bias

Sine type determines the computational technique used. The parameters in the two types are related through:

Samples per period = 2*pi / (Frequency * Sample time)

Number of offset samples = Phase * Samples per period / (2*pi)

Use the sample-based sine type if numerical problems due to running for large times (e.g. overflow in absolute time) occur.

Parameters

Sine type: Time based ▼

Time (t): Use simulation time ▼

Amplitude:

7

Bias:

0

Frequency (rad/sec):

3

Phase (rad):

pi/3

OK   Cancel   Help   Apply

Figure 2-9. *Settings of the Sine Wave block*

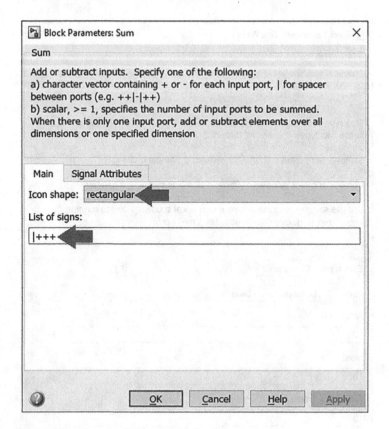

Figure 2-10.   *Settings of the Sum block*

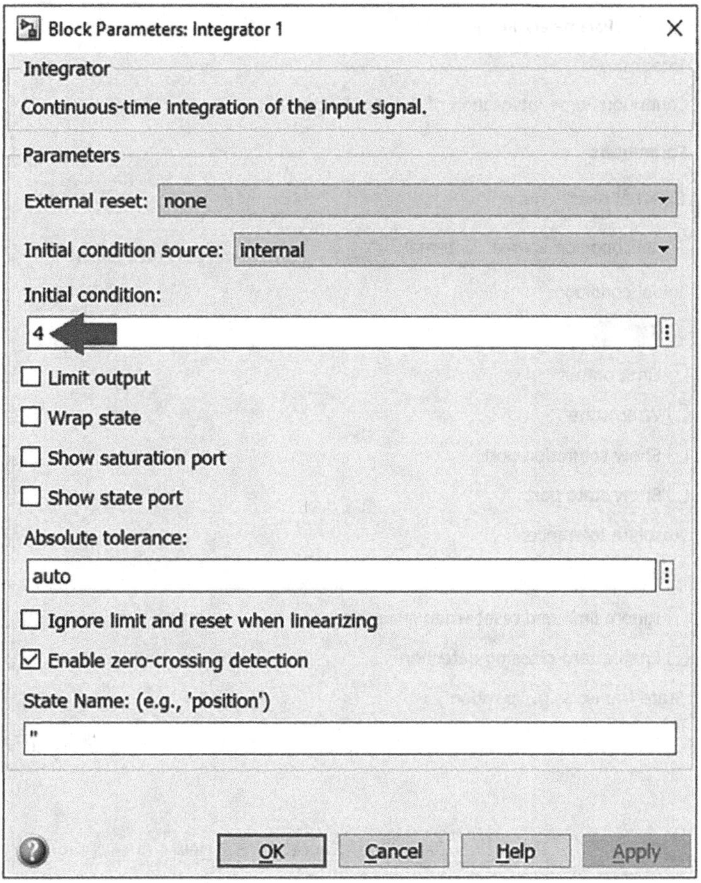

Figure 2-11. *Settings of the Integrator 1 block*

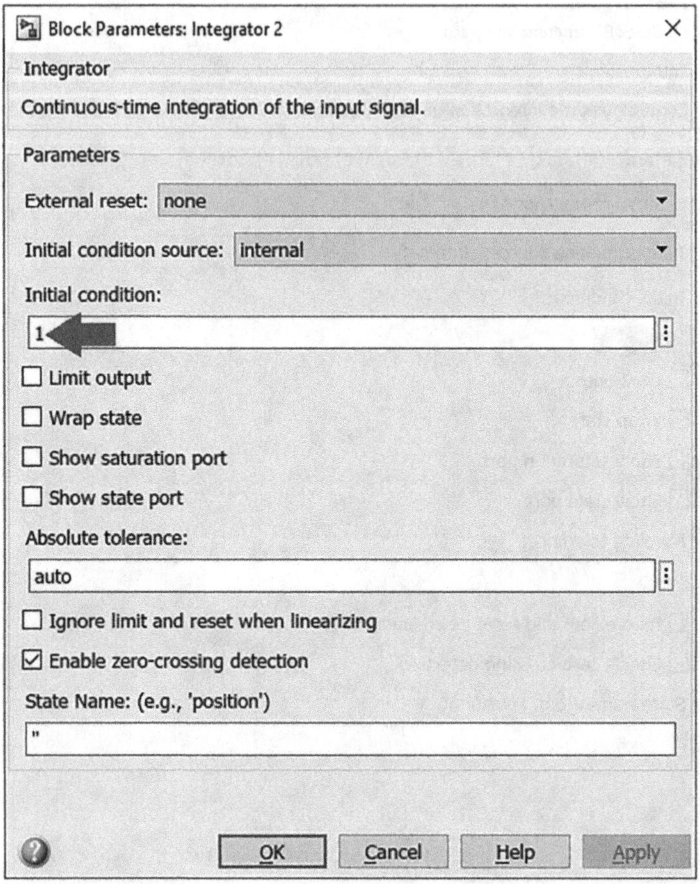

Figure 2-12. *Settings of the Integrator 2 block*

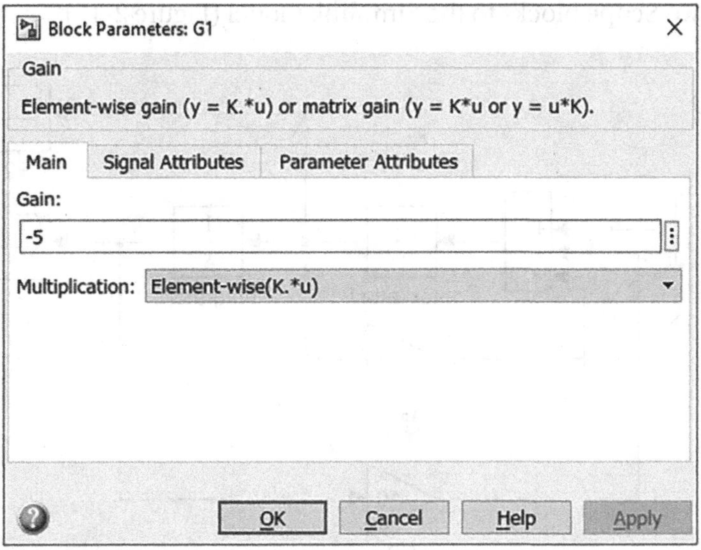

Figure 2-13. *Settings of the G1 block*

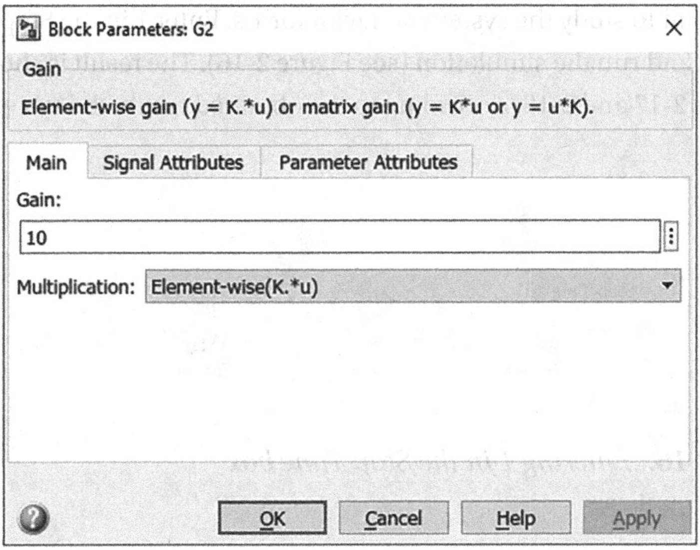

Figure 2-14. *Settings of the G2 block*

Add two Scope blocks to the Simulink model (Figure 2-15).

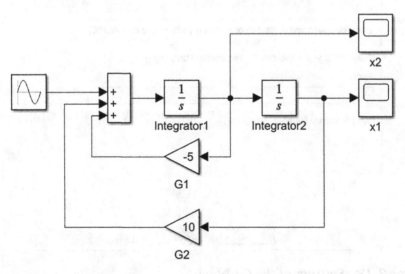

Figure 2-15. *Addition of two Scope blocks to see the x_1 and x_2*

We want to study the system behavior for 1 s. Enter 1 in the Stop Time box and run the simulation (see Figure 2-16). The result is shown in Figures 2-17 and 2-18. According to the obtained result, the system is unstable.

Figure 2-16. *Entering 1 in the Stop Time box*

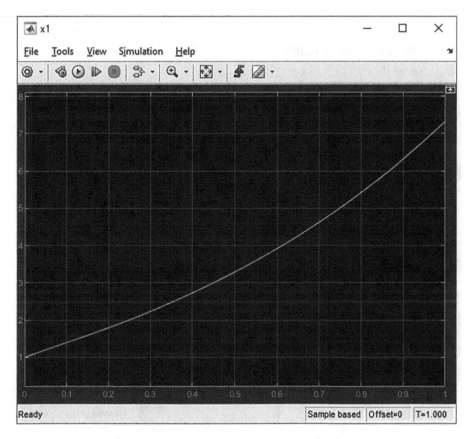

Figure 2-17. *Simulation result (x_1)*

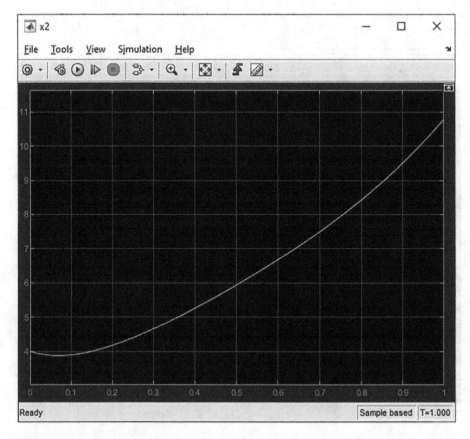

Figure 2-18. *Simulation result (x_2)*

In this example we used two Integrator blocks to simulate a second-order system. In the next example, we will learn how to decrease the number of Integrator blocks of our Simulink model to one.

Example 2: Simulation of Differential Equations with Only One Integrator Block

In this example, we want to implement the state space equation of Example 1 with only one Integrator block. The state space equation of Example 1 is rewritten in the following:

$$\dot{x}_1 = x_2, \dot{x}_2 = 10x_1 - 5x_2 + 7sin\left(3t + \frac{\pi}{3}\right), x_0 = [14] \qquad (2.3)$$

This state space equation has the following form

$$\dot{x} = Ax + u, \; x_0 = [14] \qquad (2.4)$$

where $x = [x_1; x_2]$, $A = [0 \; 1; 10 - 5]$, and $u = \left[0; 7sin\left(3t + \frac{\pi}{3}\right)\right]$. The model shown in Figure 2-19 implements the state space equation with only one Integrator block. Settings of the blocks are shown in Figures 2-20 and 2-21. This model used a Constant block (see Figure 2-22) to implement the zero of vector $u = \left[0 \; 7sin\left(3t + \frac{\pi}{3}\right)\right]$.

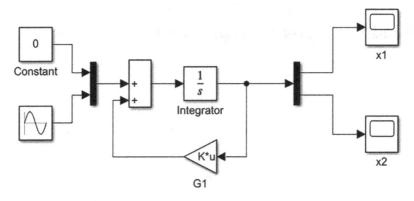

Figure 2-19. *Simulink model of Example 2*

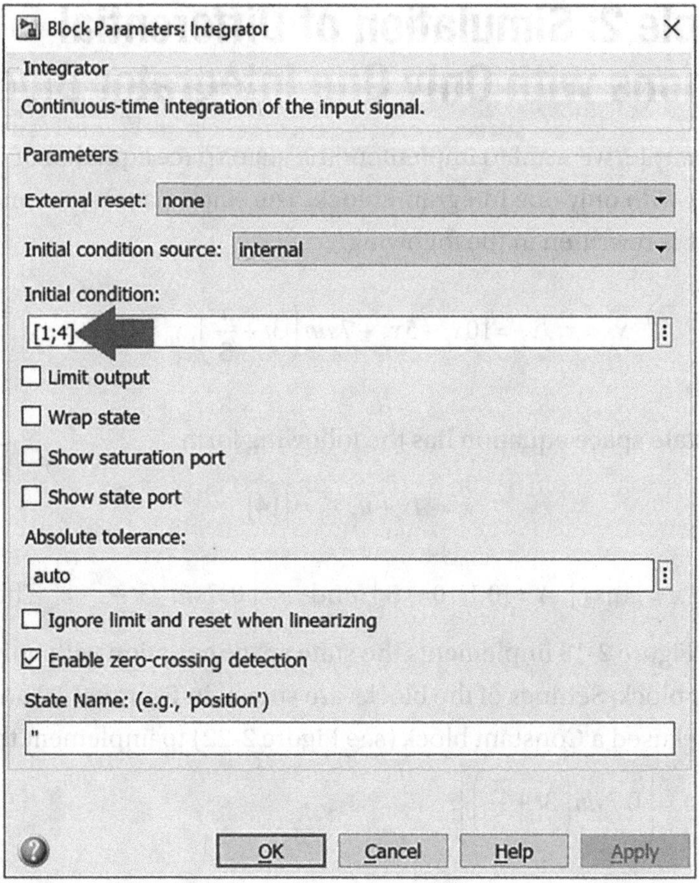

Figure 2-20. *Settings of the Integrator block*

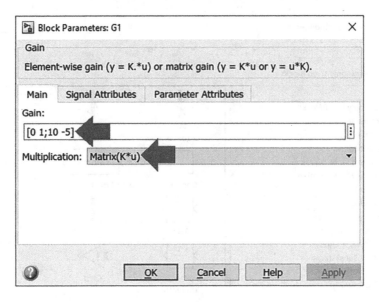

Figure 2-21. *Settings of the G1 block*

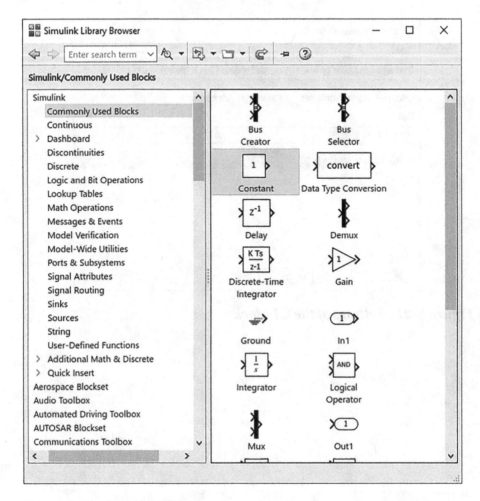

Figure 2-22. *Constant block*

Run the simulation. The result shown in Figure 2-23 is obtained. Both of the signals are shown on one scope. The model in Figure 2-24 shows how to separate the signals and send each signal to a separate scope. This model used a demultiplexer (Demux) block (see Figure 2-25) to separate the signals.

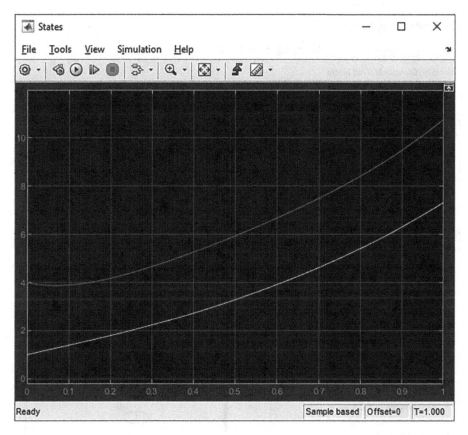

Figure 2-23. *Simulation result*

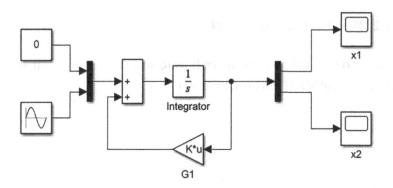

Figure 2-24. *The simulation result is shown on two Scope blocks*

63

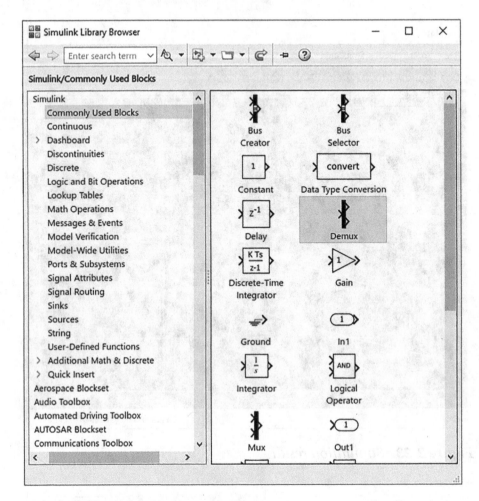

Figure 2-25. *Demultiplexer block*

In the next example, we will learn how to simulate a nonlinear system with the aid of the MATLAB Function block.

Example 3: Simulation of Differential Equations with the MATLAB Function Block

In this example we want to simulate the following equation:

$$\ddot{y} + \left(\sqrt{t} + \sin(t) \right) \dot{y} - t^2 y = 7\sin\left(3t + \frac{\pi}{3} \right), y(0) = 1, \dot{y}(0) = 4 \qquad (2.5)$$

Let's convert the equation to state space. The new variables x_1 and x_2 are defined as

$$x_1 = y, x_2 = \dot{y} = \frac{dy}{dt} \qquad (2.6)$$

So the state space model of the given system is

$$\dot{x}_1 = x_2, \dot{x}_2 = t^2 x_1 - \left(\sqrt{t} + \sin(t) \right) x_2 + 7\sin\left(3t + \frac{\pi}{3} \right) \qquad (2.7)$$

This model can be written as

$$\dot{x} = Ax + u \qquad (2.8)$$

where $x = [x_1 \ x_2]$, $A = \left[0\, 1; t^2 - \left(\sqrt{t} + \sin(t) \right) \right]$, and $u = \left[0; 7\sin\left(3t + \frac{\pi}{3} \right) \right]$.

The obtained state space equation is implemented with the block diagram shown in Figure 2-26. This model used MATLAB Function and Clock blocks (Figures 2-27 and 2-28).

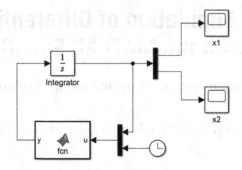

Figure 2-26. *Simulink model of Example 3*

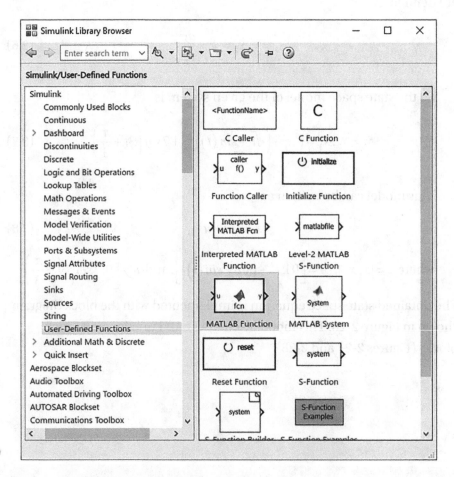

Figure 2-27. *MATLAB Function block*

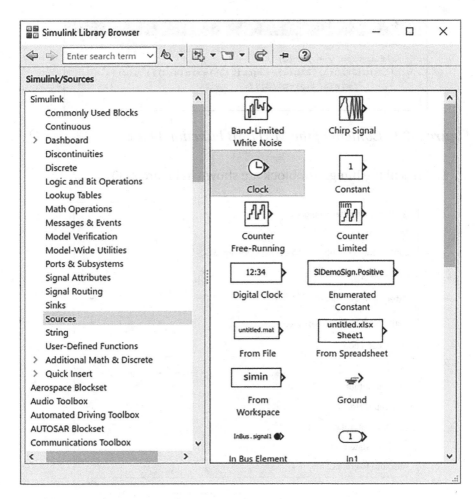

Figure 2-28. *Clock block*

Double-click the MATLAB Function block and enter the code shown in Figure 2-29. u(1) indicates variable x_1, u(2) indicates variable x_2, and u(3) indicates variable t. So Figure 2-29 is the translation of

$$\left[x_2; t^2 x_1 - \left(\sqrt{t} + sin(t) \right) x_2 + 7 sin\left(3t + \frac{\pi}{3} \right) \right]$$ into MATLAB language.

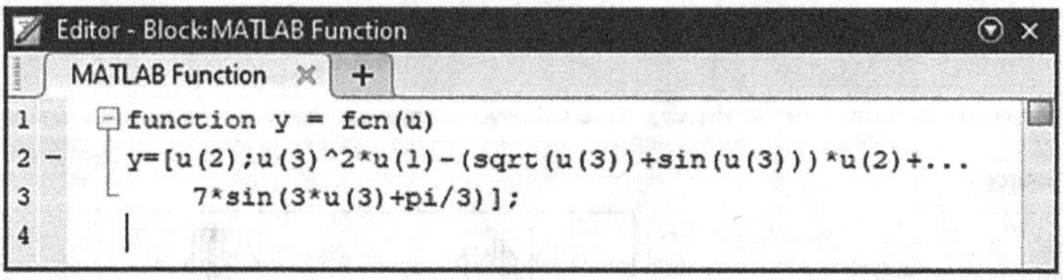

```
Editor - Block: MATLAB Function                                    ⊙ ×
  MATLAB Function  ✕  +
1   ⊟ function y = fcn(u)
2 -   │ y=[u(2);u(3)^2*u(1)-(sqrt(u(3))+sin(u(3)))*u(2)+...
3     └   7*sin(3*u(3)+pi/3)];
4     │
```

Figure 2-29. *Content of the MATLAB Function block*

Settings of the Integrator block are shown in Figure 2-30.

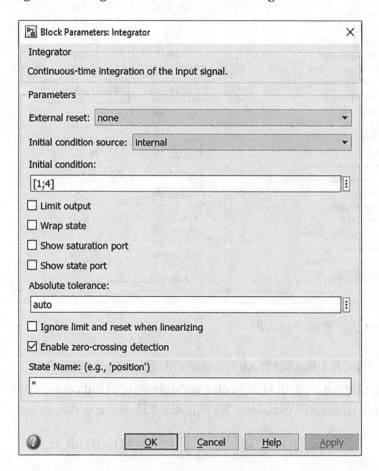

Figure 2-30. *Settings of the Integrator block*

Run the simulation. The result shown in Figures 2-31 and 2-32 is obtained.

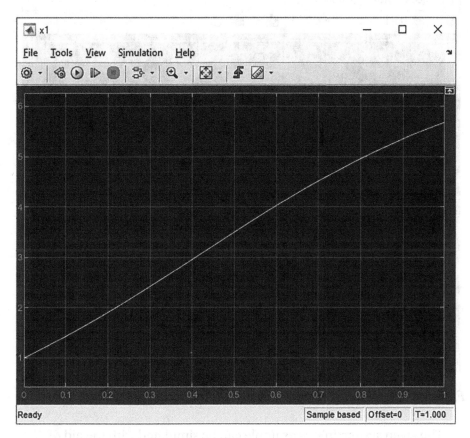

Figure 2-31. *Simulation result (x_1)*

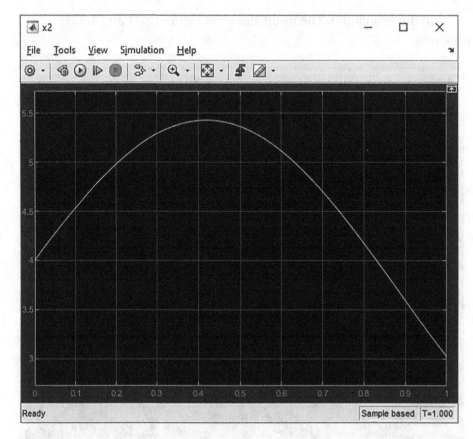

Figure 2-32. *Simulation result (x_2)*

The given system in this example can be simulated with the aid of the following block diagram as well. This Simulink model used more blocks in comparison to the model shown in Figure 2-26. If you run the Simulink model shown in Figure 2-33, you will obtain the results shown in Figures 2-31 and 2-32.

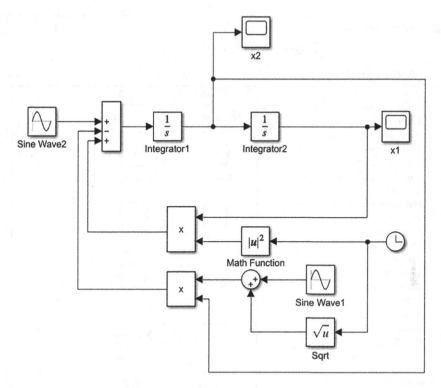

Figure 2-33. *Simulink model of Example 3 with discrete blocks*

The model shown in Figure 2-33 used Sqrt (see Figure 2-34) and Math Function (see Figure 2-35) blocks.

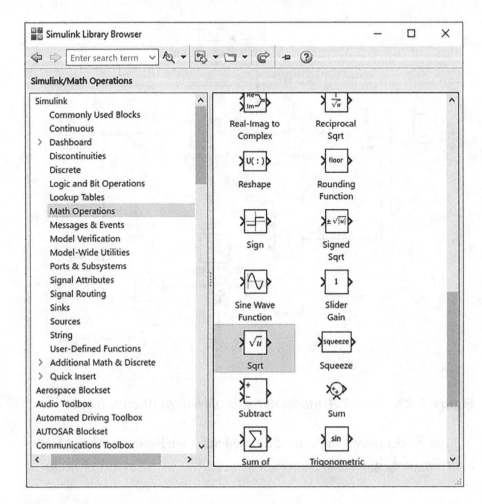

Figure 2-34. *Sqrt block*

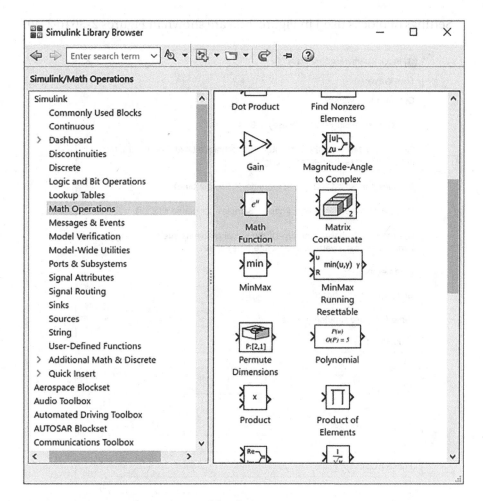

Figure 2-35. *Math Function block*

Settings of blocks used in Figure 2-33 are shown in Figures 2-36 to 2-40.

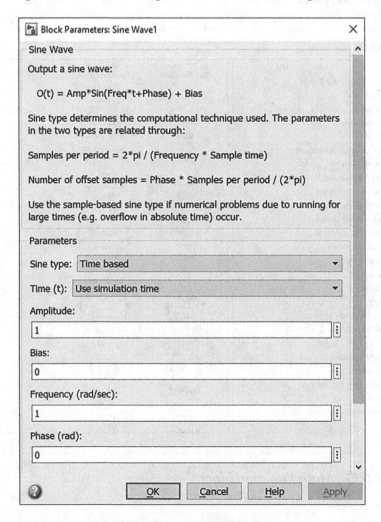

Figure 2-36. *Settings of the Sine Wave1 block*

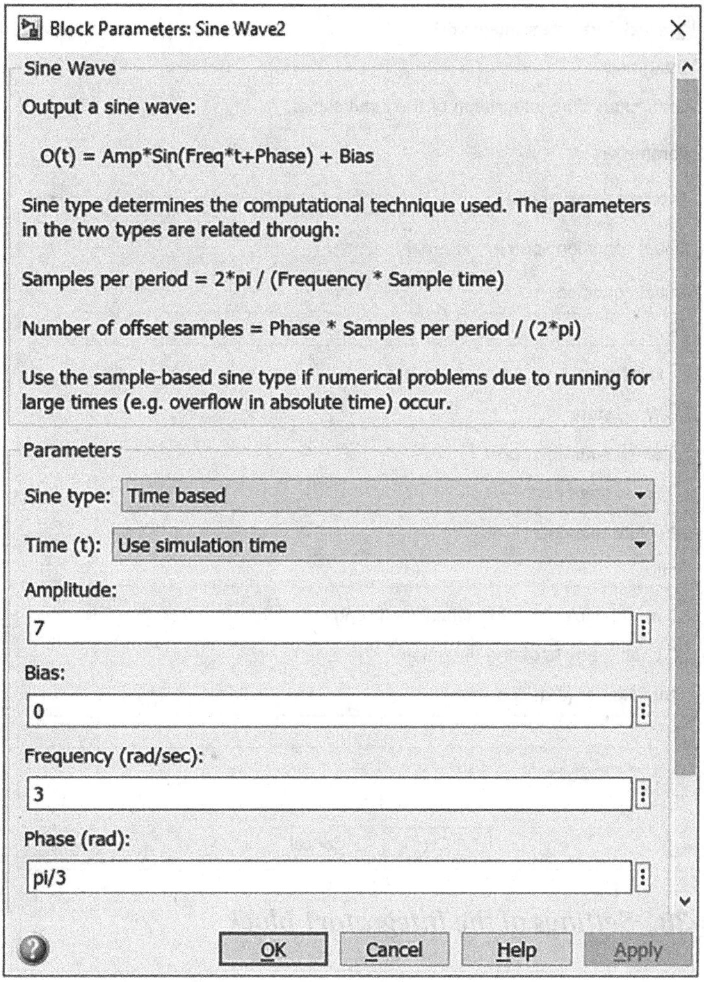

Block Parameters: Sine Wave2 ✕

Sine Wave

Output a sine wave:

O(t) = Amp*Sin(Freq*t+Phase) + Bias

Sine type determines the computational technique used. The parameters in the two types are related through:

Samples per period = 2*pi / (Frequency * Sample time)

Number of offset samples = Phase * Samples per period / (2*pi)

Use the sample-based sine type if numerical problems due to running for large times (e.g. overflow in absolute time) occur.

Parameters

Sine type: Time based ▾

Time (t): Use simulation time ▾

Amplitude:

7

Bias:

0

Frequency (rad/sec):

3

Phase (rad):

pi/3

OK   Cancel   Help   Apply

Figure 2-37. Settings of the Sine Wave2 block

75

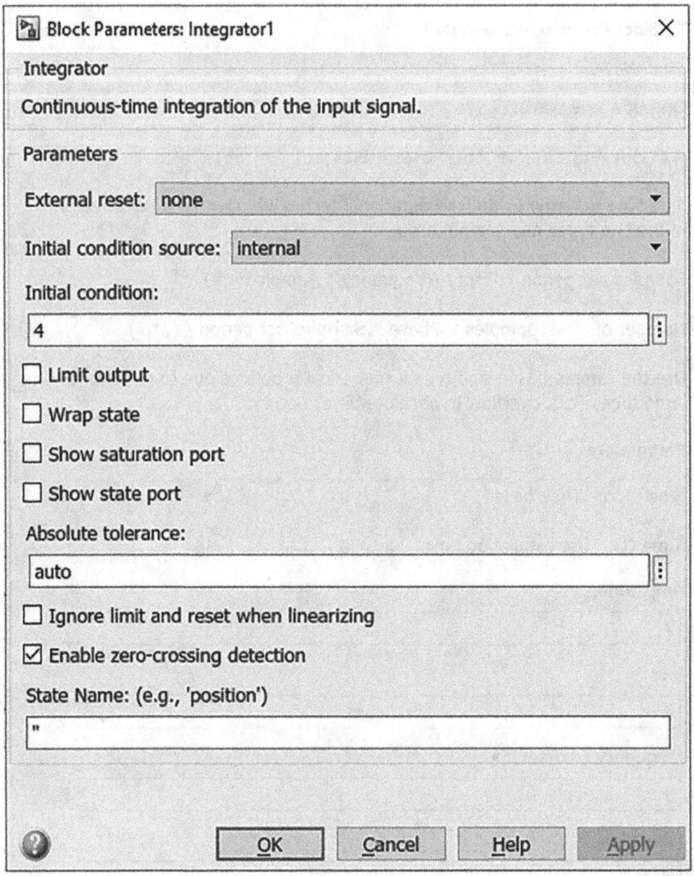

Figure 2-38. *Settings of the Integrator1 block*

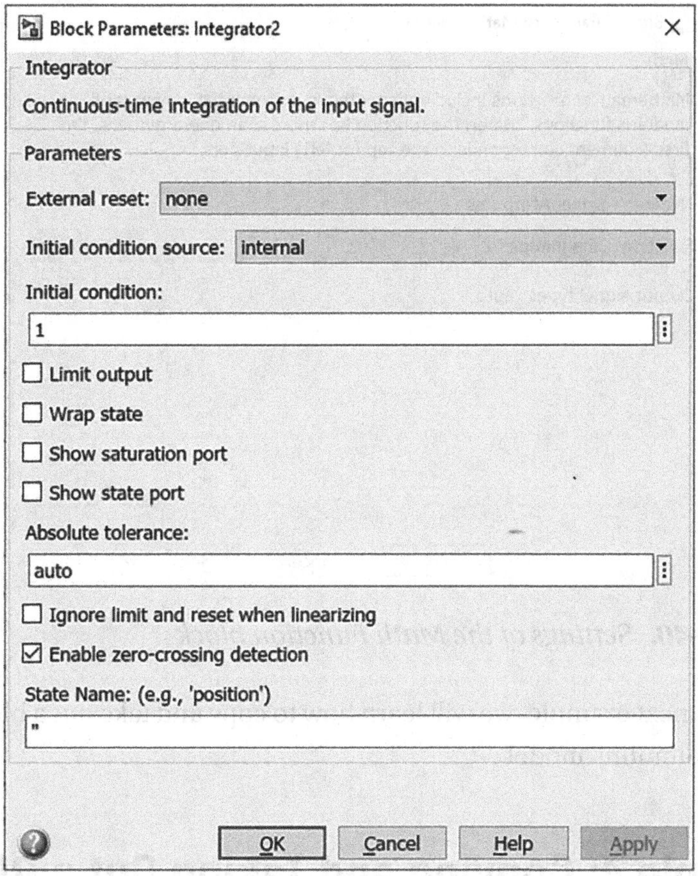

Figure 2-39. *Settings of the Integrator2 block*

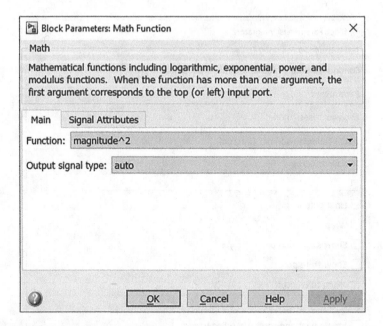

Figure 2-40. *Settings of the Math Function block*

In the next example, we will learn how to copy and take out a block from our Simulink model.

Example 4: Copying and Taking Out a Block from the Model

In this example we will show how to copy and take out a block from its location easily. Consider the model shown in Figure 2-41. Assume that you need one more scope. One way is to click the Library Browser icon and drag a new Scope block to the model. However, there is a simpler way. You can hold down the Ctrl key, click the Scope block, and drag the block outward. Once you release the mouse button, one copy of the block will be generated for you (see Figure 2-42).

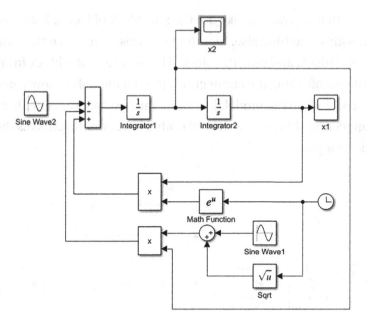

Figure 2-41. *Select scope x2 by clicking it*

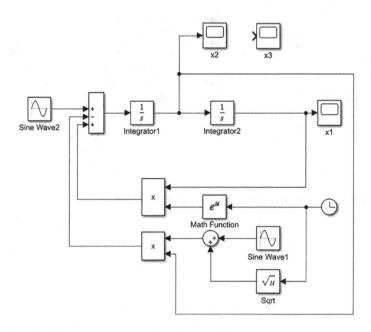

Figure 2-42. *Making a copy of a Scope block*

Assume that we want to take out the Sqrt block of Figure 2-43 and replace it with something else. In order to do this, hold down the Shift key, click the Sqrt block, and drag the block. This separates the block from the model without affecting the connections (see Figure 2-44). Now you can add the new block to the model. Just bring the new block terminals close to the connection shown with the red dotted line. Simulink makes the connection for you.

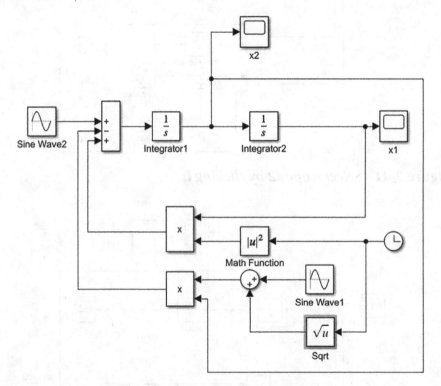

Figure 2-43. *Select the Sqrt block by clicking it*

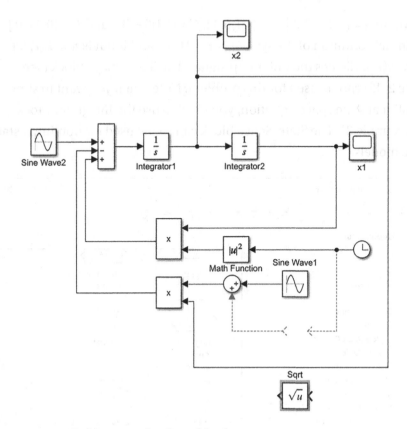

Figure 2-44. *Taking out the Sqrt block*

In the next example, we will learn how to use the State-Space block to simulate linear state space models.

Example 5: State-Space Block

In this example we will see how to simulate a linear state space system. Assume that you want to simulate the following state space system

$$\dot{x} = Ax + Bu$$

$$y = Cx + Du \tag{2.9}$$

where $A = [1\ 2; -1\ 3]$, $B = [1\ 1; 5\ 3]$, $C = [1\ 1; 6 - 3]$, and $D = [0\ 0; 0\ 0]$. The initial condition of the system is $x_0 = [1; 3]$, and input is $u = [R(t)\ 0]$, where $R(t)$ indicates the unit ramp signal. The State-Space block (see Figure 2-45) can be used for this problem. Note that if you want to simulate a nonlinear state space equation, you need to use the Integrator block (see Example 3). The State-Space block cannot be used for nonlinear state space models.

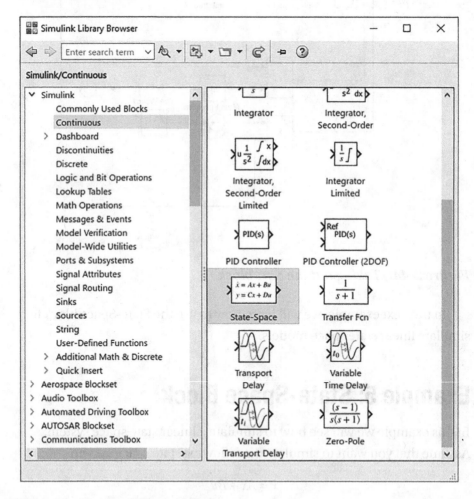

Figure 2-45. *State-Space block*

The Simulink model is shown in Figure 2-46. This diagram used the Ramp block shown in Figure 2-47 to stimulate the system with a unit ramp signal. Settings of the State-Space block are shown in Figure 2-48.

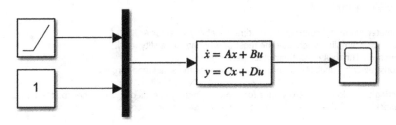

Figure 2-46. *Simulink model of Example 5*

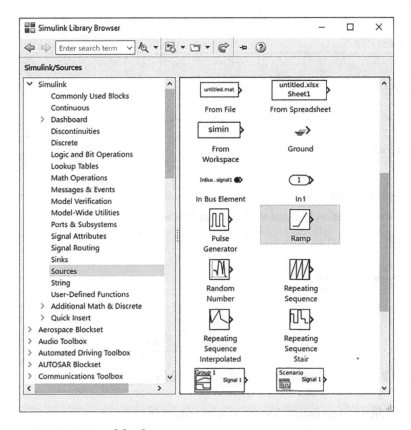

Figure 2-47. *Ramp block*

```
Block Parameters: State-Space                                              ×

State Space                                                                ^

State-space model:
  dx/dt = Ax + Bu
     y = Cx + Du

'Parameter tunability' controls the runtime tunability level for A, B, C, D.
'Auto': Allow Simulink to choose the most appropriate tunability level.
'Optimized': Tunability is optimized for performance.
'Unconstrained': Tunability is unconstrained across the simulation targets.

Selecting the 'Allow non-zero values for D matrix initially specified as zero' checkbox requires
the block to have direct feedthrough and may cause algebraic loops.

Parameters

A:
 [1 2;-1 3]                                                              :

B:
 [1 1;5 3]                                                              :

C:
 [1 1;6 -3]                                                             :

D:
 [0 0;0 0]                                                              :

Initial conditions:
 [1;3]                                                                  :

Parameter tunability:  Auto                                              ▼

☐ Allow non-zero values for D matrix initially specified as zero

Absolute tolerance:

 auto                                                                   :

State Name: (e.g., 'position')
 "                                                                          
                                                                        v

 ?                        OK        Cancel       Help       Apply
```

Figure 2-48. *Settings of the State-Space block*

The simulation result is shown in Figure 2-49.

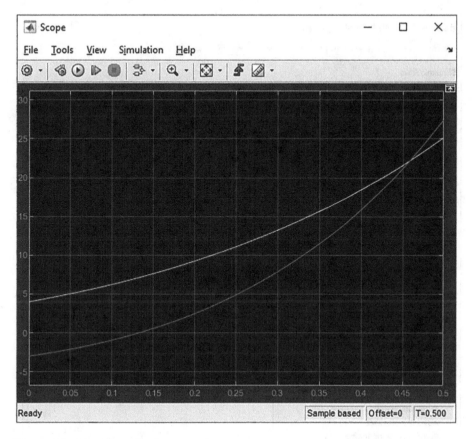

Figure 2-49. *Simulation result*

In the next example, we will learn how to transfer the simulation results from the Simulink environment to MATLAB Workspace.

Example 6: To Workspace Block

You can use the To Workspace block (see Figure 2-50) to transfer the signal from the Simulink environment to MATLAB Workspace. Let's send the output of the previous example to Workspace. Add a To Workspace block to the Simulink model of the previous example (see Figure 2-51).

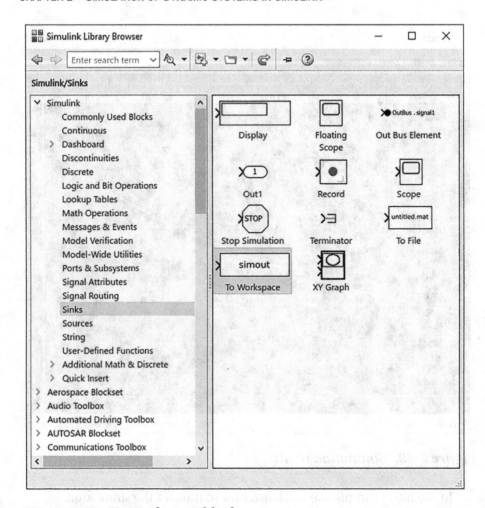

Figure 2-50. *To Workspace block*

out.simout
1
$\dot{x} = Ax + Bu$
$y = Cx + Du$

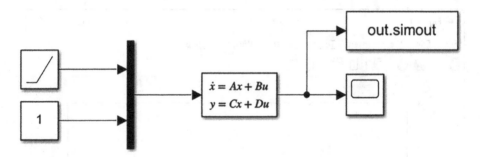

Figure 2-51. *Addition of the To Workspace block to the Simulink model*

Run the simulation. After running the simulation, a new variable named "out" will be added to Workspace (Figure 2-52).

Workspace
Name
Value
out
1x1 SimulationOutput

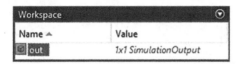

Figure 2-52. *Variable "out" is added to Workspace*

Enter the commands shown in Figure 2-53. t, y1, and y2 indicate time, first output, and second output, respectively. The result of this code is shown in Figures 2-54 and 2-55. This result is the same as the result shown in Figure 2-49.

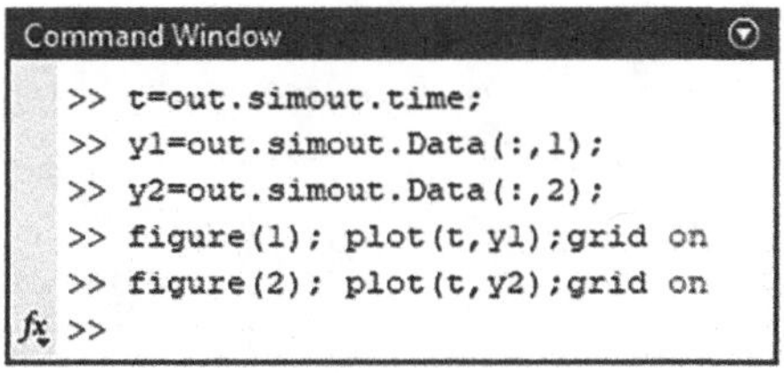

Command Window
>> t=out.simout.time;
>> y1=out.simout.Data(:,1);
>> y2=out.simout.Data(:,2);
>> figure(1); plot(t,y1);grid on
>> figure(2); plot(t,y2);grid on
fx >>

Figure 2-53. *Reading the data imported from Simulink and drawing its graph*

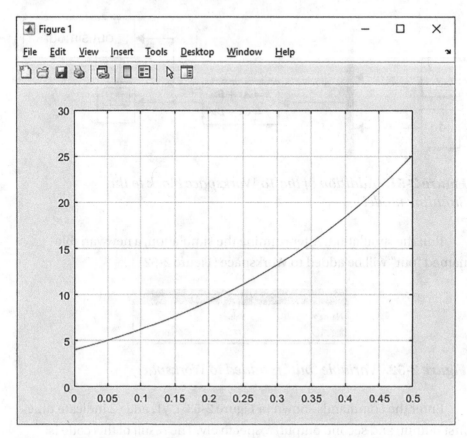

Figure 2-54.   *Output of code in Figure 2-53 (1)*

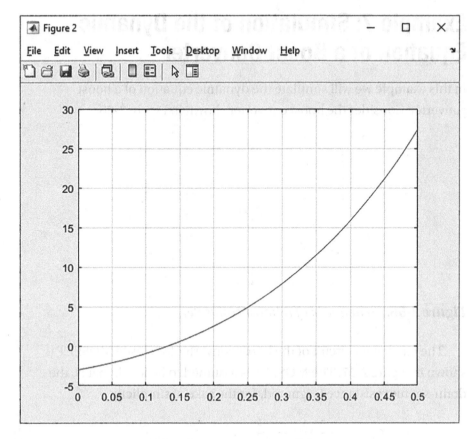

Figure 2-55. *Output of code in Figure 2-53 (2)*

In the next example, we will learn how to simulate a boost converter with the aid of its dynamic equation. In Chapter 5 we will learn how to simulate a DC-DC converter with the aid of Simscape blocks (i.e., blocks like voltage sources, inductors, diodes, MOSFETs, etc.).

Example 7: Simulation of the Dynamic Equation of a Boost Converter

In this example we will simulate the dynamic equation of a boost converter. Consider the boost converter shown in Figure 2-56.

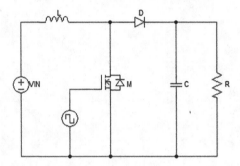

Figure 2-56. *Schematic of a boost converter*

The equivalent circuit of the boost converter for closed MOSFET is shown in Figure 2-57. The MOSFET is assumed to be ideal, that is, the drain-source resistance is ignored, for the sake of simplicity.

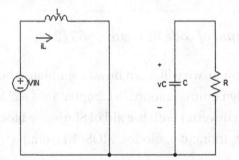

Figure 2-57. *Equivalent circuit of the boost converter for closed MOSFET*

The dynamic equation of this circuit is

$$\frac{d}{dt}i_L = \frac{V_{IN}}{L}, \frac{d}{dt}v_C = -\frac{v_C}{R.C} \tag{2.10}$$

The equivalent circuit of the boost converter for open MOSFET is shown in Figure 2-58. The diode is assumed to be ideal, that is, the forward voltage drop is ignored, for the sake of simplicity.

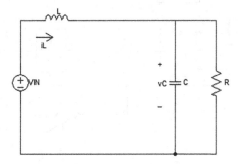

Figure 2-58. *Equivalent circuit of the boost converter for open MOSFET*

The dynamic equation of this circuit is

$$\frac{d}{dt}i_L = \frac{V_{IN}}{L} - \frac{v_C}{L}, \frac{d}{dt}v_C = \frac{i_L}{C} - \frac{v_C}{R.C} \tag{2.11}$$

The obtained two sets of equations can be written as

$$\frac{d}{dt}i_L = (1-u)\frac{-v_C}{L} + \frac{1}{L}V_{IN}, \frac{d}{dt}v_C = (1-u)\frac{i_L}{C} - \frac{v_C}{R.C} \tag{2.12}$$

where u indicates the status of the MOSFET. When the MOSFET is closed, $u = 1$; and when the MOSFET is opened, $u = 0$. The model shown in Figure 2-59 implements these equations. This model used Pulse Generator (see Figure 2-60) and Switch (see Figure 2-61) blocks. Note that values of components are defined in MATLAB Workspace (see Figure 2-62).

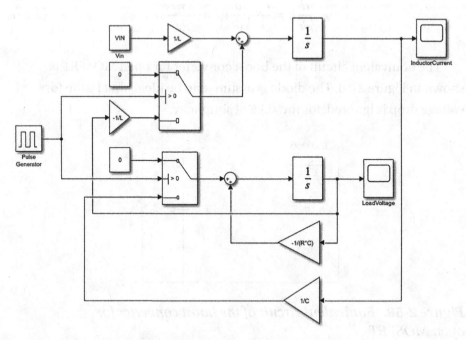

Figure 2-59. *Implementation of equation (2.12)*

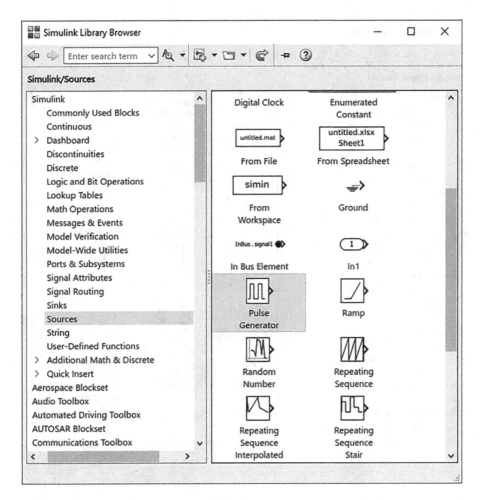

Figure 2-60. *Pulse Generator block*

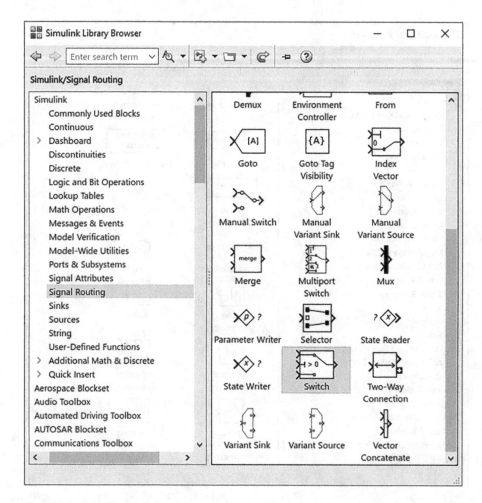

Figure 2-61. *Switch block*

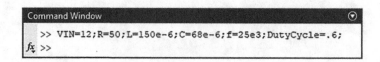

Figure 2-62. *Values of components are defined in Workspace*

Settings of the blocks are shown in Figures 2-63 and 2-64.

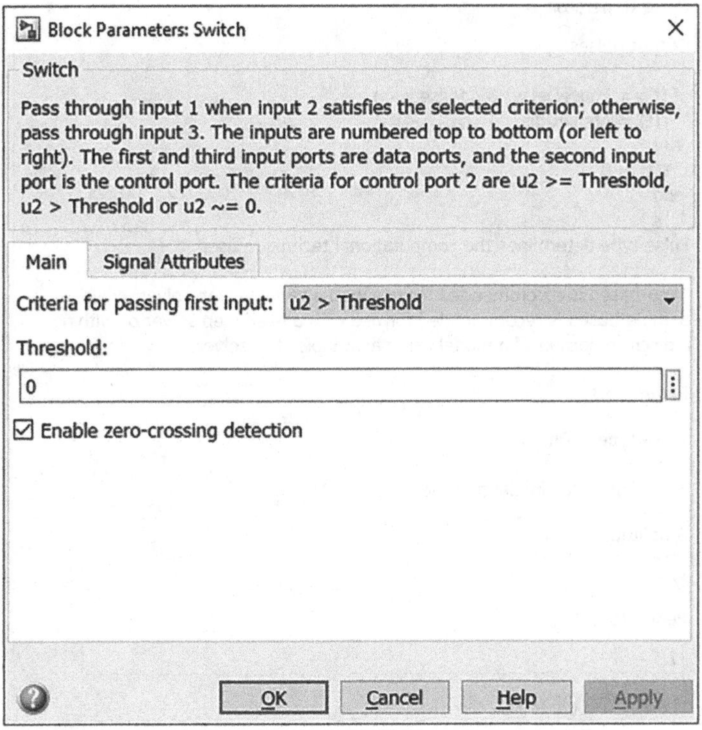

Figure 2-63. *Switch block settings*

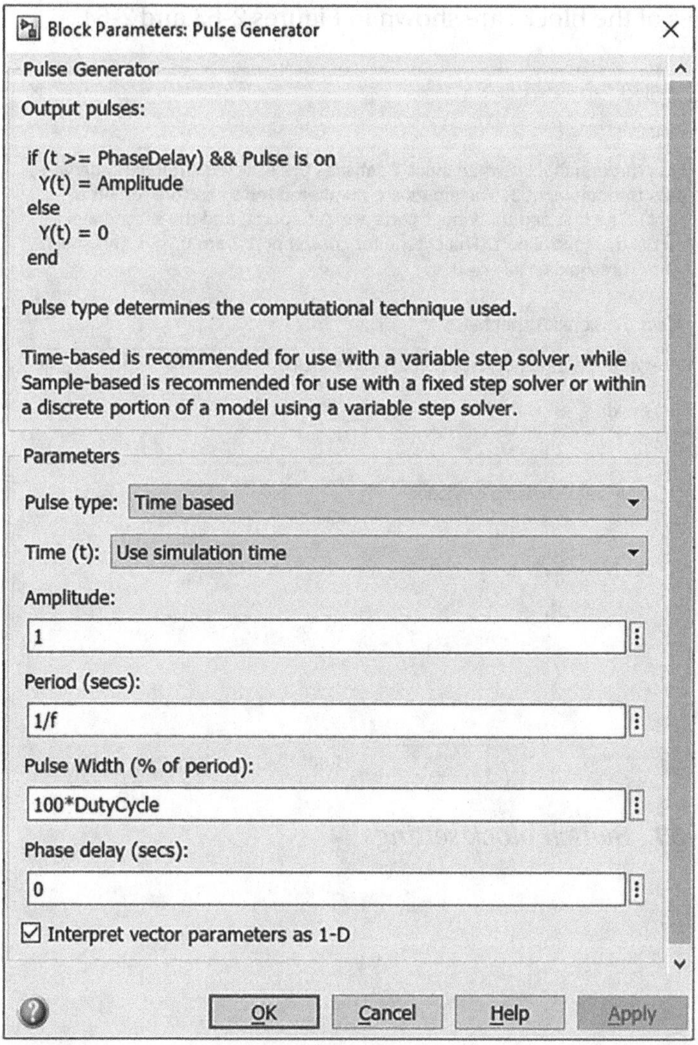

Figure 2-64. *Pulse Generator block settings*

Run the simulation. The results shown in Figures 2-65 and 2-66 are obtained. According to the obtained results, the steady-state voltage of the capacitor is about 30 V, and the steady-state inductor current has minimum of 0.5457 A and maximum of 2.453 A. You need to zoom the waveform in order to see these values.

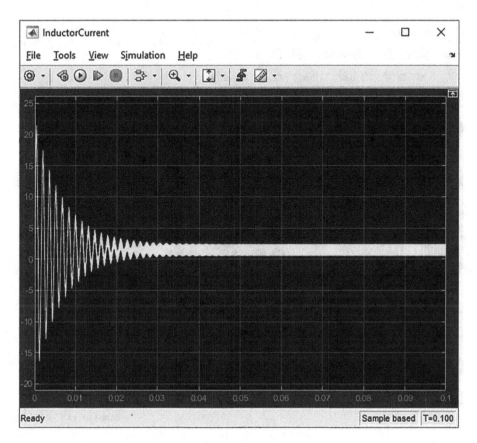

Figure 2-65. *Simulation result (inductor current)*

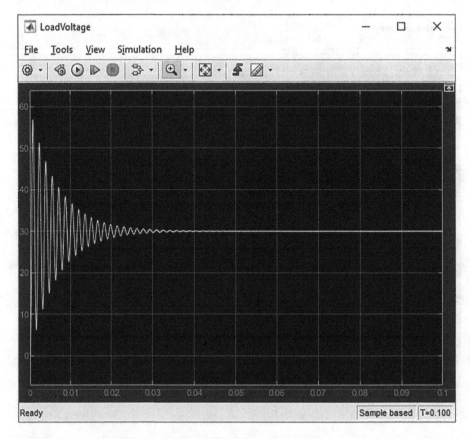

Figure 2-66. *Simulation result (capacitor voltage)*

In the previous examples, we learned how to simulate continuous time systems (i.e., systems described by a differential equation). In the next example, we will learn how to simulate discrete time systems (i.e., systems described by a difference equation).

Example 8: Simulation of Discrete Time Equations (I)

In this example we will simulate a discrete time equation. Consider the $2 \times x(n-1) + 6 \times x(n-2) = x(n)$, $x(-1) = 11$, and $x(-2) = 7$. Let's do some hand calculations for the first three terms: $x(0) = 2 \times 11 + 6 \times 7 = 64$, $x(1) = 2 \times 64 + 6 \times 11 = 194$, and $x(2) = 2 \times 194 + 6 \times 64 = 772$. The Simulink model shown in Figure 2-67 implements the given equation. This model used the Unit Delay block (see Figure 2-68). You can use the Delay block (see Figure 2-69) as well. If you want to use the Delay block, you need to double-click it and enter 1 in the Delay length box.

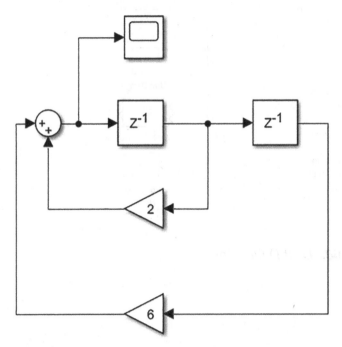

Figure 2-67. *Simulink model of Example 8*

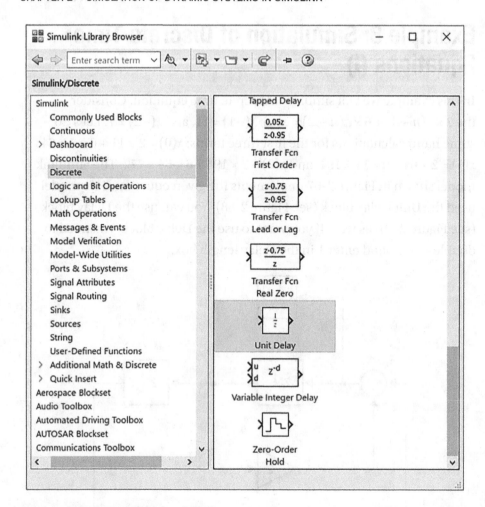

Figure 2-68. *Unit Delay block*

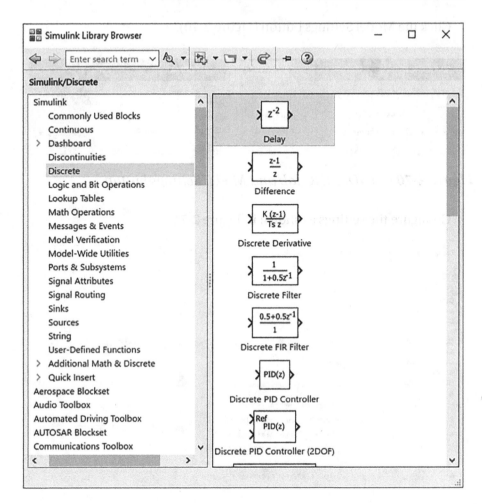

Figure 2-69. *Delay block*

Click the Model Settings button (Figure 2-70).

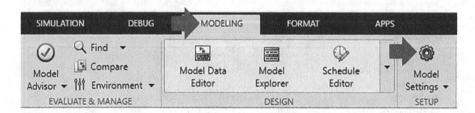

Figure 2-70. *MODELING tab and Model Settings button*

Configure the settings as shown in Figure 2-71.

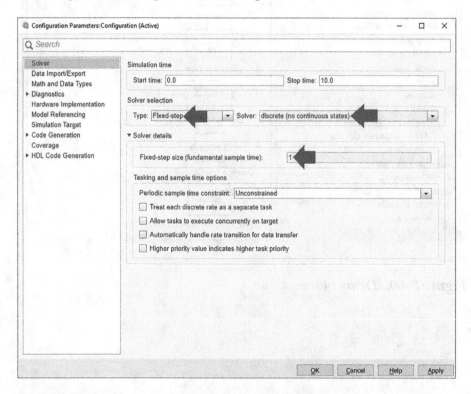

Figure 2-71. *The discrete solver must be selected for discrete time simulations*

Run the simulation. The result is shown in Figure 2-72. The obtained result is the same as hand calculations.

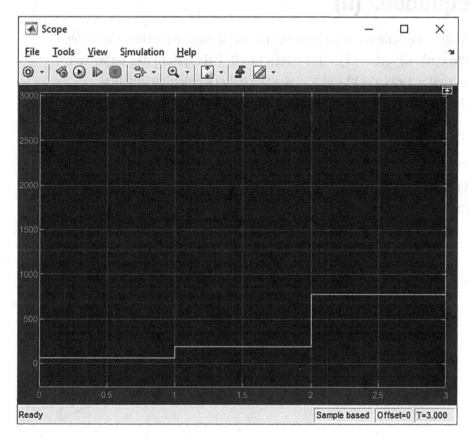

Figure 2-72. *Simulation result*

In this example we used a Delay block to simulate the given system. In the next example, we will use the MATLAB Function block to simulate a discrete time system.

Example 9: Simulation of Discrete Time Equations (II)

In this example we will simulate a discrete time equation. Consider the $y(n) - 3 \times y(n-1) = 4^{n-1}$, $y(-1) = 0$. This system can be written as $y(n) = 3 \times y(n-1) + 4^{n-1}$, $y(-1) = 0$. Let's calculate the first three terms: $y(0) = 3 \times 0 + 4^{-1} = 0.25$, $y(1) = \dfrac{3}{4} + 1 = \dfrac{7}{4} = 1.75$, and

$y(2) = \dfrac{21}{4} + 4 = \dfrac{37}{4} = 9.25$. The Simulink model shown in Figure 2-73

implements this equation. This model used a Zero-Order Hold block (see Figure 2-74) to produce variable n from continuous variable t. The code inside of the MATLAB Function block is shown in Figure 2-75.

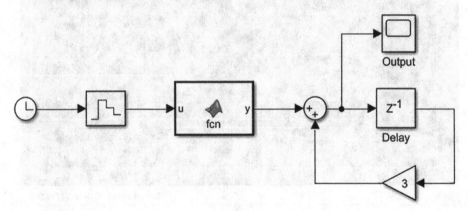

Figure 2-73. *Simulink model of Example 9*

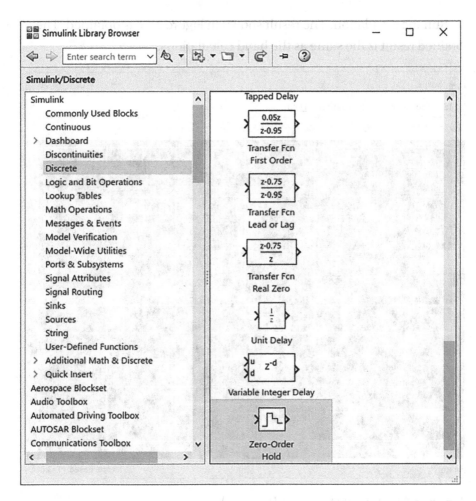

Figure 2-74. *Zero-Order Hold block*

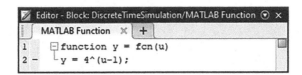

Figure 2-75. *Content of the MATLAB Function block*

Run the simulation. The result shown in Figure 2-76 is obtained. The obtained result is the same as the hand calculations.

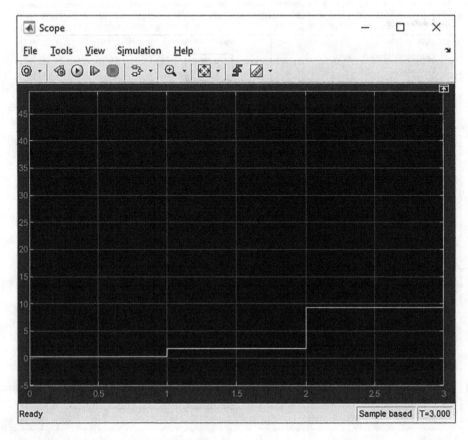

Figure 2-76. *Simulation result*

Summary

In this chapter you learned how to simulate a dynamic system in the Simulink environment. To do so, the given time domain differential equations must be converted into a state space model. The obtained state space model can be implemented with the aid of Integrator blocks. You learned how to decrease the number of integrators used in the Simulink model, how to transfer the simulation results from Simulink into MATLAB, and how to simulate discrete time models.

In the next chapter, we will learn how to simulate uncontrolled AC-DC converters with the aid of Simscape™ blocks.

CHAPTER 3

Important Measurements on Signals

In the previous chapter, we learned how to simulate a differential equation in the Simulink environment. In this chapter we will use Simscape™ to create models of physical systems within the Simulink environment. Simscape provides many blocks for different types of systems. However, we will study the blocks related to power electronics only. We will use the Simscape blocks to simulate a simple half-wave rectifier. We will use the Scope block to observe the load waveforms. Then we will learn how to measure important quantities like average and Root Mean Square (RMS) values of a signal. The techniques shown in this chapter will be used widely in the book.

Example 1: Single-Phase Half-Wave Diode Rectifier

In this example, we want to simulate a single-phase half-wave rectifier shown in Figure 3-1.

© Farzin Asadi 2022
F. Asadi, *Simulation of Power Electronics Circuits with MATLAB®/Simulink®*,
Maker Innovations Series, https://doi.org/10.1007/978-1-4842-8220-5_3

Figure 3-1. *Single-phase half-wave rectifier*

Enter the Simulink environment (Figure 3-2).

Figure 3-2. *simulink command*

The Simulink Start Page window appears. Click the Blank Model (Figure 3-3).

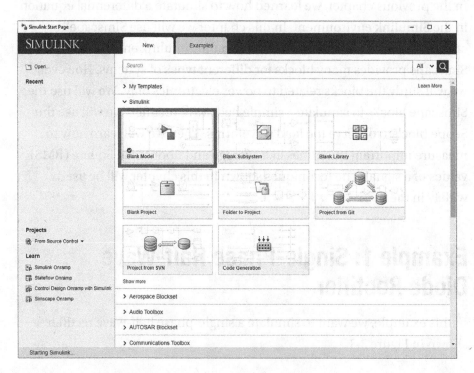

Figure 3-3. *Simulink Start Page*

Now the Simulink environment with a blank project is ready (Figure 3-4).

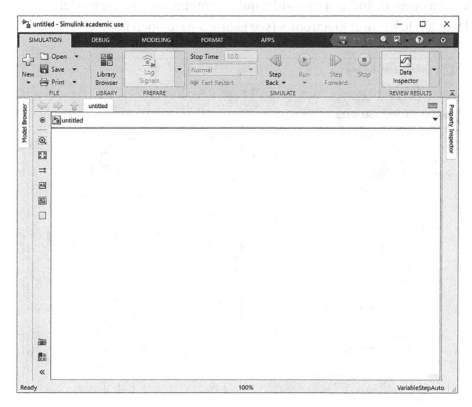

Figure 3-4. *Simulink environment*

Click Library Browser (Figure 3-5).

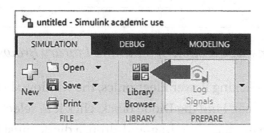

Figure 3-5. *Library Browser button*

After clicking Library Browser, the Simulink Library Browser window will be opened, and you can add required components to the model. Double-click Power Electronics (see Figure 3-6) to open it.

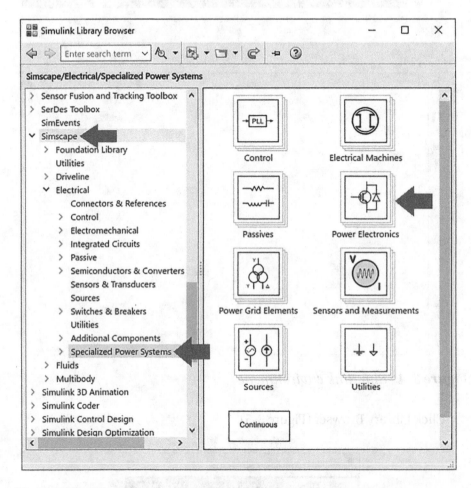

Figure 3-6. *Simscape section of Simulink Library Browser*

After double-clicking Power Electronics, the window shown in Figure 3-7 will appear. Find the Diode block, click it to select it, and drag and drop it to the model. After drag-and-drop, a diode must be added to the Simulink model (see Figure 3-8).

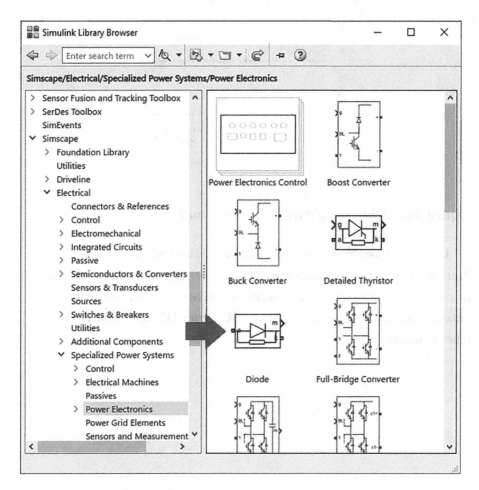

Figure 3-7. *Diode block*

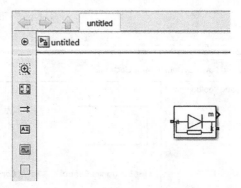

Figure 3-8. *Addition of a diode to the Simulink model*

Go to the Passives section (see Figure 3-9) and add a Series RLC
Branch element to the model (see Figure 3-10). Series RLC Branch can
be used to simulate series RLC, purely resistive (R), purely inductive (L),
purely capacitive (C), series RL, series RC, series LC, and open-circuit
types of loads.

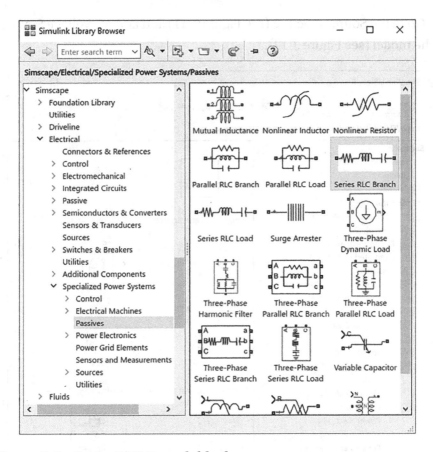

Figure 3-9. *Series RLC Branch block*

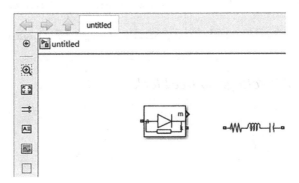

Figure 3-10. *Addition of the Series RLC Branch block to the Simulink model*

Go to the Sources section (see Figure 3-11) and add AC Voltage Source to the model (see Figure 3-12).

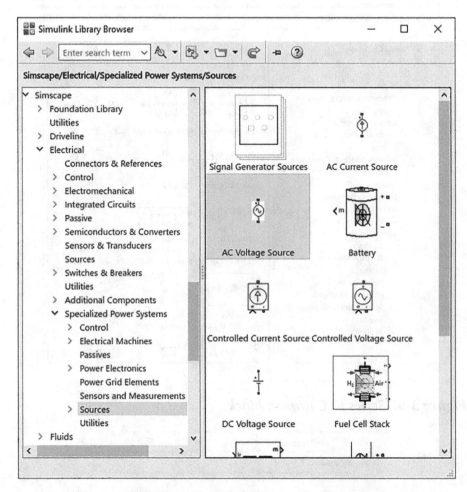

Figure 3-11. *AC Voltage Source block*

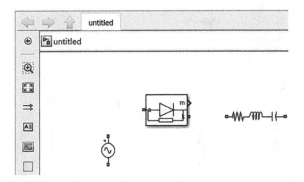

Figure 3-12. *Addition of the AC Voltage Source block to the Simulink model*

Let's rotate the Series RLC Branch element. To do this, click it (see Figure 3-13) and press Ctrl+R (see Figure 3-14). Ctrl+R rotates the block 90 degrees clockwise. If you want to rotate a block counterclockwise, then you need to press Ctrl+Shift+R.

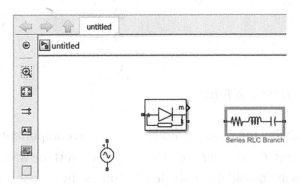

Figure 3-13. *Selection of Series RLC Branch*

117

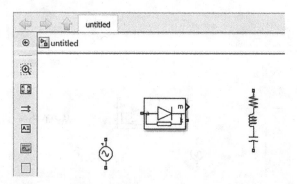

Figure 3-14. *Series RLC Branch is rotated*

There is another way to rotate a block as well: you can right-click the block and use Rotate & Flip from the pop-up menu (Figure 3-15).

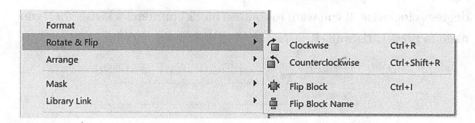

Figure 3-15. *Rotate & Flip*

When you bring the mouse pointer close to the component terminals, it will be changed to crosshair and permits you to start the wiring. After seeing the crosshair, hold down the left button on the mouse and drag the connection toward the destination node and release the button on the destination node. Use this method to connect the components together (Figure 3-16).

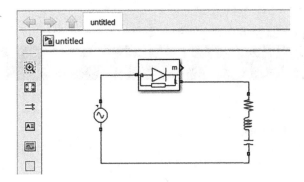

Figure 3-16. *Model of a single-phase diode rectifier in the Simulink environment*

Double-click Series RLC Branch. The window shown in Figure 3-17 appears and permits you to enter the parameters. If you click the Help button, the documentation of the block (see Figure 3-18) will be shown.

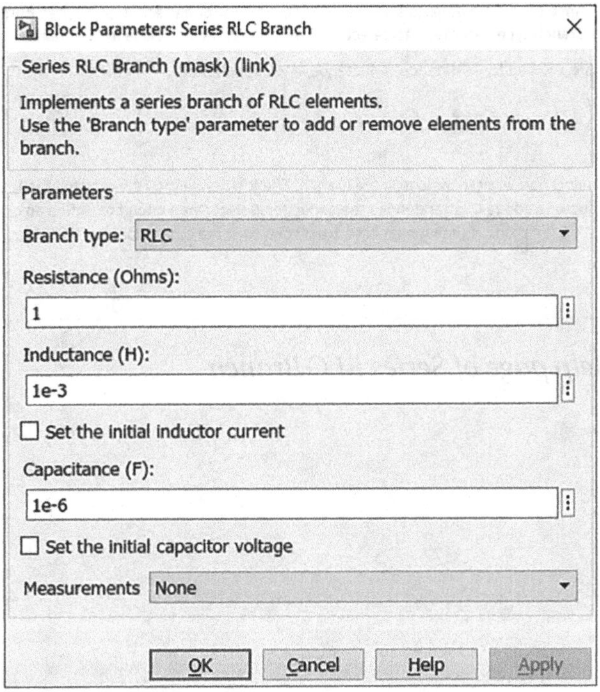

Figure 3-17. *Parameters of Series RLC Branch*

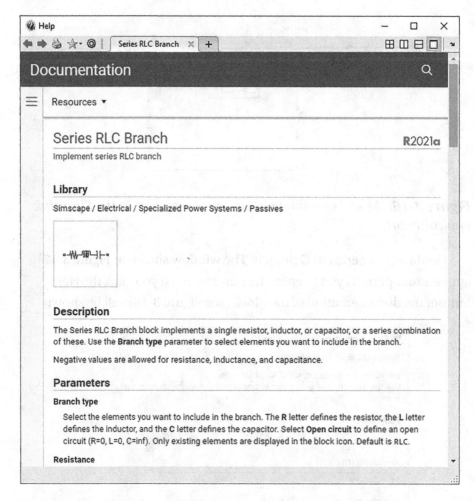

Figure 3-18. *Help page of Series RLC Branch*

Use the Branch type drop-down list (see Figure 3-19) to select a purely resistive (R) load. Enter 10 in the Resistance (Ohms) box (see Figure 3-20) to set the resistance to 10 Ω.

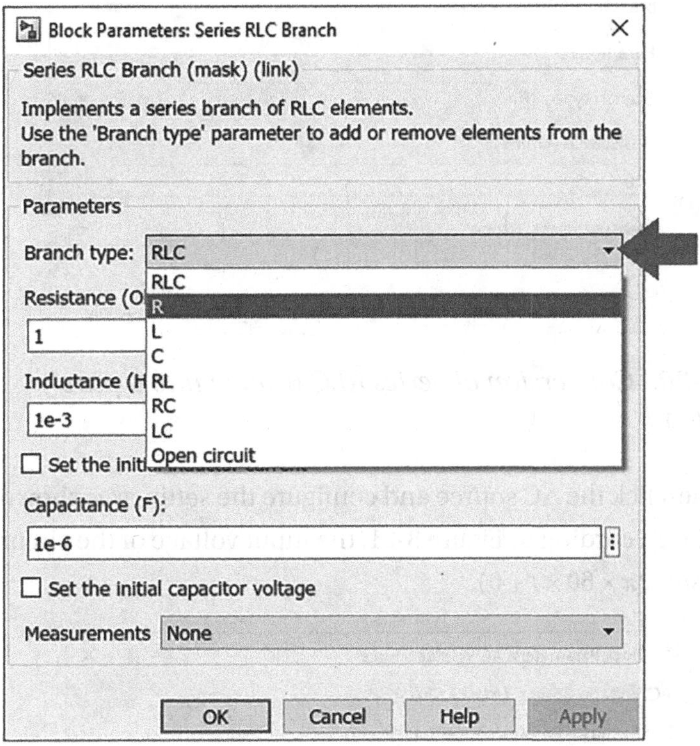

Figure 3-19. *Branch type drop-down list*

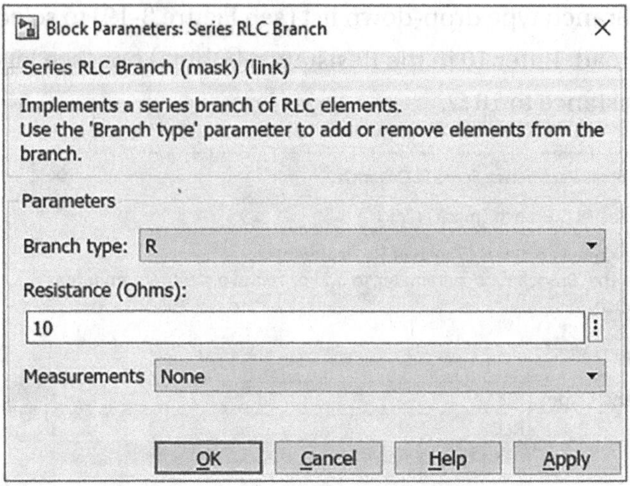

Block Parameters: Series RLC Branch   ×

Series RLC Branch (mask) (link)

Implements a series branch of RLC elements.
Use the 'Branch type' parameter to add or remove elements from the branch.

Parameters

Branch type: R   ▼

Resistance (Ohms):

10   ⋮

Measurements None   ▼

OK   Cancel   Help   Apply

Figure 3-20. *Conversion of Series RLC Branch into a purely resistive load*

Double-click the AC source and configure the settings as shown in Figure 3-21. According to Figure 3-21, the input voltage of the circuit is $v(t) = 311 \sin(2\pi \times 60 \times t + 0)$.

Block Parameters: AC Voltage Source   ×

AC Voltage Source (mask) (link)

Ideal sinusoidal AC Voltage source.

Parameters   Load Flow

Peak amplitude (V):   311   ⋮

Phase (deg):   0   ⋮

Frequency (Hz):   60   ⋮

Sample time: 0   ⋮

Measurements None   ▼

OK   Cancel   Help   Apply

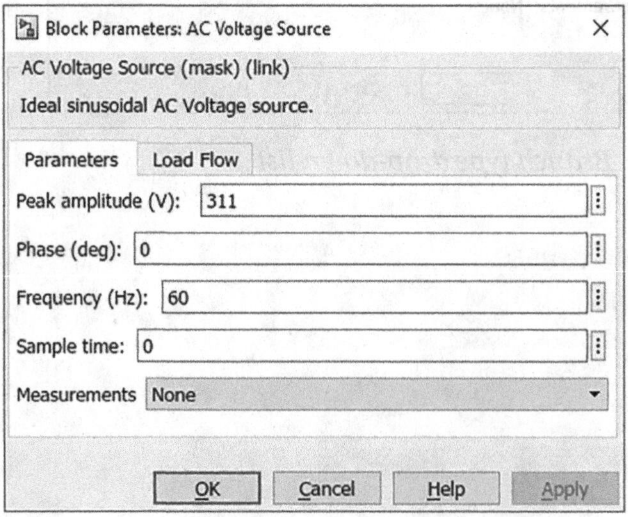

Figure 3-21. *Settings of the AC Voltage Source block*

Double-click the diode button. The window shown in Figure 3-22 appears and permits you to change the diode parameters.

Block Parameters: Diode	✕

Diode (mask) (link)

Implements a diode in parallel with a series RC snubber circuit. In on-state the Diode model has an internal resistance (Ron) and inductance (Lon). For most applications the internal inductance should be set to zero. The Diode impedance is infinite in off-state mode.

Parameters

Resistance Ron (Ohms) :

```
0.001
```

Inductance Lon (H) :

```
0
```

Forward voltage Vf (V) :

```
0.8
```

Initial current Ic (A) :

```
0
```

Snubber resistance Rs (Ohms) :

```
500
```

Snubber capacitance Cs (F) :

```
250e-9
```

☑ Show measurement port

| OK | Cancel | Help | Apply |

Figure 3-22. *Parameters of the Diode block*

The equivalent circuit of the Simulink diode is shown in Figure 3-23. The Rs and Cs indicate the snubber resistor and capacitor, respectively. Values of these components are set by the Snubber resistance Rs (Ohms) and Snubber capacitance Cs (F) boxes in Figure 3-22, respectively. Default values of Rs and Cs are 500 Ω and 250 nF, respectively. You can simulate a purely resistive snubber by entering inf in the Snubber capacitance Cs (F) box.

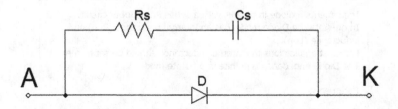

Figure 3-23. *Model of the Diode block*

The equivalent circuit of the forward biased diode is shown in Figure 3-24. Values of Ron, Lon, and VF are set by Resistance Ron (Ohms), Inductance Lon (H), and Forward voltage Vf (V) boxes, respectively.

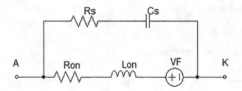

Figure 3-24. *Model of the forward biased Diode block*

The equivalent circuit of the reverse biased diode is shown in Figure 3-25.

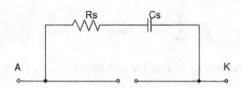

Figure 3-25. *Model of the reverse biased Diode block*

The snubber resistor and capacitor are not required in this book. You can minimize the effect Rs and Cs have on the circuit by entering a big value in the Snubber resistance Rs (Ohms) box. All the simulations in this book use the diode parameters shown in Figure 3-26.

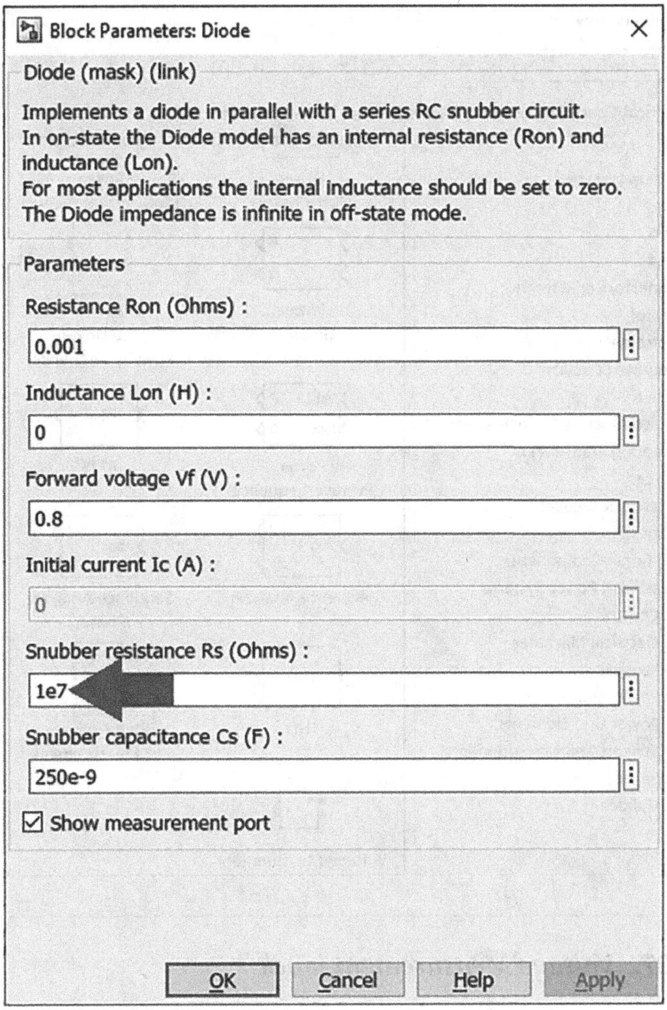

Figure 3-26. Settings of the Diode block

The Voltage Measurement (see Figure 3-27) and Current Measurement (see Figure 3-28) blocks can be used to measure the circuit voltage and current, respectively. Add a Voltage Measurement block to the model (see Figure 3-29).

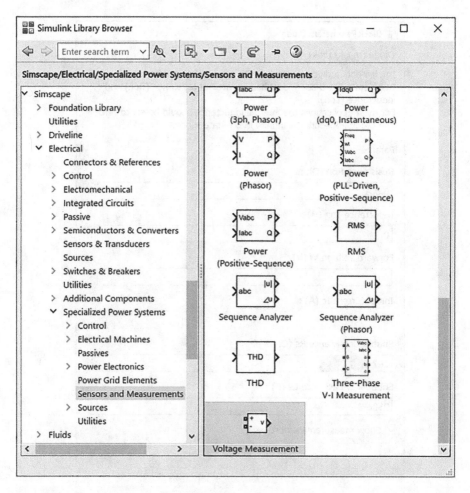

Figure 3-27. *Voltage Measurement block*

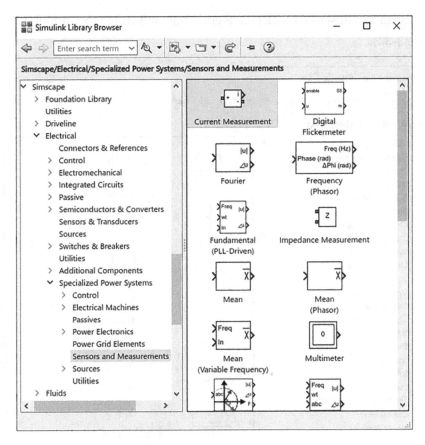

Figure 3-28. *Current Measurement block*

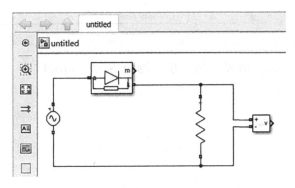

Figure 3-29. *Addition of the Voltage Measurement block to the Simulink model*

Add an oscilloscope block (see Figure 3-30 or 3-31) to the model (see Figure 3-32).

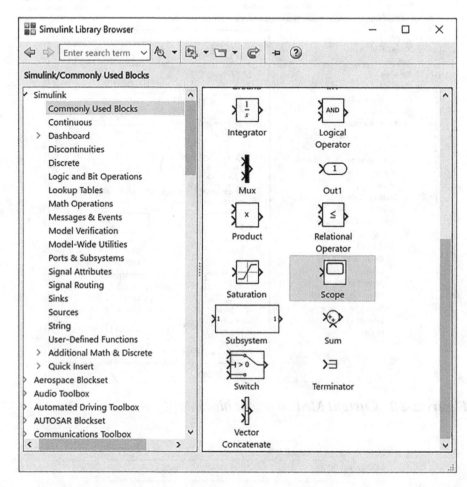

Figure 3-30. *Commonly Used Blocks* ➤ *Scope block*

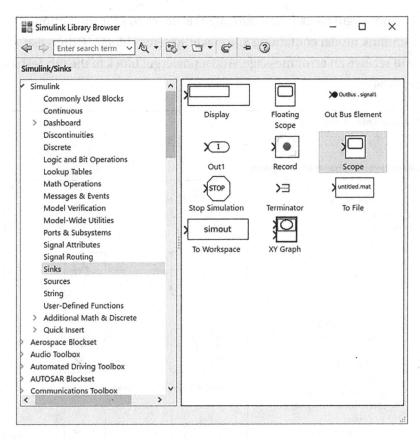

Figure 3-31. *Sinks ➤ Scope block*

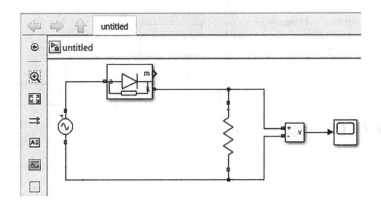

Figure 3-32. *Addition of the Scope block to the Simulink model*

The powergui block (see Figure 3-33) is necessary for simulation of any Simulink model containing SimPowerSystems™ blocks. Otherwise, you will receive an error message. Add a powergui block to the model (see Figure 3-34).

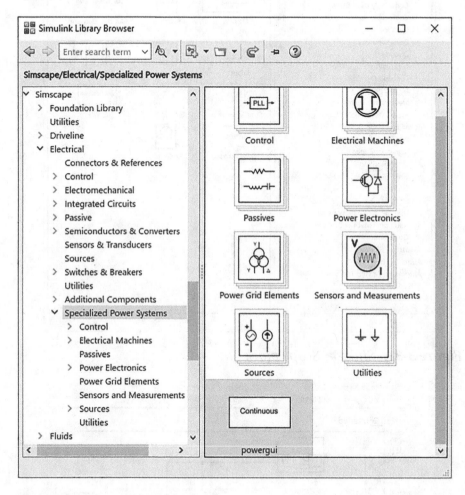

Figure 3-33. *powergui block*

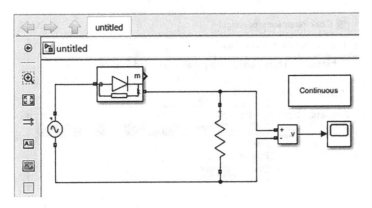

Figure 3-34. *Addition of the powergui block to the Simulink model*

Double-click the powergui block. The window shown in Figure 3-35 appears. You have four options for simulation type. Continuous uses a variable-step solver from Simulink to solve the circuit. Discrete uses a fixed step size determined by the user to solve the circuit. Phasor and discrete phasor are suitable for power system analysis and are not used in this book. Continuous and discrete are good solvers for power electronic circuits. If you want to use the discrete solver, ensure to select the time step, which is smaller than the switching period of the system. For instance, for a DC-DC converter with switching frequency (f) of 100 KHz, the time step of simulation must be less than $1/(10.f)= 1$ μs. Even, using 0.1 μs is recommended. When you do a discrete simulation and the output waveforms are not smooth enough, decreasing the step size can be a good idea to obtain smoother waveforms.

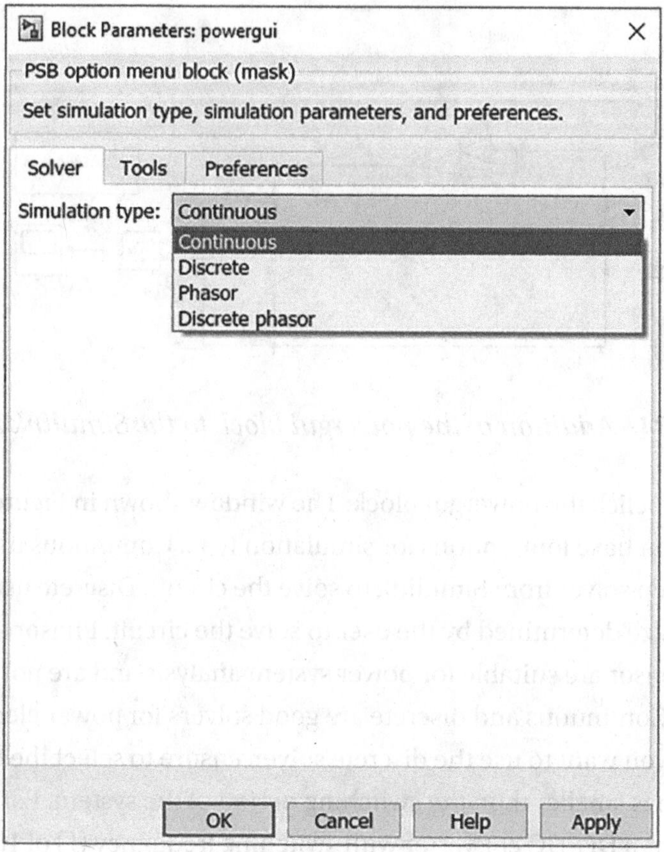

Figure 3-35. *Simulation type drop-down list*

Configure the settings of the powergui block as shown in Figure 3-36.

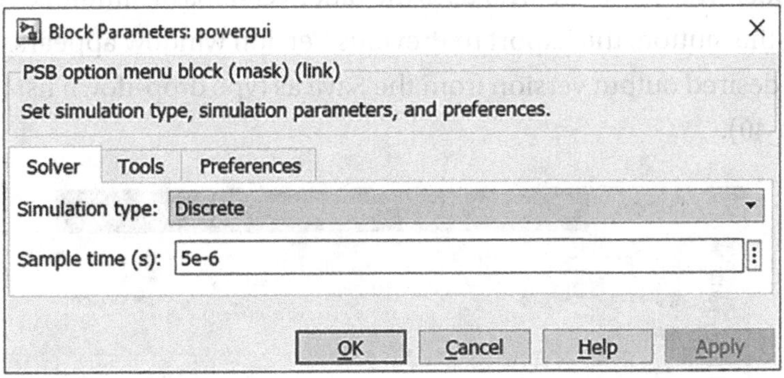

Figure 3-36. *powergui block settings*

We want to study the behavior of the circuit for 100 ms interval. Enter 100e-3 in the Stop Time box (Figure 3-37). The Stop Time box determines the end time of simulation.

Figure 3-37. *Stop Time box settings*

You can save the model by clicking the Save icon (Figure 3-38).

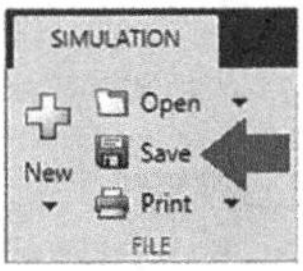

Figure 3-38. *Save button*

Use the Previous Version button (see Figure 3-39) if you want to share your model with someone who uses the older versions of Simulink. After clicking this button, the Export to Previous Version window appears. Use the desired output version from the Save as type drop-down list (see Figure 3-40).

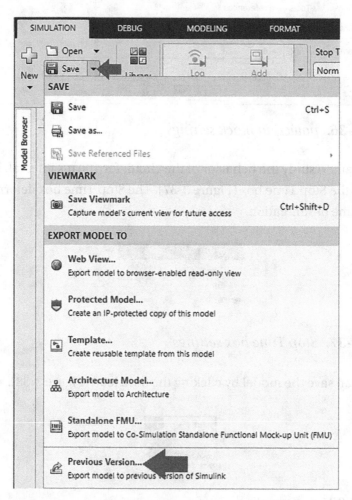

Figure 3-39. *Previous Version button*

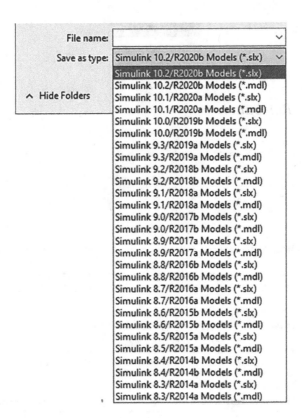

Figure 3-40. *Different types of output files*

Use the Run button (or press Ctrl+T) to run the simulation (see Figure 3-41). If you try to simulate the model without the powergui block, the error message shown in Figure 3-42 will appear.

Figure 3-41. *Run button*

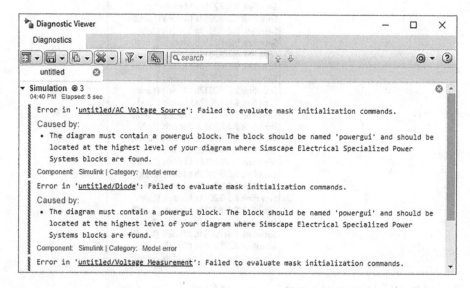

Figure 3-42. *Diagnostic Viewer*

Double-click the Scope block to see its waveform (Figure 3-43).

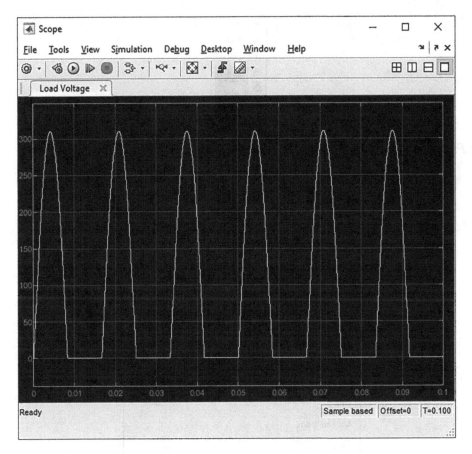

Figure 3-43. *Simulation result*

The oscilloscope block has black background, yellow waveforms, and gray scales by default. You can use the Style button (see Figure 3-44) to change these colors. After clicking the Style button, the window shown in Figure 3-45 appears and permits you to select the desired color for each section.

Figure 3-44. *Style button*

Figure 3-45. *Style: Scope window*

Sometimes the Simulink model contains many oscilloscopes. Use the Highlight Simulink block (see Figure 3-46 or 3-47) to see which waveform belongs to which oscilloscope. After clicking the Highlight Simulink block, the related oscilloscope block will be highlighted (see Figure 3-48). Another way to show which waveform belongs to which oscilloscope is to use meaningful names for the oscilloscope blocks (i.e., names like load voltage, load current, etc.). This method is shown in Example 3.

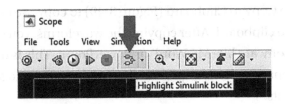

Figure 3-46. *Highlight Simulink block button*

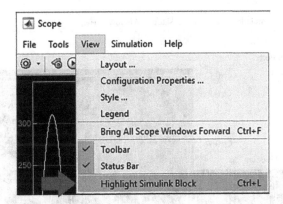

Figure 3-47. *View ▶ Highlight Simulink Block*

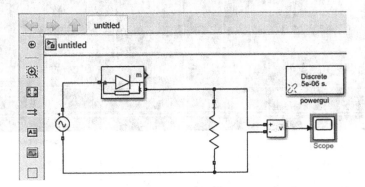

Figure 3-48. *the Scope block is highlighted*

You can use Copy to Clipboard (Figure 3-49) to copy the oscilloscope waveform to the clipboard. After copying the waveforms, you can paste them in other software like MS Word® or PowerPoint®. This is useful when you want to prepare a report or presentation and you need to show your simulation results.

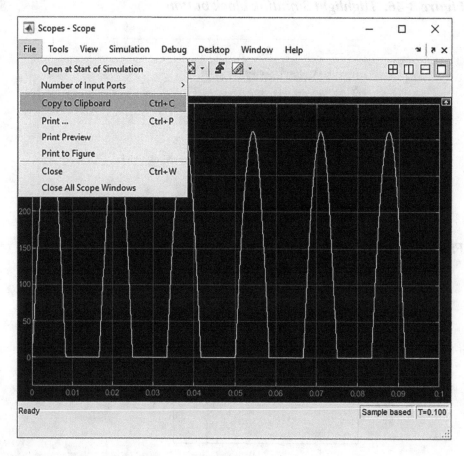

Figure 3-49.   *File ➤ Copy to Clipboard*

In the next example, we will learn how to use the Scope block to do some useful measurements.

Example 2: Measurement with the Oscilloscope Block

You can use the oscilloscope to measure the frequency, value of a waveform at a specific time, and maximum/minimum value, average value, and Root Mean Square (RMS) value of the waveform. In this example, we want to measure these parameters for the waveform obtained in Example 1. Click the Cursor Measurement icon (see Figure 3-50).

Figure 3-50. *Cursor Measurement icon*

After clicking the Cursor Measurement icon, two vertical cursors and a small window will be added to the screen (Figure 3-51). Move these cursors to the desired points. The coordinates of cursors will be shown in the Cursor Measurement window. If you put one cursor at the beginning of a period and the other one at the end of a period, the 1/ΔT row shows the frequency to you.

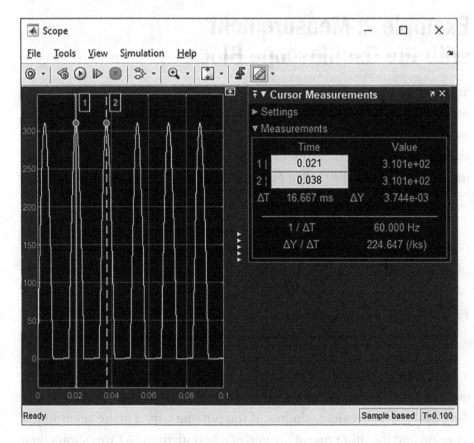

Figure 3-51. *Two vertical cursors and a Cursor Measurement window are added to the Scope block*

Let's measure the average value and RMS value of a waveform. Use the Zoom X button (see Figure 3-52) to select one full cycle from the steady-state region of the waveform (see Figure 3-53). The load of Example 1 is resistive, so we have no transients, and we can select even the first cycle of the output voltage. However, for dynamic loads, you must select the full cycle from the steady-state region of the waveform.

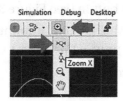

Figure 3-52. *Zoom X button*

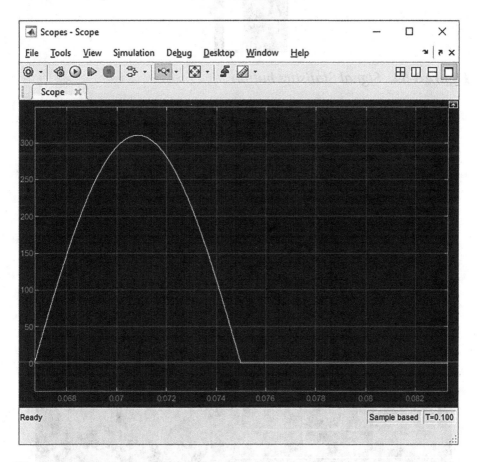

Figure 3-53. *One cycle of output is selected*

Click the Signal Statistics button (see Figure 3-54). According to Figure 3-55, the maximum value is 310.2, minimum value is about zero, average value is 98.71 V, and RMS value is 155.1 V. Note that the average value is shown in the Mean row.

Figure 3-54. *Signal Statistics button*

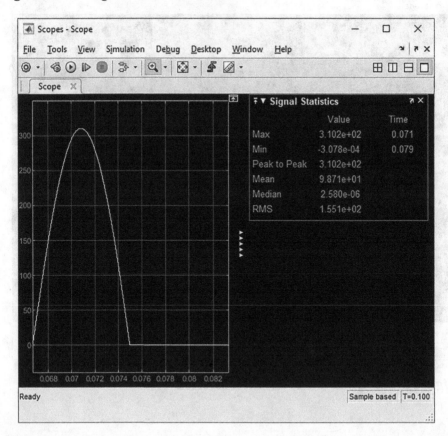

Figure 3-55. *The Signal Statistics window shows the Max, Min, Peak to Peak, Mean, Median, and RMS of the signal*

Up to now we used the Voltage Measurement and Current Measurement blocks to measure the voltage and current, respectively. Another way to measure voltage and current is to use the Multimeter block. This is studied in the next example.

Example 3: Measurement with the Multimeter Block

In this example we want to simulate the circuit shown in Figure 3-56 and see the waveforms of the capacitor voltage and current. The initial values of the inductor current and capacitor voltage are shown in Figure 3-56. Using the Voltage Measurement and Current Measurement blocks (see Figures 3-27 and 3-28) is not the only way to measure the voltage and current of a circuit. Using the Multimeter block (see Figure 3-57) is another way to measure the voltage/current. We use the Multimeter block in this example.

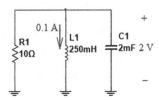

Figure 3-56. *Simple parallel RLC circuit*

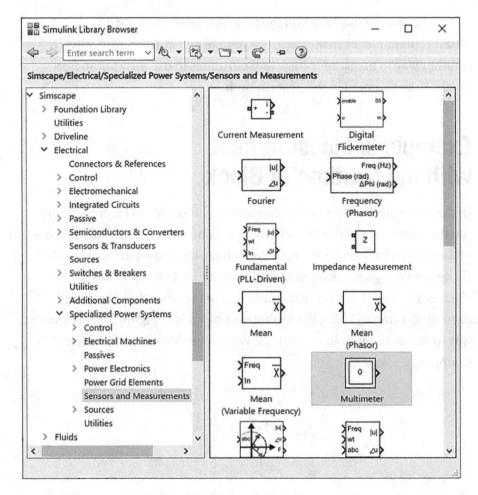

Figure 3-57. *Multimeter block*

Many of the components in the Electrical section of Simscape have a plus sign on one of the terminals (see Figure 3-58). This plus sign permits the reference direction of current/voltage measurement to be defined for the Multimeter block: the current that enters this plus sign is assumed to be positive, and the voltage that is measured by the Multimeter block is

$$V_{terminal\ with\ +\ sign} - V_{terminal\ without\ +\ sign}.$$

Figure 3-58. *The left terminal has a plus sign on it*

Draw the model shown in Figure 3-59. This model uses three Series RLC Branch blocks. Simulink gives the Series RLC Branch, Series RLC Branch1, and Series RLC Branch2 names to these blocks. You can change these default names to what you want. In order to change the name, click the block; this shows the block name. Now you can click the current name and enter the new name. In this example default names are changed to R, L, and C. By default, Simulink shows the block name when you put the mouse pointer on it and hides the name when the mouse pointer is not on the block. If you want to show the block name continuously behind the block, you need to right-click the block and turn on Show Block Name (see Figure 3-60). If you want to show the names of a group of blocks, you can click an empty point of the model and draw a rectangle around the desired blocks. Then right-click one of the selected blocks, and use Format ➤ Show Block Name ➤ On to show the block names.

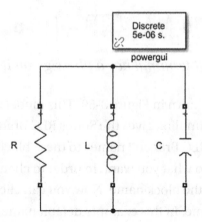

Figure 3-59. *Simulink model of Figure 3-56*

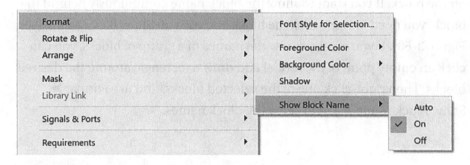

Figure 3-60. *Showing/hiding a block name*

Settings of components are shown in Figures 3-61, 3-62, and 3-63. Note that the Set the initial inductor current and Set the initial capacitor voltage boxes are checked in Figures 3-62 and 3-63, respectively. In Figure 3-63, Branch voltage and current is selected for the Measurements drop-down list. So the voltage and current of a capacitor will be measurable by a Multimeter block.

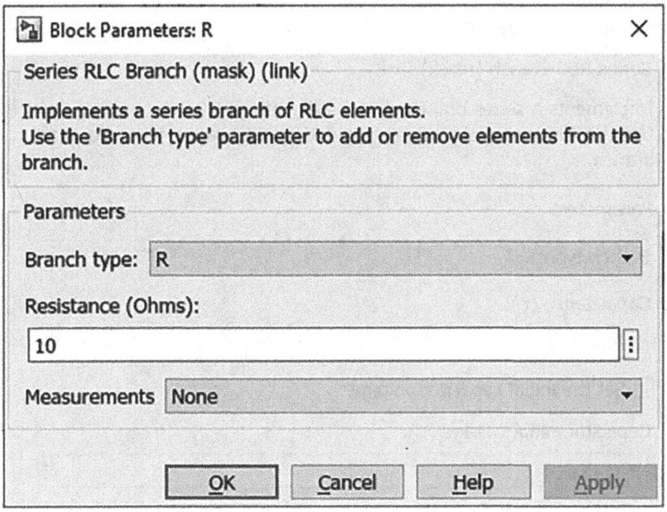

Figure 3-61. *Resistor settings*

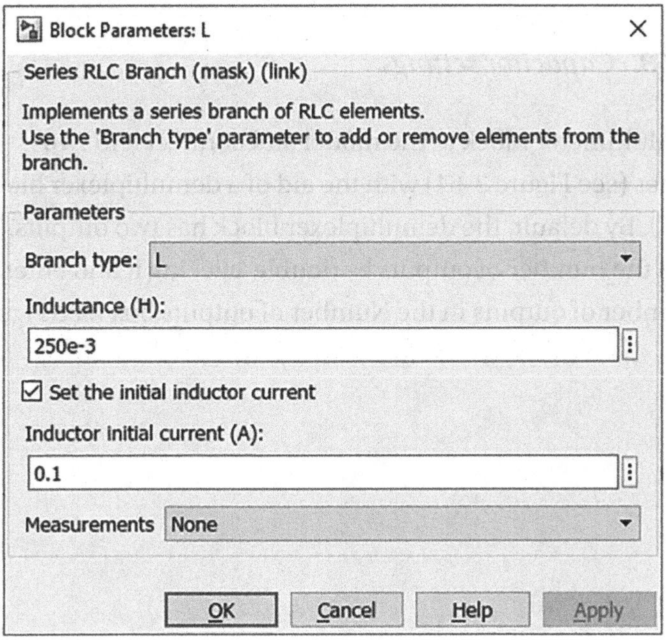

Figure 3-62. *Inductor settings*

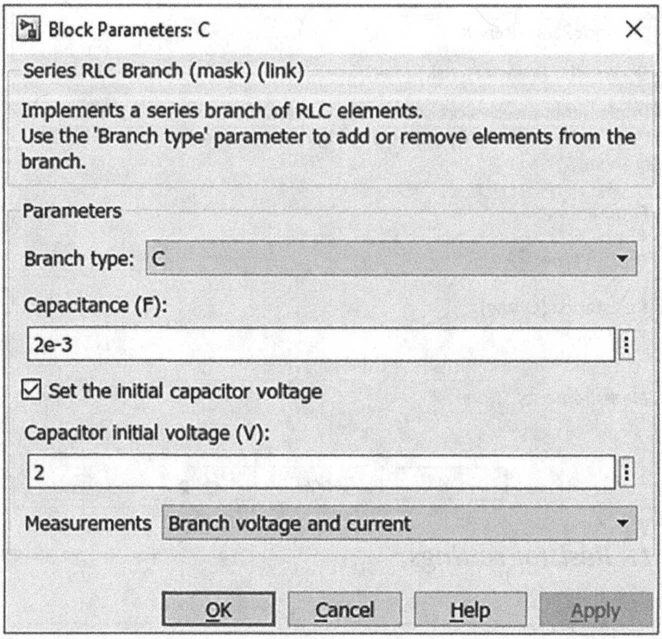

Figure 3-63. *Capacitor settings*

Add a Multimeter block to the model and connect it to two oscilloscopes (see Figure 3-64) with the aid of a demultiplexer block (see Figure 3-65). By default, the demultiplexer block has two outputs. You can change the number of outputs by double-clicking it and entering the desired number of outputs in the Number of outputs box (see Figure 3-66).

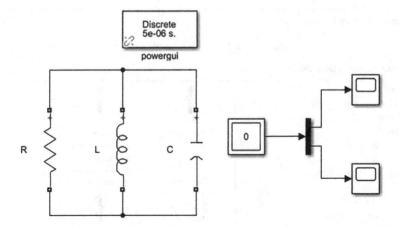

Figure 3-64. *Addition of Multimeter, Demux, and Scope blocks to the Simulink model*

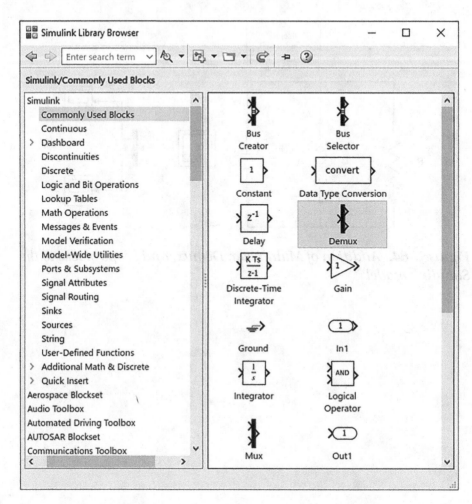

Figure 3-65. *Demux block*

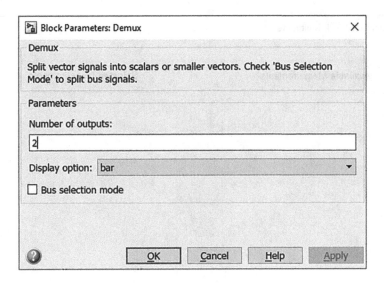

Figure 3-66. *Settings of the Demux block*

Double-click the Multimeter block in Figure 3-64. The window shown in Figure 3-67 appears.

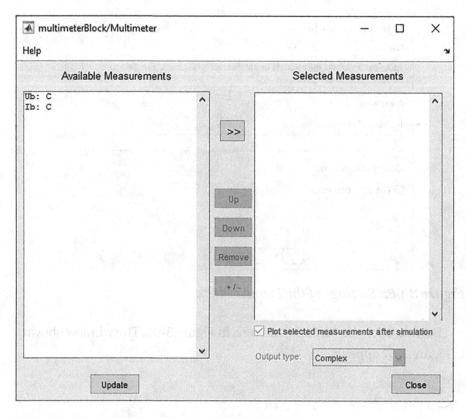

Figure 3-67.   *Settings of the Multimeter block*

Select Ib: C by clicking it (Figure 3-68). Ib: C indicates the current of component C.

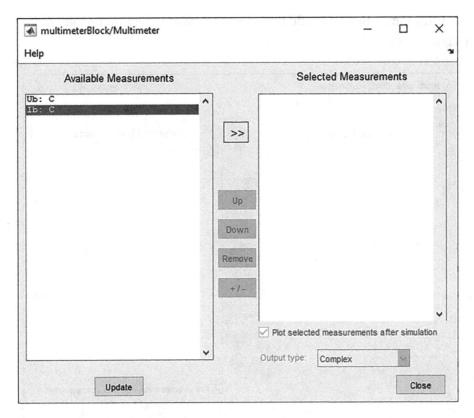

Figure 3-68. *Ib: C is selected*

Click the >> button to add the selected measurement to the right list
(Figure 3-69).

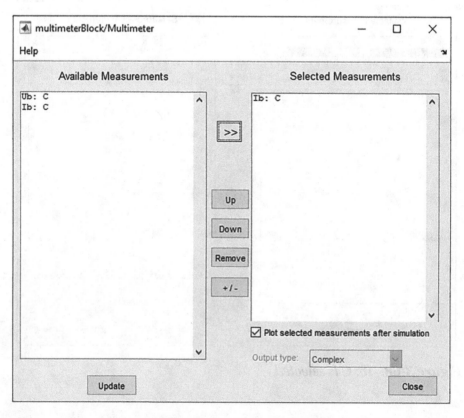

Figure 3-69. *Ib: C is added to the Selected Measurements list. Ib: C
indicates the current of capacitor C*

Use the same steps to add Ub: C to the right list. Ub: C indicates the
voltage of component C. After adding Ub: C to the right list, click the
Close button.

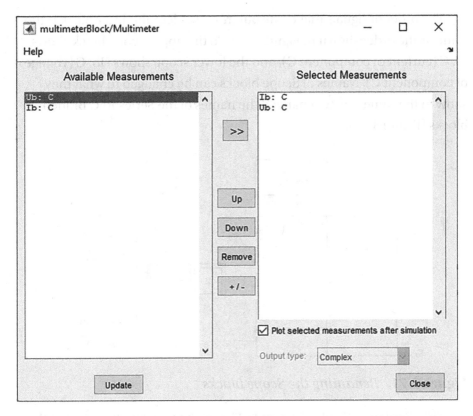

Figure 3-70. *Ub: C is added to the Selected Measurements list. Ub: C indicates the voltage of capacitor C*

The order of signals that come out from the demultiplexer block is the same as the order shown in Figure 3-70. So the upper Scope block shows Ib: C (current of component C), and the lower scope shows Ub: C (voltage of component C). Names of Scope blocks can be changed to what they show in the same way we changed the names of the Series RLC Branch blocks (Figure 3-71).

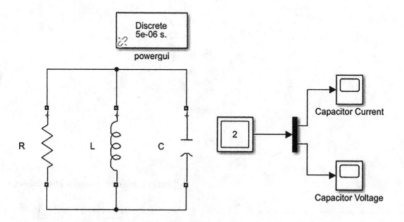

Figure 3-71. *Renaming the Scope blocks*

The simulation result is shown in Figures 3-72 and 3-73. Note that the Scope block names appear on top of the window. This helps us understand quickly what the scope shows.

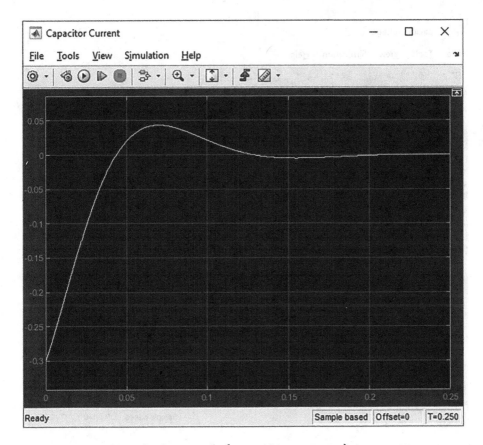

Figure 3-72. *Simulation result (capacitor current)*

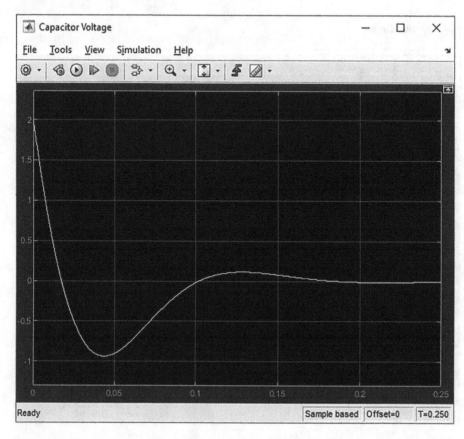

Figure 3-73. *Simulation result (capacitor voltage)*

In the next example, we will learn how to use the measurement port of blocks to measure their voltage and current.

Example 4: Measurement Port

Many of the Simscape components (specially switches) have a port with letter m on it. The m port is the measurement terminal and measures the current and voltage of the block. For instance, consider the model of Example 1, which is shown in Figure 3-74 again.

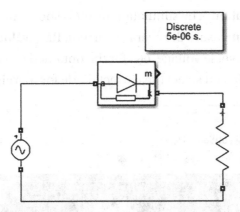

Figure 3-74. *Model of a simple half-wave rectifier*

Connect a demultiplexer block and two scopes to the measurement port (Figure 3-75). The upper signal in the output of the demultiplexer block is the current that goes from the anode to the cathode. The lower signal in the output of the demultiplexer block is the $V_{AC} = V_A - V_C$ where V_A indicates the anode voltage and V_C indicates the cathode voltage.

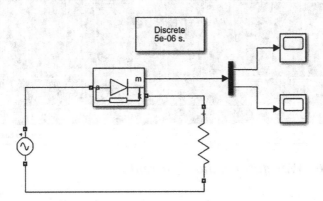

Figure 3-75. *The measurement port of the diode is used to observe the diode current and voltage*

Run the simulation. The simulation result is shown in Figures 3-76 and 3-77. You can measure the average current, RMS value of the current, maximum of the reverse voltage, etc. for the obtained waveforms. Such measurements help you select the correct diode for this circuit.

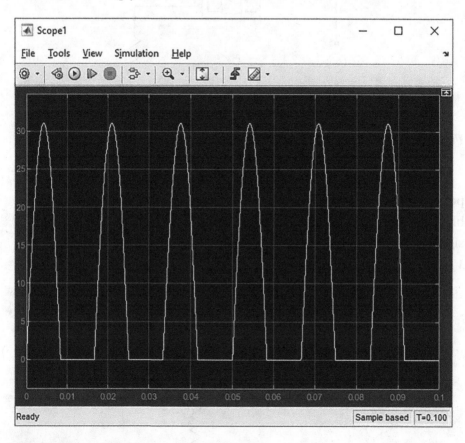

Figure 3-76. *Waveform of diode current*

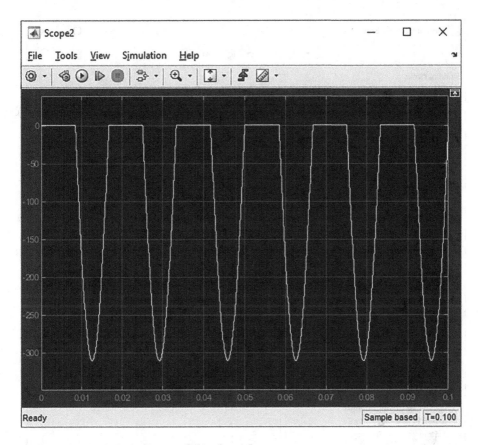

Figure 3-77. *Waveform of diode voltage*

It is better to connect the unused ports to a Terminator block (see Figure 3-78). Note that unconnected ports do not stop your simulation from working; however, they can produce simulation warnings. Figure 3-79 shows a Terminator block, which is connected to the unused measurement port of the diode.

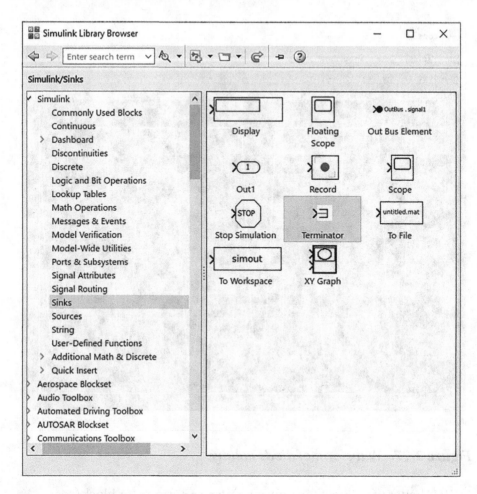

Figure 3-78. *Terminator block*

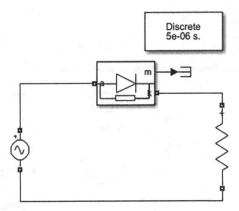

Figure 3-79. *Connecting a Terminator block to the measurement port of the diode*

In the next example, we will learn how to use the Mean and RMS blocks to measure the average and RMS values of signals.

Example 5: Mean and RMS Blocks

A method for calculation of average and RMS values of waveforms is studied in Example 2. Simulink has two specific blocks for calculation of average value (mean) and RMS value of a signal. These blocks are shown in Figures 3-80 and 3-81. The output of these blocks can be connected to the Scope or Display block (see Figure 3-82). Connection to the Display block has the advantage of reading the value quickly. This example shows how these two blocks can be used.

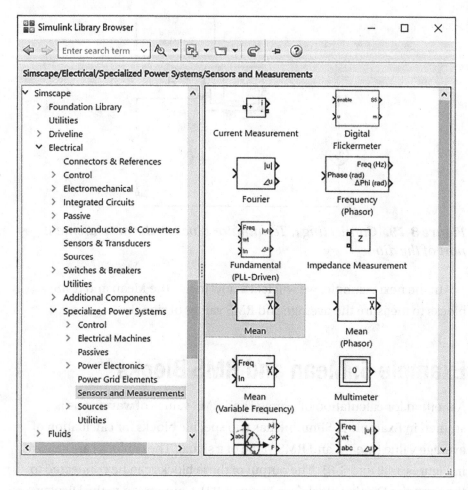

Figure 3-80. *Mean block*

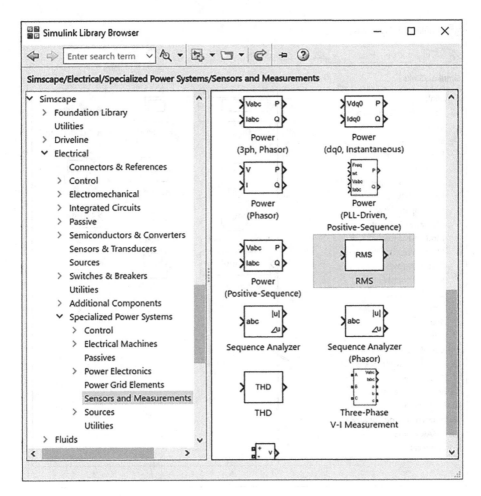

Figure 3-81. RMS block

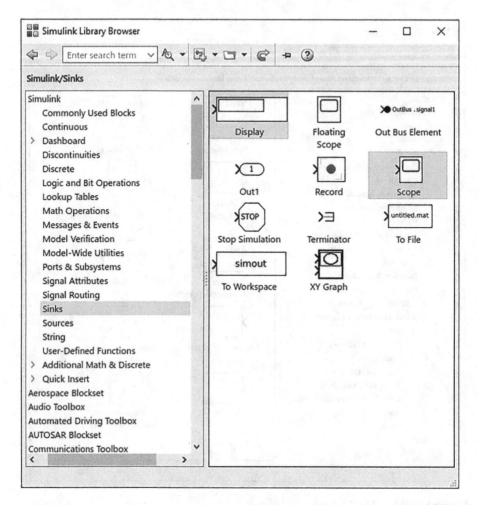

Figure 3-82. *Display and Scope blocks*

Consider the model shown in Figure 3-83. This is a half-wave rectifier with an RL load. The resistance of the load is 100 Ω, and its inductance is 0.1 H. The AC source has a peak of 100 V, and its frequency is 60 Hz. The Snubber resistance Rs (Ohms) parameter of the diode is 1e7, which means 10 MΩ. Other parameters of the diode have default values.

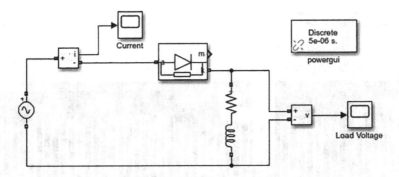

Figure 3-83. *Diode rectifier with RL load*

Enter 834e-3 in the Stop Time box (Figure 3-84). This simulates the behavior of the circuit for 50 cycles of input $(\dfrac{834\,ms}{\dfrac{1}{60}\,s} \oplus 50)$. The circuit has enough time to reach the steady state.

Figure 3-84. *Stop time of the simulation is 834 ms*

Run the simulation. Double-click the Current scope to see the circuit current (see Figure 3-85). Use the Zoom X icon (see Figure 3-85) or Tools ➤ Zoom X (see Figure 3-86) to see the steady-state waveform better (see Figure 3-87).

169

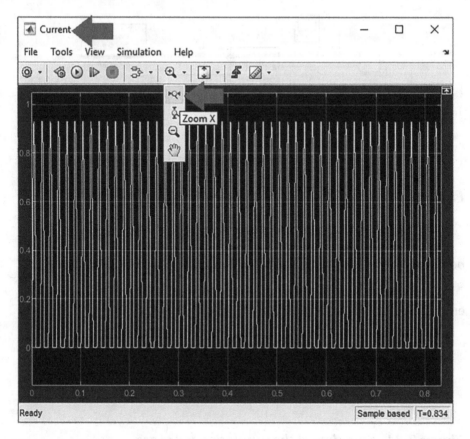

Figure 3-85. *Zoom X icon*

Figure 3-86. *Tools ➤ Zoom X*

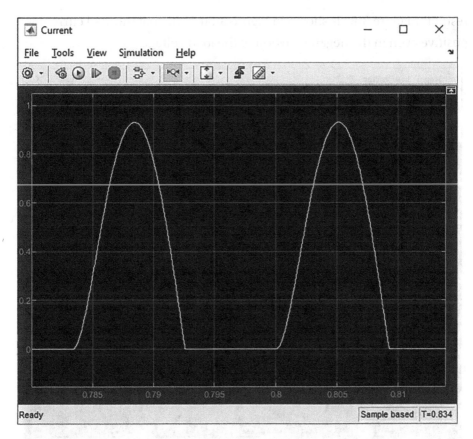

Figure 3-87. *Waveform of load current*

Use the same method to see the load voltage (see Figure 3-88).
Note that in the RL load, the load voltage has a negative section as
well; however, such a thing does not happen for a purely resistive load.
However, even in the negative region of the load voltage, the current is
positive, that is, current flows from the anode toward the cathode. This can
be verified with the aid of added blocks shown in Figure 3-89. The model
in Figure 3-89 shows both the load voltage and current on the same scope
simultaneously. The load voltage is decreased by a factor of 100 since the
load voltage is bigger than the load current. Such a scaling permits you
to have a better view and makes the comparison easier. The simulation

171

result for Figure 3-89 is shown in Figure 3-90. Note that the load current is positive even in the negative region of the load voltage.

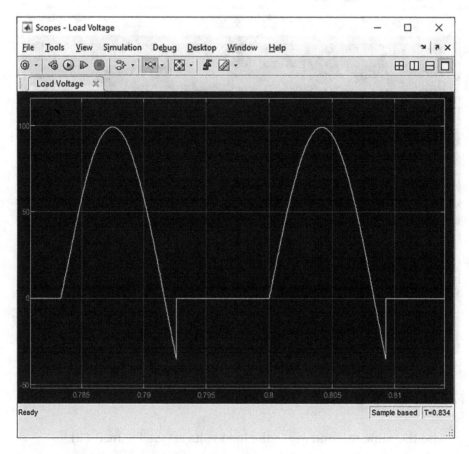

Figure 3-88. *Waveform of load voltage*

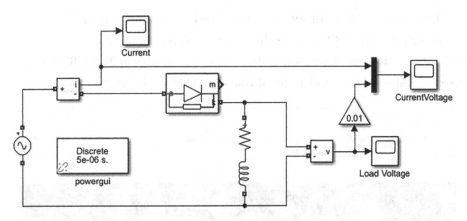

Figure 3-89. *The CurrentVoltage Scope block shows the load current and voltage simultaneously*

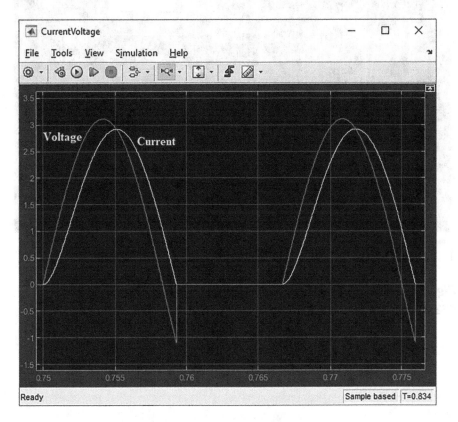

Figure 3-90. *Load current and voltage*

Let's measure the duration in which the load voltage is negative. According to Figure 3-91, the width of this region is 962.953 μs. The calculations in Figure 3-92 show that 962.953 μs equals to 20.7998°. So the diode conducts for a total angle of 180°+20.7998°= 200.7998°.

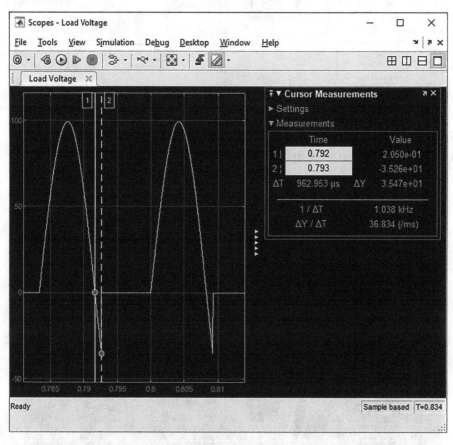

Figure 3-91. *The length of the negative portion of the graph is* *962.953 μs*

Figure 3-92. *962.953 μs equals to 20.7998°*

Let's measure the average value and RMS value of load voltage and current. Change the model to that shown in Figure 3-93.

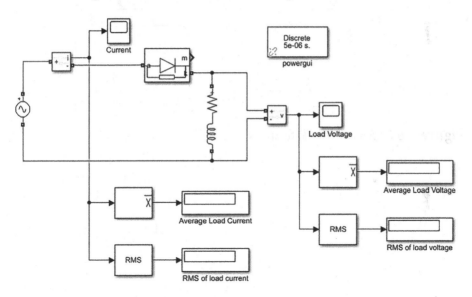

Figure 3-93. *Measurement of RMS and mean values of load current and voltage*

Settings of the Mean and RMS blocks are shown in Figures 3-94 and 3-95, respectively. The frequency of the waveform must be entered into the Fundamental frequency (Hz) box. In this example, the frequency of load voltage/current is the same as the frequency of the input AC source.

175

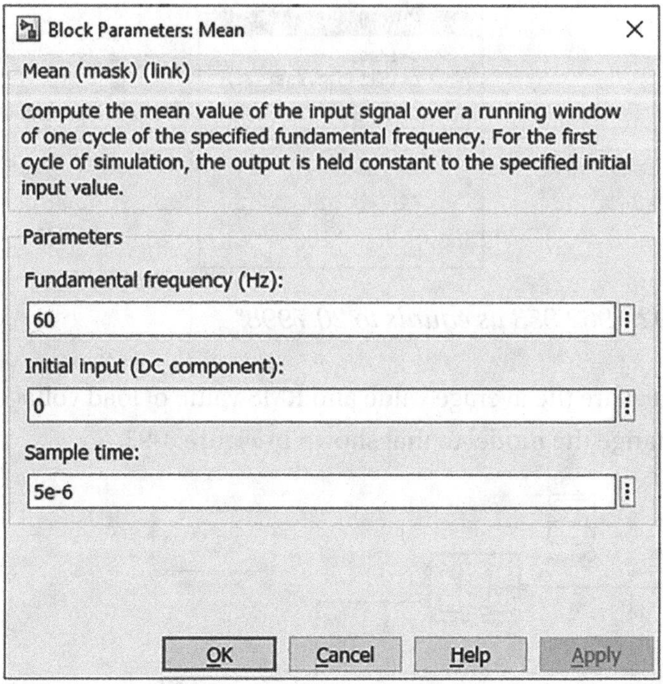

Figure 3-94. *Mean block settings*

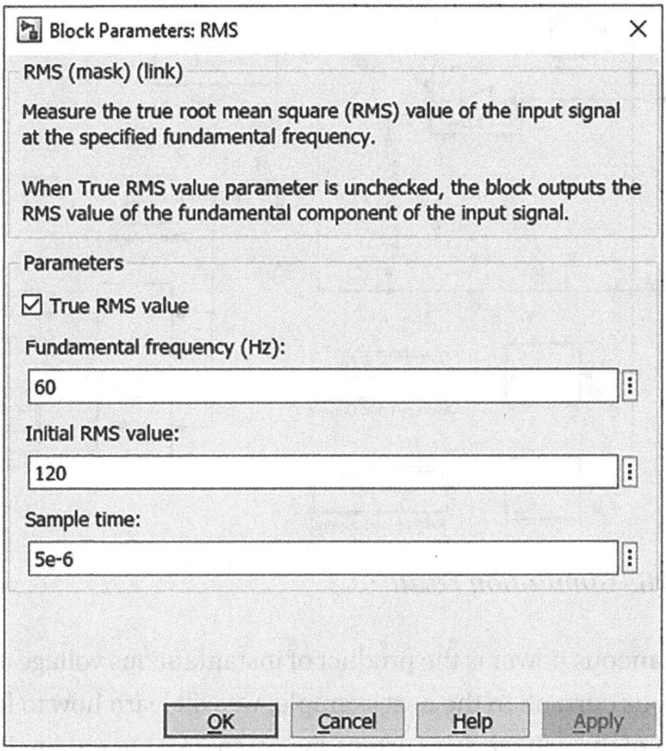

Figure 3-95. *RMS block settings*

Run the simulation. According to Figure 3-96, the average value of load current is 0.3041 A, and the RMS value of load current is 0.4685 A. The average value of load voltage is 30.4 V, and the RMS value of load voltage is 49.74 V.

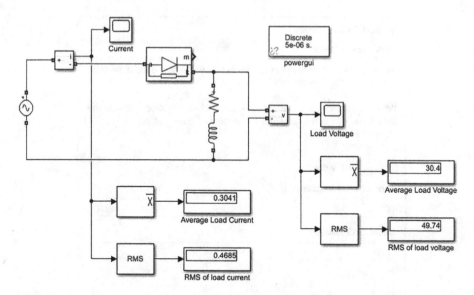

Figure 3-96. *Simulation result*

Instantaneous power is the product of instantaneous voltage and instantaneous current. In the next example, we will learn how to form the product of the voltage and current signals in order to obtain the instantaneous power signal. If we pass the obtained instantaneous power signal through a Mean block, then we will obtain the average power.

Example 6: Instantaneous Power and Average Power

This example shows how you can see the instantaneous power waveform and measure the average power of the load. Consider the model shown in Figure 3-97. Component values are the same as those of Example 5. Settings of the Mean block are shown in Figure 3-98. The multiplication can be done with the aid of the Product block (see Figure 3-99). Another way to do the multiplication is to use the Divide block (see Figure 3-100).

After adding the Divide block to the model, double-click it and enter ** in the Number of inputs box (see Figure 3-101). This converts the block into a multiplier.

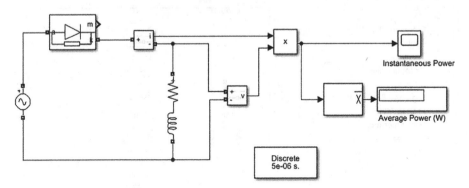

Figure 3-97. *Voltage and current are multiplied to form the instantaneous power. Instantaneous power is used to measure the average power*

> **Block Parameters: Mean**   ×
>
> Mean (mask) (link)
>
> Compute the mean value of the input signal over a running window of one cycle of the specified fundamental frequency. For the first cycle of simulation, the output is held constant to the specified initial input value.
>
> Parameters
>
> Fundamental frequency (Hz):
>
> 60
>
> Initial input (DC component):
>
> 0
>
> Sample time:
>
> 0
>
> OK   Cancel   Help   Apply

Figure 3-98. *Mean block settings*

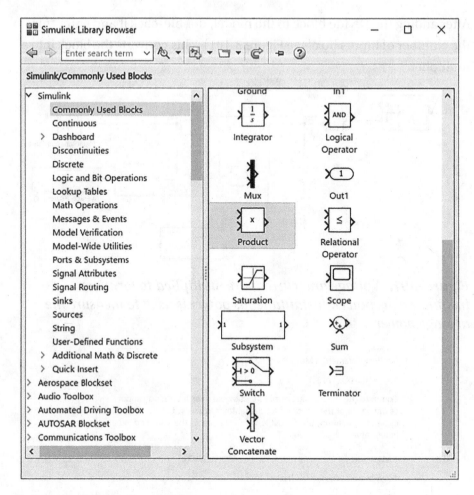

Figure 3-99. *Product block*

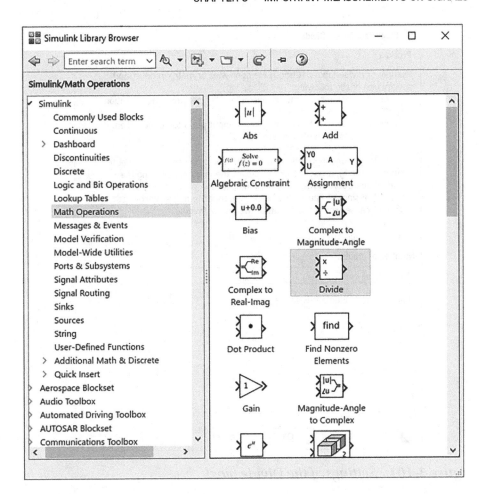

Figure 3-100. *Divide block*

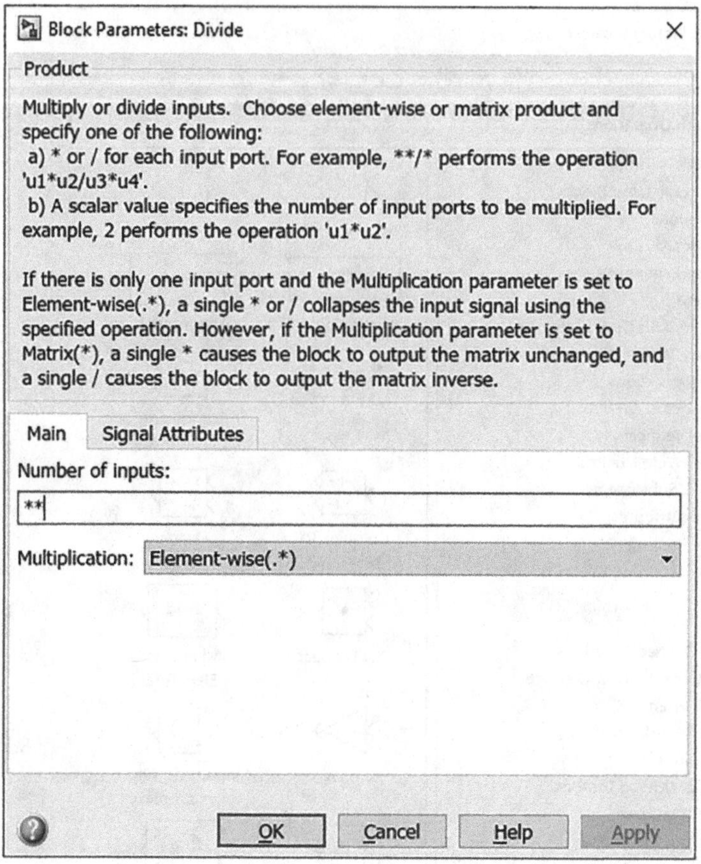

Figure 3-101. *Settings of the Divide block*

Run the simulation. According to Figure 3-102, the average power is 21.95 W.

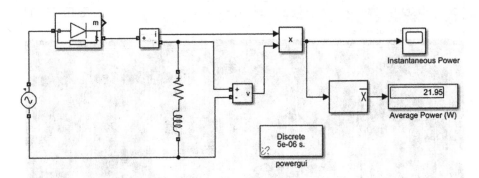

Figure 3-102. *Simulation result*

The instantaneous load power is shown in Figure 3-103. According to Figure 3-104, the frequency of this waveform is 60 Hz. That is why the Fundamental frequency (Hz) box of the Mean block (see Figure 3-98) is filled with 60.

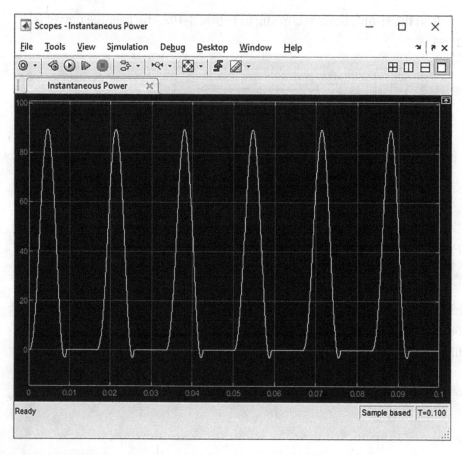

Figure 3-103. *Simulation result*

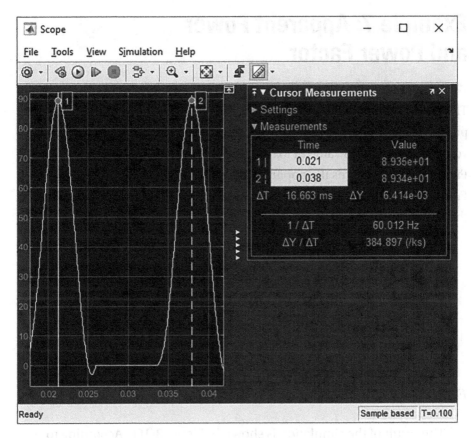

Figure 3-104. *Simulation result*

In this example we learned how to measure the average power. In the next example, we will learn how to measure the apparent power. The RMS block will be used for this purpose. We will obtain the circuit power factor by dividing the average power by the measured apparent power.

Example 7: Apparent Power and Power Factor

We want to measure the apparent power and power factor of Example 5. The power factor is defined as the ratio of average power to apparent power. The apparent power is the product of the RMS value of source voltage and the RMS value of load current. The model shown in Figure 3-105 measures the apparent power and power factor. The Fundamental frequency (Hz) box of the RMS block is filled with 60 since the frequency of load voltage/current is 60 Hz.

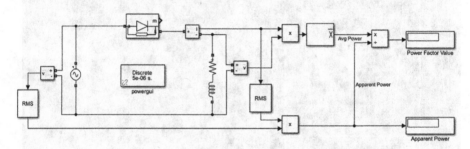

Figure 3-105. *Simulink model of Example 7*

The result of the simulation is shown in Figure 3-106. According to Figure 3-106, the apparent power and power factor are 33.13 VA and 0.6626, respectively.

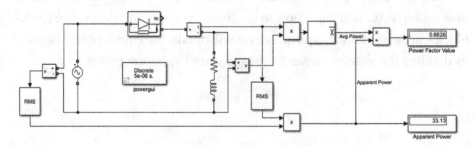

Figure 3-106. *Simulation result*

In the next chapter, we will learn how to use the Goto and From blocks to make your Simulink model tidy and easy to understand.

Summary

In this chapter we learned how to simulate a power electronic converter with the aid of Simscape blocks. We learned how to measure important quantities like average and RMS values as well.

In the next chapter, we will study the simulation of rectifiers. Rectifiers are circuits to convert AC into DC. Rectifiers are used in DC motor drives, AC motor drives input stage, and battery charger circuits.

CHAPTER 4

Simulation of Uncontrolled Rectifier Circuits

Rectifiers are AC-DC converters. They can be used to drive DC motors and charge batteries. Rectifiers are divided into two groups: uncontrolled (diode) rectifiers and controlled (thyristor) rectifiers. Output voltage of uncontrolled rectifiers is a constant value and is not controllable, while output voltage of controlled rectifiers is variable and controllable.

In this chapter we will learn how to simulate uncontrolled rectifiers in the Simulink environment. We will study both single-phase and three-phase uncontrolled rectifiers. We will learn how to see the output waveform with the aid of the Scope block, how to measure the average and RMS values of the output voltage, how to measure the rectifier power factor, how to measure the output voltage harmonics, and how to measure the conduction losses of the circuit.

© Farzin Asadi 2022
F. Asadi, *Simulation of Power Electronics Circuits with MATLAB*/*Simulink*,
Maker Innovations Series, https://doi.org/10.1007/978-1-4842-8220-5_4

Example 1: Goto and From Blocks

The model shown in Figure 3-106 has many wires and is a little bit crowded. This model can be redrawn with the aid of Goto and From blocks (see Figure 4-1) in a better and more understandable way.

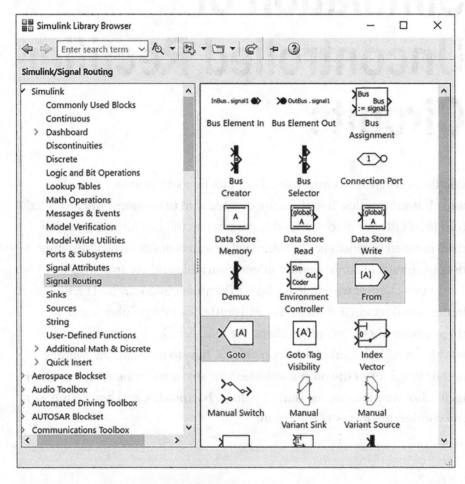

Figure 4-1. *Goto and From blocks*

The Goto block passes its input to its corresponding From block. From and Goto blocks allow you to pass a signal from one block to another

without actually connecting them. For instance, the model shown in
Figure 4-2 is equivalent to the model in Figure 4-3.

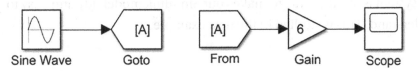

Figure 4-2. *A simple model with Goto and From blocks*

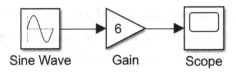

Figure 4-3. *This model is the same as the model shown in Figure 4-2*

The model shown in Figure 4-4 uses the Goto and From blocks to
do the measurements. Such a model is tidier and easier to understand
in comparison with a model that uses wires to connect the voltmeter/
ammeter to the measurement blocks.

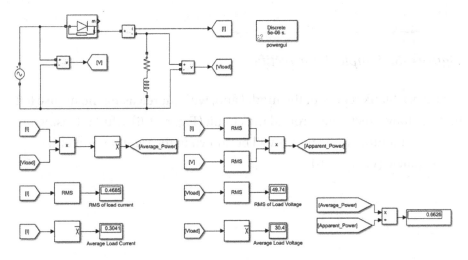

Figure 4-4. *Use of Goto and From blocks to measure the desired
quantities*

191

In this example we learned how to use the Goto and From blocks to make your Simulink model tidy and easy to understand. Making a subsystem is another way to make your Simulink model tidy and easy to understand. This is studied in the next example.

Example 2: Making a Subsystem

Making a subsystem is a way to hide some details from the Simulink model and make an easier-to-understand model. Let's convert the rectifier circuit of Figure 4-5 into a subsystem and make the model simpler. Connect a Terminator block to the diode measurement port.

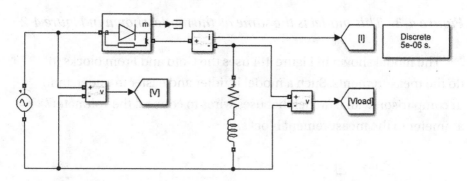

Figure 4-5. *Simple diode rectifier*

Click a blank region of the model and, without releasing the mouse left button, draw a rectangle around the circuit (Figure 4-6). After releasing the mouse left button, three points will be shown in the right bottom end of the rectangle (Figure 4-6).

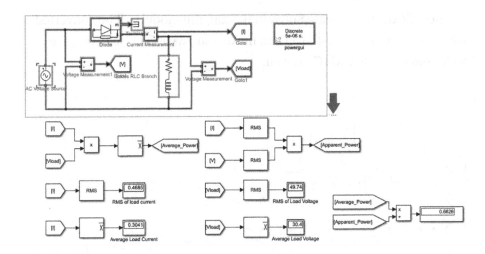

Figure 4-6. *Power stage components are selected*

Put the mouse cursor on the shown three dots. A menu will appear almost immediately (Figure 4-7). Click Create Subsystem (first icon from the left).

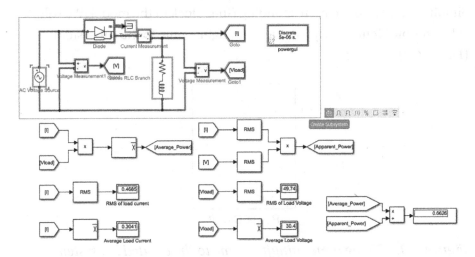

Figure 4-7. *Click Create Subsystem to make a subsystem*

After clicking the Create Subsystem icon, the model will be converted to that shown in Figure 4-8. You can make a subsystem by selecting the blocks and pressing Ctrl+G, as well.

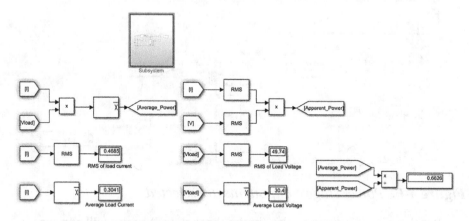

Figure 4-8. *Selected blocks are converted into a subsystem*

Note that the From blocks in Figure 4-8 are highlighted because Simulink can't find the corresponding Goto block in the model. We will solve this problem shortly. Give a meaningful name to the subsystem (Figure 4-9).

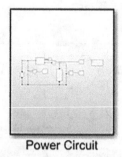

Power Circuit

Figure 4-9. *Giving a meaningful name to the created subsystem*

Double-click the created subsystem (see Figure 4-10). Double-click the Goto blocks one by one and select global for Tag visibility (see Figure 4-11).

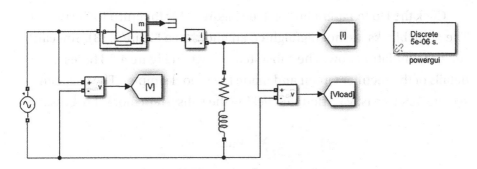

Figure 4-10. *Blocks inside the subsystem*

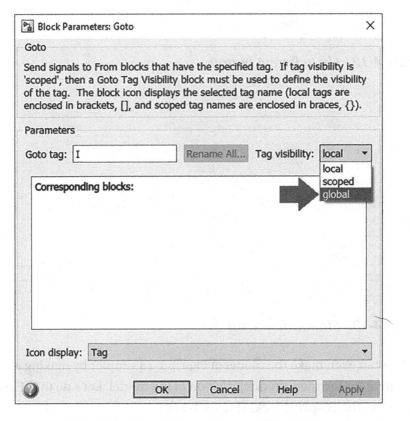

Figure 4-11. *global is selected for the Tag visibility drop-down list*

Click the Up to Parent button (see Figure 4-12) to return to the model. The From blocks are not highlighted anymore (see Figure 4-13). You can run the simulation now. The subsystem shown in Figure 4-13 hides the details of the rectifier circuit and made the model simpler. The user can see the details easily by double-clicking the subsystem block if necessary.

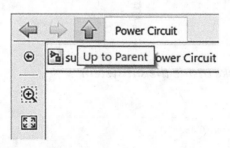

Figure 4-12. *Up to Parent button*

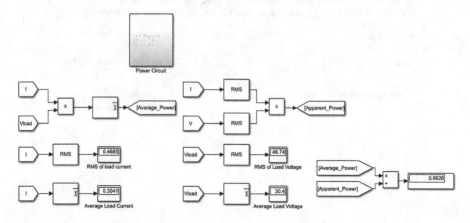

Figure 4-13. *Simulation result*

You can even make the model of Figure 4-13 simpler by making a subsystem for the measurement section of the model. Let's do this. First of all, remove the Display blocks (Figure 4-14).

196

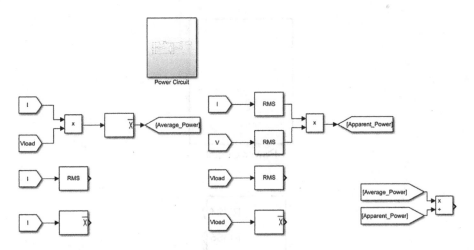

Figure 4-14. *Removing the Display blocks*

Draw a rectangle around the measurement blocks (see Figure 4-15) and convert them into a subsystem (see Figure 4-16).

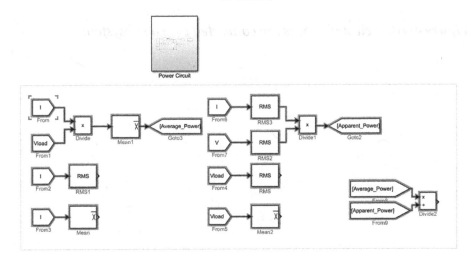

Figure 4-15. *Selected blocks*

197

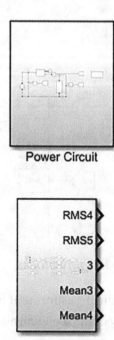

Figure 4-16. *Selected blocks are converted into a subsystem*

Give a suitable name to the new subsystem (Figure 4-17).

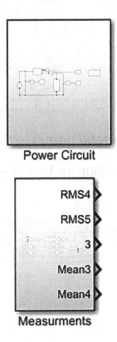

Power Circuit

RMS4
RMS5
3
Mean3
Mean4

Measurments

Figure 4-17. *Giving a meaningful name to the created subsystem*

Double-click the Measurements subsystem and give meaningful names to the output ports (Figure 4-18).

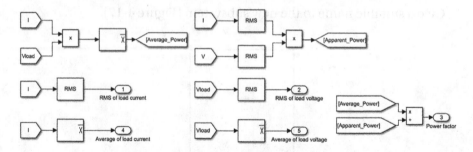

Figure 4-18.   *Giving meaningful names to the output ports*

Return to the model by clicking the Up to Parent button (Figure 4-19).

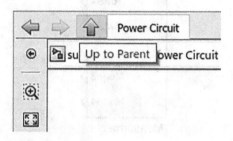

Figure 4-19.   *Up to Parent button*

Connect the Display blocks to the outputs of the Measurements subsystem and run the simulation (Figure 4-20).

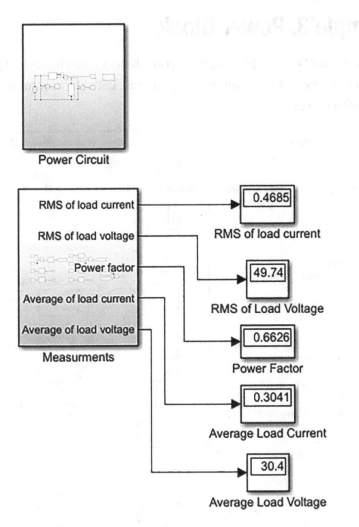

Figure 4-20. *Simulation result*

In Example 6 of Chapter 3, we learned a way to measure the average power. In the next example, you will learn another method to measure the average power.

Example 3: Power Block

The Power and Power (3ph, Instantaneous) blocks (see Figure 4-21) can be used to measure the power of linear circuits. Let's see how to use these blocks with two examples.

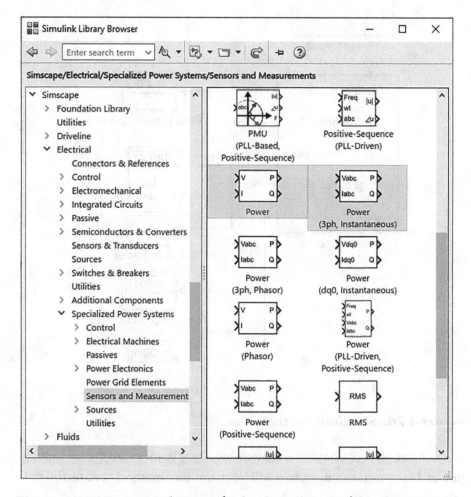

Figure 4-21. *Power and Power (3ph, Instantaneous) blocks*

The model shown in Figure 4-22 uses the Power block to measure the load power. The AC source has a peak of 100 V and frequency of 60 Hz. The load is RL. The load resistance is 100 Ω, and its inductance is 0.1 H. According to Figure 4-22, the average of load power is 43.78 W. The reactive power of the load is 16.5 VAR. Remember that inductive loads have positive reactive powers. The commands in Figure 4-23 show that the obtained result is correct.

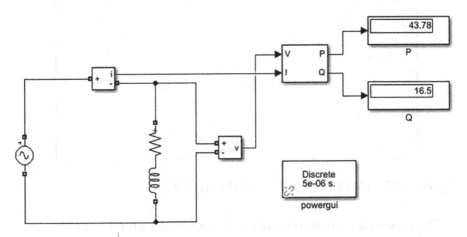

Figure 4-22. *Simulation result*

```
Command Window                                            ⊙
  >> R=100;L=0.1;f=60;w=2*pi*f;Vm=100;Vrms=Vm/sqrt(2);
  >> XL=L*w;
  >> Z=R+j*XL;
  >> Irms=Vrms/abs(Z);
  >> S=Vrms*Irms;
  >> phi=angle(Z);
  >> P=S*cos(phi)

  P =

    43.7781

  >> Q=S*sin(phi)

  Q =

    16.5040

fx >> |
```

Figure 4-23. *MATLAB analysis of the circuit*

The power factor of the circuit can be calculated with the aid of commands shown in Figure 4-24.

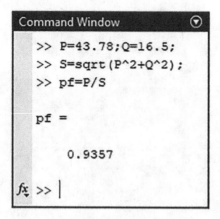

```
Command Window              ⊙
  >> P=43.78;Q=16.5;
  >> S=sqrt(P^2+Q^2);
  >> pf=P/S

  pf =

      0.9357

fx >> |
```

Figure 4-24. *Calculation of the power factor*

Note that you cannot use the Power block to measure the power of nonlinear circuits. For instance, consider the circuit shown in Figure 4-25 (a diode is added to the model of Figure 4-22). This circuit is nonlinear since the circuit current is not composed of only one component with the frequency of the AC source. In other words, the current is full of harmonics. According to Figure 4-25, the average of load power is 10.94 W, and the reactive power is 4.128 VAR. These values are not correct. The correct values are 21.95 W and 24.8125 VAR. (See Figures 3-102 and 3-106. Remember that $Q = \sqrt{S^2 - P^2}$. Q, S, and P indicate reactive power, apparent power, and active power, respectively.)

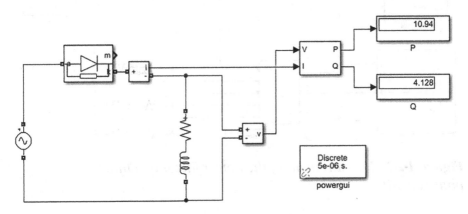

Figure 4-25. *Simulation result*

As our second example, we want to measure the power of a linear three-phase circuit. Consider the model shown in Figure 4-26. This model uses the Three-Phase Source (see Figure 4-27), Power (3ph, Instantaneous) (see Figure 4-28), and Three-Phase V-I Measurement (see Figure 4-29) blocks. The load resistance and inductance are 10 Ω and 0.1 H, respectively. Note that the Three-Phase Source block only simulates the Y-connected three-phase source. If you need delta-connected three-phase sources, you can use three separate AC Voltage Source blocks. The Phase (deg) box of these three sources must be filled with 0, 120, and –120 to create the phase difference between them. It is a good idea to put small resistors (e.g., 1 mΩ) in series with these sources (see Figure 4-30) to avoid the convergence problem.

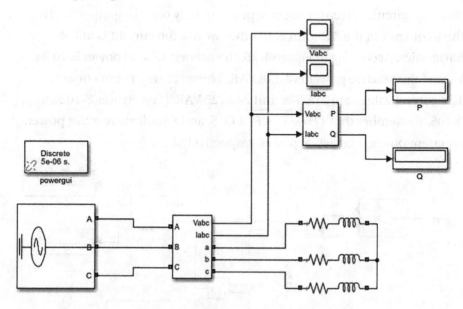

Figure 4-26. *Measurement of the power factor of a three-phase circuit*

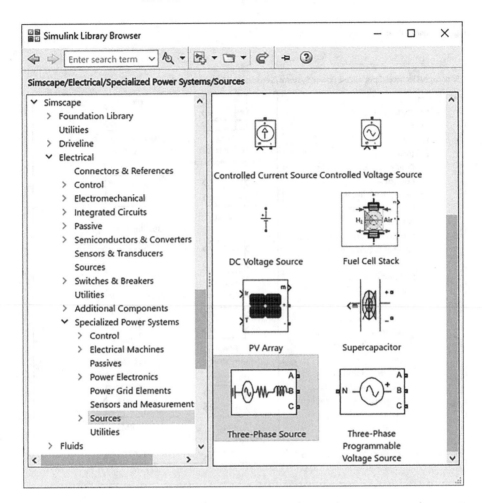

Figure 4-27. *Three-Phase Source block*

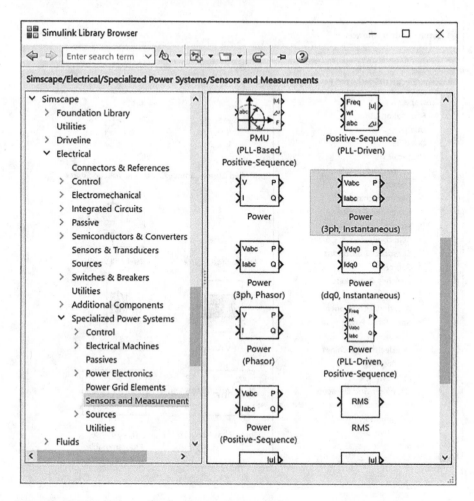

Figure 4-28. *Power (3ph, Instantaneous)*

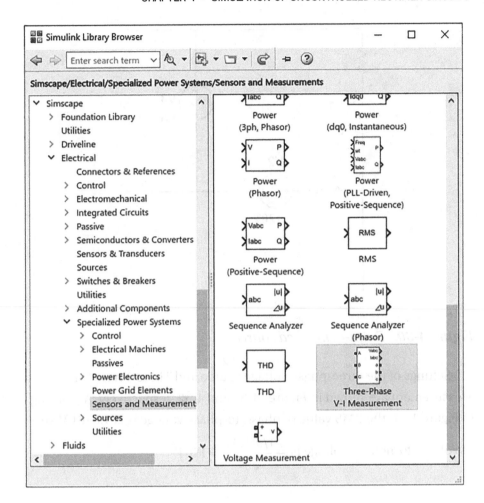

Figure 4-29. *Three-Phase V-I Measurement*

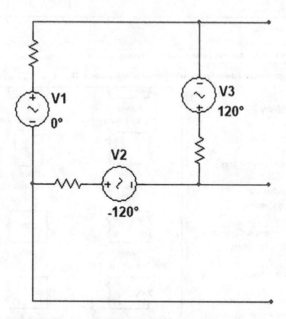

Figure 4-30. *Delta-connected sources*

Settings of the three-phase voltage source and Three-Phase V-I Measurement are shown in Figures 4-31 and 4-32, respectively. According to Figure 4-31, the RMS value of phase-to-phase voltage is 207.8461 V, so the phase-to-neutral voltage is $\dfrac{207.8461\,V}{\sqrt{3}} = 120\,V$.

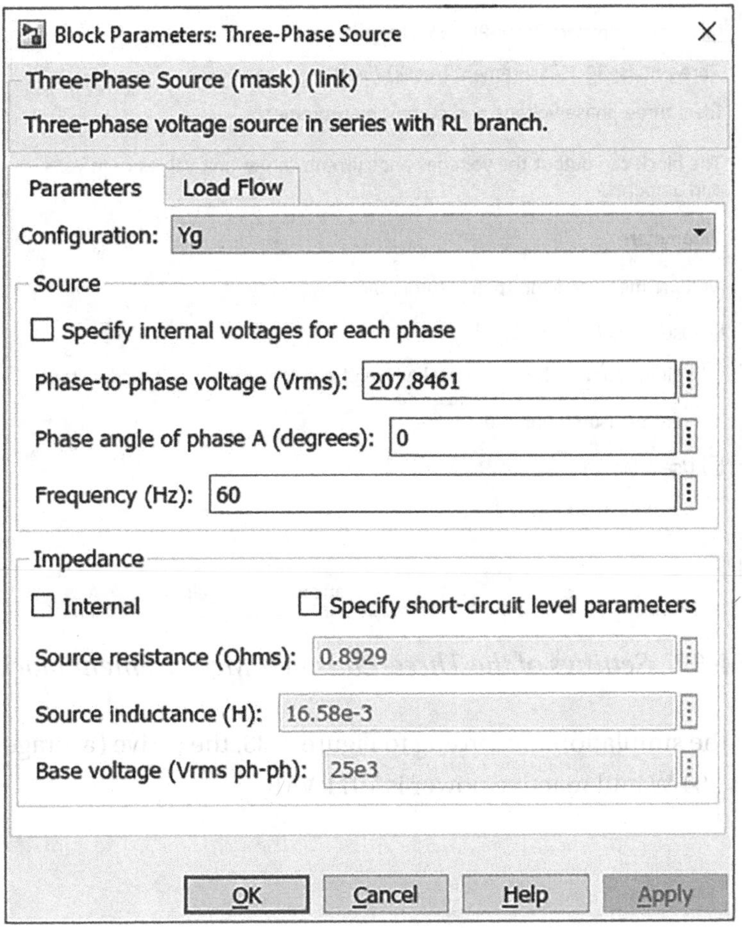

Figure 4-31. *Settings of the Three-Phase Source block*

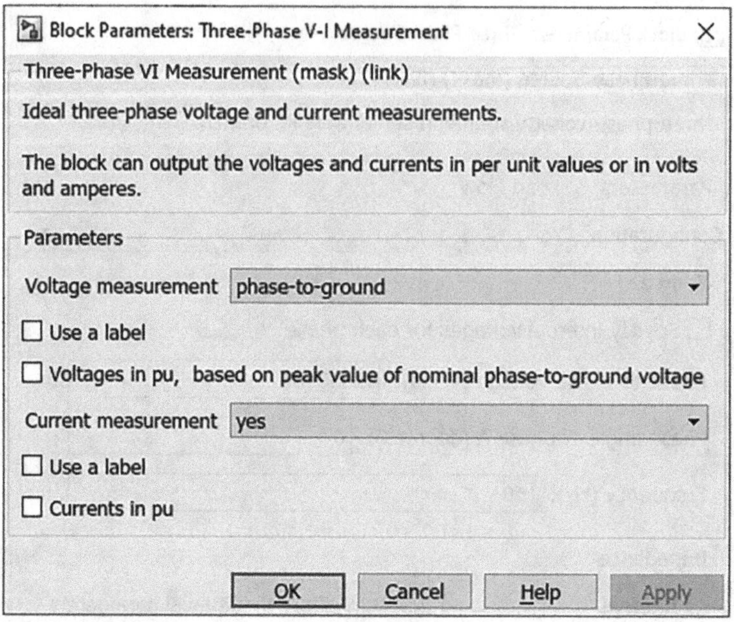

Figure 4-32. *Settings of the Three-Phase V-I Measurement block*

Run the simulation. According to Figure 4-33, the active (average) power is 284 W and reactive power is 1071 VAR.

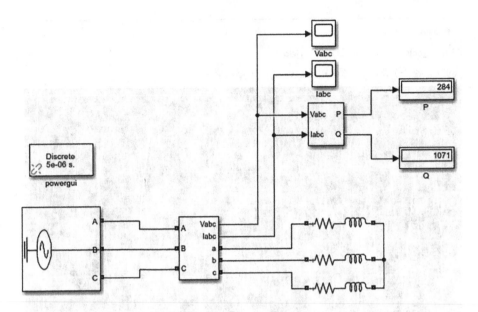

Figure 4-33. *Simulation result*

The phase voltages and phase currents that are measured by the Three-Phase V-I Measurement block are shown in Figures 4-34 and 4-35, respectively. The RMS value of phase voltage is 120 V. So the peak is $120\sqrt{2} = 169.7\,V$.

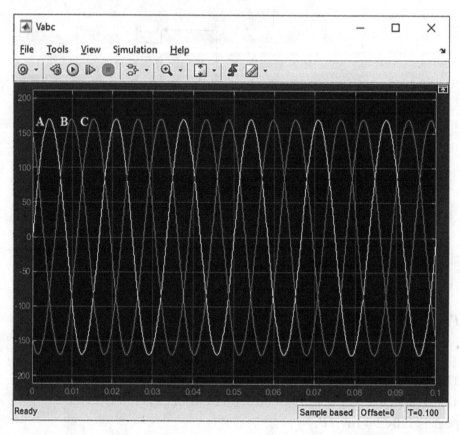

Figure 4-34. *Simulation result (voltage between phases and ground)*

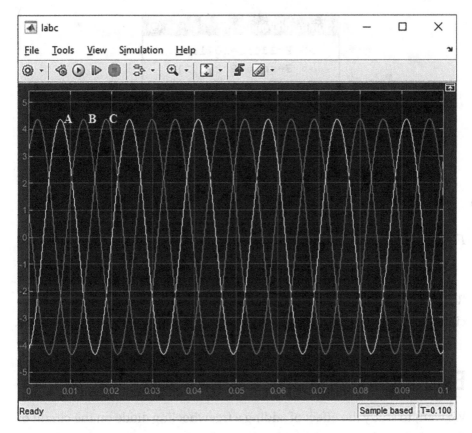

Figure 4-35. *Simulation result (phase currents)*

The commands shown in Figure 4-36 measure the power factor of the circuit according to the simulation result shown in Figure 4-33.

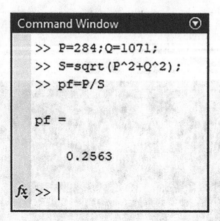

Figure 4-36. *Calculation of the power factor*

In Example 5 of Chapter 3, we simulated a half-wave rectifier with an RL load. In the next example, we want to add a freewheeling diode to that circuit and see the effect of the freewheeling diode on the circuit operation.

Example 4: Freewheeling Diode

We want to study the effect of adding a freewheeling diode on the circuit of Example 5 in Chapter 3. Consider the model shown in Figure 4-37.

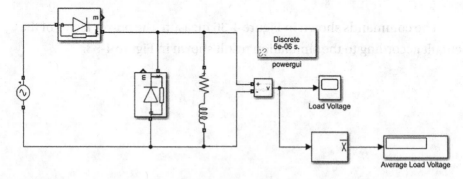

Figure 4-37. *Simulink model of Example 4*

Run the simulation. According to Figure 4-38, the average value of load voltage is 31.25 V, which shows a slight increase in comparison with the circuit without a freewheeling diode. The reason of this increase can be understood by taking a look at the waveform of load voltage. The load voltage for the circuit with a freewheeling diode is shown in Figure 4-39. As shown in Figure 4-39, the load voltage has no negative region, and the average value is the area under the positive half cycle divided by the value of period. When the circuit has no freewheeling diode, the area under the negative region of the waveform is subtracted from the area under the positive half cycle, the result of which is then divided by the value of period. In other words, the numerator is slightly decreased, while the denominator is constant. So the average load voltage for the circuit without a freewheeling diode is slightly less than the average value of load voltage for the circuit with a freewheeling diode.

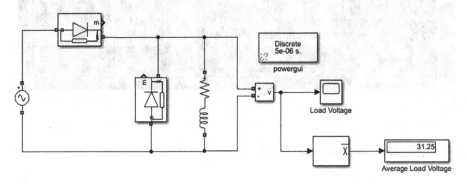

Figure 4-38. *Simulation result*

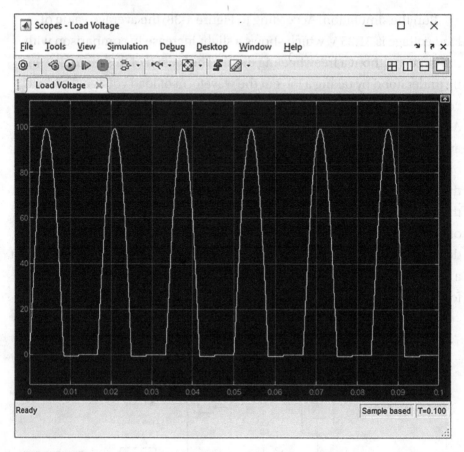

Figure 4-39. *Simulation result*

In the next example, we will learn how to disable a block so it has no effect on the simulation.

Example 5: Disabling a Block

You can disable a block and remove its effect on the simulation without deleting it. For instance, assume that we want to disable the freewheeling diode of Example 4. To do this, click the freewheeling diode. Then click the three dots behind it (see Figure 4-40). After clicking the three dots, a menu appears (see Figure 4-41). Click the % button. This disables the block. Disabled blocks are shown with a light-gray color (see Figure 4-42).

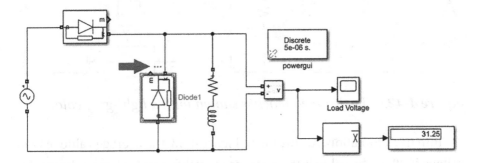

Figure 4-40. *The diode block is selected*

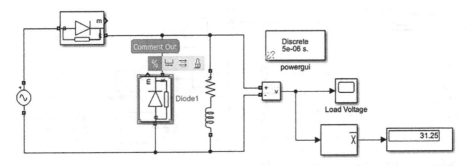

Figure 4-41. *The Comment Out icon disables the block*

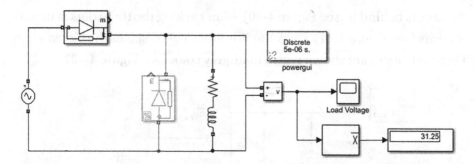

Figure 4-42. *The disabled block is shown with a light-gray color*

Run the simulation. According to Figure 4-43, the average value of load voltage is 30.4. The value is the same as the value we obtained in Example 5 of Chapter 3 (see Figure 3-96).

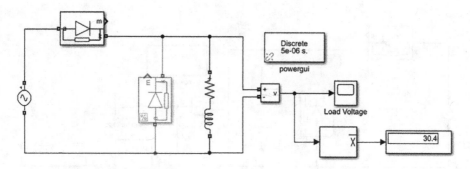

Figure 4-43. *Simulation result*

In order to enable a disabled block, click it; and when the three dots appear, click them. Then click the % button (Figure 4-44).

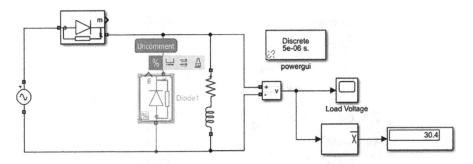

Figure 4-44. *The Uncomment button enables a disabled block*

There is another way to disable and enable a block. To disable a block, right-click it and click Comment Out from the pop-up menu (Figure 4-45). To enable a disabled block, right-click it and click Uncomment from the pop-up menu (Figure 4-46).

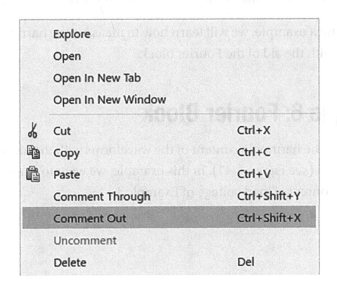

Figure 4-45. *Comment Out disables an active block*

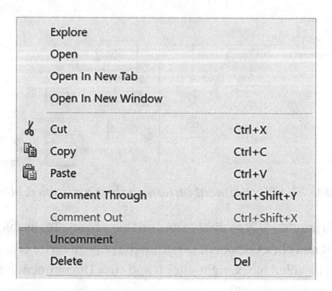

Figure 4-46. *Uncomment enables a disabled block*

In the next example, we will learn how to measure the harmonics of a waveform with the aid of the Fourier block.

Example 6: Fourier Block

You can see the harmonic content of the waveforms with the aid of the Fourier block (see Figure 4-47). In this example, we want to study the harmonic content of load voltage of Example 4.

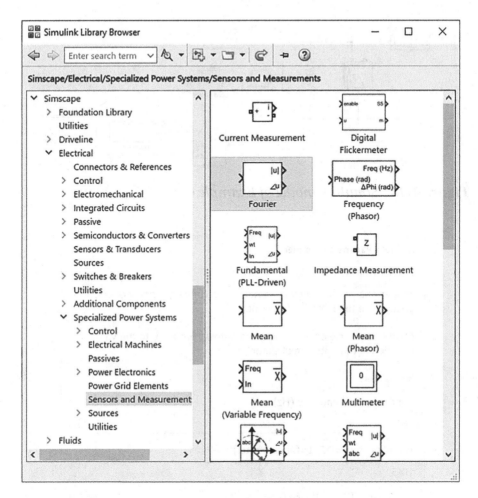

Figure 4-47. *Fourier block*

Consider the model shown in Figure 4-48. We want to measure the DC component (average value) and the magnitude and phase of the fundamental, second, third, fourth, and fifth harmonics. This block gives the phase in degrees. Settings of the Fourier block are shown in Figure 4-49. Remember that the fundamental frequency of the load voltage is 60 Hz.

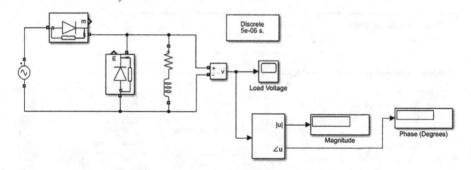

Figure 4-48. *Simulink model of Example 6*

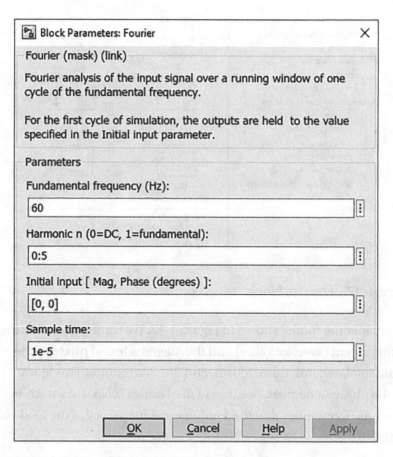

Figure 4-49. *Settings of the Fourier block*

Run the simulation. The result shown in Figure 4-50 is obtained.

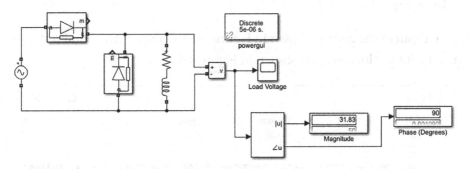

Figure 4-50. *Simulation result*

Click the Display blocks and drag their sides to make them bigger (Figure 4-51).

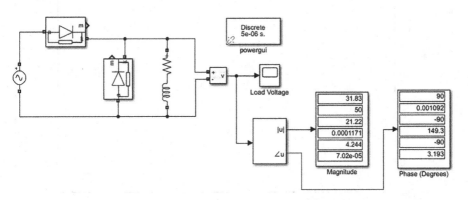

Figure 4-51. *Display blocks are dragged to show the numbers better*

The following code draws the graph of the obtained result:

```
syms t
w=2*pi*60;
D=pi/180;
ezplot(31.83*sin(0*w*t+90*D)+50*sin(w*t+0.001092*D)+21.22*sin
(2*w*t-...
90*D)+0.0001171*sin(3*w*t+149.3*D)+4.244*sin(4*w*t-90*D)+...
```

```
7.02e-5*sin(5*w*t+3.193*D),[0,16.7e-3])
grid minor
```

Output of the code is shown in Figure 4-52. Compare the obtained result with the load voltage shown in Figure 4-53.

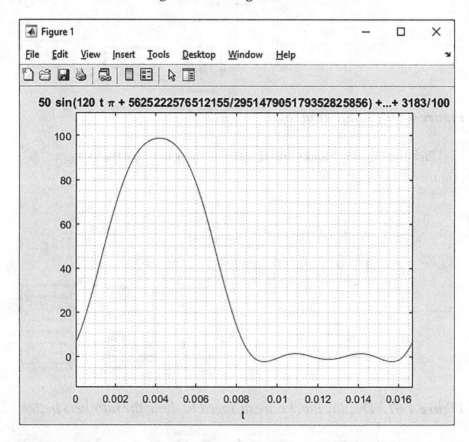

Figure 4-52. *Graph of summation of harmonics shown in Figure 4-51*

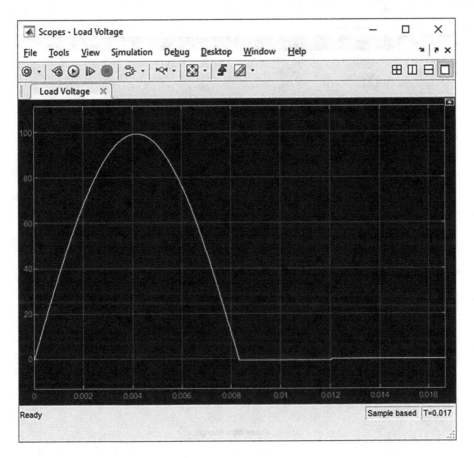

Figure 4-53. *Waveform of load voltage*

Simulink has a sample simulation related to the Fourier block (see Figure 4-54). You can open this example by typing power_Fourier in the command window (see Figure 4-55).

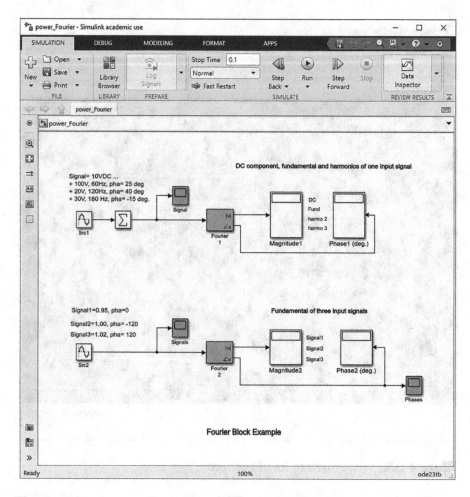

Figure 4-54. *power_Fourier model*

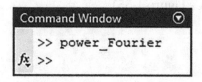

Figure 4-55. *Opening the model shown in Figure 4-54*

Up to this point, we focused on single-phase rectifiers. The next example studies the simulation of three-phase rectifiers.

Example 7: Three-Phase Diode Rectifier

In this example, we want to simulate a three-phase uncontrolled (diode) rectifier. Consider the model shown in Figure 4-56. The load resistor is 10 Ω. The Ground block can be found in the Utilities section (see Figure 4-57). The Snubber resistance Rs (Ohms) parameter of the diodes is 1e7, which means 10 MΩ. Other parameters of the diodes have default values. The Multimeter blocks measure the voltage and current of the load resistor. Both of the Mean blocks have Fundamental frequency (Hz) of 6×f where f indicates the frequency of the AC source. In this example f= 50 Hz, so the Fundamental frequency (Hz) box is filled with 300.

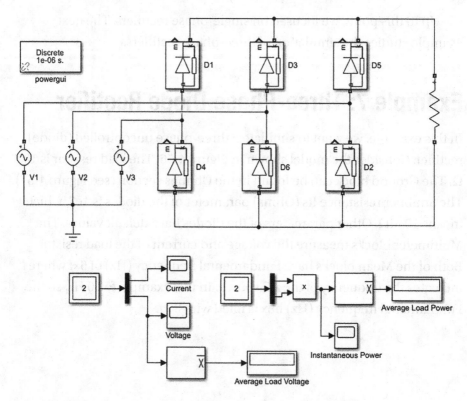

Figure 4-56. *Simulink model of Example 7*

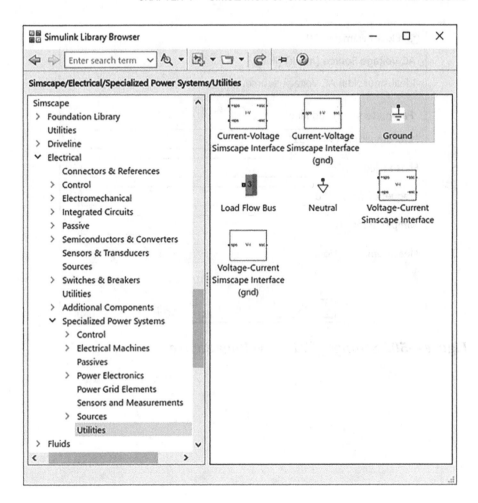

Figure 4-57. *Ground block*

Settings of V1, V2, and V3 are shown in Figures 4-58, 4-59, and 4-60, respectively.

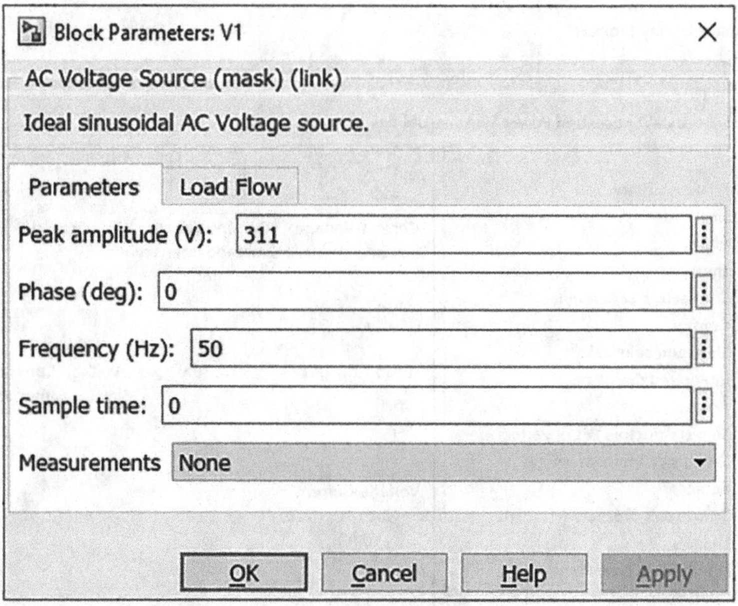

Figure 4-58. *Settings of V1 AC Voltage Source*

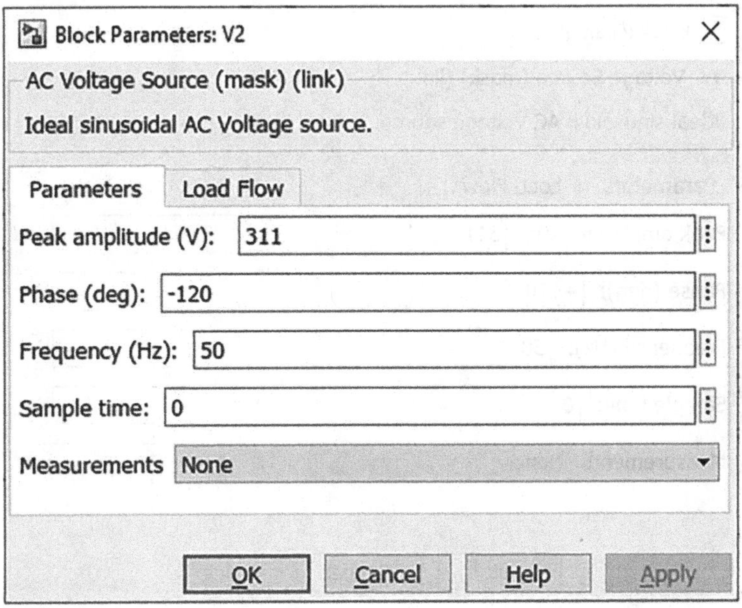

Figure 4-59. Settings of V2 AC Voltage Source

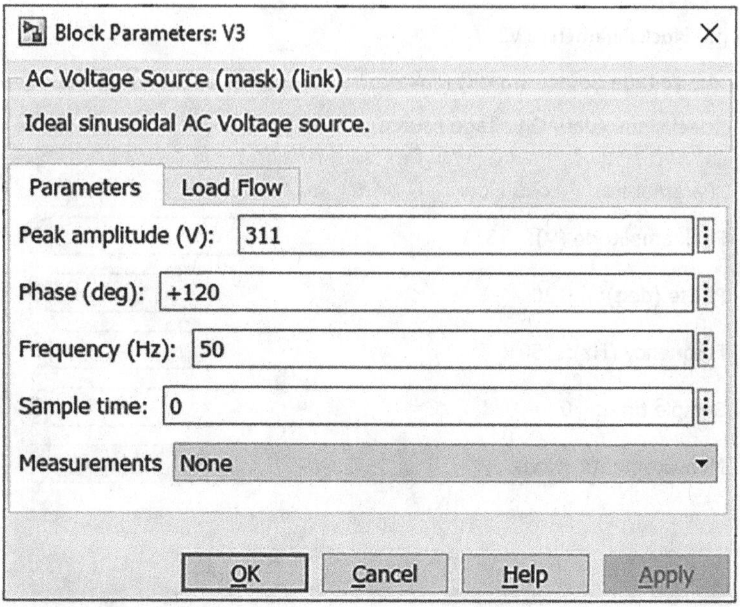

Figure 4-60. *Settings of V3 AC Voltage Source*

The average output voltage of a three-phase diode rectifier with ideal diodes (diodes without any forward voltage drop) can be calculated with the aid of the $V_{O,DC} = \dfrac{3\sqrt{2}}{\pi} \times V_{LL}$ formula. V_{LL} indicates the line-line voltage. According to the calculations shown in Figure 4-61, the average output voltage must be about 514.3899 V.

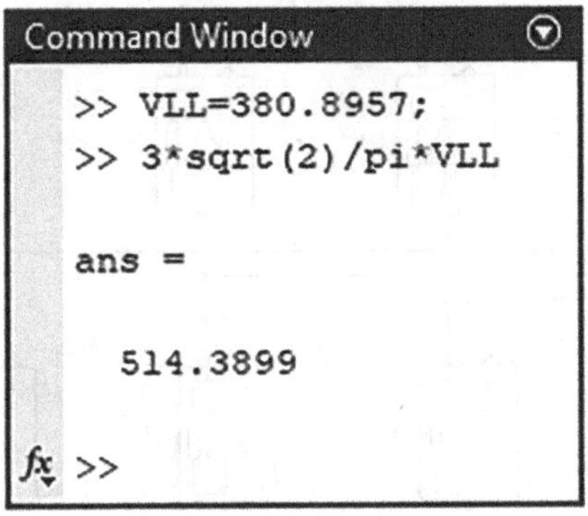

```
Command Window                    ⊙
  >> VLL=380.8957;
  >> 3*sqrt(2)/pi*VLL

  ans =

    514.3899

fx >>
```

Figure 4-61. *Calculation of the average output voltage of the rectifier*

Run the simulation. The simulation result is shown in Figure 4-62. According to this result, the average load voltage is 512.7 V, and the power consumed by the load is 26.33 kW. The average output voltage is close to the theoretical value. Note that in this simulation, the diodes have a small voltage drop. So a small deviation is expected.

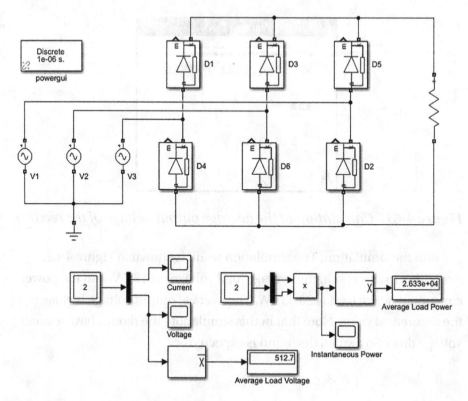

Figure 4-62. *Simulation result*

The load voltage and instantaneous load power waveforms are shown in Figures 4-63 and 4-64, respectively. Note that the frequency of these waveforms is 6×50 Hz=300 Hz. That is why the Fundamental frequency (Hz) box of Mean blocks is filled with 300.

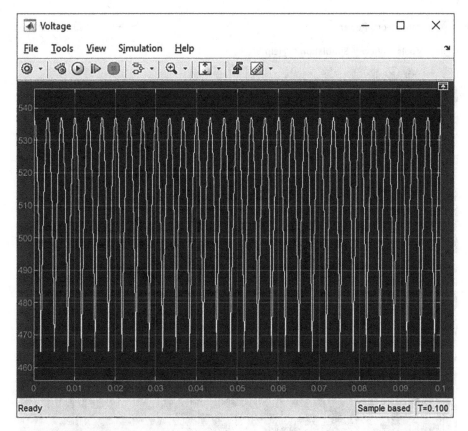

Figure 4-63. *Simulation result*

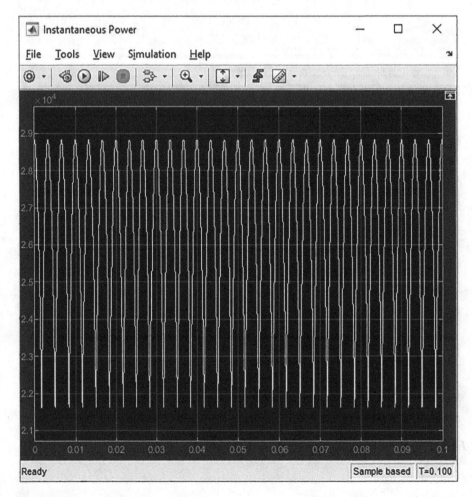

Figure 4-64. *Simulation result*

You can remove the three independent AC sources and use a ready-to-use Three-Phase Source block as well (see Figure 4-65). Settings of the Three-Phase Source block are shown in Figure 4-66. The line-line voltage is calculated with the aid of calculations shown in Figure 4-67.

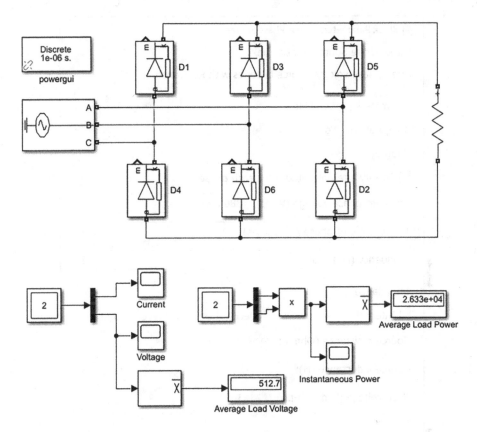

Figure 4-65. *Simulation result*

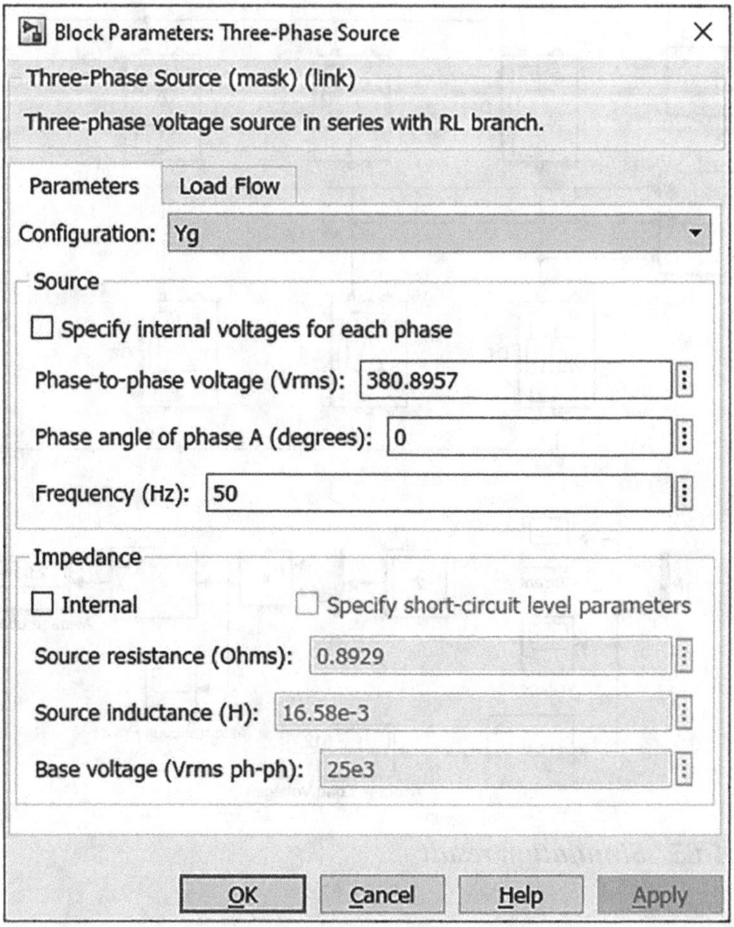

Figure 4-66. *Settings of Three-Phase Source*

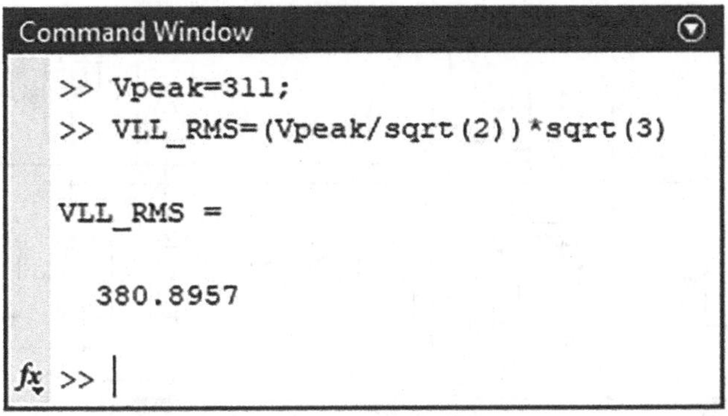

```
Command Window                                    ⊙

 >> Vpeak=311;
 >> VLL_RMS=(Vpeak/sqrt(2))*sqrt(3)

 VLL_RMS =

    380.8957

fx >> |
```

Figure 4-67.   *Calculation of line-line voltage*

In this example we learned how to simulate a three-phase uncontrolled rectifier. In the next example, we will measure the power factor of the studied three-phase rectifier.

Example 8: Measurement of the Power Factor of a Three-Phase Uncontrolled Rectifier

In this example, we want to measure the power factor of Example 7. Consider the model shown in Figure 4-68. This model measures the average power and apparent power of one phase and multiplies the measured average and apparent power by three to obtain the total average and apparent power of the AC source. Fundamental frequency (Hz) of RMS blocks is filled with 50, and Fundamental frequency (Hz) of the Mean block is filled with 100.

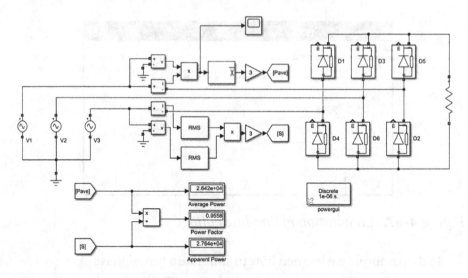

Figure 4-68. *Simulink model of Example 8*

According to the simulation result, the average power is 26.42 kW
and apparent power is 27.64 kVA and power factor is 0.9558. Note that
the average power of source is a little bit bigger than the average power of
load. The difference between these two powers is dissipated in the diodes.
According to the calculation shown in Figure 4-69, each diode dissipates
15 W. According to Figure 4-70, the efficiency of conversion is 99.6593%.

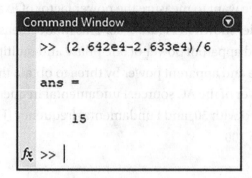

Figure 4-69. *Calculation of one diode's conduction losses*

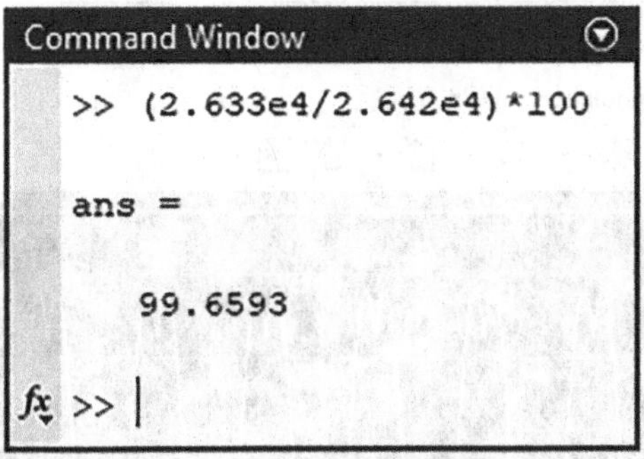

```
Command Window                          ⊙
  >> (2.633e4/2.642e4)*100

  ans =

      99.6593

fx >> |
```

Figure 4-70. *Calculation of efficiency of the converter*

The power waveform for one phase is shown in Figure 4-71. The frequency of this waveform is 100 Hz. That is why the Fundamental frequency (Hz) box of the Mean block is filled with 100.

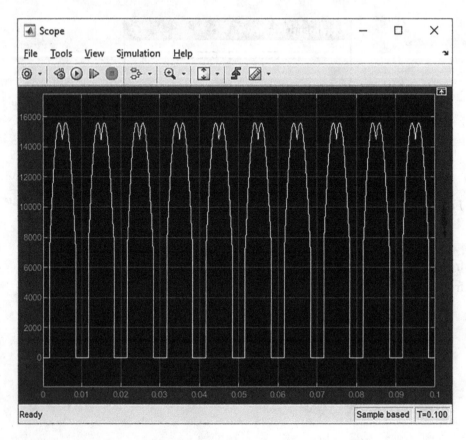

Figure 4-71. *Simulation result*

You can remove the three independent AC sources and use a ready-to-use Three-Phase Source as well (see Figure 4-72). Settings of Three-Phase Source are shown in Figure 4-66.

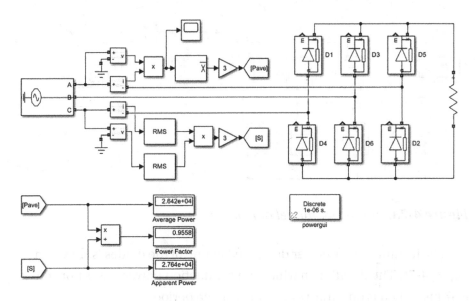

Figure 4-72. *Simulation result*

In the next example, we will learn how to measure the conduction loss of diodes.

Example 9: Measurement of Conduction Loss

In this example we will measure the conduction loss of the diodes of Example 7. The model shown in Figure 4-73 measures the conduction loss of one of the diodes. The Fundamental frequency (Hz) box of the Mean block is filled with 50.

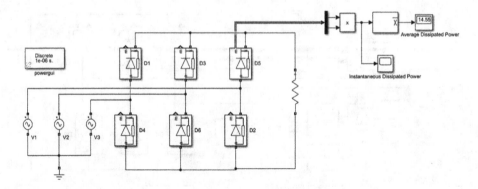

Figure 4-73. *Simulink model of Example 9*

The instantaneous power dissipated in one of the diodes is shown in Figure 4-74. The duration in which the conduction power loss is nonzero is 6.67 ms, which is one-third of the line voltage period.

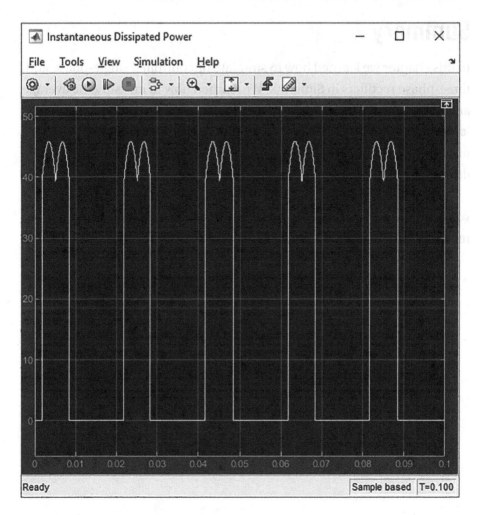

Figure 4-74. *Simulation result*

Summary

In this chapter we learned how to simulate uncontrolled single-phase and three-phase rectifiers in Simulink. We learned how to measure the average and RMS values of the output voltage, power factor, average power of the load, and the harmonics of load voltage or current. We learned how to disable a block, make a subsystem, and use the Goto and From blocks to draw more understandable Simulink models as well.

In the next chapter, we will study the controlled rectifiers. Output voltage of controlled rectifiers is variable in contrast with uncontrolled rectifiers, which provide a constant voltage.

CHAPTER 5

Simulation of Controlled Rectifier Circuits

In the previous chapter, we learned how to simulate uncontrolled rectifiers in the Simulink environment. This chapter focuses on the simulation of controlled (thyristor) rectifiers. We will learn how to simulate single-phase half-wave and full-wave controlled rectifiers, three-phase controlled rectifiers, and circuits that contain mutual inductance.

Example 1: Single-Phase Half-Wave Thyristor Rectifier

We want to simulate a single-phase half-wave thyristor rectifier with an RL load (R=10 Ω and L= 10 mH). The model of this example is shown in Figure 5-1. This model uses Thyristor (see Figure 5-2) and Pulse Generator (see Figure 5-3) blocks. Input AC source has a peak of 169.7 V and frequency of 60 Hz. The Snubber resistance Rs (Ohms) parameter of the thyristor is 1e7. Other parameters of the thyristor have default values.

© Farzin Asadi 2022
F. Asadi, *Simulation of Power Electronics Circuits with MATLAB*/Simulink*,
Maker Innovations Series, https://doi.org/10.1007/978-1-4842-8220-5_5

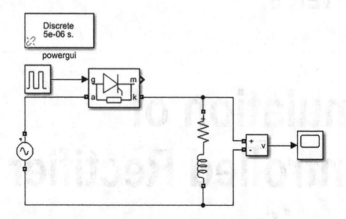

Figure 5-1. *Simulink model of Example 1*

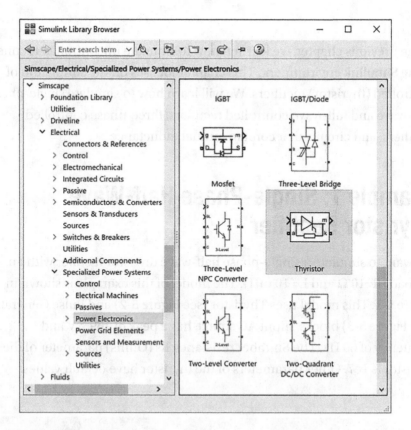

Figure 5-2. *Thyristor block*

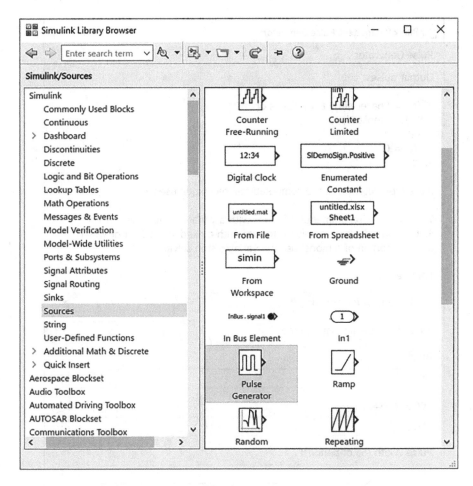

Figure 5-3. *Pulse Generator block*

Settings of the Pulse Generator block are shown in Figure 5-4. The number entered in the Phase delay (secs) box of the Pulse Generator block controls the triggering angle of the thyristor. Phase delay (secs) in Figure 5-4 has a value of 1/60/4, which means $\dfrac{1}{240}$. So the triggering angle of the thyristor is

$$\frac{Number\ entered\ to\ the\ Phase\ delay\ (secs)\ box}{Number\ entered\ to\ the\ Period\ (secs)\ box} = \frac{\dfrac{1}{240}}{\dfrac{1}{60}} \times 360 = 90°.$$

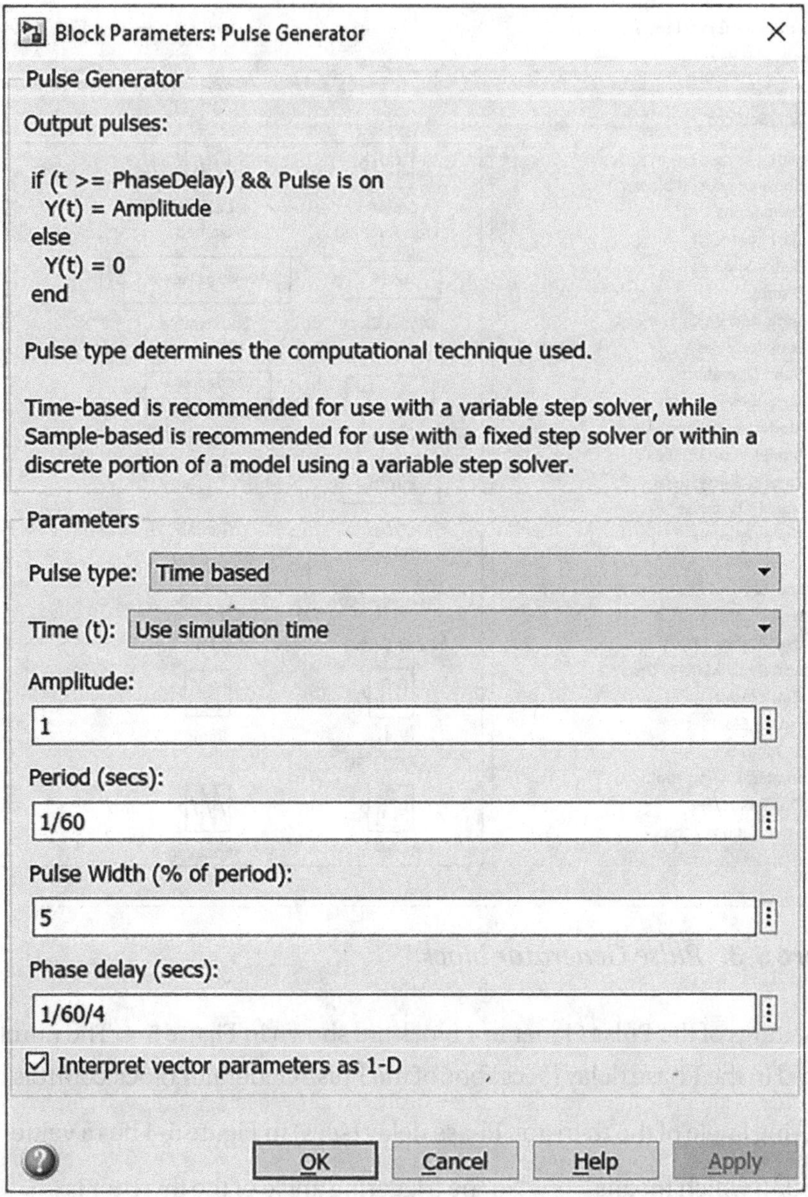

Block Parameters: Pulse Generator   ×

Pulse Generator

Output pulses:

if (t >= PhaseDelay) && Pulse is on
  Y(t) = Amplitude
else
  Y(t) = 0
end

Pulse type determines the computational technique used.

Time-based is recommended for use with a variable step solver, while Sample-based is recommended for use with a fixed step solver or within a discrete portion of a model using a variable step solver.

Parameters

Pulse type: Time based   ▼

Time (t): Use simulation time   ▼

Amplitude:

1

Period (secs):

1/60

Pulse Width (% of period):

5

Phase delay (secs):

1/60/4

☑ Interpret vector parameters as 1-D

OK   Cancel   Help   Apply

Figure 5-4. *Settings of the Pulse Generator block*

The simulation result is shown in Figure 5-5. You can measure the average value and RMS value of this waveform with the aid of Mean and RMS blocks, or you can use Signal Statistics of the Scope block.

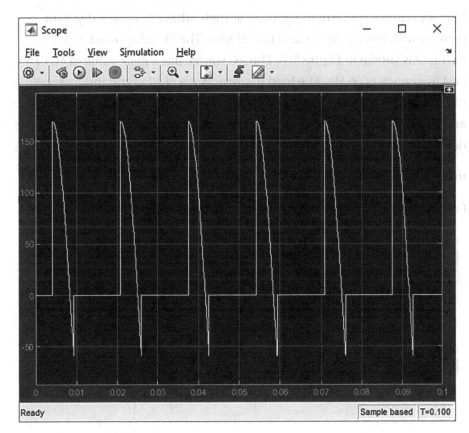

Figure 5-5. *Simulation result*

In this example we simulated a half-wave rectifier. In the next example, we will simulate a full-wave rectifier.

Example 2: Single-Phase Full-Wave Thyristor Rectifier (I)

In this example, we want to simulate a single-phase full-wave thyristor rectifier with two thyristors and two diodes. The Simulink model of this example is shown in Figure 5-6. The AC source has a peak value of 169.7 V and frequency of 60 Hz. The load has resistance of 10 Ω and inductance of 10 mH. The Snubber resistance Rs (Ohms) parameter of the diode and thyristor is 1e7. Other parameters of the diode and thyristor have default values. This model uses a Transport Delay block (see Figure 5-7) to trigger the second thyristor. The value of time delay is $\dfrac{1}{2} \times \dfrac{1}{f} = \dfrac{1}{120}$ (see Figure 5-8). f shows the frequency of the AC source.

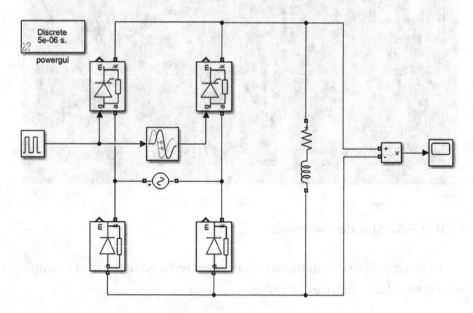

Figure 5-6. *Simulink model of Example 2*

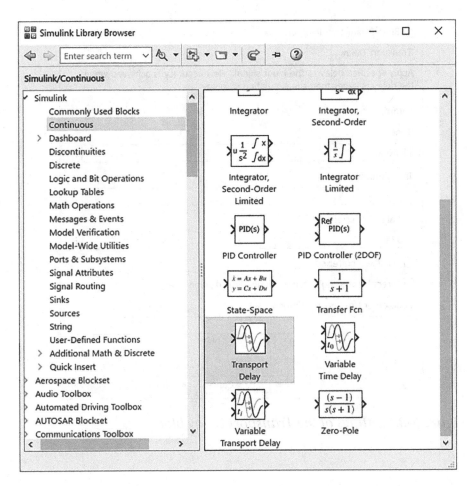

Figure 5-7. *Transport Delay block*

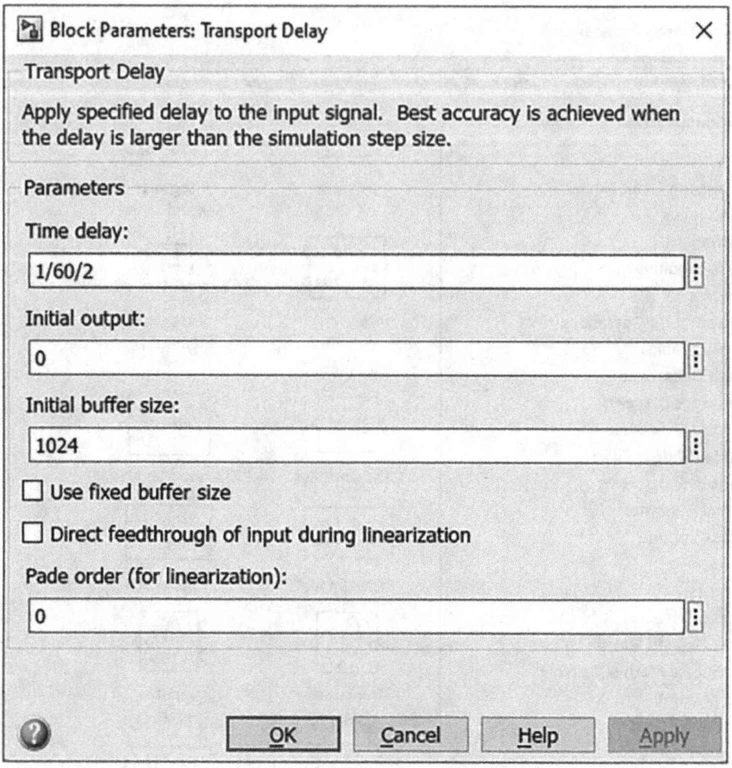

Figure 5-8. *Settings of the Transport Delay block*

Settings of the Pulse Generator block are shown in Figure 5-9. According to Figure 5-8, the firing angle is 60°.

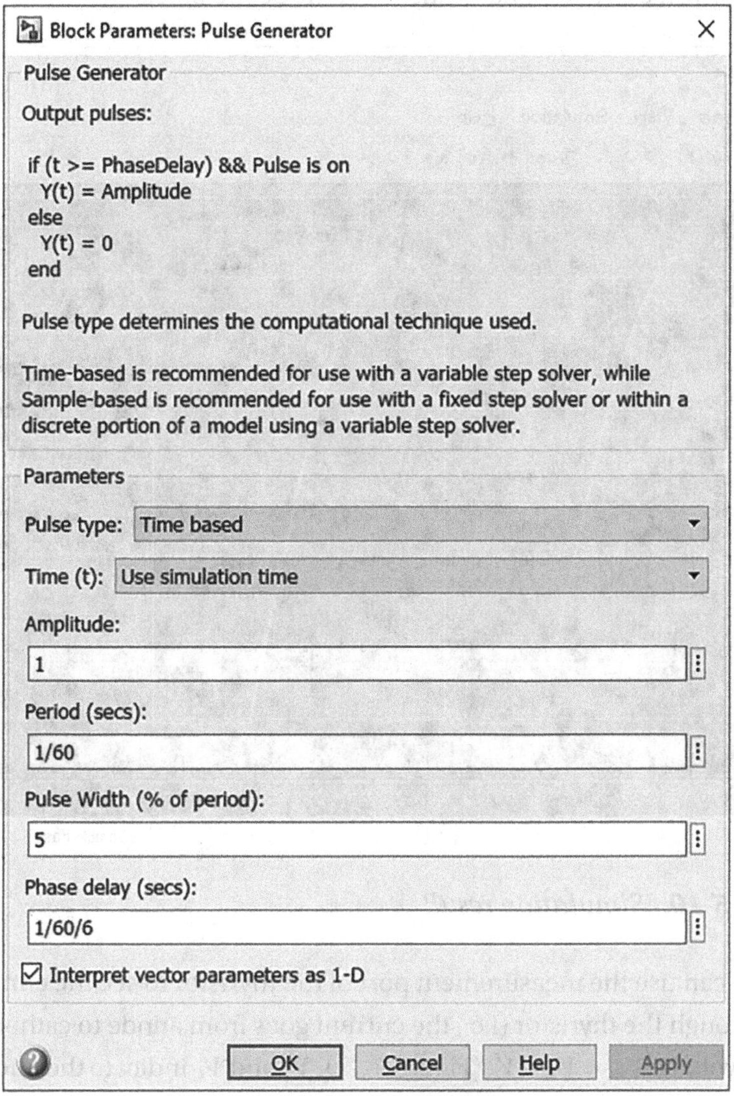

Block Parameters: Pulse Generator ✕

Pulse Generator

Output pulses:

```
if (t >= PhaseDelay) && Pulse is on
  Y(t) = Amplitude
else
  Y(t) = 0
end
```

Pulse type determines the computational technique used.

Time-based is recommended for use with a variable step solver, while Sample-based is recommended for use with a fixed step solver or within a discrete portion of a model using a variable step solver.

Parameters

Pulse type: Time based   ▼

Time (t):   Use simulation time   ▼

Amplitude:

| 1 |

Period (secs):

| 1/60 |

Pulse Width (% of period):

| 5 |

Phase delay (secs):

| 1/60/6 |

☑ Interpret vector parameters as 1-D

    OK   Cancel   Help   Apply

Figure 5-9. *Settings of the Pulse Generator block*

The simulation result is shown in Figure 5-10. You can measure the average value and RMS value of this waveform with the aid of Mean and RMS blocks, or you can use Signal Statistics of the Scope block.

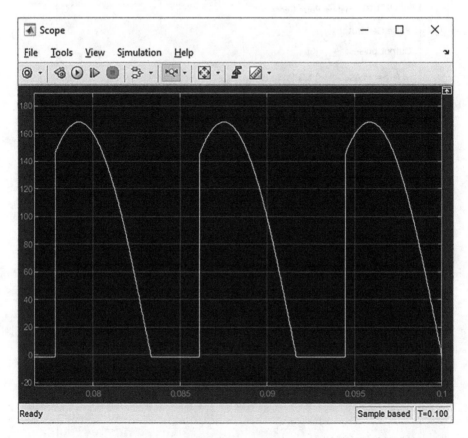

Figure 5-10. *Simulation result*

You can use the measurement port of the thyristor to see the current pass through the thyristor (i.e., the current goes from anode to cathode) and its voltage $V_{AC} = V_A - V_C$ (Figure 5-11). V_A and V_C indicate the anode voltage and cathode voltage, respectively.

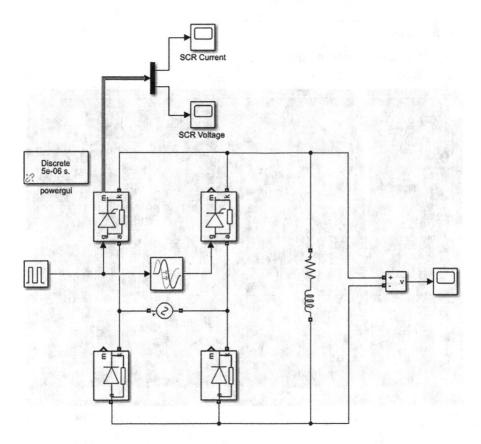

Figure 5-11. *The measurement port is used to observe the current and voltage waveforms of one of the thyristors*

Waveforms of SCR Current and SCR Voltage scopes (Figure 5-11) are shown in Figures 5-12 and 5-13, respectively. Maximum, average, and RMS values of current that passes through the thyristor and the peak of the anode-cathode voltage help you select the suitable thyristor for your application.

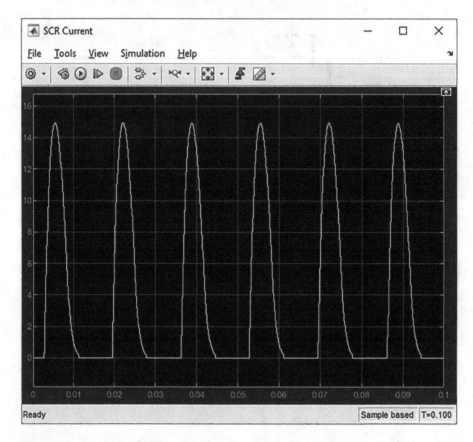

Figure 5-12. *Simulation result*

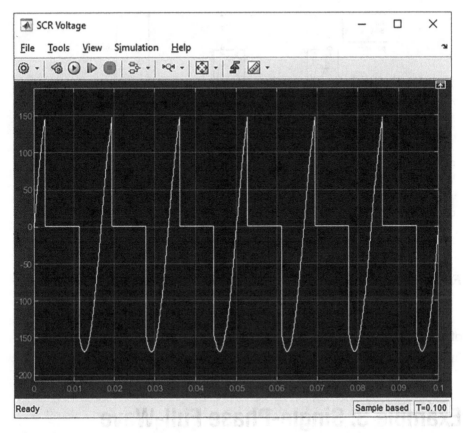

Figure 5-13. *Simulation result*

The measurement port of the diode can be used to measure the current that passes through the diode (i.e., the current goes from anode to cathode) and its voltage $V_{AC} = V_A - V_C$ (Figure 5-14). V_A and V_C indicate the anode voltage and cathode voltage, respectively. These waveforms help you select the suitable diode for the circuit.

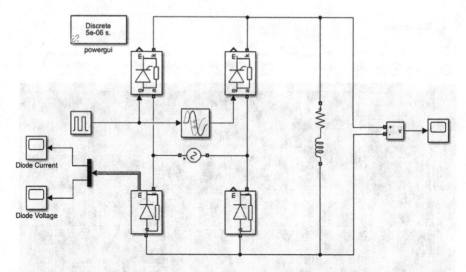

Figure 5-14. *Measurement of the diode voltage and current*

In this example we simulated a full-wave rectifier, which is composed of two thyristors and two diodes. In the next example, we will simulate a full-wave rectifier that has four thyristors and no diodes.

Example 3: Single-Phase Full-Wave Thyristor Rectifier (II)

In this example, we want to simulate a single-phase full-wave rectifier with four thyristors. The Simulink model of this example is shown in Figure 5-15. In this example, the two diodes of Example 2 are replaced with two thyristors. Settings of other blocks are the same as Example 2. The load voltage waveform of this circuit is the same as Figure 5-10.

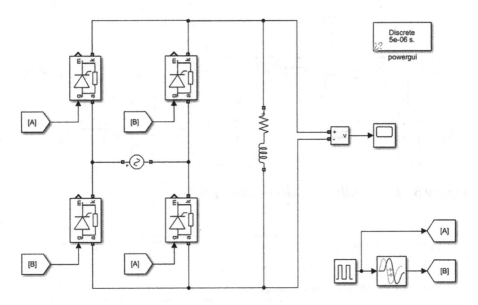

Figure 5-15. *Simulink model of Example 3*

In the previous examples, we studied the single-phase controlled rectifiers. In the next example, we will simulate a three-phase controlled rectifier.

Example 4: Three-Phase Thyristor Rectifier

In this example, we want to simulate a three-phase rectifier. The model of this example is shown in Figure 5-16. The load is RL with R=10 Ω and L=10 mH. This model uses the PLL (3ph) (see Figure 5-17), Pulse Generator (Thyristor, 6-Pulse) (see Figure 5-18), Constant (see Figure 5-19), and Universal Bridge (see Figure 5-20) blocks. The equivalent circuit of Universal Bridge is shown in Figure 5-21.

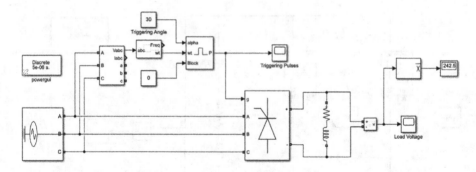

Figure 5-16. *Simulink model of Example 4*

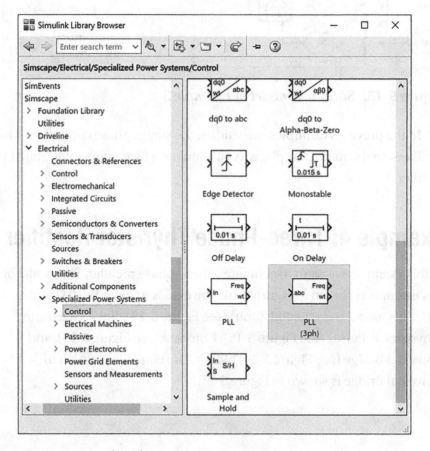

Figure 5-17. *PLL (3ph) block*

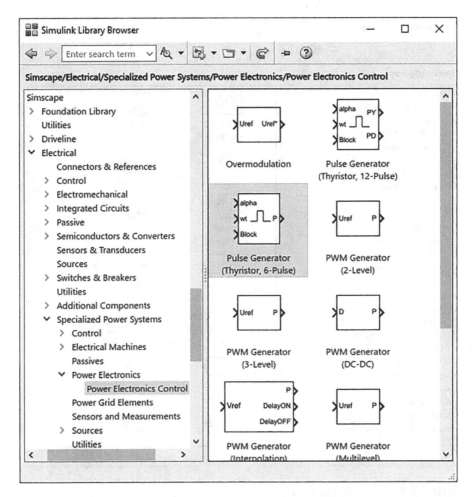

Figure 5-18. *Pulse Generator (Thyristor, 6-Pulse) block*

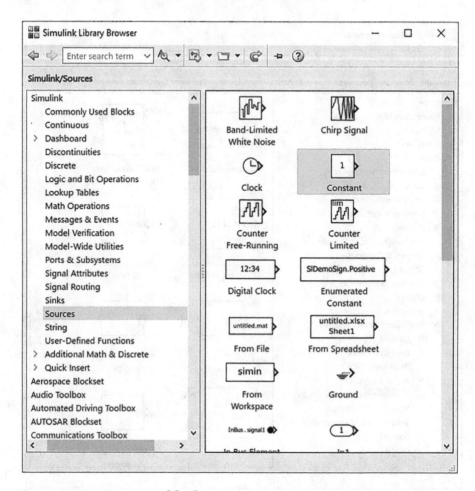

Figure 5-19. *Constant block*

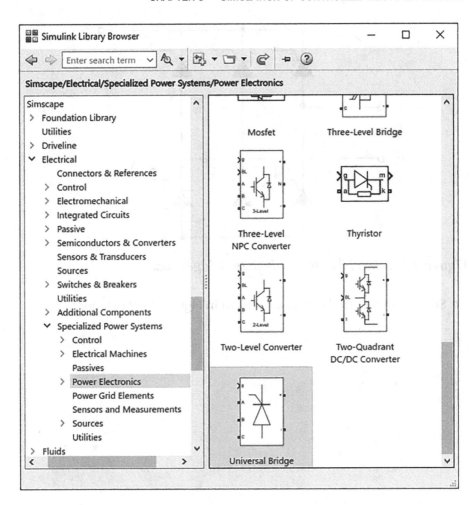

Figure 5-20. *Universal Bridge block*

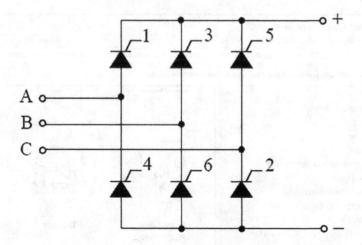

Figure 5-21. *Model of the Universal Bridge block*

Settings of the used blocks are shown in Figures 5-22 to 5-26.

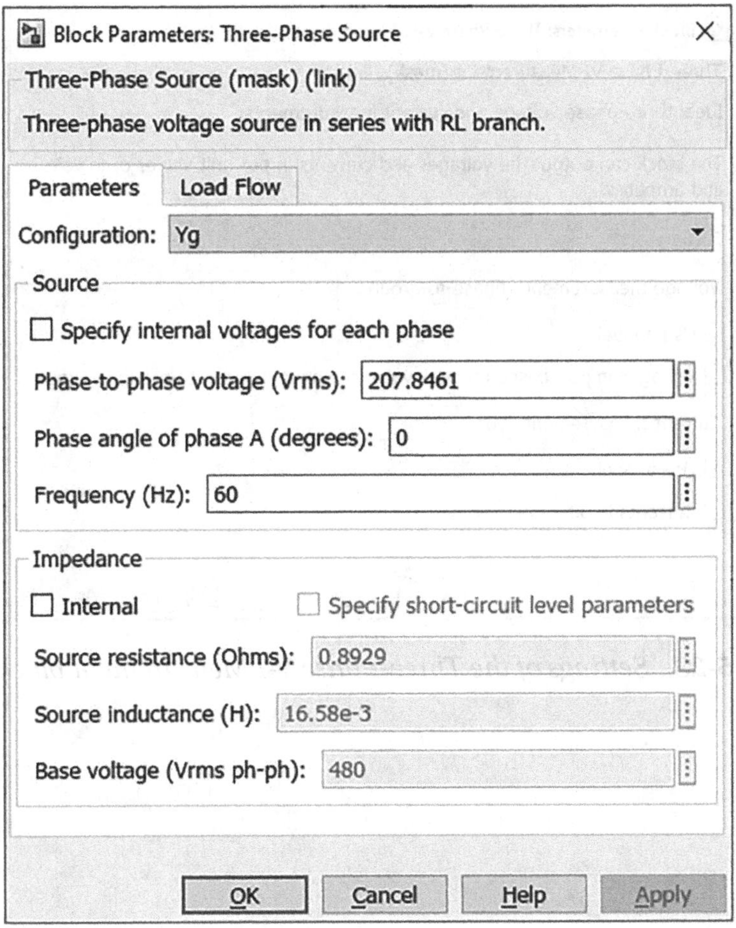

Figure 5-22. *Settings of the Three-Phase Source block*

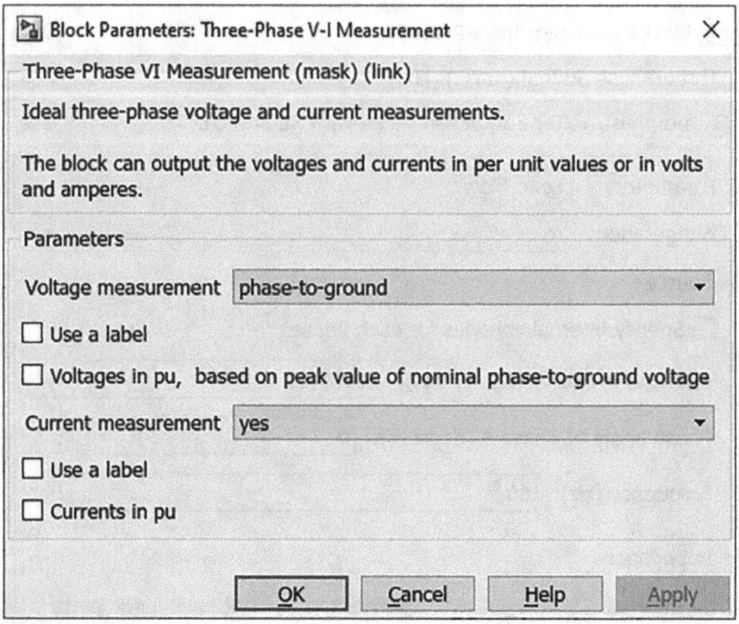

Figure 5-23. *Settings of the Three-Phase V-I Measurement block*

Block Parameters: PLL (3ph)   ✕

PLL (3ph) (mask) (link)

This Phase Locked Loop (PLL) system can be used to synchronize on
a set of variable frequency, three-phase sinusoidal signals. If the
Automatic Gain Control is enabled, the input (phase error) of the PLL
regulator is scaled according to the input signals magnitude.

For optimal performance, set regulator gains [Kp Ki Kd] = [180
3200 1] and check the Enable Automatic Gain Control parameter.

Input : Vector containing the normalized three-phase signals [Va Vb
Vc]
Output 1: Measured frequency (Hz) = w/(2pi)
Output 2: Ramp w.t varying between 0 and 2*pi, synchronized on
zero crossings of the fundamental (positive-sequence) of phase A.

Parameters

Minimum frequency (Hz):

| 45 |

Initial inputs [Phase (degrees), Frequency (Hz)]:

| [0, 60] |

Regulator gains [Kp, Ki, Kd]:

| [180, 3200, 1] |

Time constant for derivative action (s):

| 1e-4 |

Maximum rate of change of frequency (Hz/s):

| 12 |

Filter cut-off frequency for frequency measurement (Hz):

| 25 |

Sample time:

| 0 |

☑ Enable automatic gain control

[OK]   [Cancel]   [Help]   [Apply]

Figure 5-24. *Settings of the PLL (3ph) block*

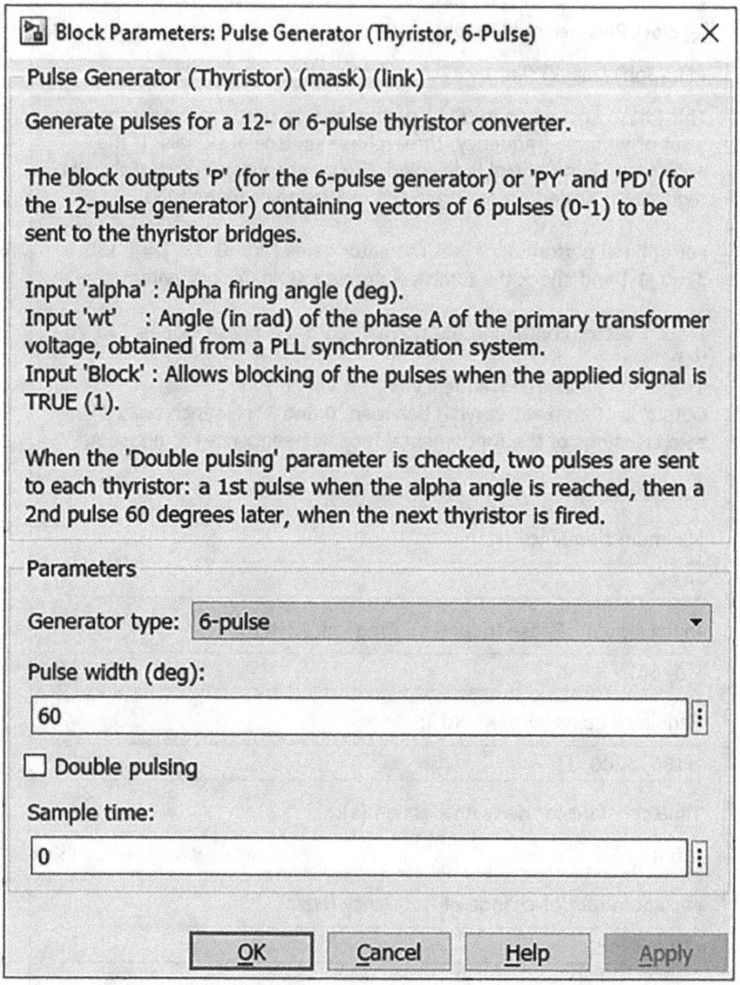

Figure 5-25. *Settings of the Pulse Generator (Thyristor, 6-Pulse) block*

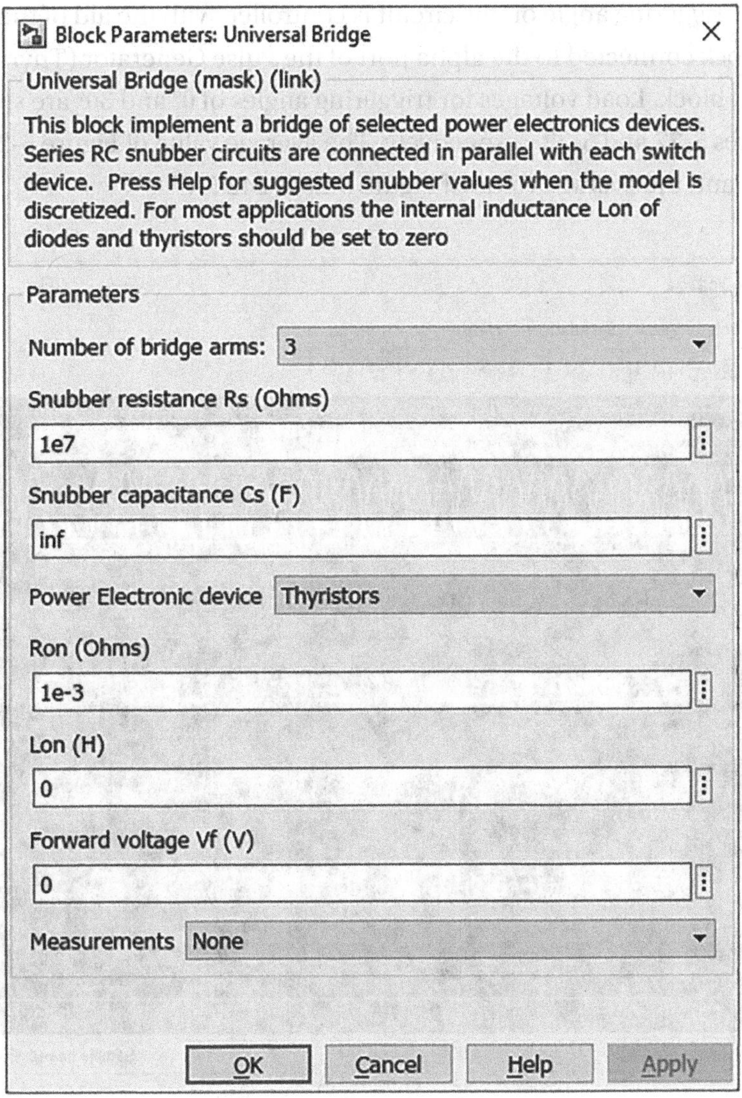

Figure 5-26. *Settings of the Universal Bridge block*

The triggering angle of this circuit is controlled with the aid of the Constant block connected to the alpha port of the Pulse Generator (Thyristor, 6-Pulse) block. Load voltages for triggering angles of 0° and 30° are shown in Figures 5-27 and 5-28, respectively. The average value of Figure 5-27 is 280.6 V, and the average value of Figure 5-28 is 242.5 V.

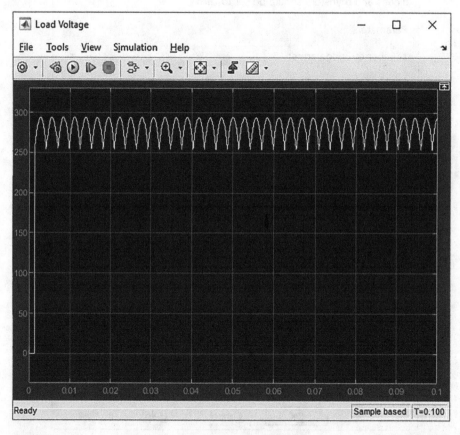

Figure 5-27. *Simulation result (firing angle is 0°). The average value of this waveform is 280.6 VDC*

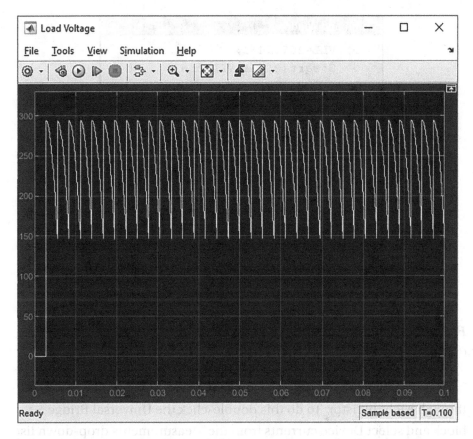

Figure 5-28. *Simulation result (firing angle is 30°). The average value of this waveform is 242.5 VDC*

The average output voltage of a three-phase thyristor rectifier with ideal thyristors (forward voltage drop is ignored) can be calculated with the aid of the $V_{O,DC} = \dfrac{3\sqrt{2}}{\pi} \times V_{LL} \, cos(\alpha)$ formula. V_{LL} indicates the line-line voltage, and α indicates the triggering angle. According to the calculations shown in Figure 5-29, the average output voltage for $\alpha = 0°$ and $\alpha = 30°$ equals to 280.6909 V and 243.0854 V, respectivley. These values are quite close to the obtained results since the closed thyristors are modeled with 1 mΩ resistors (see Figure 5-26) without any forward voltage drop.

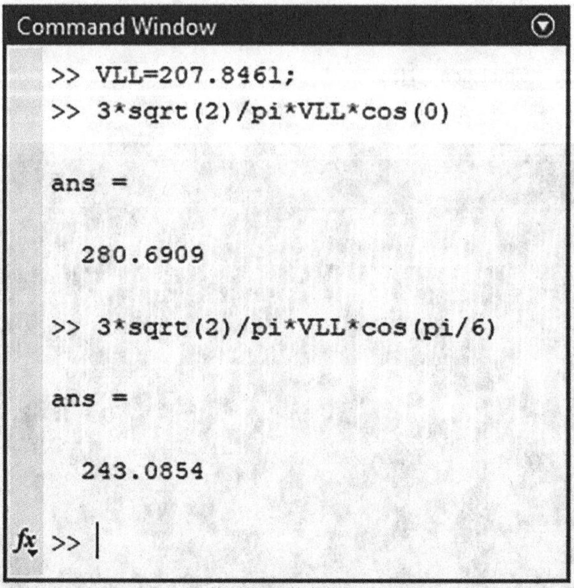

```
Command Window                                    ⌄

>> VLL=207.8461;
>> 3*sqrt(2)/pi*VLL*cos(0)


ans =

  280.6909

>> 3*sqrt(2)/pi*VLL*cos(pi/6)

ans =

  243.0854

fx >> |
```

Figure 5-29. *Calculation of the average output voltage for firing angles of 0° and 30°*

Assume that you want to measure the average current that passes through each thyristor. To do this double-click the Universal Bridge block and select Device currents from the Measurements drop-down list (Figure 5-30).

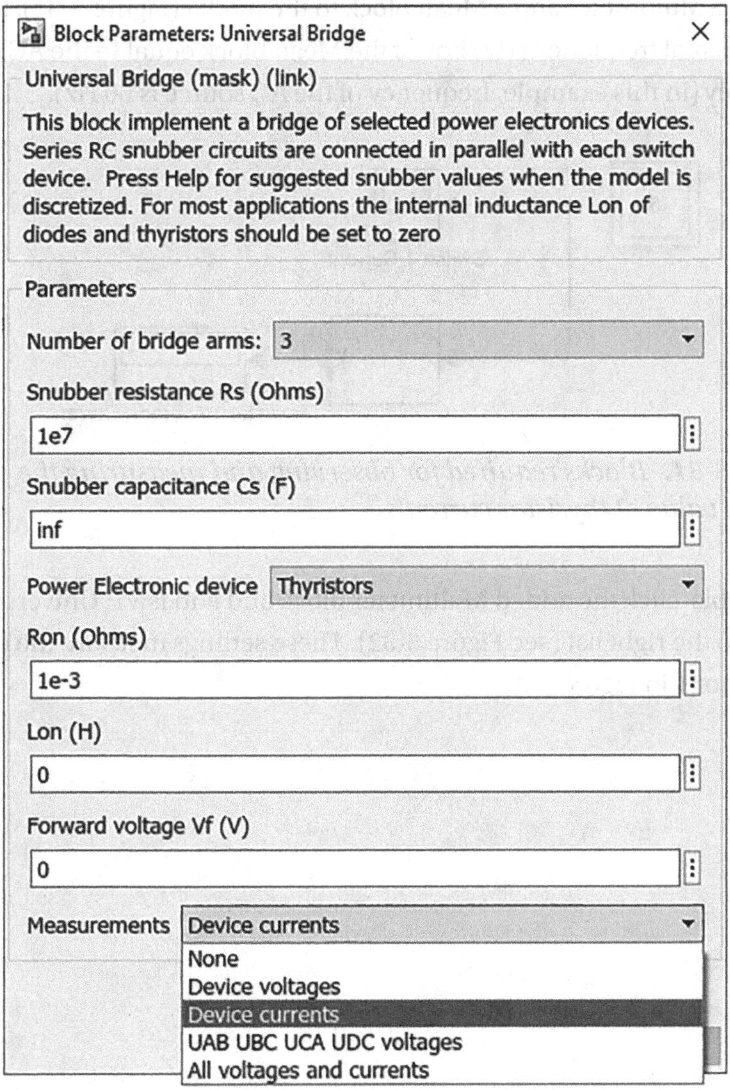

Figure 5-30. *Measuring the current of thyristors*

Add a Multimeter and a Mean block to the model (Figure 5-31). Set the Fundamental frequency (Hz) box of the Mean block equal to the AC source frequency (in this example, frequency of the AC source is 60 Hz).

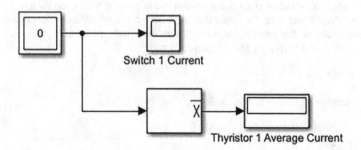

Figure 5-31. *Blocks required for observing and measuring the average value of thyristor currents*

Double-click the added Multimeter block and add Isw1: Universal Bridge to the right list (see Figure 5-32). These settings measure the current of thyristor 1 in Figure 5-21.

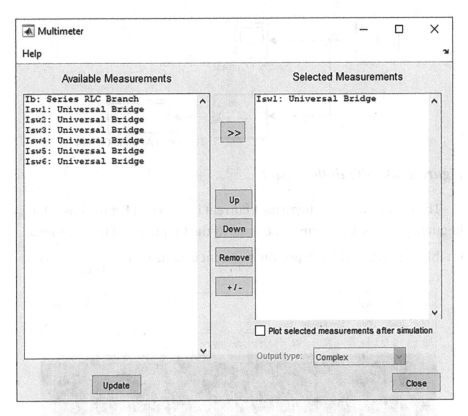

Figure 5-32. *Isw1: Universal Bridge is added to the Selected Measurements list. Isw1: Universal Bridge shows the current of thyristor 1*

Run the simulation (triggering angle is 0°). The average current of thyristor 1 (or any of other thyristors) is 9.355 A (Figure 5-33).

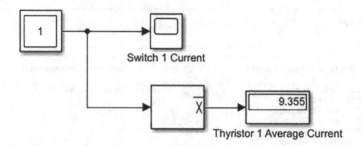

Figure 5-33. *Simulation result*

The waveform of the thyristor 1 current is shown in Figure 5-34. The frequency of this waveform is the same as the frequency of the AC source (in this example, 60 Hz). The switch current is nonzero for $\dfrac{1}{3 \times 60} = 5.6\,ms$.

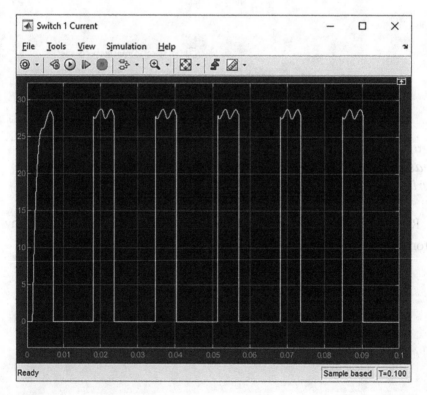

Figure 5-34. *Simulation result*

Let's measure the average current of the load and compare the average current of the thyristors with it. We expect the average current of thyristors to be one-third of the average current of the load (because each thyristor conducts the load current for 120°). Figure 5-35 verifies our expectation.

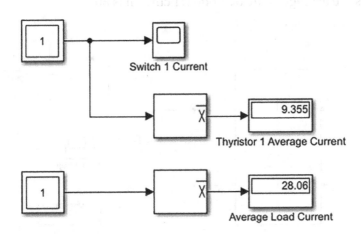

Figure 5-35. *Simulation result*

The output voltage ripple decreases if we add a capacitor to the rectifier output. In the next example, we will simulate a single-phase rectifier with an output filter capacitor, and we will investigate the effect of the filter capacitor on the current drawn from the input AC source.

Example 5: Effect of a Filter Capacitor on the Rectifier Circuit

In this example we want to see the effect of a filter capacitor on the output voltage ripple and the current that passes through the bridge switches. The Simulink model of this example is shown in Figure 5-36 (the filter capacitor is not added yet). The load is purely resistive with value of 10 Ω. Peak of the AC source is 100 V, and its frequency is 60 Hz. Settings of Universal Bridge are shown in Figure 5-37. The equivalent circuit of the Universal Bridge block with two arms is shown in Figure 5-38. The Fundamental frequency (Hz) box of the Mean block that measures the average value of load voltage is 120. The Fundamental frequency (Hz) box of the Mean block that measures the average value of diode D1 current is 60.

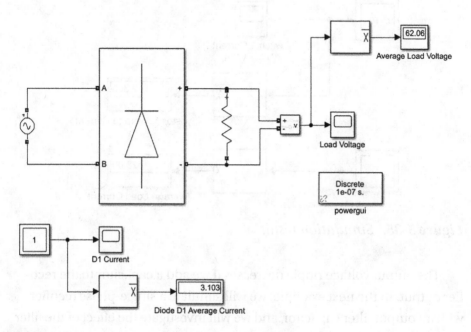

Figure 5-36. *Simulink model of Example 5*

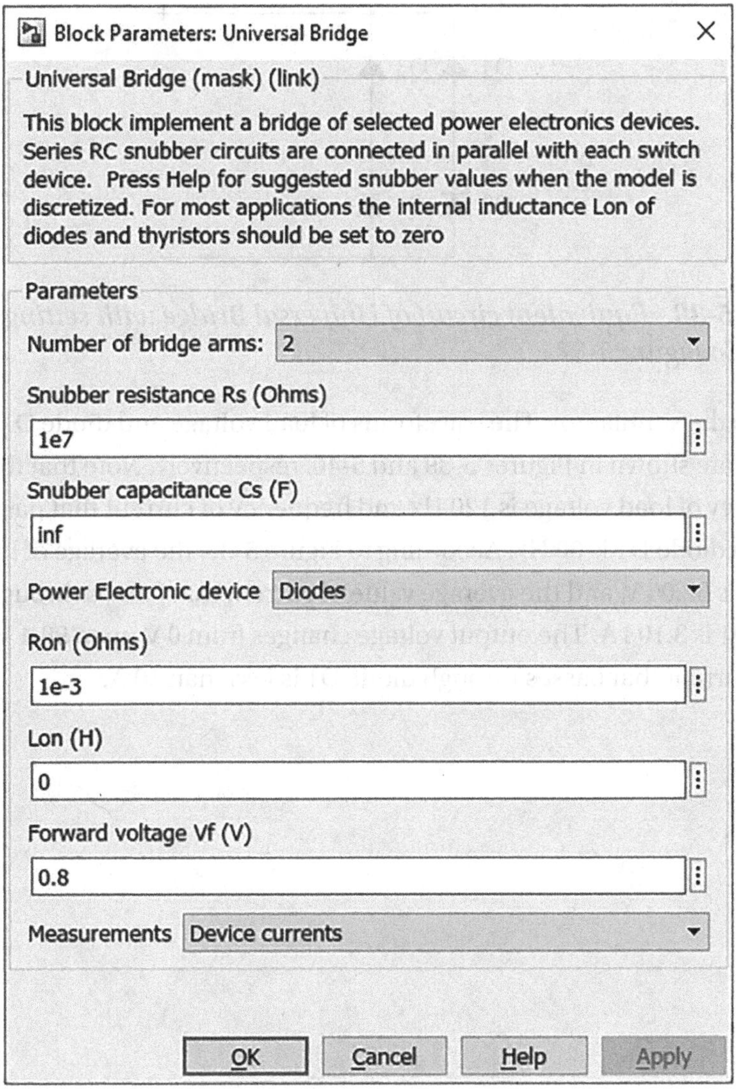

Figure 5-37. *Settings of the Universal Bridge block*

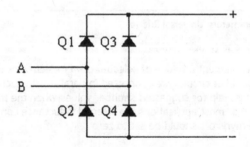

Figure 5-38. *Equivalent circuit of Universal Bridge with settings shown in Figure 5-37*

Run the simulation. The waveforms of load voltage and diode D1 current are shown in Figures 5-39 and 5-40, respectively. Note that the frequency of load voltage is 120 Hz and frequency of current that passes through diode D1 is 60 Hz. According to Figure 5-36, the average of load voltage is 62.06 V, and the average value of current that passes through diode D1 is 3.103 A. The output voltage changes from 0 V up to 98.4 V. Peak of the current that passes through diode D1 is less than 10 A.

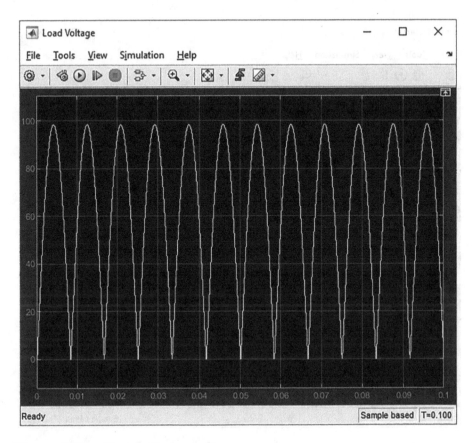

Figure 5-39. *Simulation result*

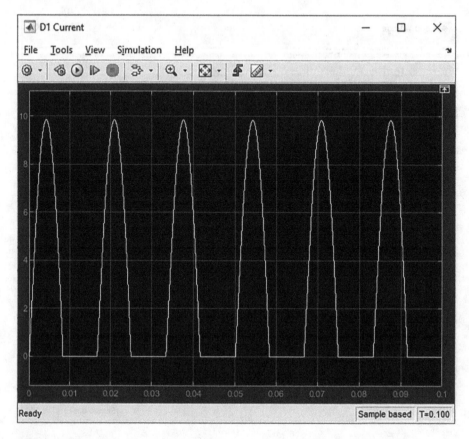

Figure 5-40. *Simulation result*

Add a filter capacitor with a value of 1000 µF to the circuit and run the simulation. According to Figure 5-41, the average of load voltage is 79.17 V, and the average value of current that passes through diode D1 is 3.959 A.

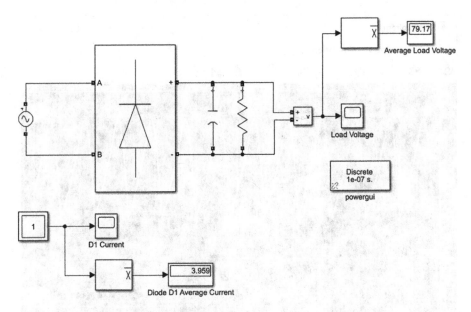

Figure 5-41. *Simulation result*

The waveforms of load voltage and diode D1 current are shown in Figures 5-42 and 5-43, respectively. Note that the frequency of load voltage is 120 Hz and frequency of current that passes through diode D1 is 60 Hz. The output voltage changes from 56.72 V up to 98.4 V. Peak of the current that passes through diode D1 is about 39 A.

So, when you add a filter capacitor to the rectifier output, the voltage ripple decreases; however, the current drawn from the source (or the current that flows through the diodes) becomes narrow pulses with high values. These narrow high-current pulses increase the chance of burning the diodes. Therefore, you can't increase the filter capacitor without bound. You need to consider the safe region for the diodes as well.

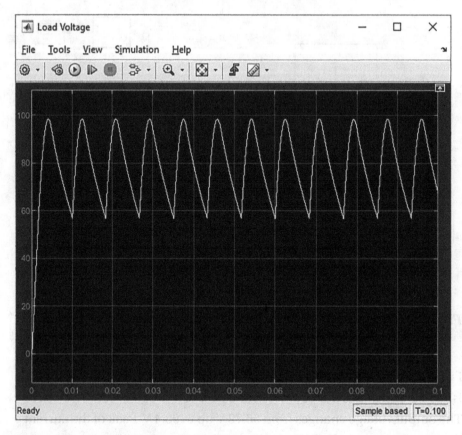

Figure 5-42. *Simulation result*

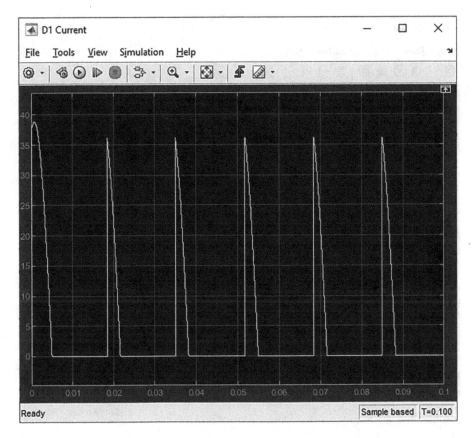

Figure 5-43. *Simulation result (time step of the powergui block is 10^{-7})*

Figure 5-43 is produced with a powergui time step of 1e-7. Figure 5-44 shows the diode D1 current with a powergui time step of 5e-6. It is a good idea to decrease the time step of simulation when you want to see the impulse-type signals. Figure 5-43 is smoother in comparison with Figure 5-44.

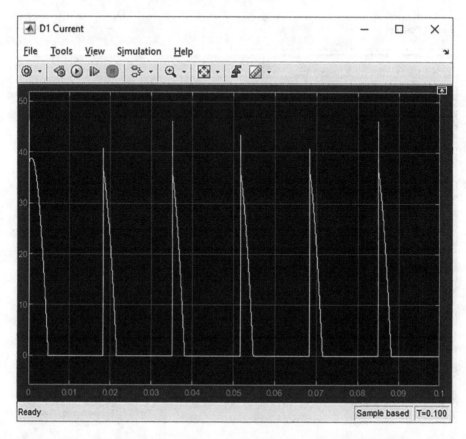

Figure 5-44. *Simulation result (time step of the powergui block is* 5×10^{-6}*)*

The current of the filter capacitor is shown in Figure 5-45. The average of this waveform is 0 A (why?). The maximum of capacitor current is 37.63 A, and the RMS value of current that passes through the capacitor is about 12 A. So you need to select a capacitor that is able to handle these values of current.

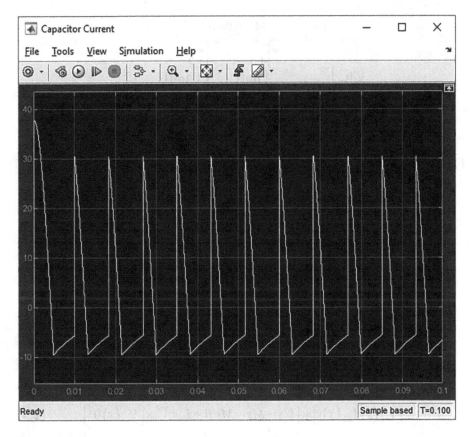

Figure 5-45. *Simulation result*

In the next example, we will learn how to simulate coupled inductors in the Simulink environment.

Example 6: Coupled Inductors

In this example we want to show how coupled inductors can be simulated in Simulink. Consider the circuit shown in Figure 5-46. Vin is a step voltage, and M is the mutual inductance between L1 and L2. The coupling coefficient between the two coils is $k = \dfrac{M}{\sqrt{L_1 L_2}} = \dfrac{0.9m}{\sqrt{1m \times 1.1m}} = 0.8581$.

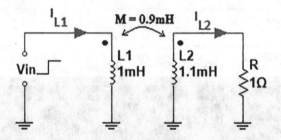

Figure 5-46. *A simple circuit with magnetic coupling*

From basic circuit theory

$$\{ L_1 \frac{di_{L1}}{dt} - M \frac{di_{L2}}{dt} = V_{in}(t) \; R i_{L2} + L_2 \frac{di_{L2}}{dt} - M \frac{di_{L1}}{dt} = 0 \qquad (2.1)$$

Take the Laplace transform of both sides:

$$\left[L_1 s - Ms - Ms \; R + L_2 s \right] \times \left[I_{L1}(s) \; I_{L2}(s) \right] = \left[V_{in}(s) \, 0 \right] \qquad (2.2)$$

So

$$\left[I_{L1}(s) \; I_{L2}(s) \right] = \left[L_1 s - Ms - Ms \; R + L_2 s \right]^{-1} \times \left[V_{in}(s) \, 0 \right] \qquad (2.3)$$

$V_{in}(s) = \dfrac{1}{s}$, so

$$\left[I_{L1}(s) \; I_{L2}(s) \right] = \left[\frac{(11s+10000) \times 10000}{s^2 \times (29s+100000)} \quad \frac{90000}{s(29s+100000)} \right] \qquad (2.4)$$

You can use the commands shown in Figure 5-47 in order to see the time domain graph of I_{L1} and I_{L2}. Graphs of I_{L1} and I_{L2} are shown in Figures 5-48 and 5-49, respectively.

```
Command Window                                              ⊙
  >> s=tf('s');
  >> I1=(11*s+10000)*10000/s/(29*s+100000);
  >> I2=90000/(29*s+100000);
  >> step(I1,[0:0.06/100:0.06]), grid on
  >> step(I2), grid on
fx >>
```

Figure 5-47. *MATLAB commands to draw $I_{L1}(t)$ and $I_{L2}(t)$*

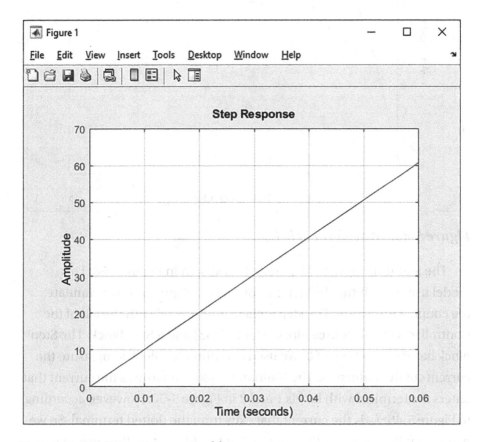

Figure 5-48. *Waveform of $I_{L1}(t)$*

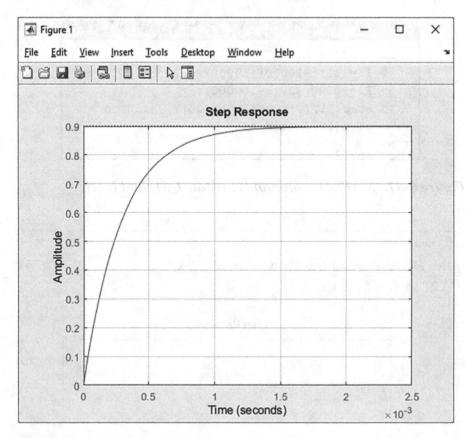

Figure 5-49.   *Waveform of $I_{L2}(t)$*

The Simulink model of Figure 5-46 is shown in Figure 5-50. This model uses the Mutual Inductance block (see Figure 5-51) to simulate the coupled inductors. The step voltage is produced with the aid of the Controlled Voltage Source block (Figure 5-52) and a Step block. The Step block has the step time of 0. We used a Multimeter block to measure the currents of the inductors. The Multimeter block measures the current that enters the terminal with labels 1 and 2 in Figure 5-50. However, according to Figure 5-46, I_{L2} is the current that exits from the dotted terminal. So we need to multiply the Multimeter reading by –1 to obtain the current that exits from the dotted terminal.

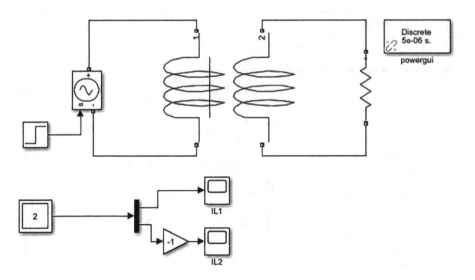

Figure 5-50. *Simulink model of Figure 5-46*

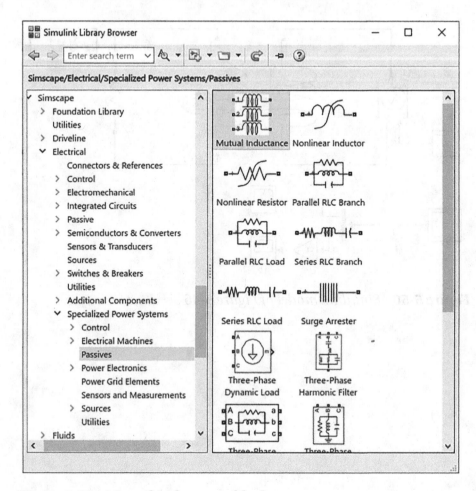

Figure 5-51. *Mutual Inductance block*

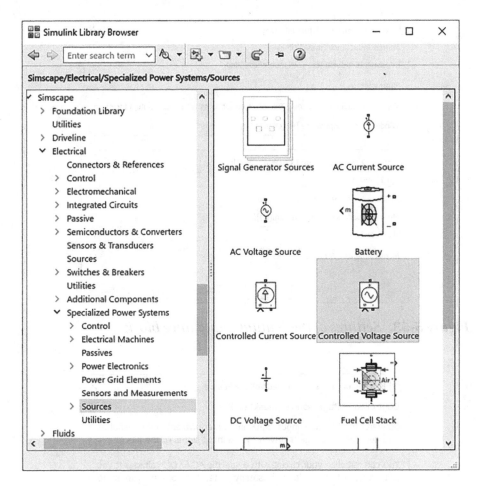

Figure 5-52. *Controlled Voltage Source block*

Settings of the Mutual Inductance block and the Controlled Voltage Source block are shown in Figures 5-53 and 5-54, respectively.

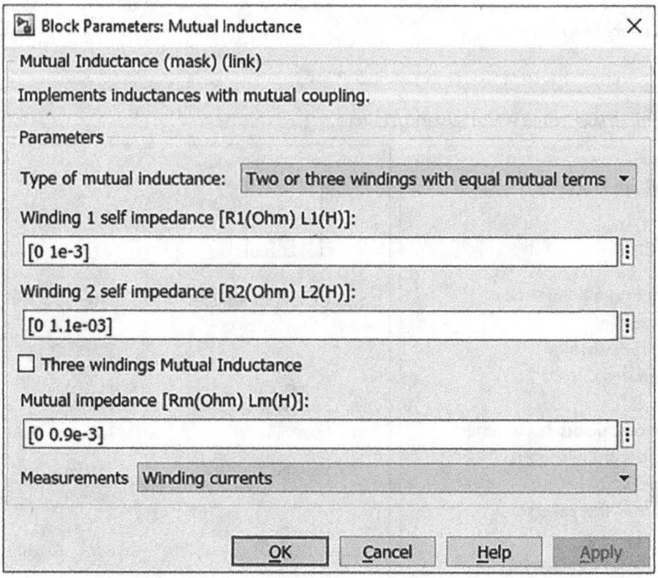

Figure 5-53. *Settings of the Mutual Inductance block*

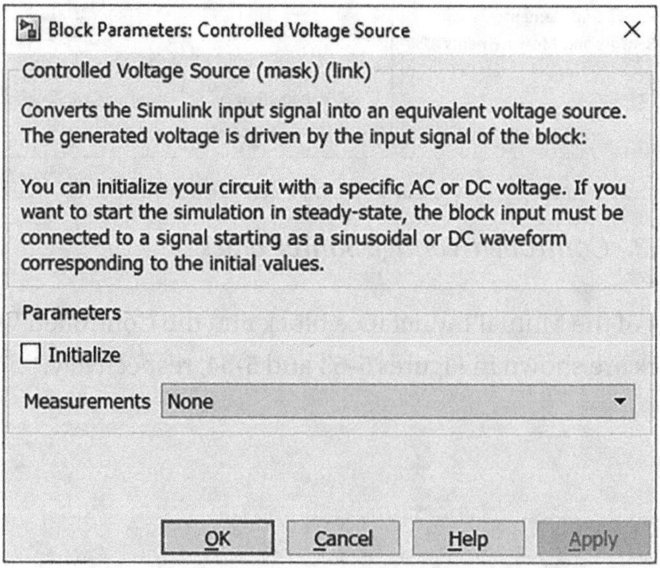

Figure 5-54. *Setting of the Controlled Voltage Source block*

Simulation results are shown in Figures 5-55 and 5-56. Obtained waveforms are the same as the waveforms shown in Figures 5-48 and 5-49.

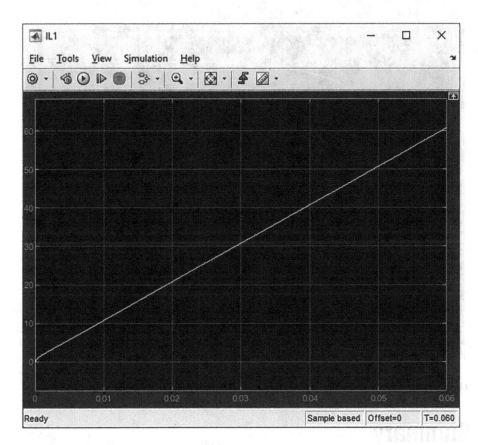

Figure 5-55. *Waveform of $I_{L1}(t)$*

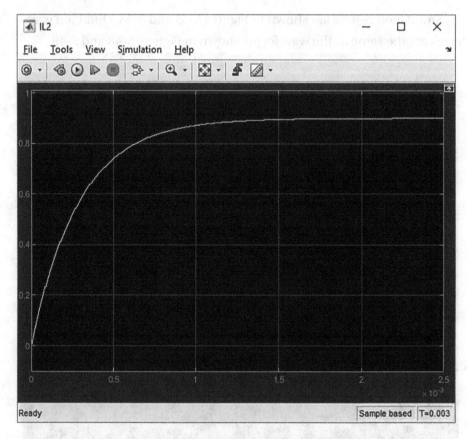

Figure 5-56. *Waveform of $I_{L2}(t)$*

Summary

In this chapter we learned how to simulate controlled single-phase and three-phase rectifiers and measure the average and RMS values of the output. You observed that addition of a capacitor to the output of the rectifier decreases the output voltage ripple. Presence of the capacitor causes the input current to change into narrow impulses, which is undesirable. Therefore, you can't increase the capacitor without bound. We learned how to simulate circuits that contain coupled inductors as well.

In the next chapter, we will learn how to simulate the DC-DC converters.

CHAPTER 6

Simulation of DC-DC Converters

DC-DC converters convert a source of direct current (DC) from one voltage level to another. For instance, assume that you want to install a digital clock in a car. The car battery is 12 V, while the digital clock requires 5 V. In this case you need a DC-DC converter in order to decrease the voltage to 5 V.

DC-DC converters can be divided into two major groups: isolated DC-DC converters and non-isolated DC-DC converters. Isolated DC-DC converters contain a transformer, while non-isolated DC-DC converters do not contain a transformer.

This chapter studies the simulation of DC-DC converters in the Simulink environment. We will learn how to simulate a Buck converter and determine its operating mode (i.e., Continuous Conduction Mode [CCM] or Discontinuous Conduction Mode [DCM]), how to generate a PWM signal, how to simulate a closed-loop Buck converter, and how to simulate a Flyback converter and measure its efficiency.

© Farzin Asadi 2022
F. Asadi, *Simulation of Power Electronics Circuits with MATLAB®/Simulink®*,
Maker Innovations Series, https://doi.org/10.1007/978-1-4842-8220-5_6

Example 1: Buck Converter

In this example we want to simulate a Buck converter. Consider the Simulink model shown in Figure 6-1. The converter is supplied from a DC Voltage Source block (see Figure 6-2). A Pulse Generator block is used to trigger the Mosfet block (see Figure 6-3). The resistor in series with the inductor and capacitor shows the Equivalent Series Resistance (ESR) of the inductor and capacitor, respectively. The input voltage is 50 V, the inductor is 400 µH with ESR of 1 mΩ, the capacitor is 100 µF with ESR of 50 mΩ, and the output load is 20 Ω. Settings of the Pulse Generator block are shown in Figure 6-4. With these settings, a pulse with frequency of 20 kHz and duty cycle of 40% will be applied to the gate of the MOSFET.

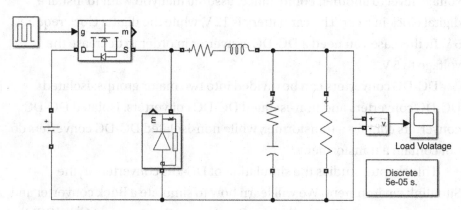

Figure 6-1. *Simulink model of Example 1*

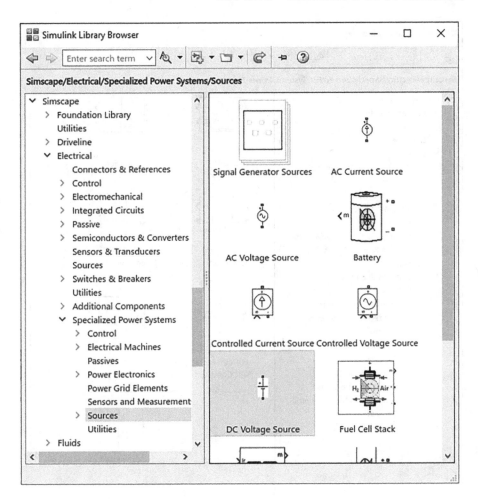

Figure 6-2. *DC Voltage Source block*

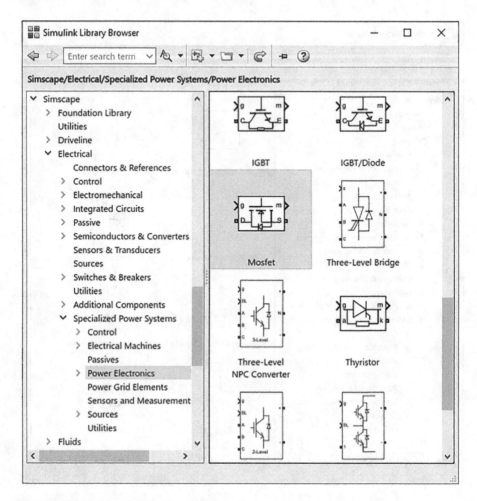

Figure 6-3. *Mosfet block*

Block Parameters: Pulse Generator   ✕

Pulse Generator

Output pulses:

if (t >= PhaseDelay) && Pulse is on
  Y(t) = Amplitude
else
  Y(t) = 0
end

Pulse type determines the computational technique used.

Time-based is recommended for use with a variable step solver, while
Sample-based is recommended for use with a fixed step solver or within a
discrete portion of a model using a variable step solver.

Parameters

Pulse type: | Time based   ▼ |

Time (t): | Use simulation time   ▼ |

Amplitude:

| 1 |⋮|

Period (secs):

| 1/20e3 |⋮|

Pulse Width (% of period):

| 40 |⋮|

Phase delay (secs):

| 0 |⋮|

☑ Interpret vector parameters as 1-D

⑦ | OK | | Cancel | | Help | Apply

Figure 6-4. *Settings of the Pulse Generator block*

Run the simulation. The waveform shown in Figure 6-5 is obtained.
You can measure the average value of output voltage by connecting a

Mean block to the output. Fundamental frequency (Hz) of this block must be filled with the switching frequency.

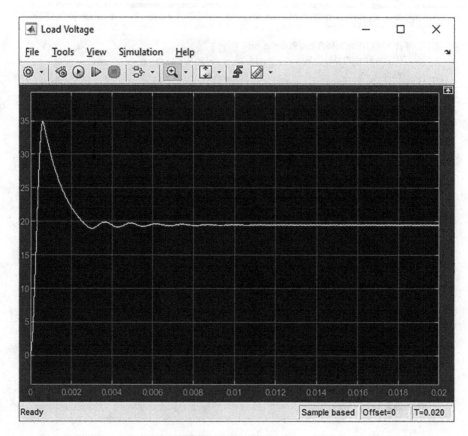

Figure 6-5. *Simulation result*

Let's measure the ripple of output voltage. To do this, use the magnifier (see Figure 6-6) to zoom into the steady-state region of the waveform (see Figure 6-7). According to Figure 6-7, the ripple is about 100 mV.

Figure 6-6. *Magnifier icon*

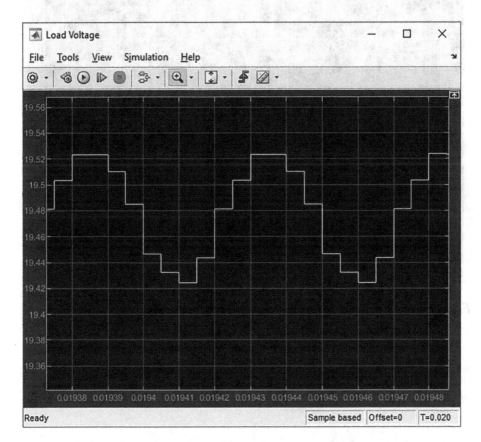

Figure 6-7. *Simulation result (time step of powergui is 5 μs)*

If you decrease the step size of the powergui block, you see a smoother graph when you zoom in the graph (however, the simulation takes more time to be done). Figure 6-8 shows the zoomed graph for step size 5e-7.

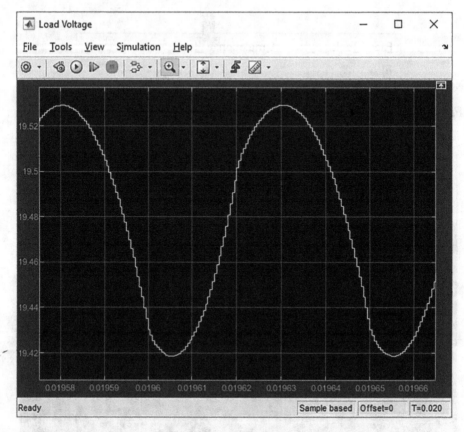

Figure 6-8. *Simulation result (time step of powergui is 0.5 μs)*

In this example we simulated a Buck converter. In the next example, we will determine its operating mode (i.e., CCM or DCM).

Example 2: Operating Mode of the DC-DC Converter

In this example, we want to determine the operating mode of the Buck converter of Example 1. In order to do this, we need to see the inductor current waveform. The model shown in Figure 6-9 uses a Multimeter block to monitor the inductor current.

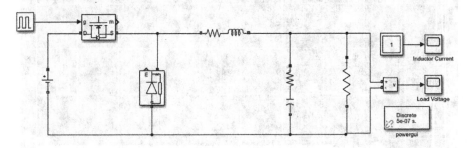

Figure 6-9. *Simulink model of Example 2*

The simulation result is shown in Figure 6-10. Use the magnifier (see Figure 6-11) to see the steady-state region of the waveform. According to Figure 6-12, the minimum of the waveform in steady state is positive. So this converter is operated in Continuous Conduction Mode (CCM).

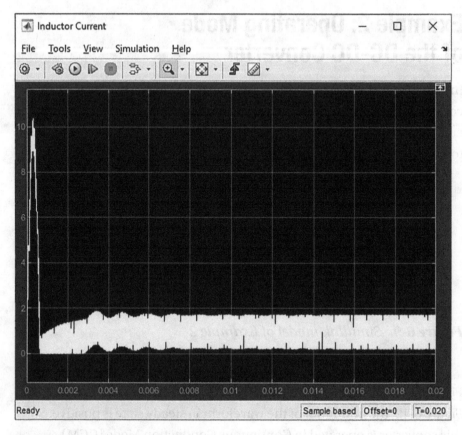

Figure 6-10. *Simulation result*

Figure 6-11. *Magnifier icon*

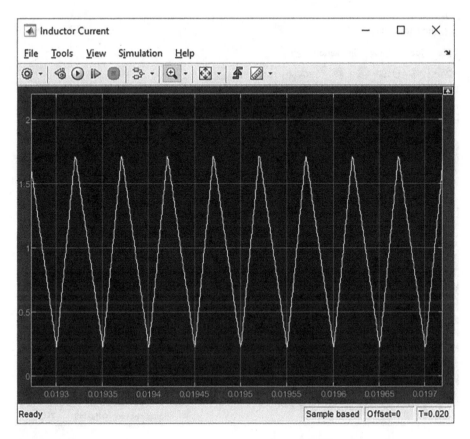

Figure 6-12. *Minimum of inductor current is bigger than zero (load is 20 Ω)*

Increase the load to 40 Ω. The inductor current changes to that shown in Figure 6-13. The converter is operated in Discontinuous Conduction Mode (DCM) for this value of the load.

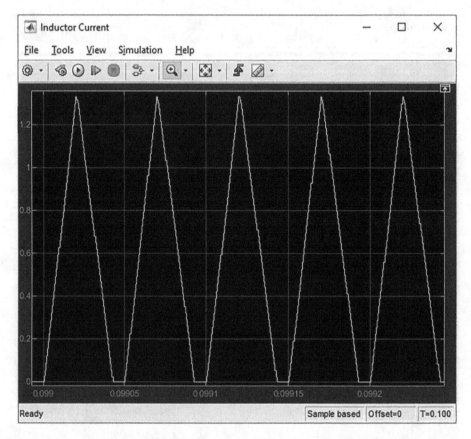

Figure 6-13. *Minimum of inductor current is zero (load is 40 Ω)*

The Buck converter simulated in Example 1 is an open-loop converter
(i.e., there is no feedback from output to set the duty cycle of pulses
applied to the gate of the MOSFET). In the next two examples, we will
study the effect disturbances like input voltage and output voltage changes
on the operation of the converter.

Example 3: Effect of Input Voltage Changes on the Output Voltage

In this example, we want to study the effect of input voltage changes on the converter of Example 1. A Controlled Voltage Source block is used to supply the converter (see Figure 6-14). Settings of the Step block are shown in Figure 6-15. So we have a sudden change in the input voltage (from 50 V to 40 V) at t= 50 ms.

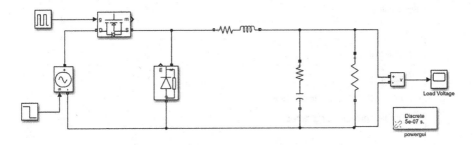

Figure 6-14. *Simulink model of Example 3*

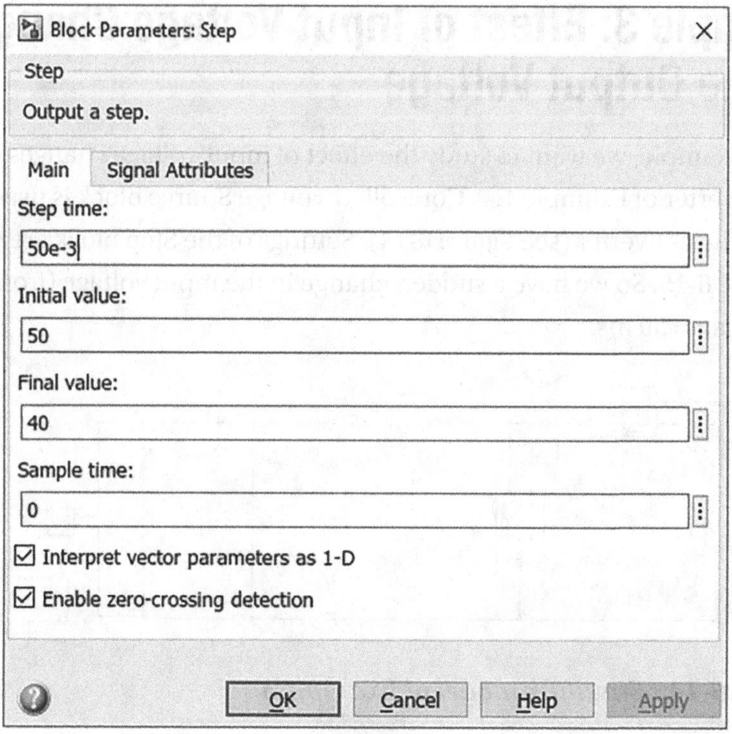

Figure 6-15. *Settings of the Step block*

The simulation result is shown in Figure 6-16. As shown, a decrease in the input voltage of the converter leads to a decrease in the output voltage. Note that we have no control mechanism, that is, feedback controller, to keep the output voltage constant. If you want to keep the output voltage constant despite the input voltage changes, you need to use a closed-loop control system.

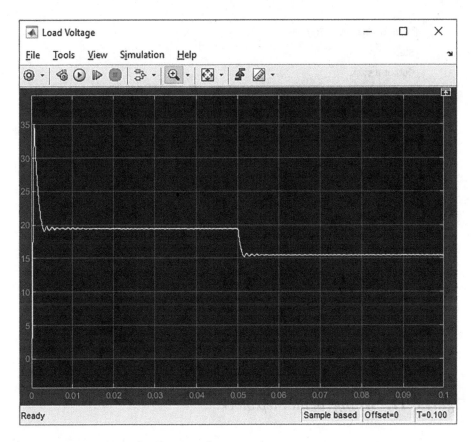

Figure 6-16. *Simulation result*

You can study the effect of input voltage increases as well. For instance, with the settings shown in Figure 6-17, the input voltage changes from 50 V to 60 V at t=50 ms. The result of the simulation is shown in Figure 6-18. An increase of input voltage leads to an increase in the output voltage.

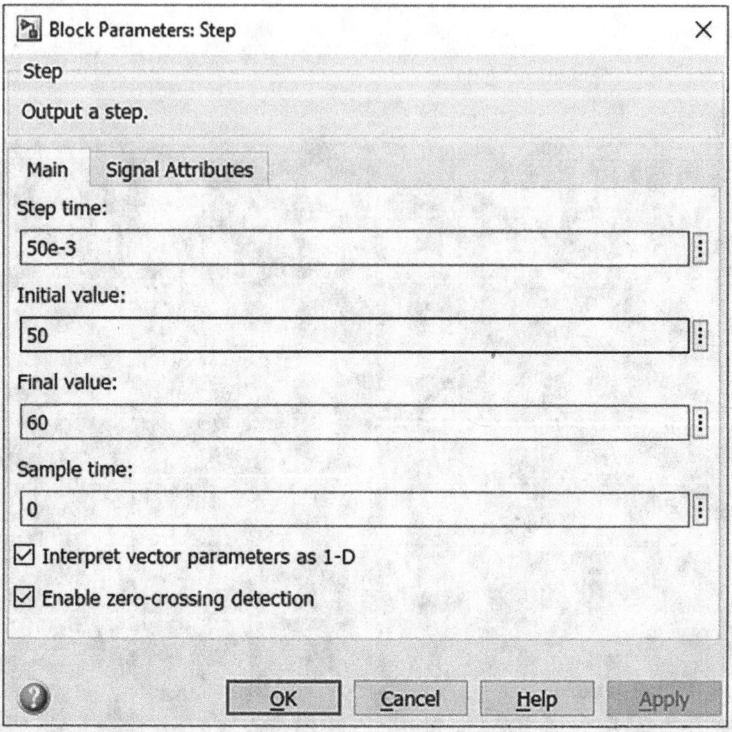

Figure 6-17. *Settings of the Step block*

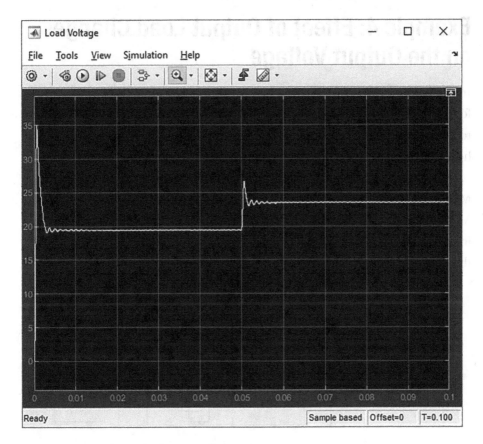

Figure 6-18. Simulation result

In this example we studied the effect of input voltage changes on the output voltage of the converter. In the next example, we will study the effect of output load changes on the output voltage of the studied Buck converter.

Example 4: Effect of Output Load Changes on the Output Voltage

In the previous example, we saw how to study the behavior of a converter for input voltage changes. Another type of disturbance that may be applied to a converter is the output load changes. In this example we will show how to decrease/increase the output load of the converter.

Consider the Simulink model shown in Figure 6-19. When the output MOSFET is open, only one resistor consumes power. When the output MOSFET is closed, two resistors consume power, so the output power is increased. Both of the output resistors are assumed to be 20 Ω. Settings of the Step block are shown in Figure 6-20.

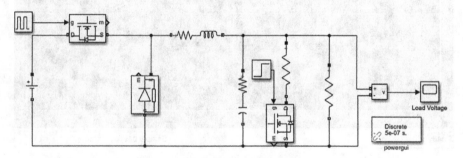

Figure 6-19. *Simulink model of Example 4*

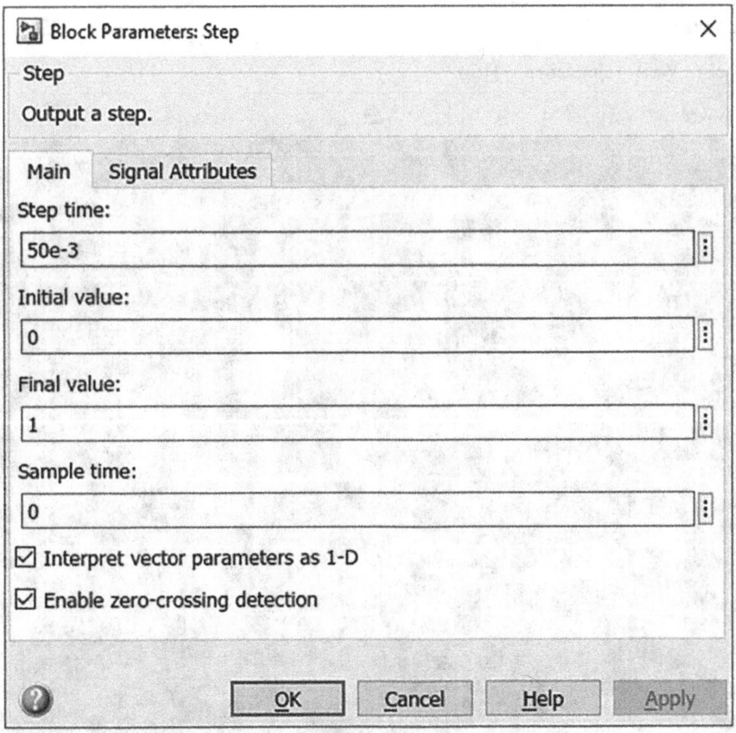

Figure 6-20. Settings of the Step block

According to the settings of the Step block, the output load is 20 Ω for [0, 50 ms] and is 20×20/(20+20)=10 Ω for [50 ms, 100 ms]. The simulation result is shown in Figure 6-21. Figure 6-22 shows the region around the instant at which the load changes. According to the obtained result, the effect of decreasing the value of the load resistor is not considerable for this specific converter.

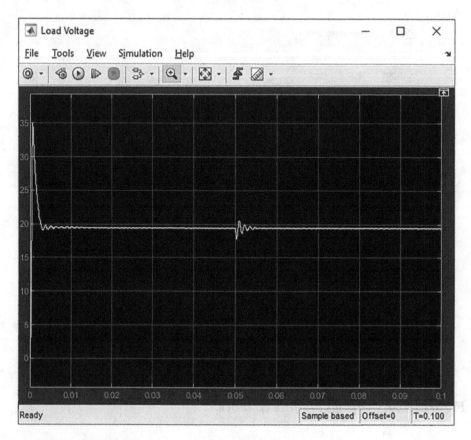

Figure 6-21. *Simulation result*

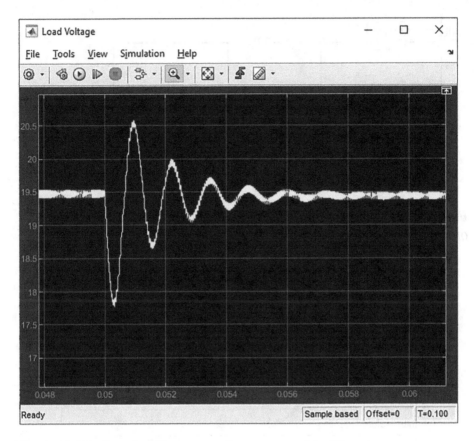

Figure 6-22. *Load voltage waveform around t= 50 ms*

Let's simulate the effect of increase in output load. Consider the Simulink model shown in Figure 6-23. When the output MOSFET is closed, only one resistor is connected to the output of the converter. When the output MOSFET is opened, two resistors in series are connected to the output of the converter. So, when the output MOSFET is opened, the value of output load is increased. Both of the output resistors are assumed to be 20 Ω. Settings of the Step block are shown in Figure 6-24.

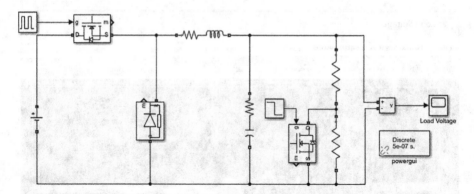

Figure 6-23. *Simulink model to simulate the effect of increase in output load*

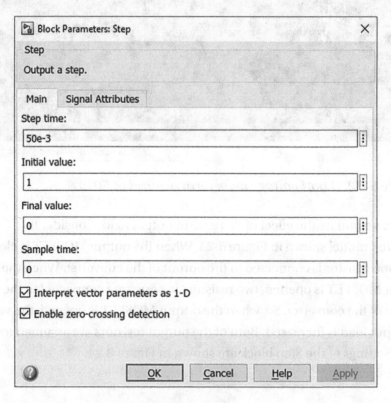

Figure 6-24. *Settings of the Step block*

According to the settings of the Step block, the output load is 20 Ω for [0, 50 ms] and is 20+20=40 Ω for [50 ms, 100 ms]. The simulation result is shown in Figure 6-25. According to the obtained result, increasing the value of the load resistor leads to increase in output voltage for this specific converter.

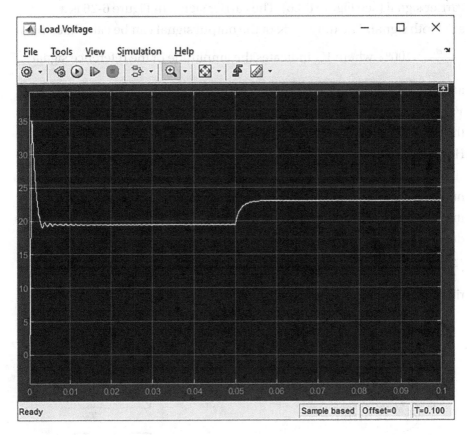

Figure 6-25. *Simulation result*

In the previous examples, we used a Pulse Generator block to generate the required gate pulses for the MOSFET switch. You can use the Pulse Generator block to simulate open-loop converters; however, it is not useful if you want to simulate closed-loop converters. The next two examples focus on the problem of generating a PWM signal for closed-loop converters.

Example 5: Generation of PWM Signals

In the previous examples, we used a Pulse Generator block to turn on and off the MOSFET. In this example, we want to produce the pulses required for the MOSFET by comparing a reference signal with a high-frequency carrier signal (see Figure 6-26). The carrier signal in Figure 6-26 is a sawtooth signal. The duty cycle of the output signal can be calculated by $\frac{V_{ref}}{V_{sawtooth}} \times 100\%$ where V_{ref} indicates the amplitude of the reference signal and $V_{sawtooth}$ indicates the amplitude of the sawtooth signal (note that $V_{ref} < V_{sawtooth}$). The frequency of output pulse equals to the frequency of the carrier signal. There is no limitation on the amplitude of the carrier. However, if you assume $V_{sawtooth} = 1$, then the value of the reference signal shows the duty cycle of output pulse obviously. Studying a simple numeric example is useful: For instance, when $V_{sawtooth} = 1$ V and $V_{ref} = 0.4$, the duty cycle of output pulse is 40%. For $V_{sawtooth} = 5$ V and $V_{ref} = 2$ V, the duty cycle of output pulse will be 40%. However, we need to do a division ($\frac{2}{5} \times 100\% = 40\%$) to find the duty cycle. By taking $V_{sawtooth} = 1$ V, we can get rid of such a division operation.

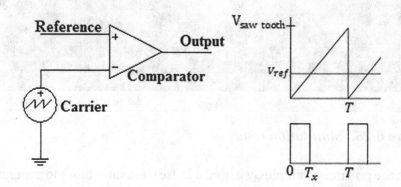

Figure 6-26. *PWM generation*

Figure 6-27 shows the Simulink model of the modulator shown in Figure 6-26. The comparison and generation of the sawtooth signal are done with the aid of Relational Operator (see Figure 6-28) and Sawtooth Generator blocks (see Figure 6-29). The duty cycle of the output signal is determined by the duty cycle Constant block. In this example, it is filled with 0.4, which produces an output pulse with a duty cycle of 40%. It is a good idea to put a Saturation block (see Figure 6-30) after the duty cycle block to ensure that the reference signal that reaches the Relational Operator block is always less than or equal to the carrier. The Lower limit and Upper limit boxes of the Saturation block must be filled with 0 and the amplitude of the carrier signal ($V_{sawtooth}$), respectively. The Fundamental frequency (Hz) box of the Sawtooth Generator block determines the frequency of output pulse. In this specific example, this box is filled with 20e3, which means 20 kHz. Note that the output of the Sawtooth Generator block is between –1 and 1. We need to add +1 to it and divide the result by 2 in order to transfer it to the 0 and 1 range.

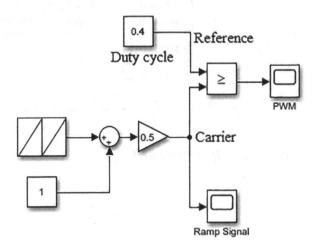

Figure 6-27. *Simulink model to generate the PWM signal*

325

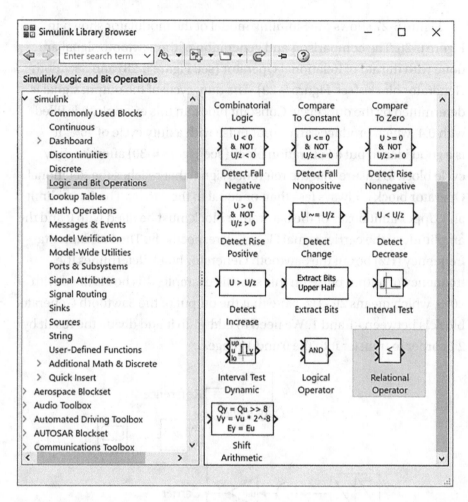

Figure 6-28. *Relational Operator block*

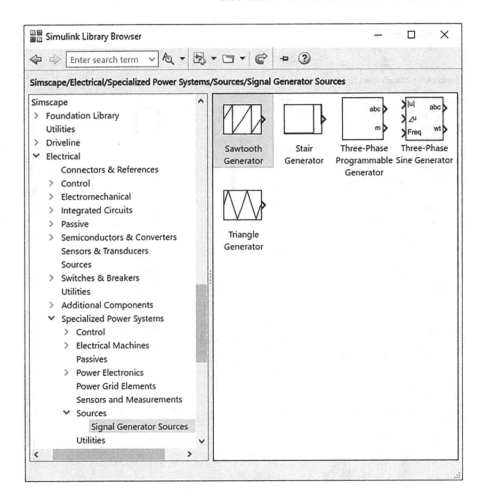

Figure 6-29. *Sawtooth Generator block*

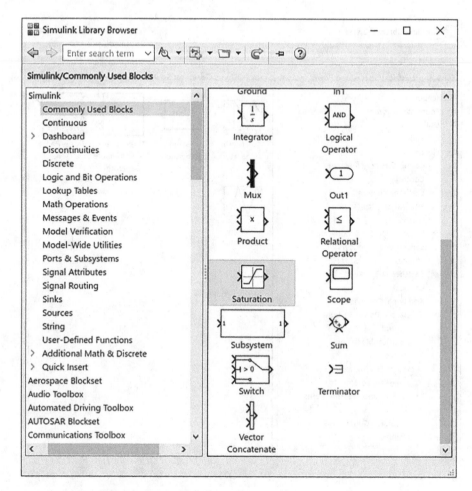

Figure 6-30. *Saturation block*

Run the simulation. The result shown in Figure 6-31 is obtained. You can use cursors to ensure that the duty cycle is 40% and frequency is 20 kHz. The sawtooth signal that enters the Relational Operator block is shown in Figure 6-32 as well.

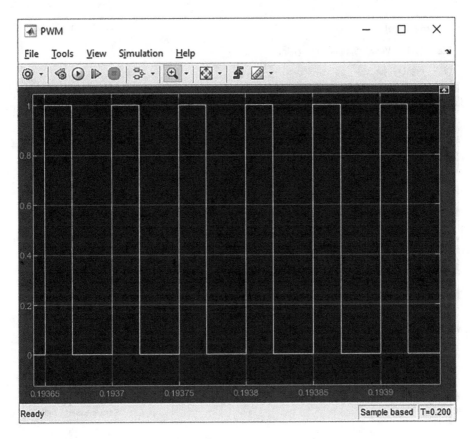

Figure 6-31. *Simulation result*

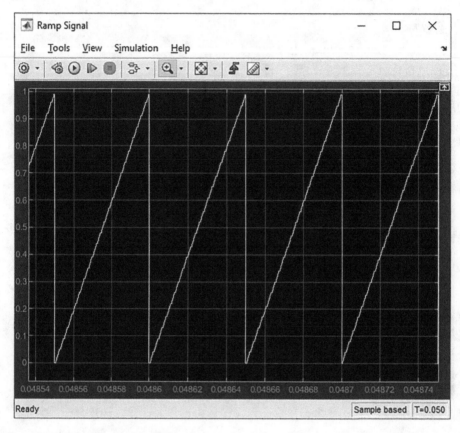

Figure 6-32. *Simulation result*

Sometimes (e.g., in a Synchronous Buck converter) you need the inverted version of the obtained control signal as well. The required Simulink model to produce the inverse (complement) of the control signal is shown in Figure 6-33. This model uses the Logical Operator block (see Figure 6-34). After adding the Logical Operator block to the Simulink model, double-click it and select NOT from the Operator drop-down list (Figure 6-35).

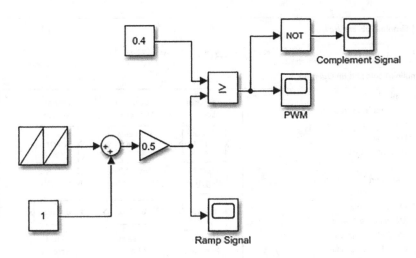

Figure 6-33. *Generation of the PWM signal and its complement*

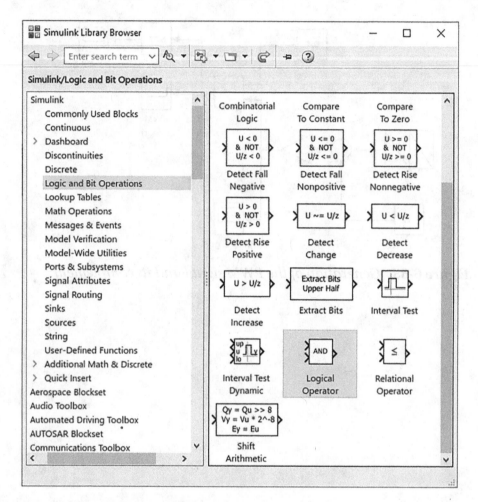

Figure 6-34. *Logical Operator block*

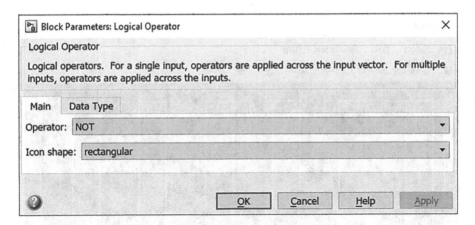

Figure 6-35. *Settings of the Logical Operator block*

Run the model shown in Figure 6-33. The simulation results are shown in Figures 6-36 and 6-37. As expected the output (PWM Scope block) has a duty cycle of 40%, and the inverted signal has a duty cycle of 60%.

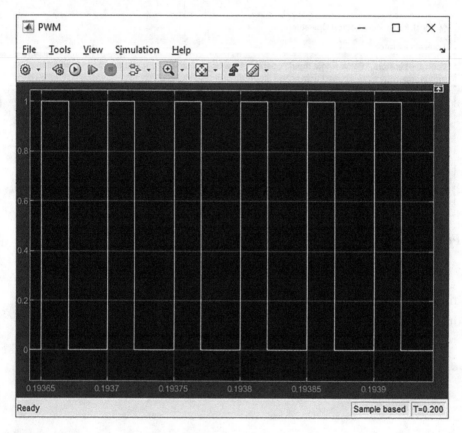

Figure 6-36. *Simulation result*

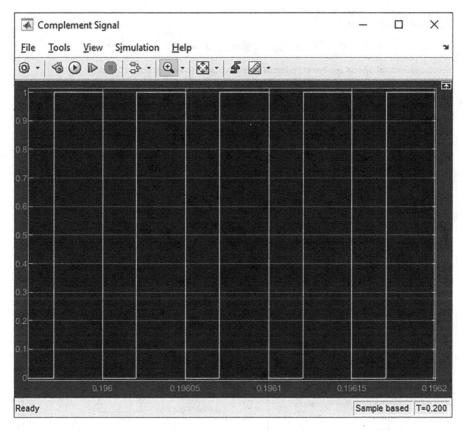

Figure 6-37. *Simulation result*

Simulink has a ready-to-use PWM generation block as well. This block is introduced in the next example.

Example 6: PWM Generator (DC-DC) Block

In the previous examples, we studied two different ways (using a Pulse Generator block or using the models shown in Figure 6-27 or 6-33) to produce the required control signal for the MOSFET. In this example we will study the third way: using the PWM Generator (DC-DC) block (see Figure 6-38).

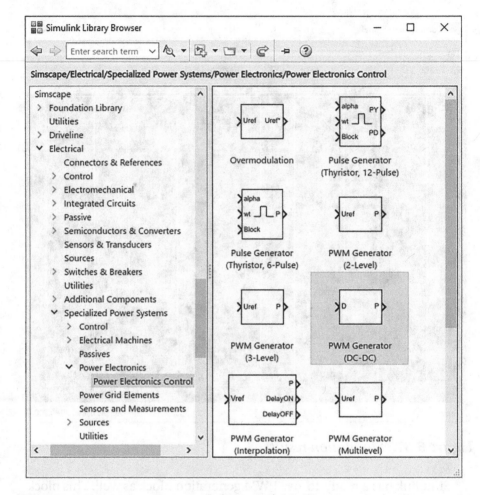

Figure 6-38. *PWM Generator (DC-DC) block*

Consider the model shown in Figure 6-39. The input voltage is 10 V, switching frequency is 100 kHz, duty cycle is 40%, inductor is 100 µH with series resistance of 0.1 Ω, capacitor is 100 µF with series resistance of 0.1 Ω, and output load is 5 Ω. The Snubber resistance Rs (Ohms) parameter of the diode and MOSFET is 1e7. Other parameters of the diode and

MOSFET have default values. It is a good idea to put a Saturation block (see Figure 6-30) before the PWM Generator (DC-DC) block. The Lower limit and Upper limit boxes of the Saturation block must be filled with 0 and 1. Note that PWM Generator (DC-DC) accepts values between 0 and 1 only.

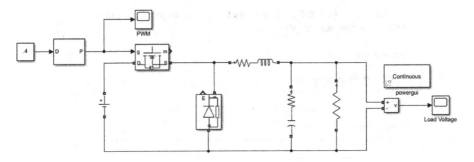

Figure 6-39. *Simulink model of Example 6*

Settings of the PWM Generator (DC-DC) block are shown in Figure 6-40.

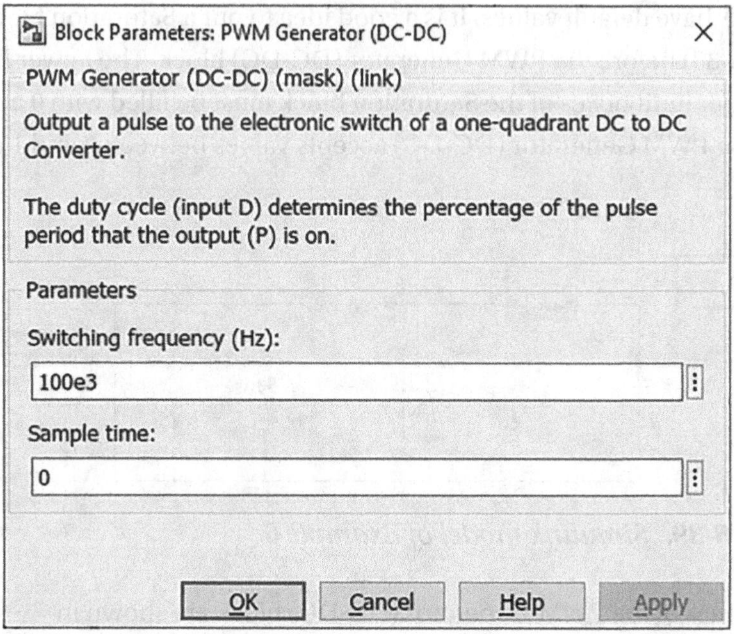

Figure 6-40. *Settings of the PWM Generator (DC-DC) block*

Run the simulation. The signal applied to the gate of the MOSFET is shown in Figure 6-41. You can use cursors to ensure that its frequency equals to 100 kHz and its duty cycle equals to 40%. The output voltage is shown in Figure 6-42. Figure 6-43 shows the zoomed view of the steady-state region. According to Figure 6-43, the frequency of the ripple is 100 kHz, maximum of steady-state voltage is 3.436 V, minimum of steady-state voltage is 3.411 V, and output voltage ripple is 3.436 – 3.411=25.41 mV. The average value of output voltage can be approximated by averaging the maximum and minimum steady-state values. So the average value of output voltage is about (3.436+3.411)/2=3.4235 V. You can use a Mean block to measure the average output voltage as well (see Figure 6-44).

The Fundamental frequency (Hz) box of the Mean block must be filled with the switching frequency of the converter (see Figure 6-45) since the frequency of the output voltage ripple equals to the frequency of switching.

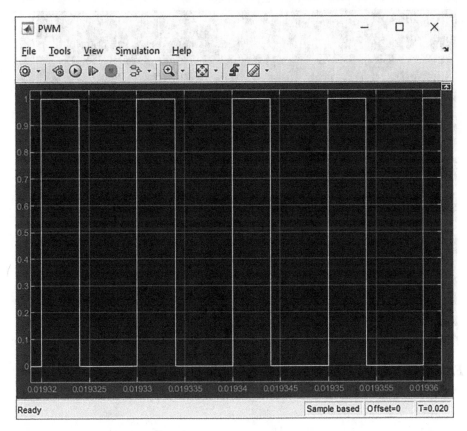

Figure 6-41. *Simulation result*

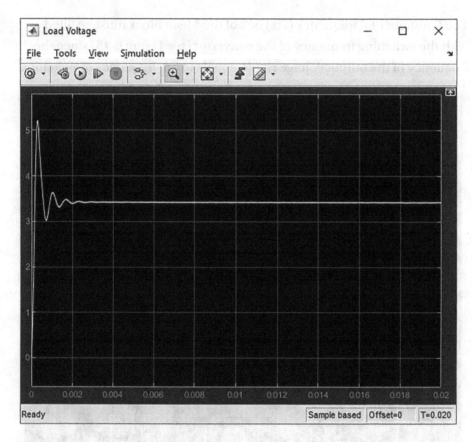

Figure 6-42. *Simulation result*

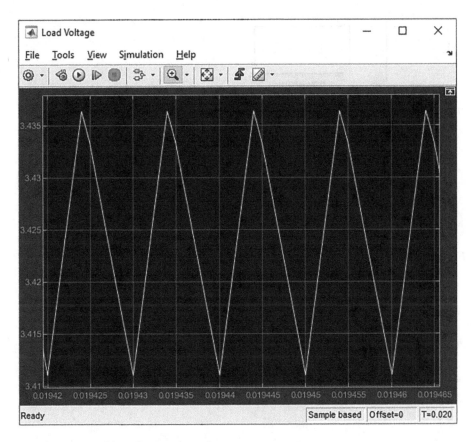

Figure 6-43. *Simulation result*

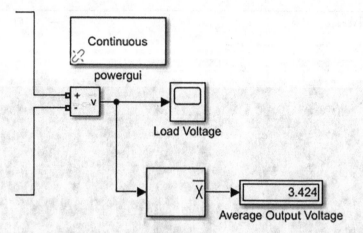

Figure 6-44. *Measurement of the average value of output voltage*

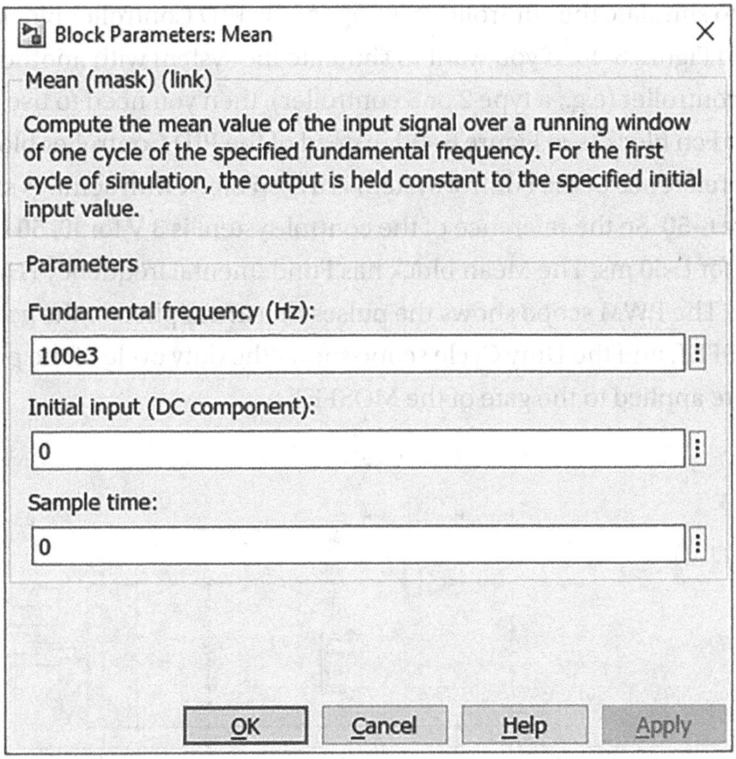

Figure 6-45. *Settings of the Mean block*

In the next example, we will simulate a closed-loop Buck converter.

Example 7: Closed-Loop Control of a Buck Converter

In the previous examples, we studied the open-loop Buck converter. In this example we want to study the voltage mode control of the Buck converter of Example 1. Consider the Simulink model shown in Figure 6-46. This model uses a PID controller. The PID Controller block (see Figure 6-47) is used to simulate the controller. Settings of the PID Controller block are shown in Figure 6-48. If you want to simulate the system with another type of controller (e.g., a type 2 or 3 controller), then you need to use the Transfer Fcn block (see Figure 6-49) instead of the PID Controller block.

The reference of the control system is a Step block with settings shown in Figure 6-50. So the reference of the control system is 3 V for [0, 50 ms] and 6 V for t>50 ms. The Mean block has Fundamental frequency (Hz) of 100 kHz. The PWM scope shows the pulses that are applied to the gate of the MOSFET, and the Duty Cycle scope shows the duty cycle of the pulses, which are applied to the gate of the MOSFET.

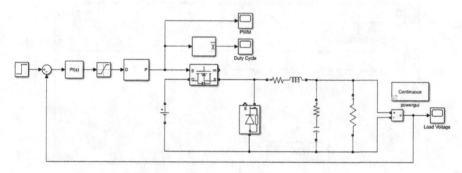

Figure 6-46. *Simulink model of Example 7*

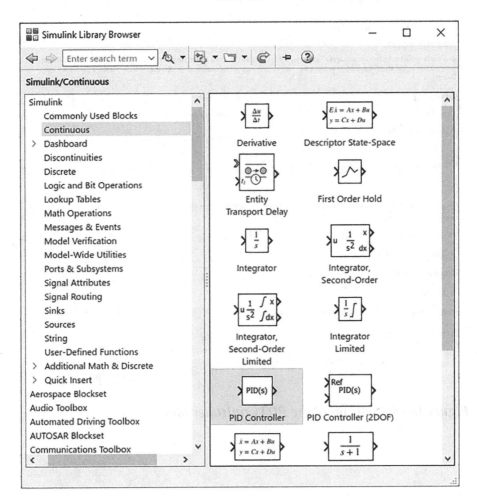

Figure 6-47. *PID Controller block*

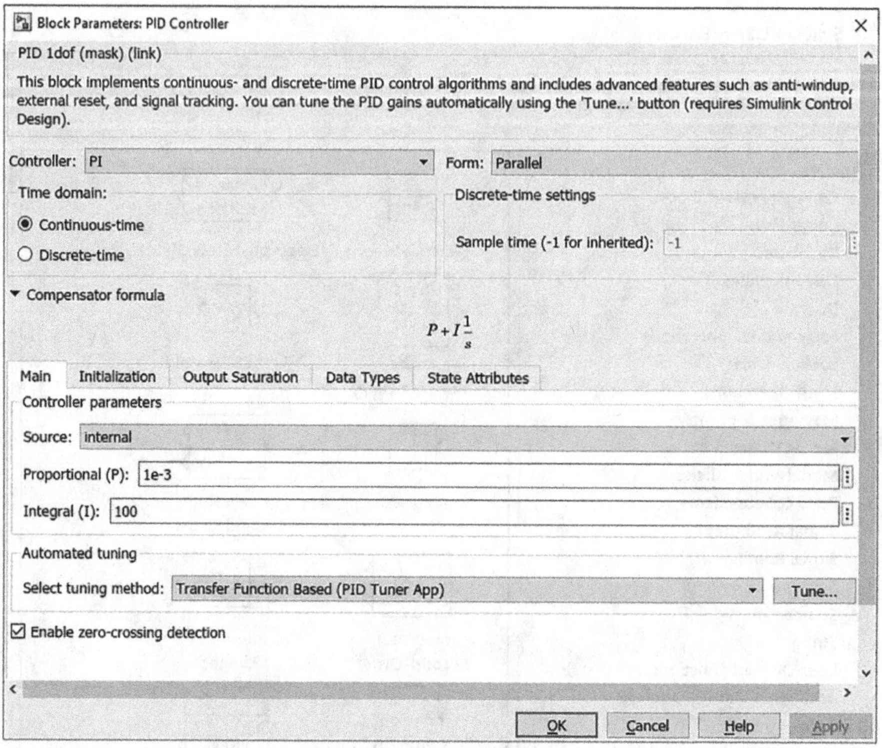

Figure 6-48. *Settings of the PID Controller block*

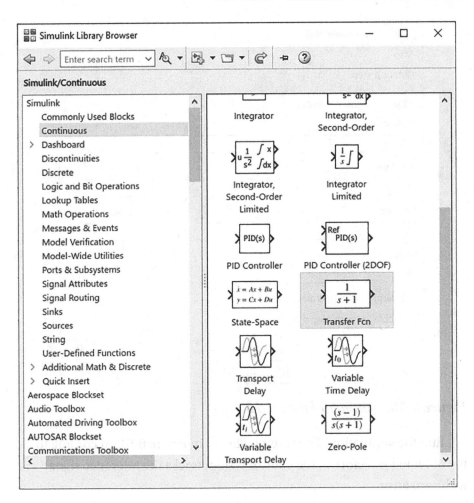

Figure 6-49. *Transfer Fcn block*

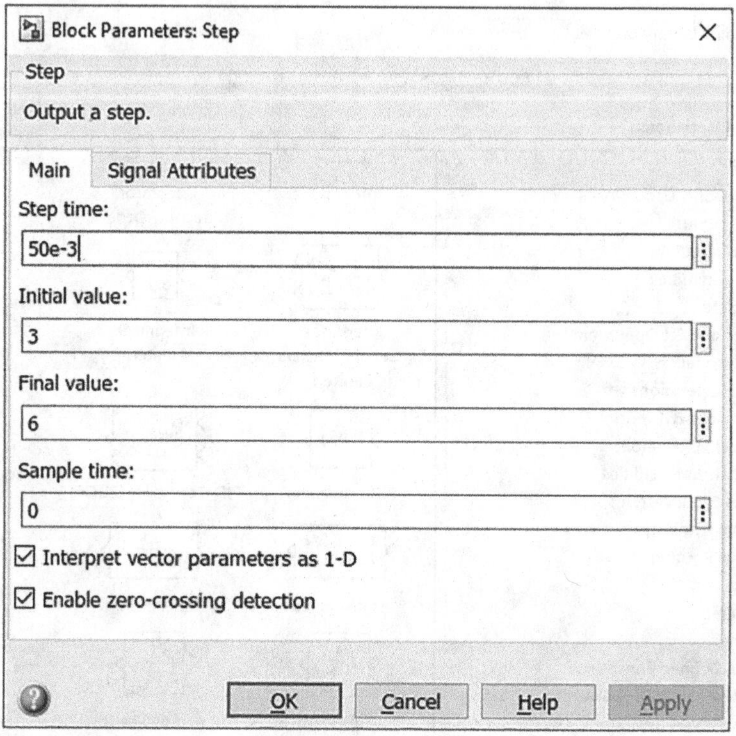

Block Parameters: Step ✕

Step

Output a step.

Main	Signal Attributes

Step time:

50e-3

Initial value:

3

Final value:

6

Sample time:

0

☑ Interpret vector parameters as 1-D

☑ Enable zero-crossing detection

| OK | Cancel | Help | Apply |

Figure 6-50. *Settings of the Step block*

Run the simulation. The result is shown in Figure 6-51. According to the obtained waveforms, the control system tracks the reference signal with zero error.

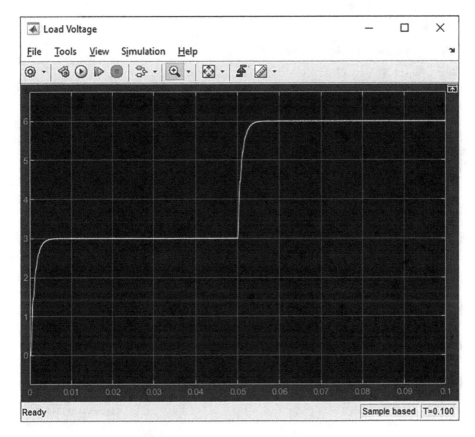

Figure 6-51. *Simulation result*

The duty cycle of the pulses that are applied to the gate of the MOSFET is shown in Figure 6-52. The controller increases the duty cycle to increase the output voltage from 3 V to 6 V.

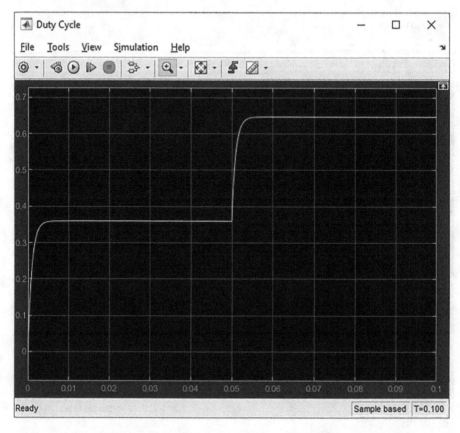

Figure 6-52. *Simulation result*

You can test the system for other scenarios. For instance, keep the reference signal of the control system on 3 V and apply a step change to the input voltage/output load of the converter. The controller keeps the output voltage constant despite these disturbances.

The Flyback converter is one of the most commonly used DC-DC converters with many applications. In the next example, we will learn how to simulate a Flyback converter in the Simulink environment.

Example 8: Flyback Converter

In this example, we want to simulate a Flyback converter that converts 24 V into 5 V. Consider the Simulink model shown in Figure 6-53. The input voltage of the converter is 24 V, the capacitor is 470 μF and its series resistance is 50 mΩ, and the output load is 5 Ω. The switching frequency of this converter is 40 kHz, and the duty cycle of the pulses applied to the gate of the MOSFET is 54%. This model uses a Linear Transformer block (see Figure 6-54). The settings of the transformer are shown in Figure 6-55. These settings simulate the transformer shown in Figure 6-56. It is a good idea to double-click the Linear Transformer block of the model and click the Help button to see the description of each parameter.

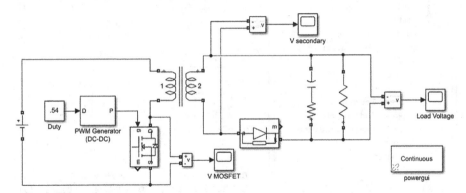

Figure 6-53. *Simulink model of Example 8*

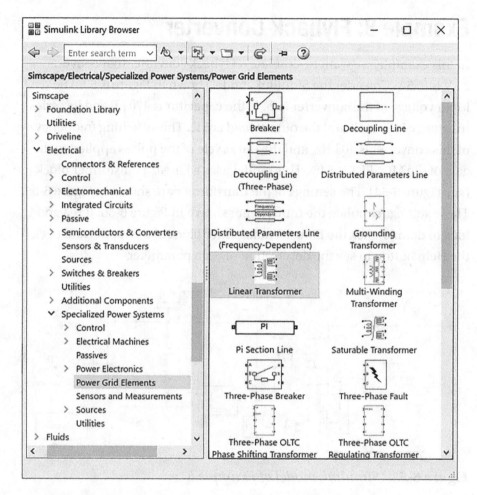

Figure 6-54. *Linear Transformer block*

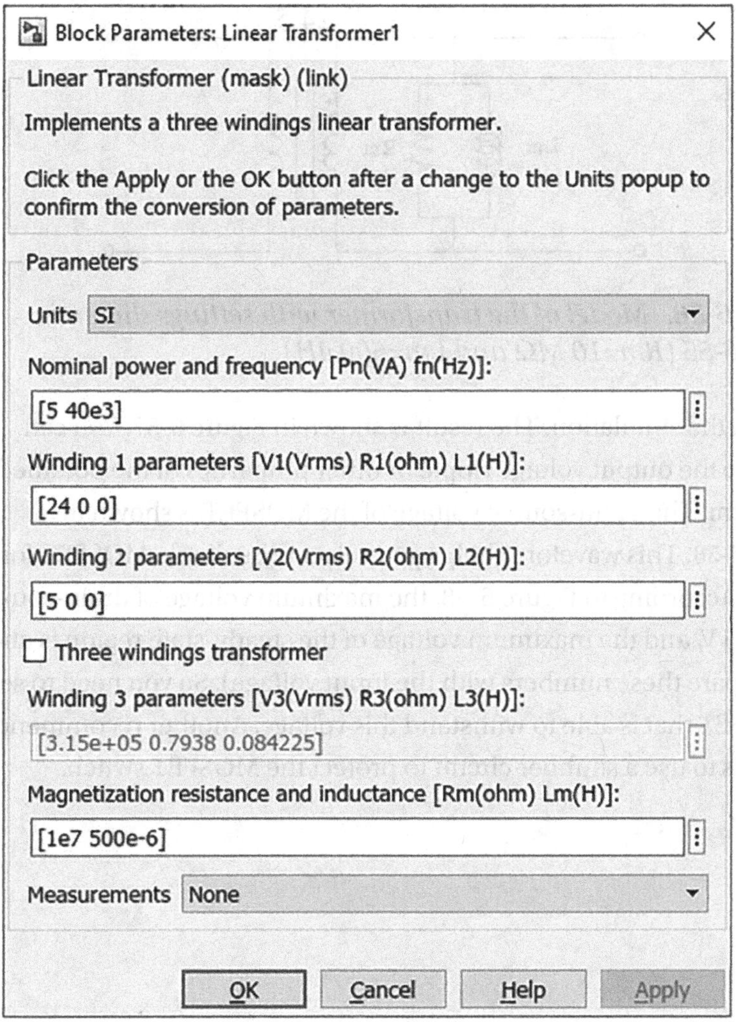

Block Parameters: Linear Transformer1   ×

Linear Transformer (mask) (link)

Implements a three windings linear transformer.

Click the Apply or the OK button after a change to the Units popup to confirm the conversion of parameters.

Parameters

Units SI   ▼

Nominal power and frequency [Pn(VA) fn(Hz)]:

[5 40e3]   ⋮

Winding 1 parameters [V1(Vrms) R1(ohm) L1(H)]:

[24 0 0]   ⋮

Winding 2 parameters [V2(Vrms) R2(ohm) L2(H)]:

[5 0 0]   ⋮

☐ Three windings transformer

Winding 3 parameters [V3(Vrms) R3(ohm) L3(H)]:

[3.15e+05 0.7938 0.084225]   ⋮

Magnetization resistance and inductance [Rm(ohm) Lm(H)]:

[1e7 500e-6]   ⋮

Measurements None   ▼

OK   Cancel   Help   Apply

Figure 6-55. *Settings of the Linear Transformer block*

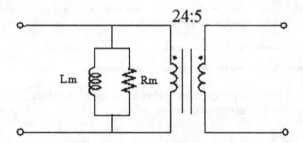

Figure 6-56. *Model of the transformer with settings shown in Figure 6-55 (Rm=10 MΩ and Lm=500 μH)*

Run the simulation. The result is shown in Figure 6-57. You can measure the output voltage ripple or other properties of the obtained waveform. The drain-source voltage of the MOSFET is shown in Figure 6-58. This waveform helps you select the suitable MOSFET for the circuit. According to Figure 6-58, the maximum voltage of drain-source is about 65 V, and the maximum voltage of the steady-state region is about 52 V (compare these numbers with the input voltage). So you need to select a MOSFET that is able to withstand this voltage. Another recommended option is to use a snubber circuit to protect the MOSFET switch.

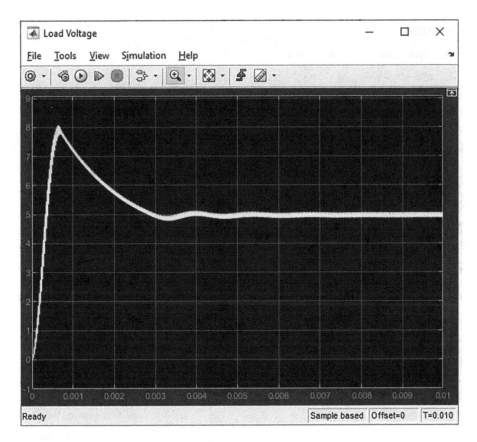

Figure 6-57. *Simulation result*

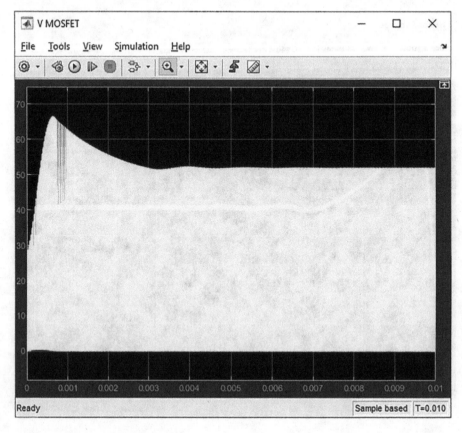

Figure 6-58. *Simulation result*

In this example we learned how to simulate a Flyback converter in the Simulink environment. In the next example, we will measure the efficiency of the studied converter.

Example 9: Efficiency of a Flyback Converter

Efficiency is defined as the ratio of output power to input power. It is quite common to multiply this ratio with 100 and describe the efficiency in percentage. In this example, we will calculate the efficiency of the

Flyback converter of Example 9. Consider the Simulink model shown in Figure 6-59. We used two Multimeter blocks to measure the input and output powers. The small resistor in series with the input voltage source acts as a current sensor. Settings of this block are shown in Figure 6-60. The value of input voltage is measured by selecting the Voltage in the Measurements box (see Figure 6-61). So the instantaneous input power can be calculated by multiplying the value of source voltage and the current that passes from Sense Resistor, and its average is calculated with the aid of the Mean block. The Fundamental frequency (Hz) box of Mean blocks is filled with the switching frequency (40 kHz). The output power is calculated by selecting the Branch voltage and current in the Measurements box (see Figure 6-62). These two measurements are multiplied together to form the instantaneous input power. Then, a Mean block calculates the average output power. The ratio of the average output power to the average input power gives the efficiency.

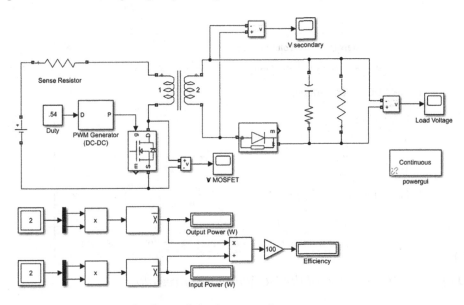

Figure 6-59. *Simulink model of Example 9*

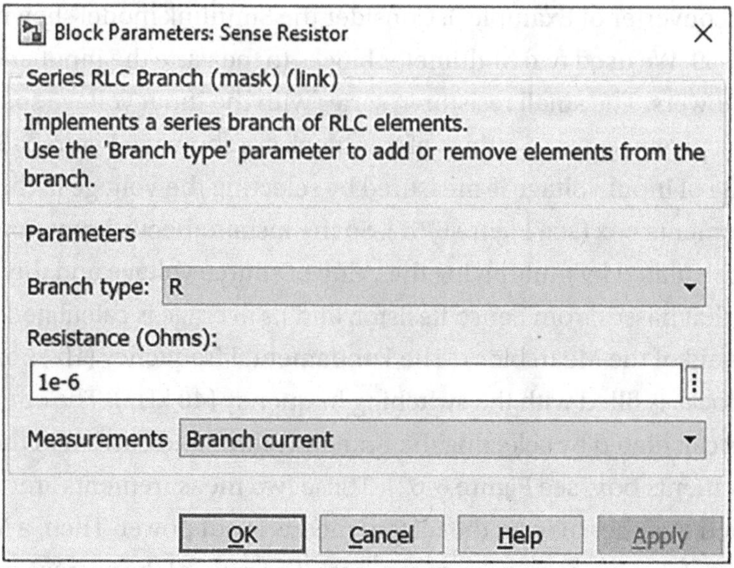

Figure 6-60. *Settings of the Sense Resistor block*

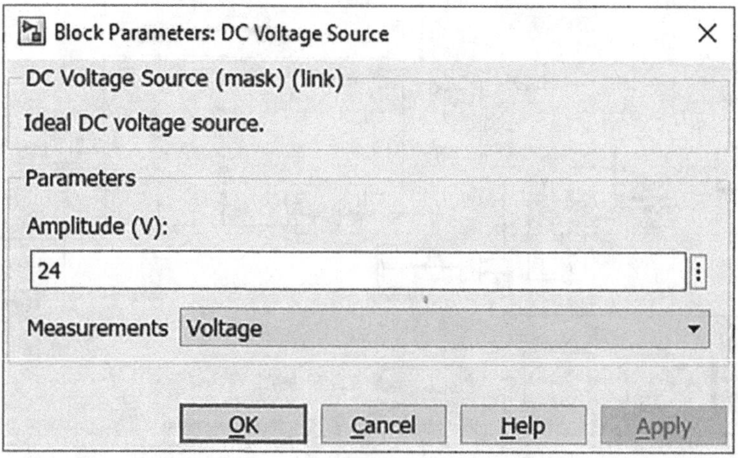

Figure 6-61. *Settings of the DC Voltage Source block*

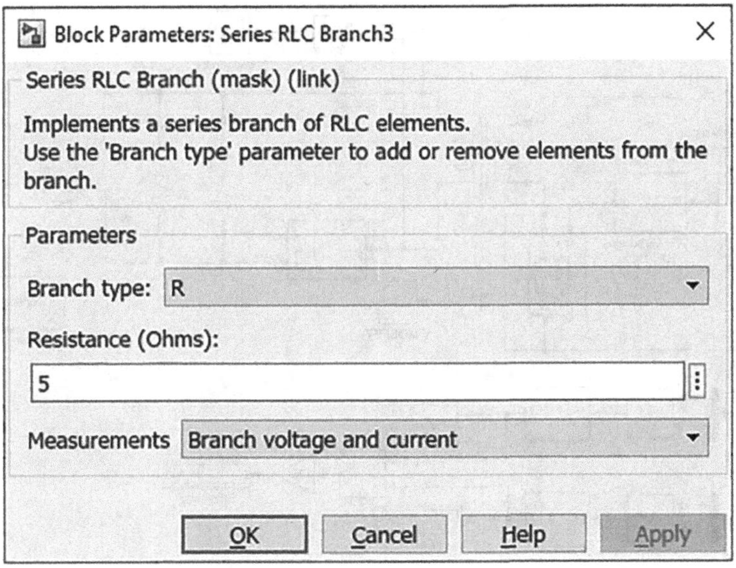

Figure 6-62. *Settings of output load*

Run the simulation. According to Figure 6-63, the efficiency is about 84.45%. Try to find the element that consumed the other 15.55% of input power.

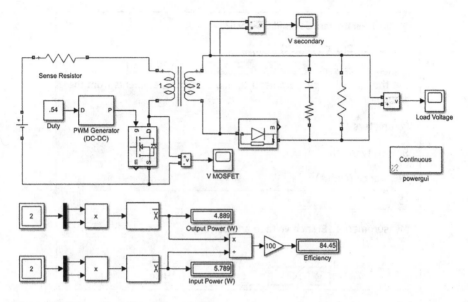

Figure 6-63. *Simulation result*

Summary

In this chapter we learned how to simulate open-loop and closed-loop DC-DC converters. You observed that disturbances like input voltage or output load changes affect the output voltage of open-loop converters considerably, while their effect is negligible for a closed-loop converter. We learned different methods of generating a PWM signal and a method of efficiency measurement, as well. In the next chapter, we will learn how to simulate DC-AC converters (inverters).

CHAPTER 7

Simulation of Inverters

In Chapters 4 and 5, we learned how to simulate the rectifiers (AC-DC converters). In this chapter we will focus on the simulation of inverters (DC-AC converters). Inverters are used in applications like adjustable-speed AC motor drives, Uninterruptible Power Supplies (UPS), induction heating, and running AC appliances from an automobile battery.

In this chapter we will learn how to simulate a single-phase and a three-phase PWM inverter and how to measure their Total Harmonic Distortion (THD).

Example 1: Single-Phase PWM Inverter

In this example we want to simulate a single-phase full-bridge inverter with unipolar PWM. Consider the Simulink model shown in Figure 7-1. The input voltage is 100 V, and the load is RL with resistance of 25 Ω and inductance of 1 mH. The required triangular carrier signal is generated with the aid of a Repeating Sequence block (see Figure 7-2). Settings of the Repeating Sequence block are shown in Figure 7-3. The frequency of this block determines the switching frequency of the inverter. In this example the switching frequency is 23×50=1150 Hz. Settings of Sine Wave1 and Sine Wave2 blocks are shown in Figures 7-4 and 7-5, respectively. Note that

© Farzin Asadi 2022

F. Asadi, *Simulation of Power Electronics Circuits with MATLAB®/Simulink®*,
Maker Innovations Series, https://doi.org/10.1007/978-1-4842-8220-5_7

there is a 180° phase difference between these two sinusoidal sources. The frequency of Sine Wave1 and Sine Wave2 blocks must be equal to each other and determines the frequency of the output. The effective value of the output (RMS value of load voltage) can be changed by changing the modulation index. The modulation index is the ratio of the amplitude of sinusoidal reference signals to the amplitude of the high-frequency triangular carrier signal. According to the settings shown in Figures 7-3, 7-4, and 7-5, the modulation index is 0.7. The Simulink model shown in Figure 7-1 is equivalent to the Simulink model of Figure 7-6. You can use this model if you prefer.

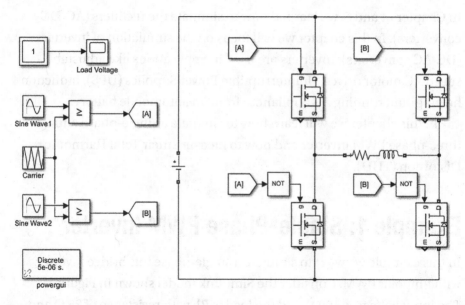

Figure 7-1. *Simulink model of Example 1*

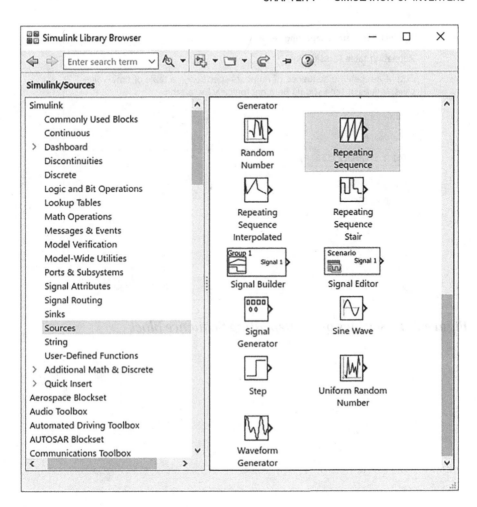

Figure 7-2. *Repeating Sequence block*

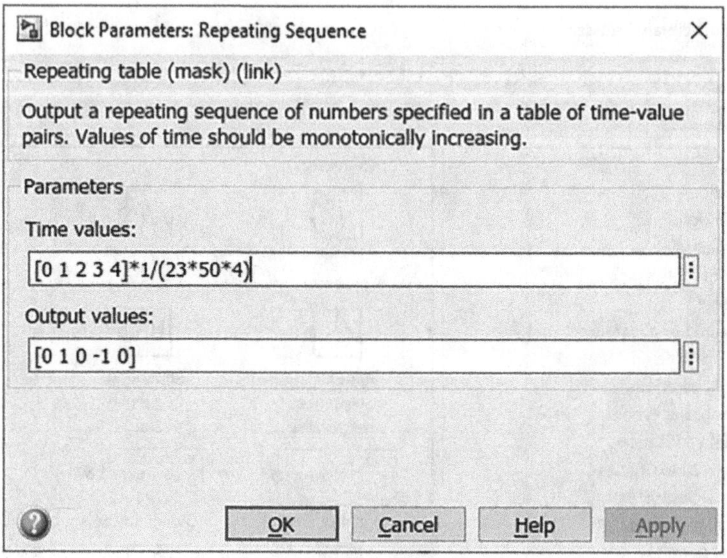

Figure 7-3. Settings of the Repeating Sequence block

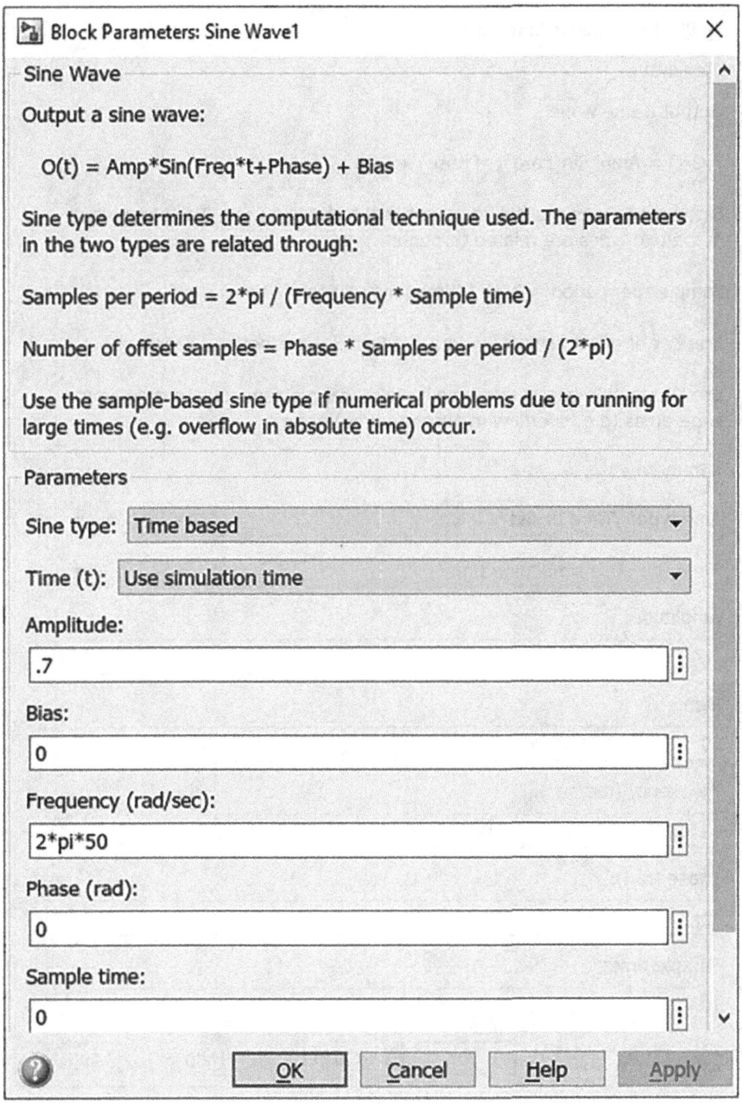

Figure 7-4. *Settings of the Sine Wave1 block*

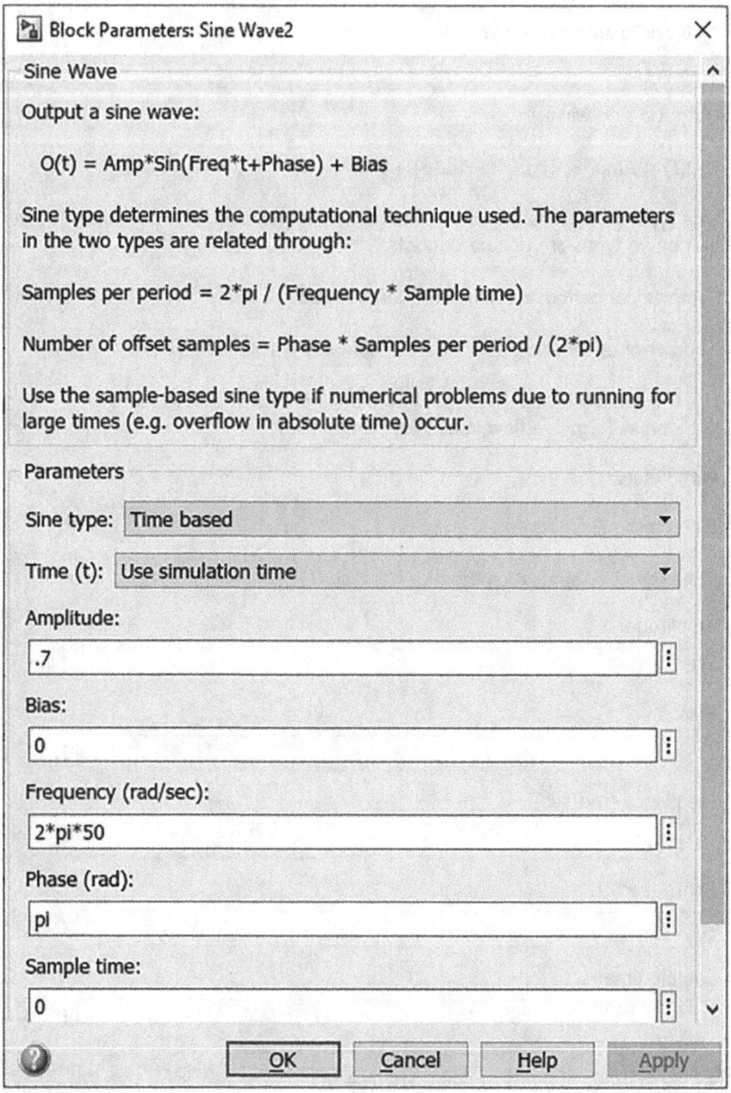

Figure 7-5. *Settings of the Sine Wave2 block*

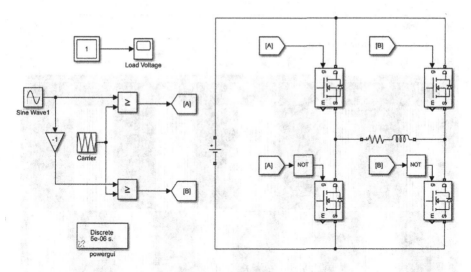

Figure 7-6. *Equivalent model of Figure 7-1*

Run the simulation. The load voltage is shown in Figure 7-7. The load voltage is composed of pulses with amplitudes –100 V, 0 V, and +100 V. The output voltage is not similar to a sinusoidal waveform. Let's draw the average of the load voltage. The model shown in Figure 7-8 calculates the average value in each switching period. The Fundamental frequency (Hz) box of the Mean block is filled with 23*50, which means 23×50= 1150 Hz. The simulation result is shown in Figure 7-9. It is sinusoidal with an amplitude of 68.48 V.

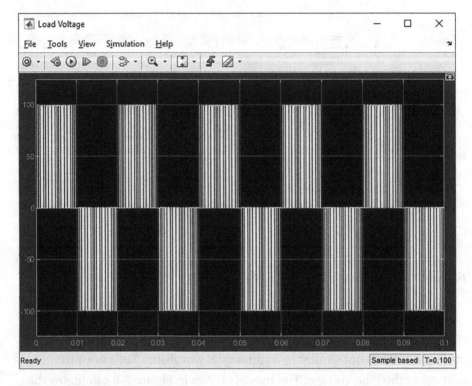

Figure 7-7. *Simulation result*

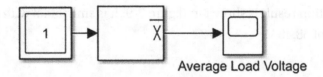

Average Load Voltage

Figure 7-8. *Measurement of the average value of load voltage*

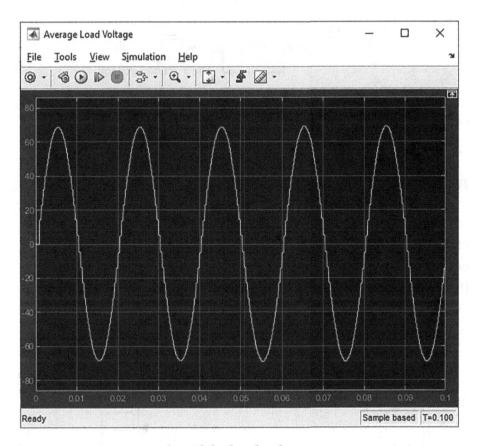

Figure 7-9. *Average value of the load voltage*

The RMS value of output voltage can be found with the aid of the RMS block (see Figure 7-10). The Fundamental frequency (Hz) box of the RMS block must be filled with the frequency of output voltage (frequency of output voltage is 50 Hz in this example). For modulation index of 0.7, the RMS value of load voltage is 66.2 V.

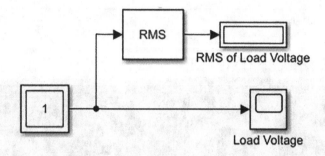

Figure 7-10. *Measurement of the RMS value of load voltage*

Magnitude of harmonics in the load voltage can be found with the aid of the Fourier block (see Figure 7-11). The Fundamental frequency (Hz) box of the Fourier block must be filled with the frequency of output voltage (frequency of output voltage is 50 Hz in this example). For modulation index of 0.7, the amplitude of the fundamental harmonic is 69.32 V.

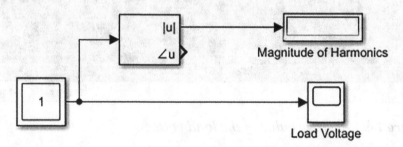

Figure 7-11. *Measurement of harmonics of load voltage*

In this example we simulated a single-phase PWM inverter. In the next example, we will measure the THD of the studied inverter with the aid of the THD block.

Example 2: THD Block

In this example we want to calculate the Total Harmonic Distortion (THD) of output voltage of the inverter of the previous example. The THD of the inverter can be calculated with the aid of the THD block (see Figure 7-12). Load voltage THD can be measured with the aid of blocks shown in Figure 7-13. The Fundamental frequency of input signal (Hz) box of the THD block must be filled with the frequency of output voltage of the inverter (frequency of output voltage is 50 Hz in Example 1). The THD of the inverter is 90.78% for modulation index of 0.7. The THD of load current is 69.4% for modulation index of 0.7. The inductive part of the load acts as a filter and decreases the high-frequency component of the load current. So the THD of current is smaller than the THD for voltage. For purely resistive loads, the THD of current is equal to the THD of voltage.

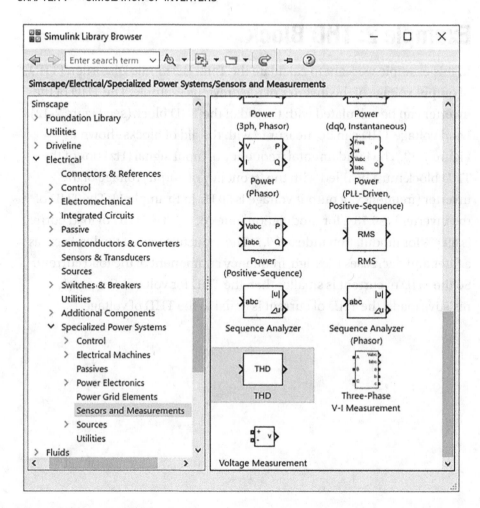

Figure 7-12. *THD block*

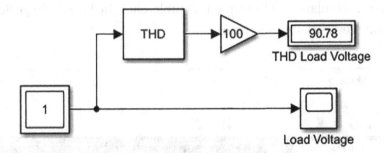

Figure 7-13. *Simulation result*

Simulink has a useful sample simulation for the THD block. Enter power_RMS_THD in the command line (Figure 7-14) and press the Enter key to open the Simulink model.

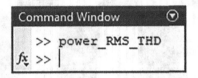

Figure 7-14. *Opening the power_RMS_THD Simulink model*

In this example we learned how to measure the THD of an inverter circuit. In the next example, we will learn how to measure the magnitude of the harmonics in the output voltage/current.

Example 3: Harmonic Analysis with the FFT Analyzer Program

In Example 1, we used the Fourier block to measure the amplitude of the harmonics of the output voltage of the inverter. There is another way to analyze the harmonic content of waveforms: using the FFT Analyzer program. In this example, we want to use the FFT Analyzer program to analyze the harmonic content of the output voltage of the inverter of Example 1.

Run the simulation of Example 1. Double-click the Load Voltage Scope block and then click the gear icon.

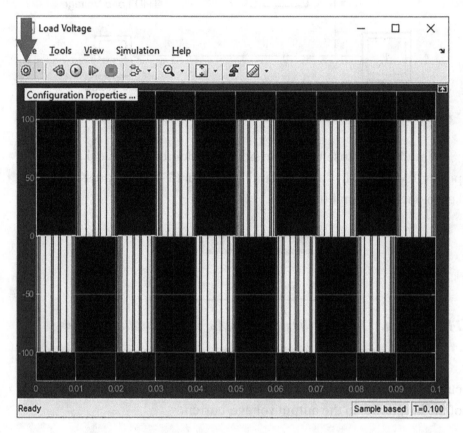

Figure 7-15. *Simulation result*

After clicking the gear icon, the Configuration Properties window will be opened. Go to the Logging tab and check Log data to workspace. Then enter LoadVoltage in the Variable name box, select Structure With Time for the Save format box, and click the OK button.

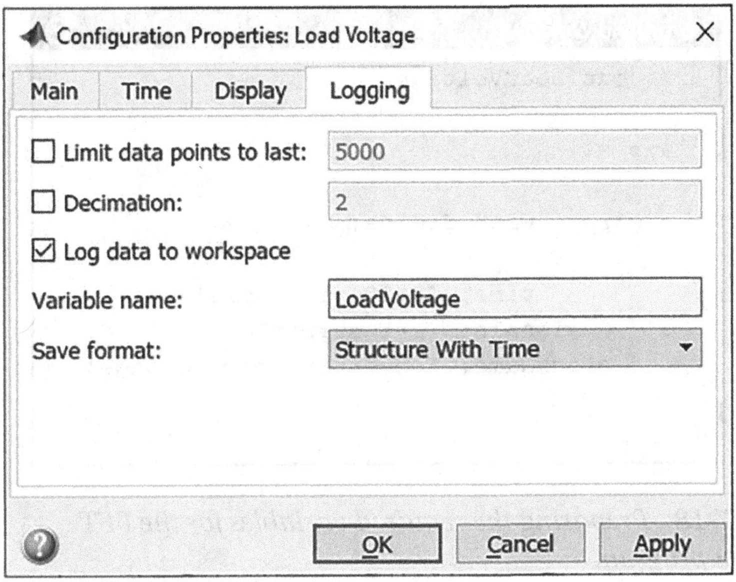

Configuration Properties: Load Voltage   ✕

| Main | Time | Display | Logging |

☐ Limit data points to last: 5000

☐ Decimation: 2

☑ Log data to workspace

Variable name: LoadVoltage

Save format: Structure With Time   ▾

OK   Cancel   Apply

Figure 7-16. *Configuration Properties window*

Run the simulation. A variable named "out" will be added to Workspace (Figure 7-17).

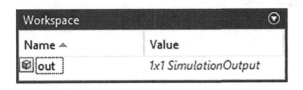

Workspace	
Name ▲	Value
▣ out	1x1 SimulationOutput

Figure 7-17. *Variable out is added to Workspace*

Enter the command shown in Figure 7-18.

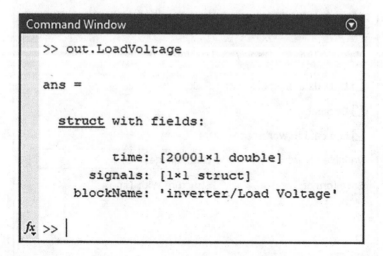

Figure 7-18. *Preparing the required variables for the FFT Analyzer program*

Go to the Simulink model and double-click the powergui block. Open the Tools tab and click the FFT Analysis button (see Figure 7-19). After clicking the FFT Analysis button, the FFT Analyzer window will be opened (see Figure 7-20). The output voltage waveform of the converter is loaded to FFT Analysis as well.

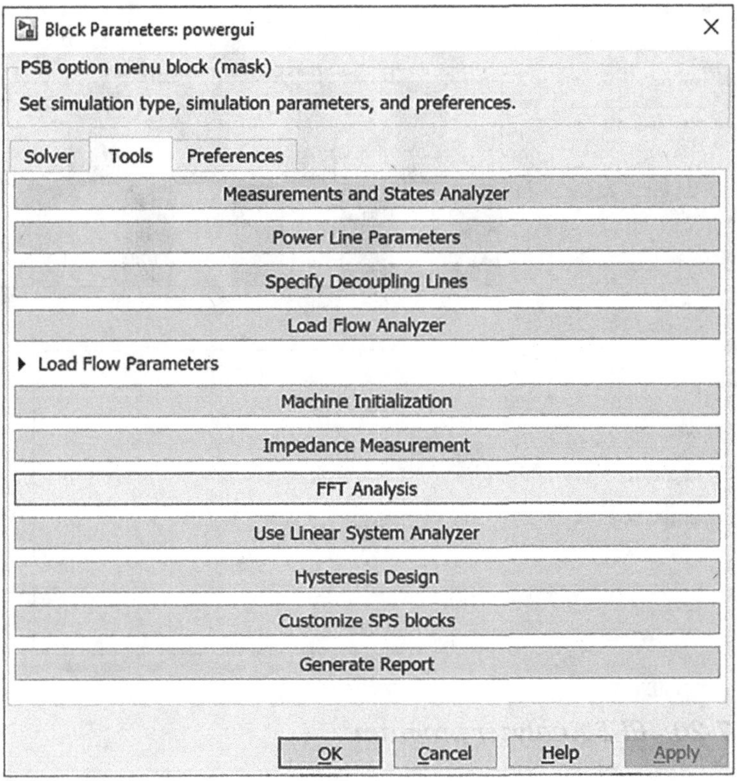

Figure 7-19. *Tools tab of the powergui block*

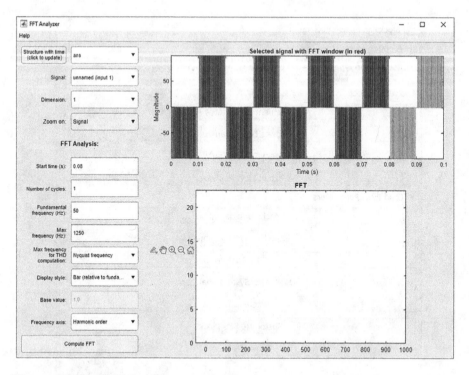

Figure 7-20. *FFT Analyzer program*

Configure the settings similar to Figure 7-21 and click the Compute FFT button. The result shown in Figure 7-22 is obtained. According to the result shown in Figure 7-22, the amplitude of the third harmonic is 0.15% of the fundamental harmonic. The amplitude (peak value) of the fundamental harmonic is 69.32 V. So the third harmonic amplitude is 0.0015×69.32=0.1040 V. Amplitude of other harmonics can be calculated in the same way.

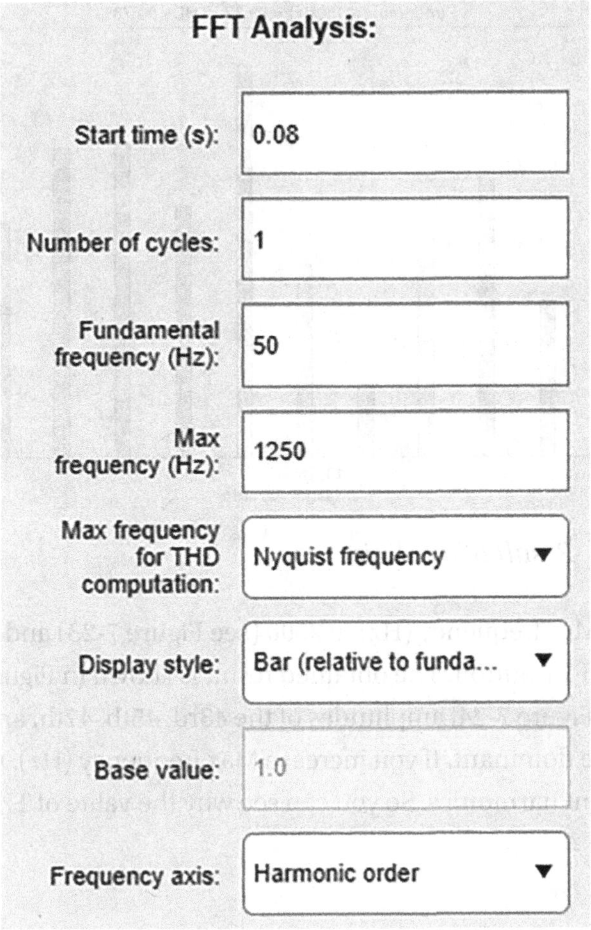

FFT Analysis:

Start time (s):	0.08
Number of cycles:	1
Fundamental frequency (Hz):	50
Max frequency (Hz):	1250
Max frequency for THD computation:	Nyquist frequency ▼
Display style:	Bar (relative to funda... ▼
Base value:	1.0
Frequency axis:	Harmonic order ▼

Figure 7-21. Settings of the FFT Analyzer program

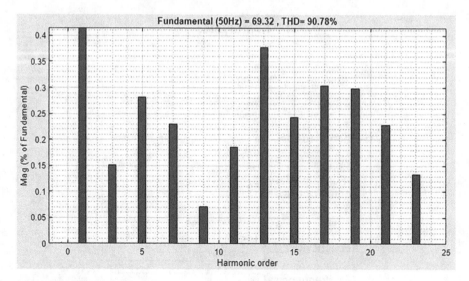

Figure 7-22. *Result of analysis*

Increase Max frequency (Hz) to 2500 (see Figure 7-23) and click the Compute FFT button. The obtained result is shown in Figure 7-24. According to Figure 7-24, amplitudes of the 43rd, 45th, 47th, and 49th harmonics are dominant. If you increase Max frequency (Hz), you can see more dominant harmonics. So you can see why the value of THD is high.

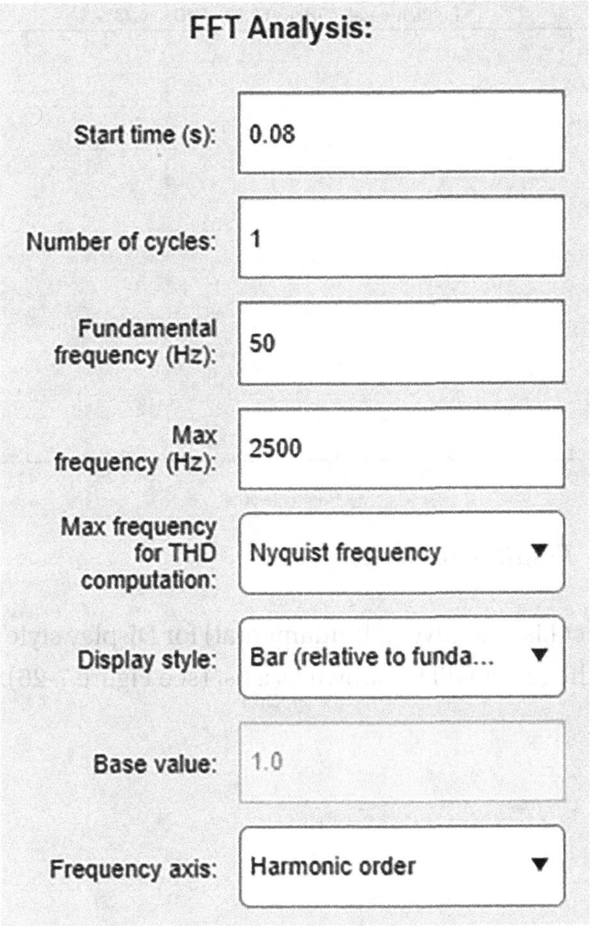

FFT Analysis:

Start time (s): `0.08`

Number of cycles: `1`

Fundamental frequency (Hz): `50`

Max frequency (Hz): `2500`

Max frequency for THD computation: `Nyquist frequency ▼`

Display style: `Bar (relative to funda... ▼`

Base value: `1.0`

Frequency axis: `Harmonic order ▼`

Figure 7-23. *Max frequency (Hz) box is filled with 2500*

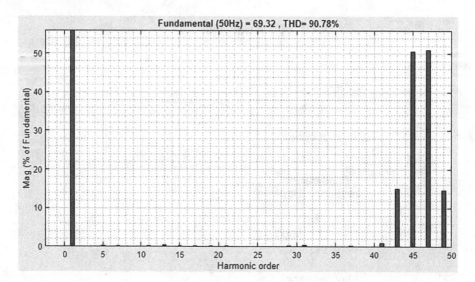

Figure 7-24. *Result of analysis*

If you select List (relative to fundamental) for Display style (see Figure 7-25), the result will be shown as a list (see Figure 7-26).

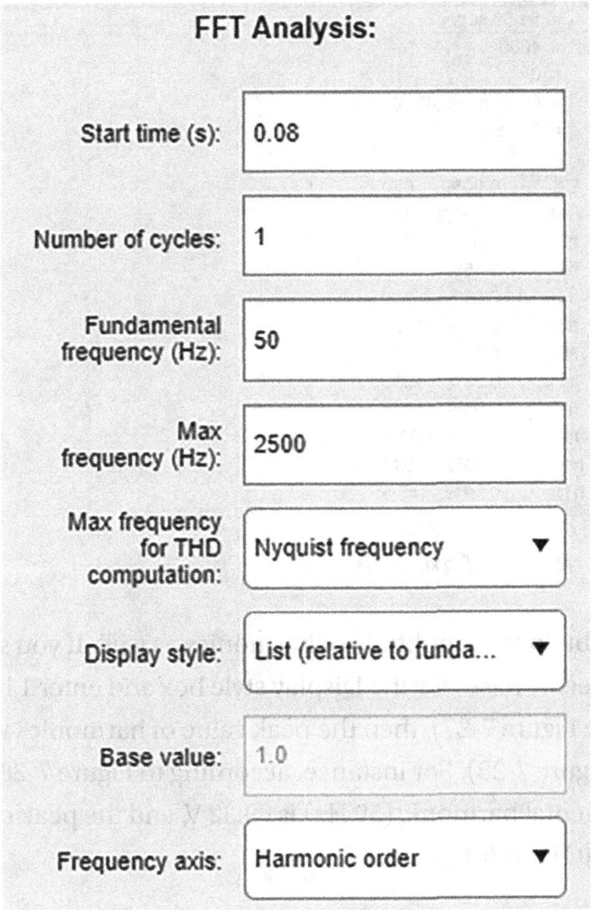

FFT Analysis:

Start time (s): | 0.08

Number of cycles: | 1

Fundamental frequency (Hz): | 50

Max frequency (Hz): | 2500

Max frequency for THD computation: | Nyquist frequency ▼

Display style: | List (relative to funda... ▼

Base value: | 1.0

Frequency axis: | Harmonic order ▼

Figure 7-25. *List (relative to fundamental) for Display style*

Sampling time	= 5e-06 sec.		
Samples per cycle	= 4000		
DC component	= 0		
Fundamental	= 69.32 peak (49.02 rms)		
THD	= 90.78%		
0 Hz	DC	0.00%	0.0°
50 Hz	Fnd	100.00%	179.7°
100 Hz	h2	0.00%	0.0°
150 Hz	h3	0.15%	74.7°
200 Hz	h4	0.00%	0.0°
250 Hz	h5	0.28%	102.9°
300 Hz	h6	0.00%	0.0°
350 Hz	h7	0.23%	196.7°
400 Hz	h8	0.00%	0.0°
450 Hz	h9	0.07%	33.0°
500 Hz	h10	0.00%	0.0°
550 Hz	h11	0.19%	-49.5°

Figure 7-26. *Result of analysis*

You can obtain the amplitude of harmonics as well. If you select List (relative to specific base) for the Display style box and enter 1 in the Base value box (see Figure 7-27), then the peak value of harmonics will be shown (see Figure 7-28). For instance, according to Figure 7-28, the peak of the fundamental harmonic (50 Hz) is 69.32 V, and the peak of the third harmonic (150 Hz) is 0.1 V.

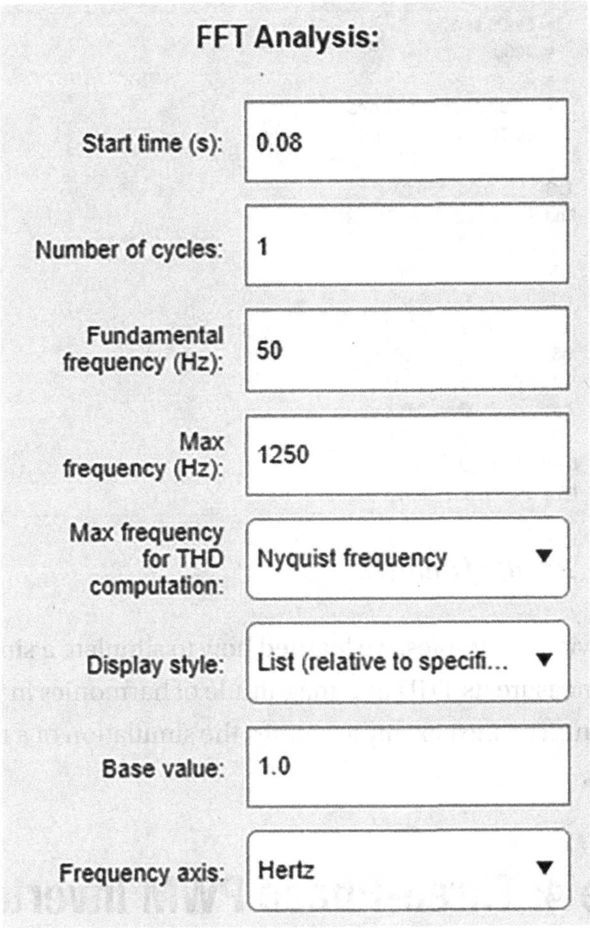

FFT Analysis:

Start time (s):	0.08
Number of cycles:	1
Fundamental frequency (Hz):	50
Max frequency (Hz):	1250
Max frequency for THD computation:	Nyquist frequency ▼
Display style:	List (relative to specifi... ▼
Base value:	1.0
Frequency axis:	Hertz ▼

Figure 7-27. *List (relative to specific base) for the Display style box*

```
Sampling time      = 5e-06 sec.
Samples per cycle  = 4000
DC component       = 0
Fundamental        = 69.32 peak (49.02 rms)
THD                = 90.78%


     0 Hz      DC      0.00    0.0°
    50 Hz      Fnd    69.32  179.7°
   100 Hz      h2      0.00    0.0°
   150 Hz      h3      0.10   74.7°
   200 Hz      h4      0.00    0.0°
   250 Hz      h5      0.19  102.9°
   300 Hz      h6      0.00    0.0°
   350 Hz      h7      0.16  196.7°
   400 Hz      h8      0.00    0.0°
   450 Hz      h9      0.05   33.0°
   500 Hz      h10     0.00    0.0°
   550 Hz      h11     0.13  -49.5°
```

Figure 7-28. *Result of analysis*

In the previous examples, we learned how to simulate a single-phase inverter and measure its THD and magnitude of harmonics in the output voltage/current. The next example studies the simulation of a three-phase PWM inverter.

Example 4: Three-Phase PWM Inverter

In this example we want to simulate a three-phase inverter. Consider the Simulink model shown in Figure 7-29. The input voltage is 100 V, and the load is balanced Y-connected RL with resistance of 25 Ω and inductance of 1 mH. The Branch voltage and current option is selected for the Measurements box (see Figure 7-30), so we can measure the load voltage and current easily with a Multimeter block. The power stage and PWM sections of this model are shown in Figures 7-31 and 7-32, respectively.

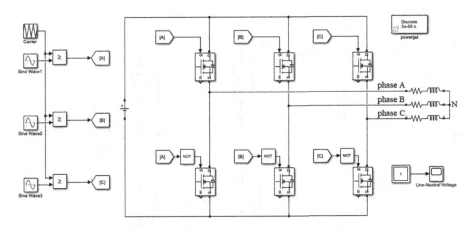

Figure 7-29. *Simulink model of Example 4*

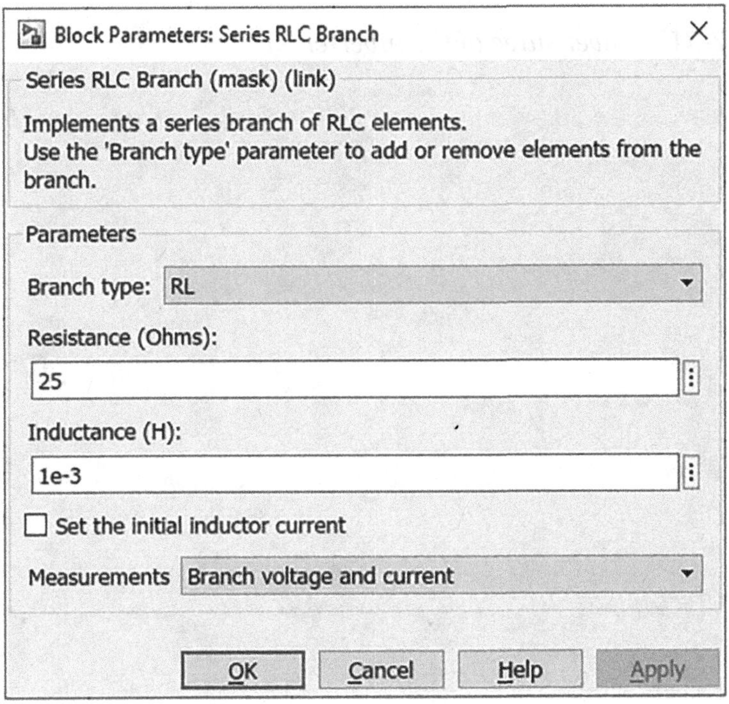

Figure 7-30. *Settings of Series RLC Branch*

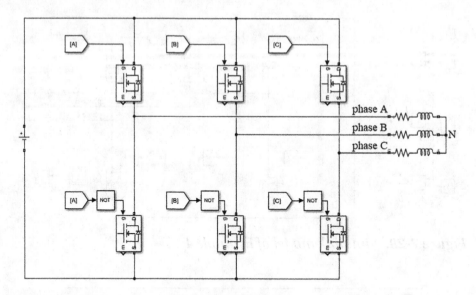

Figure 7-31. *Power stage of the inverter*

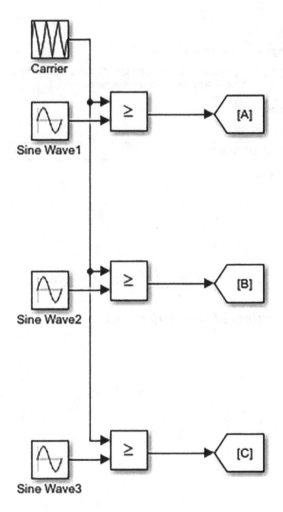

Figure 7-32. *Generation of PWM signals*

Settings of the blocks of the PWM section are shown in Figures 7-33 to 7-36. Note that there is a 120° phase difference between the sinusoidal sources. The switching frequency of this inverter is 23×50=1150 Hz.

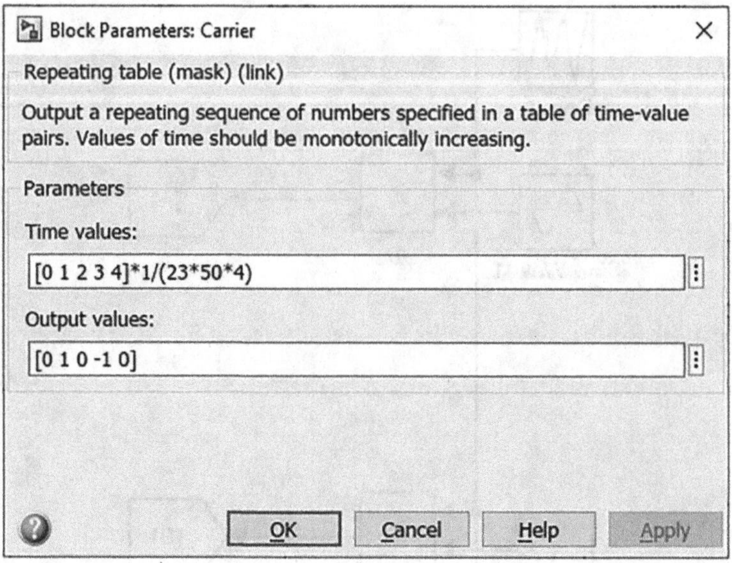

Figure 7-33. *Settings of the Carrier block*

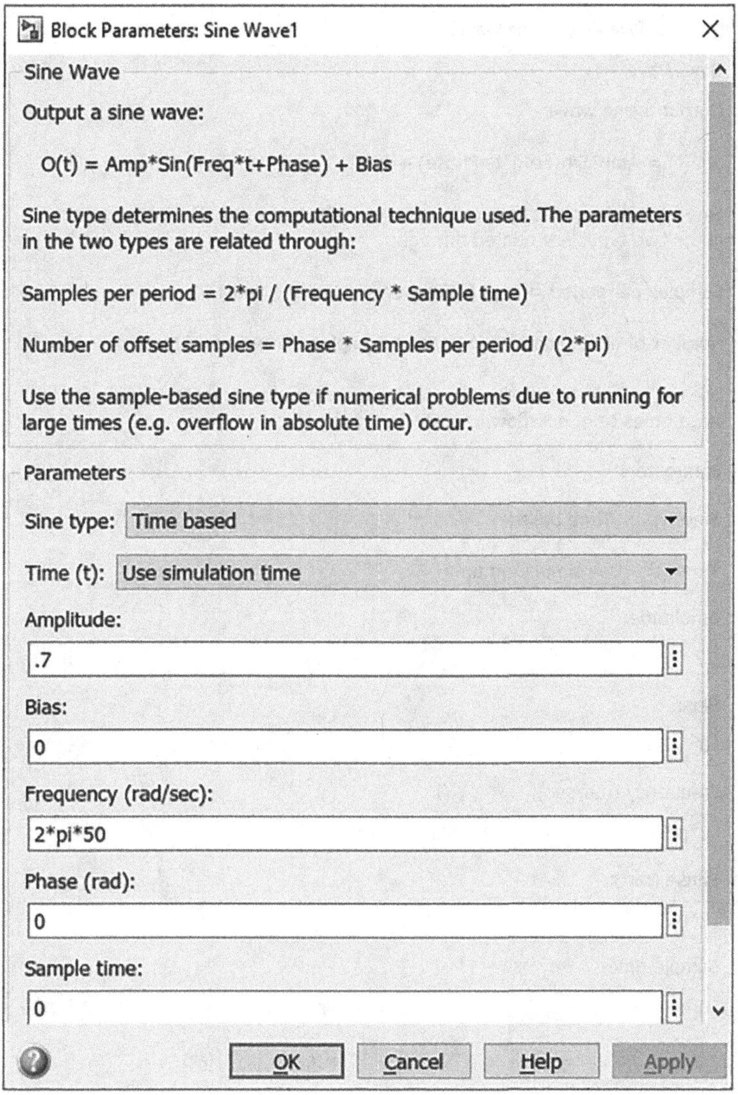

Block Parameters: Sine Wave1   ✕

Sine Wave

Output a sine wave:

  O(t) = Amp*Sin(Freq*t+Phase) + Bias

Sine type determines the computational technique used. The parameters in the two types are related through:

Samples per period = 2*pi / (Frequency * Sample time)

Number of offset samples = Phase * Samples per period / (2*pi)

Use the sample-based sine type if numerical problems due to running for large times (e.g. overflow in absolute time) occur.

Parameters

Sine type: Time based   ▼

Time (t): Use simulation time   ▼

Amplitude:

.7

Bias:

0

Frequency (rad/sec):

2*pi*50

Phase (rad):

0

Sample time:

0

ⓘ   OK   Cancel   Help   Apply

Figure 7-34.   *Settings of the Sine Wave1 block*

391

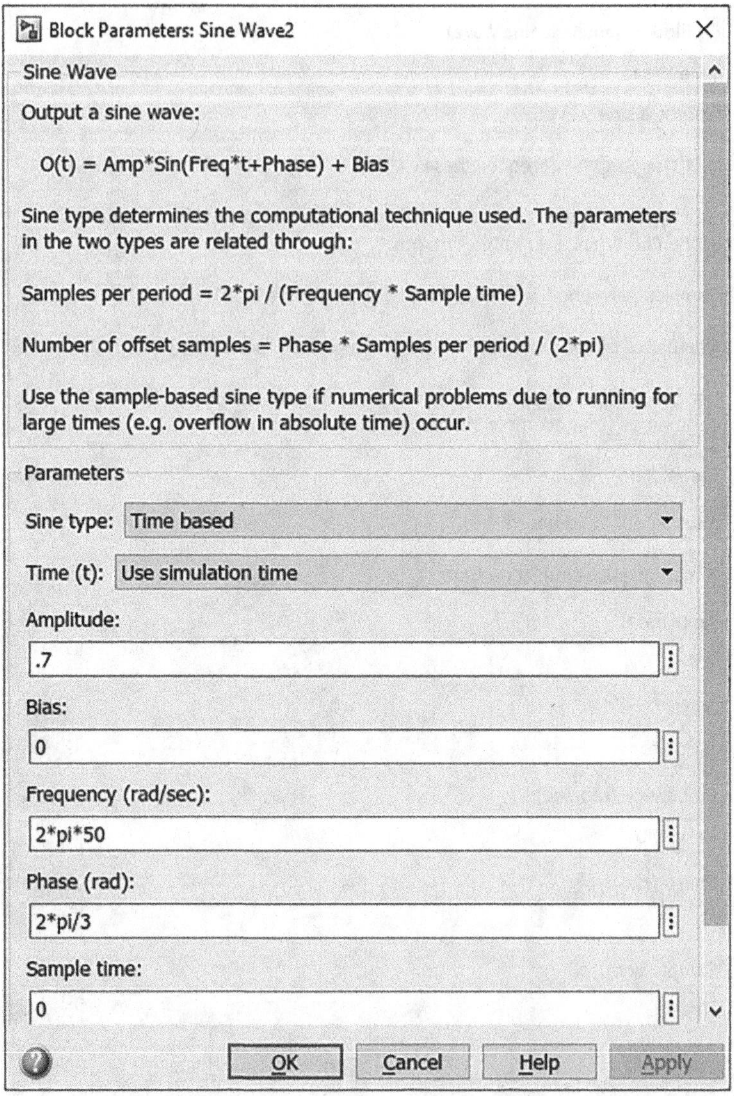

Figure 7-35. *Settings of the Sine Wave2 block*

Block Parameters: Sine Wave3   ×

Sine Wave

Output a sine wave:

O(t) = Amp*Sin(Freq*t+Phase) + Bias

Sine type determines the computational technique used. The parameters
in the two types are related through:

Samples per period = 2*pi / (Frequency * Sample time)

Number of offset samples = Phase * Samples per period / (2*pi)

Use the sample-based sine type if numerical problems due to running for
large times (e.g. overflow in absolute time) occur.

Parameters

Sine type: | Time based   ▼ |

Time (t): | Use simulation time   ▼ |

Amplitude:

| .7   ⋮ |

Bias:

| 0   ⋮ |

Frequency (rad/sec):

| 2*pi*50   ⋮ |

Phase (rad):

| -2*pi/3   ⋮ |

Sample time:

| 0   ⋮ |

⊘   [OK   ]   [Cancel]   [Help]   [Apply]

Figure 7-36. *Settings of the Sine Wave3 block*

Run the simulation. Figure 7-37 shows the voltage between phase A
and point N.

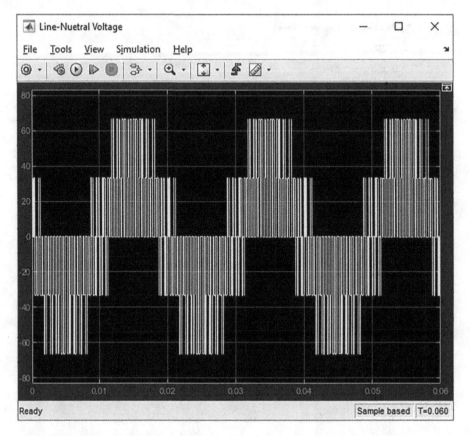

Figure 7-37. *Simulation result*

The model shown in Figure 7-38 can be used to see the line-line voltage. The upper output of the Demux block is the voltage between phase A and point N. The lower output of the Demux block is the voltage between phase B and point N. So the voltage that reaches the Scope block is the difference between phase A and phase B points.

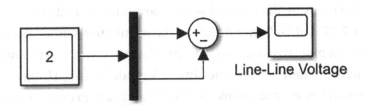

Figure 7-38. *Observing the line-line voltage*

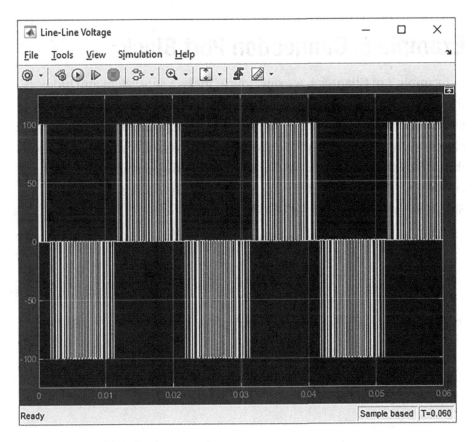

Figure 7-39. *Simulation result*

You can measure the RMS value and harmonic content of waveforms in Figures 7-37 and 7-39 with the aid of the techniques studied before.

In this example we simulated a three-phase inverter. You can make a subsystem and hide some of the Simulink model details. Using a subsystem makes your Simulink model tidy and easy to understand. In the next example, we will learn how to make subsystems that contain electrical components.

Example 5: Connection Port Block

In Example 2 of Chapter 4, we saw how to make a subsystem and hide the system details. The subsystem we made in that example had no electrical connection with the outside. When you want to make an electrical connection with the outside of the subsystem, you need to use the Connection Port block (see Figure 7-40). In this example we want to convert the power stage of the inverter into a subsystem and make the Simulink model a little bit tidier.

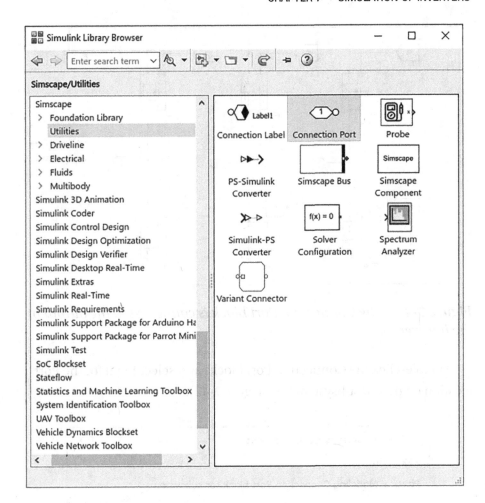

Figure 7-40. *Connection Port block*

Change the Simulink model of Example 4 to that shown in Figure 7-41.

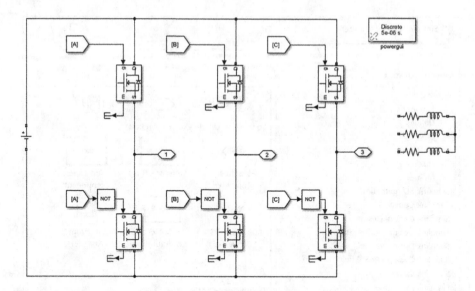

Figure 7-41. *The Connection Port block is connected to the output of the inverter*

Double-click the Connection Port blocks and select Right for the Port location on parent subsystem box (Figure 7-42).

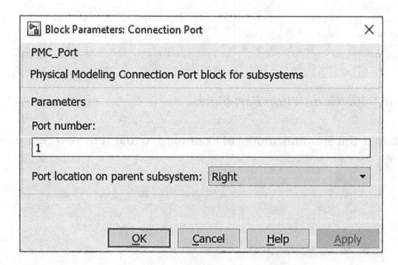

Figure 7-42. *Settings of the Connection Port blocks*

Draw a rectangle around the power stage elements (see Figure 7-43) and press Ctrl+G to make them a subsystem. The result is shown in Figure 7-44.

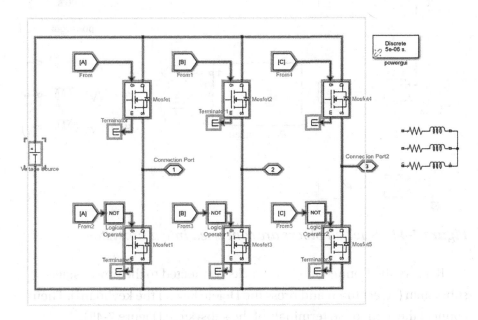

Figure 7-43. *Highlighted blocks are selected*

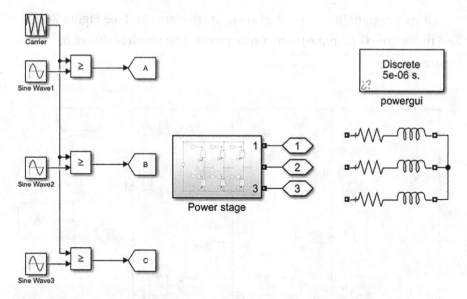

Figure 7-44. *Selected blocks are converted into a subsystem*

Remove the Connection Port blocks connected to the power stage subsystem (select them and press the Delete key on the keyboard). Then connect the load to the terminals of the subsystem (Figure 7-45).

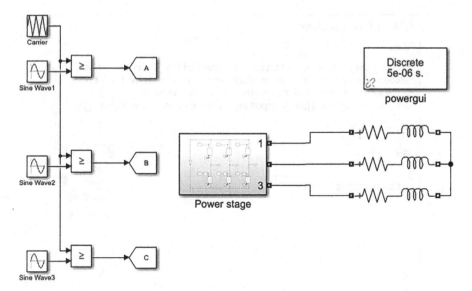

Figure 7-45. *The load is connected to the power stage subsystem*

Double-click the Goto blocks of the PWM section and change the Tag visibility box to global (Figure 7-46).

Figure 7-46. *global is selected for the Tag visibility drop-down list*

You can convert the PWM section to another subsystem and make the Simulink model tidier (Figure 7-47).

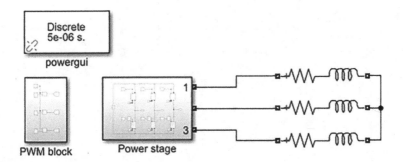

Figure 7-47. *The PWM generation section is converted into a subsystem block*

Summary

In this chapter we learned how to simulate single-phase and three-phase PWM inverters. We learned how to generate required PWM signals. We learned how to measure the magnitude of harmonics and the THD of output, as well.

In the next chapter, we will learn how to simulate electrical machines in Simulink.

CHAPTER 8

Simulation of Motors and Generators

Simulation of different types of power electronic circuits was studied in previous chapters. Simulink can be used to simulate electrical machines as well. In this chapter we will focus on the simulation of electrical machines. We will learn how to simulate DC motors, DC generators, and induction motors. The techniques shown in this chapter are very useful in the simulation of electrical drive systems.

Example 1: Simulation of a DC Motor

Simulink has ready-to-use models of different electrical machines. Electrical machines can be found in the Electrical Machines section of Simscape (see Figure 8-1). In this example, we want to show how a DC motor can be simulated in Simulink.

© Farzin Asadi 2022
F. Asadi, *Simulation of Power Electronics Circuits with MATLAB®/Simulink®*,
Maker Innovations Series, https://doi.org/10.1007/978-1-4842-8220-5_8

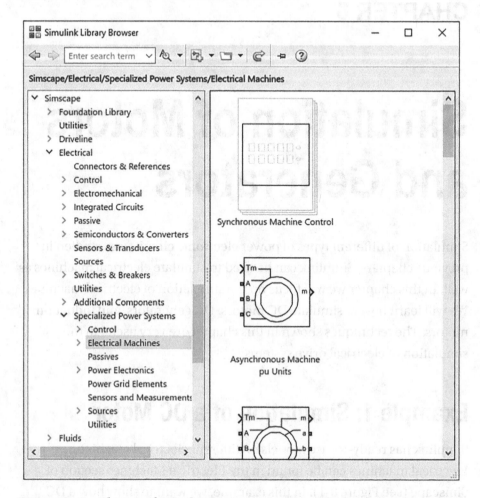

Figure 8-1. *Electrical Machines section of Simulink Library Browser*

The DC Machine block can be found in the Electrical Machines section of Simulink (see Figure 8-2). If you double-click the DC Machine block, the window shown in Figure 8-3 will appear. You can determine the type of machine with the aid of the Field type box (see Figure 8-3). Different types of symbols that are used for DC machines are shown in Figure 8-4. The parameters of the machines are determined in the Parameters tab (see Figure 8-5).

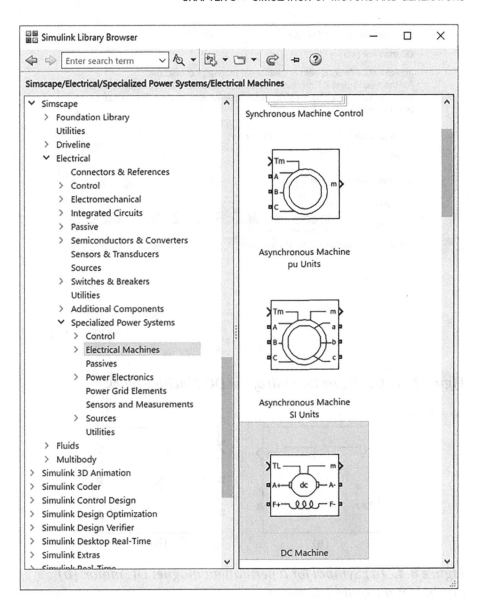

Figure 8-2. *DC Machine block*

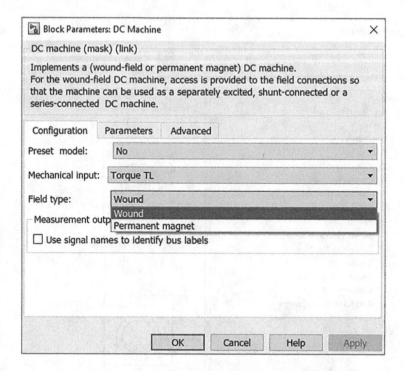

Figure 8-3. Configuration tab of the DC Machine block

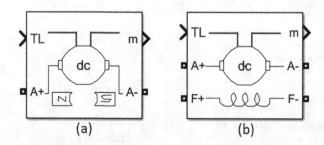

Figure 8-4. (a) Symbol for a permanent magnet DC motor. (b) Symbol for a wound DC motor

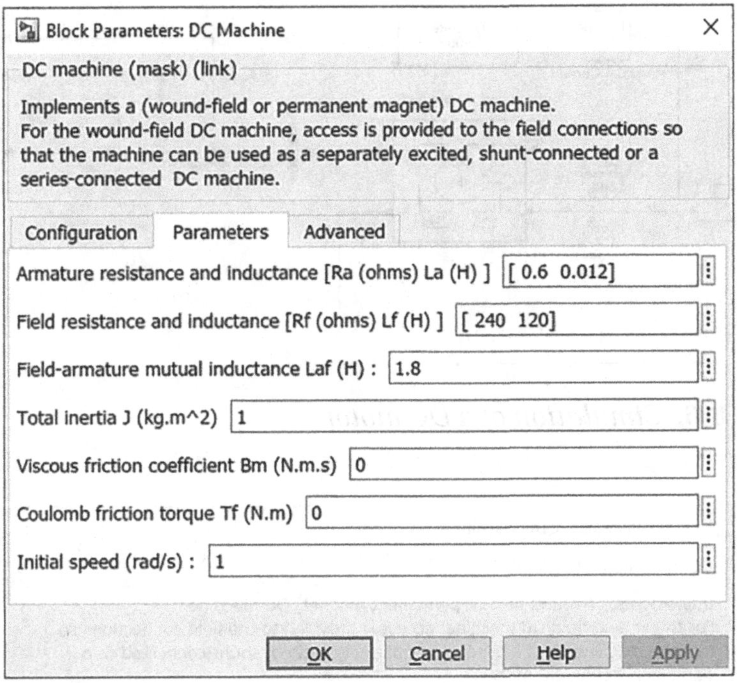

Figure 8-5. *Parameters tab of the DC Machine block*

Consider the Simulink model shown in Figure 8-6. This simulation simulates a DC motor. Input voltage is 100 V. The DC Machine block has the default parameter values. Settings of the Configuration tab of the DC Machine block are shown in Figure 8-7. The measurement port of the DC Machine block is connected to a Bus Selector block (see Figure 8-8). The Bus Selector block outputs the elements you select from the input bus. Settings of Bus Selector are shown in Figure 8-9. Settings of the Load block are shown in Figure 8-10. According to Figure 8-10, a 10 N.m load is applied at t= 2 s. Note that when the speed is positive, a positive torque signal indicates motor mode and a negative signal indicates generator mode.

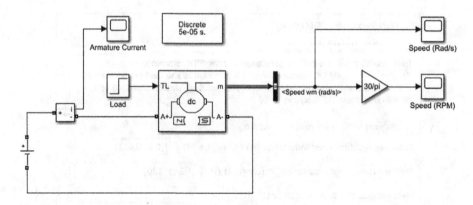

Figure 8-6. *Simulation of a DC motor*

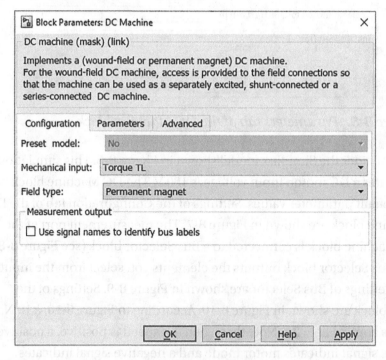

Figure 8-7. *Configuration tab of DC Machine*

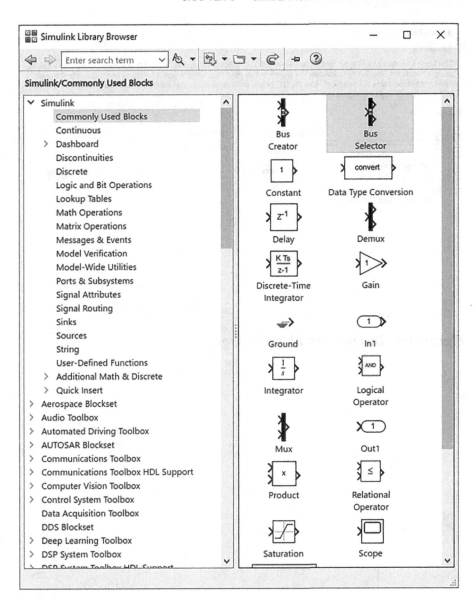

Figure 8-8. *Bus Selector block*

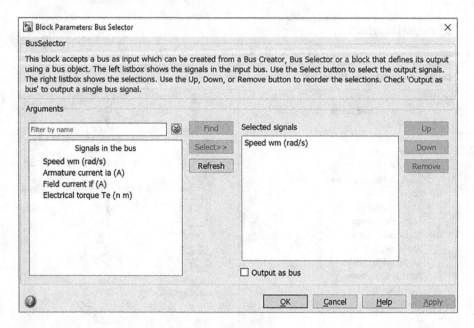

Figure 8-9. *Bus Selector block settings*

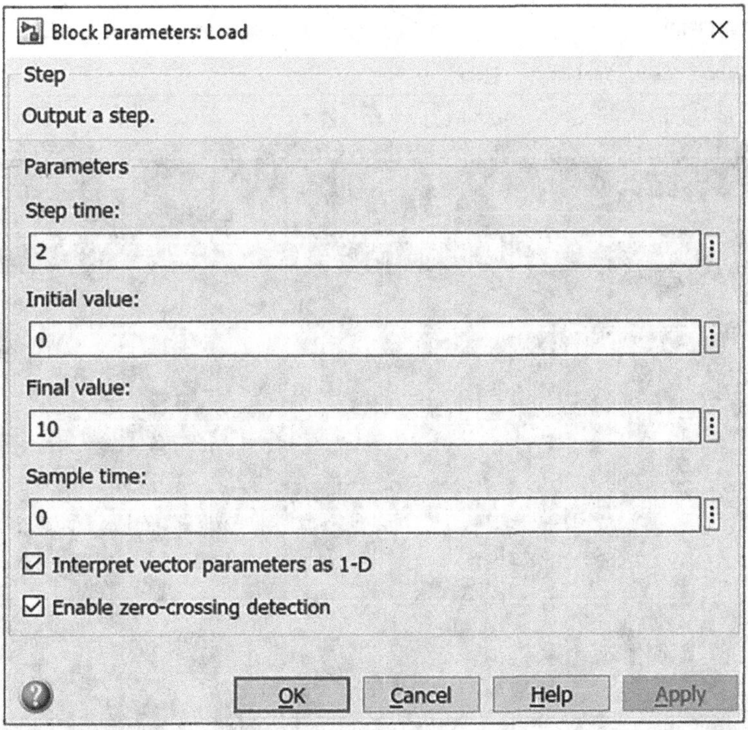

Block Parameters: Load ✕

Step

Output a step.

Parameters

Step time:

2

Initial value:

0

Final value:

10

Sample time:

0

☑ Interpret vector parameters as 1-D

☑ Enable zero-crossing detection

OK   Cancel   Help   Apply

Figure 8-10. *Load block settings*

Run the simulation. Figure 8-11 shows the speed of the shaft in RPM. The speed decreases at t=2 s since a 10 N.m load is applied to the shaft.

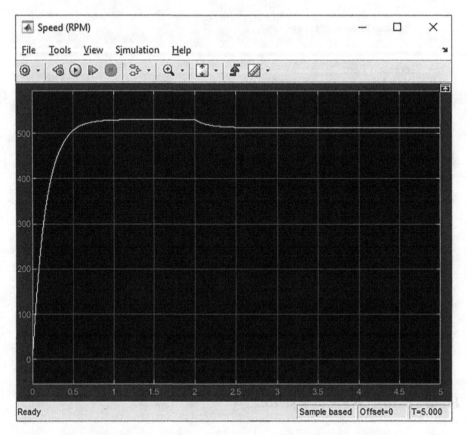

Figure 8-11. *Simulation result*

Armature current is shown in Figure 8-12. Note that the current is very large at the beginning since the back Electromotive Force (EMF) is small. As the shaft speed increases, the back EMF increases, and the armature current decreases.

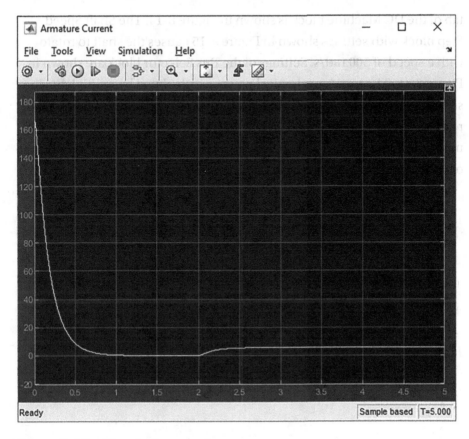

Figure 8-12. *Simulation result*

In this example we learned how to simulate a DC motor in Simulink. The next example studies the simulation of a DC generator.

Example 2: Simulation of a DC Generator

In this example we want to simulate a DC generator. Consider the Simulink model shown in Figure 8-13. The load resistor is 10 Ω. The field winding of the generator is connected to a 100 V DC Voltage Source block. The DC Machine block used the default values of parameters. The Configuration

415

tab of the DC Machine block is shown in Figure 8-14. The Shaft Speed
Step block with settings shown in Figure 8-15 causes the shaft to rotate
with a speed of 500 rad/s. Settings of the Bus Selector block are shown in
Figure 8-16. The input mechanical power is calculated by multiplying the
shaft speed with the shaft torque. The output power is the product of load
resistor voltage and load resistor current (a Multimeter block is used to
measure the voltage and current of the load resistor). Efficiency is the ratio
of output power to input power.

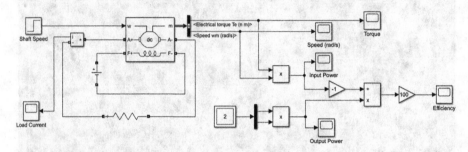

Figure 8-13. *Simulink model of Example 2*

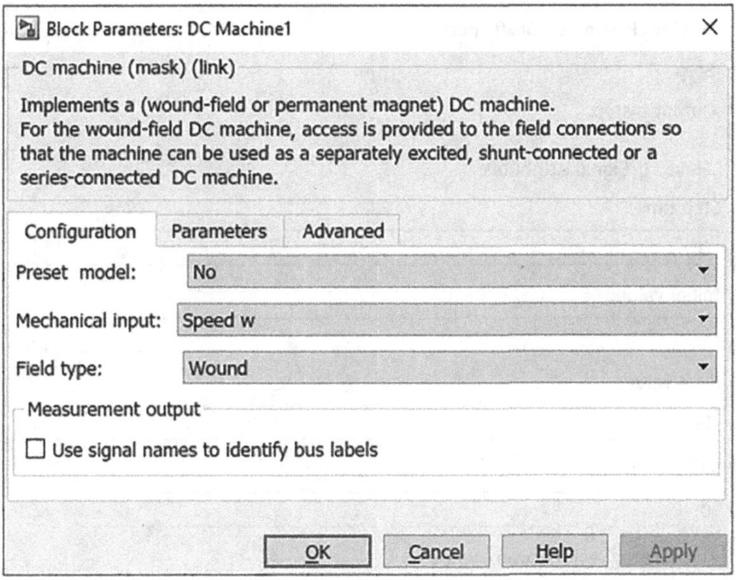

Block Parameters: DC Machine1 ✕

DC machine (mask) (link)

Implements a (wound-field or permanent magnet) DC machine.
For the wound-field DC machine, access is provided to the field connections so
that the machine can be used as a separately excited, shunt-connected or a
series-connected DC machine.

| Configuration | Parameters | Advanced |

Preset model: No ▼

Mechanical input: Speed w ▼

Field type: Wound ▼

Measurement output
☐ Use signal names to identify bus labels

OK   Cancel   Help   Apply

Figure 8-14. Settings of the DC Machine block

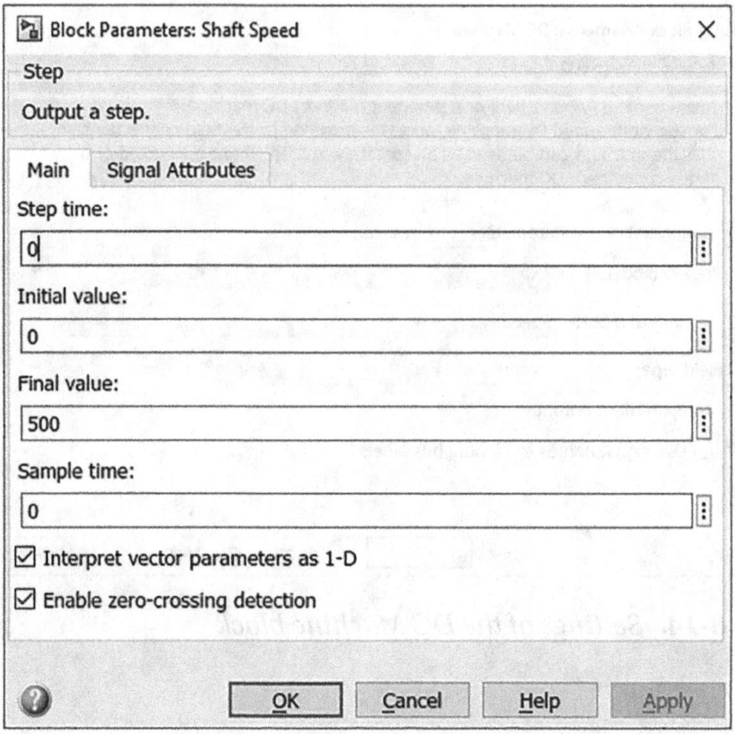

Figure 8-15. *Settings of the Shaft Speed Step block*

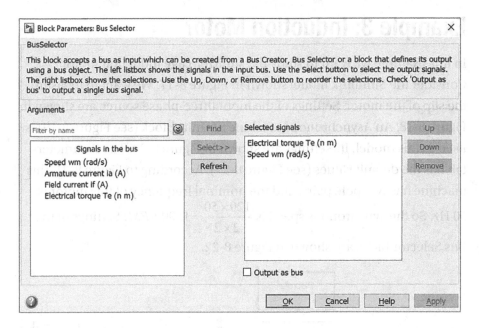

Figure 8-16. *Settings of the Bus Selector block*

Run the simulation. The input power to the generator is about 3.317 kW. The output power (load resistor power) is about 3.129 kW. The efficiency is about 94%.

In the previous two examples, we studied the simulation of a DC motor and DC generator. In the next example, we will simulate a squirrel-cage induction motor. Squirrel-cage induction motors are very prevalent in industry, in sizes from below 1 kilowatt (1.3 hp) up to tens of megawatts (tens-of-thousands horsepower). They are simple, rugged, and self-starting and maintain a reasonably constant speed from light load to full load, set by the frequency of the power supply and the number of poles of the stator winding.

Example 3: Induction Motor

In this example we want to study the squirrel-cage induction motor.
Consider the Simulink model shown in Figure 8-17. We want to measure
the slip of the motor. Settings of the input three-phase source are shown in
Figure 8-18. An Asynchronous Machine SI Units block (see Figure 8-19) is
used in this model. Its settings are shown in Figure 8-20. The Parameters
tab has the default values (see Figure 8-21). According to Figure 8-21, this
machine has two pole pairs, and the nominal frequency of this motor is
50 Hz. So the synchronous speed is $\dfrac{120 \times 50}{2 \times 2} = 1500 \; RPM$. Settings of the

Bus Selector block are shown in Figure 8-22.

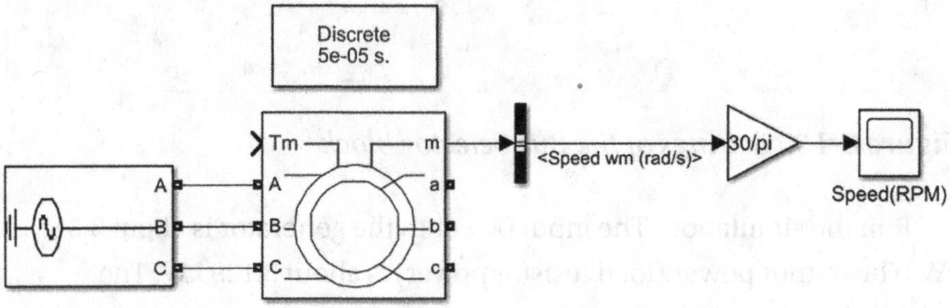

Figure 8-17. *Simulink model of Example 3*

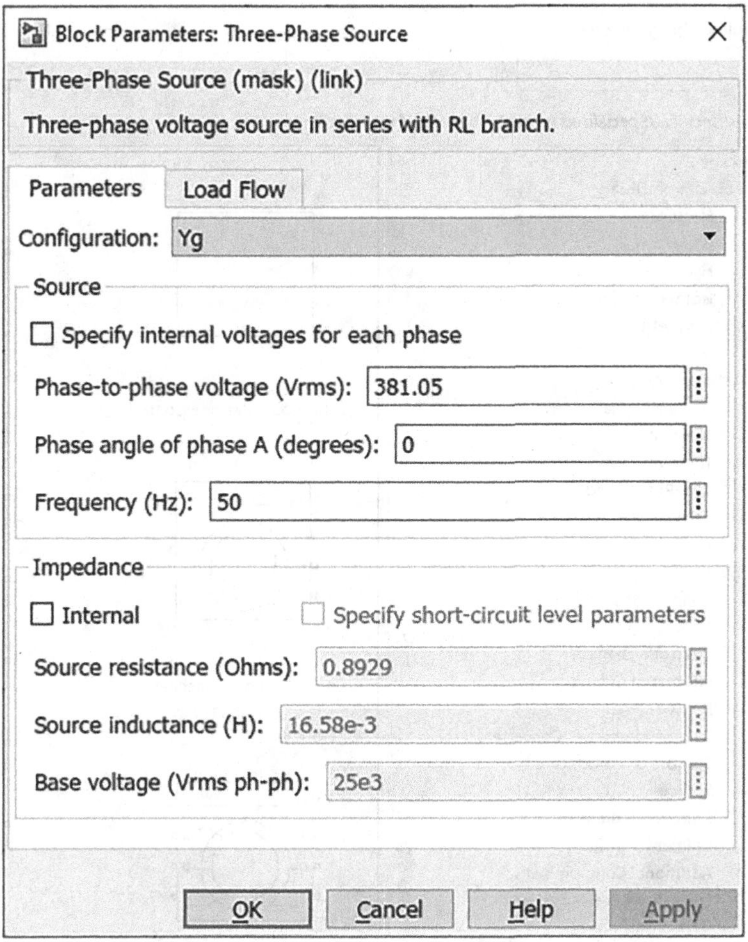

Figure 8-18. *Settings of the Three-Phase Source block*

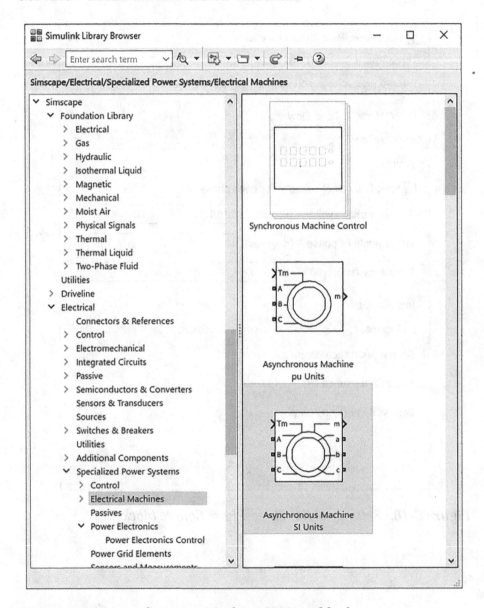

Figure 8-19. *Asynchronous Machine SI Units block*

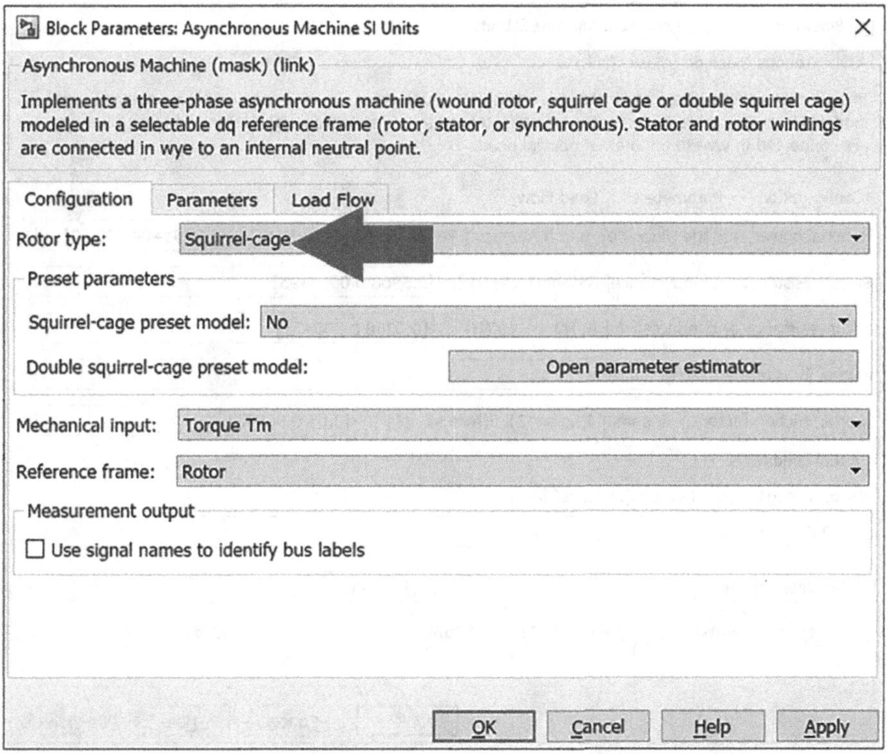

Figure 8-20. *Configuration tab of the Asynchronous Machine SI Units block*

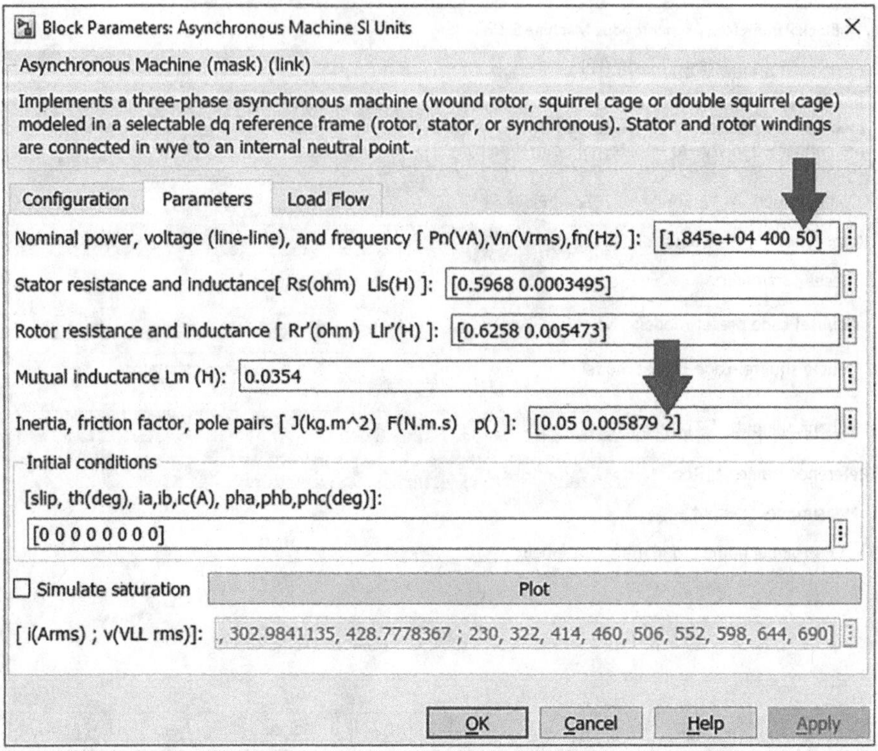

Figure 8-21. Parameters tab of the Asynchronous Machine SI Units block

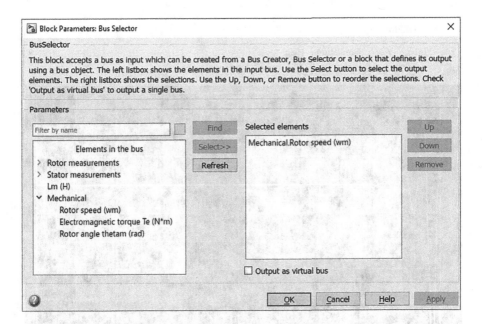

Figure 8-22. *Settings of the Bus Selector block*

Run the simulation. The result shown in Figure 8-23 is obtained. The steady-state speed is 1499.04 RPM. So the slip is $\dfrac{1500 - 1499.04}{1500} \times 100 = 0.064\%$.

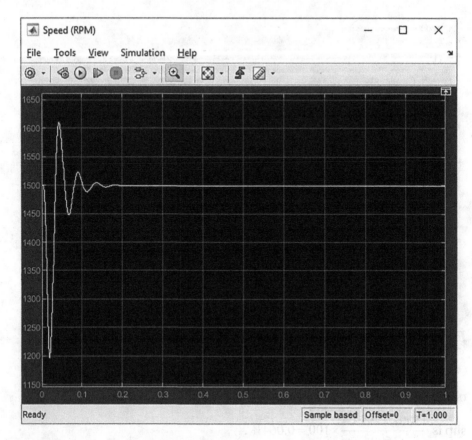

Figure 8-23. *Simulation result*

Note that in Figure 8-23, the shaft speed started from 1500 RPM. If you change the slip to 1 (see Figure 8-24), the shaft starts from 0 RPM (see Figure 8-25).

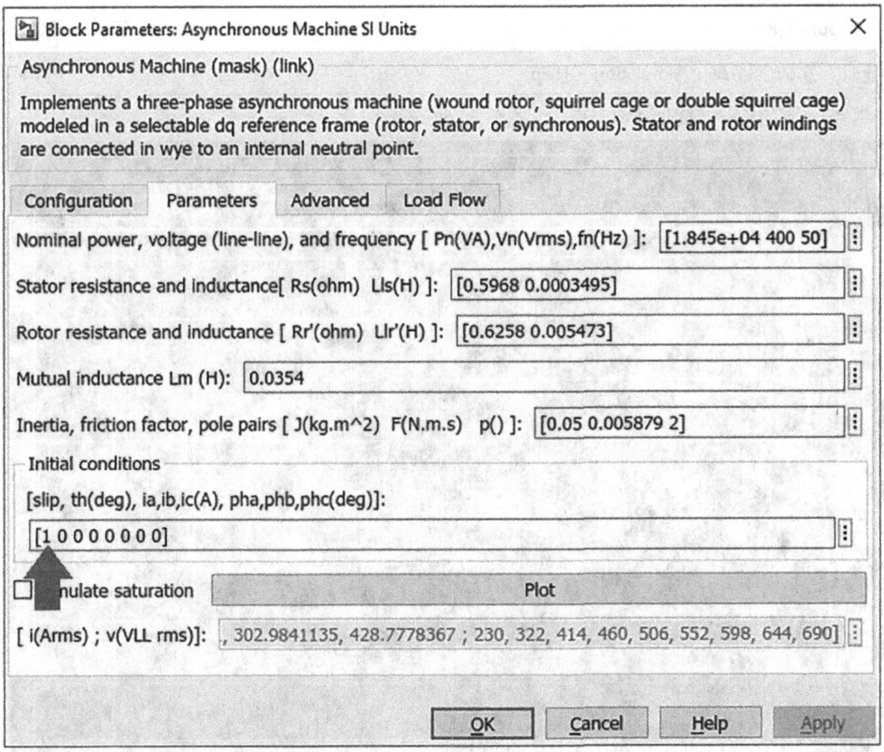

Figure 8-24. *Slip is changed to 1 in order to start the shaft from 0 RPM*

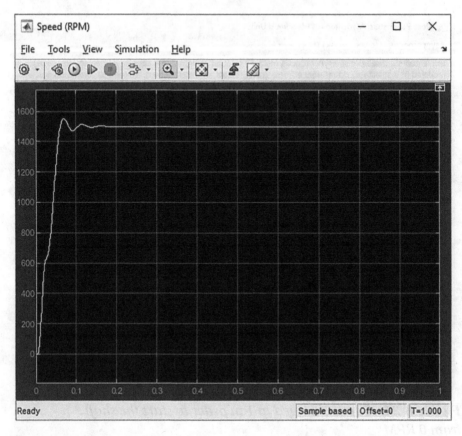

Figure 8-25. *Simulation result*

In this example we learned how to simulate squirrel-cage induction motors. In the next example, we will study the effect of harmonics on the studied motor speed.

Example 4: Effect of Harmonics on AC Motor Speed

In this example, we want to study the effect of harmonics on the motor speed. Consider the Simulink model shown in Figure 8-26.

The Asynchronous Machine SI Units block has an initial slip of 1 (see Figure 8-24) to start from 0 RPM. Other parameters have default values.

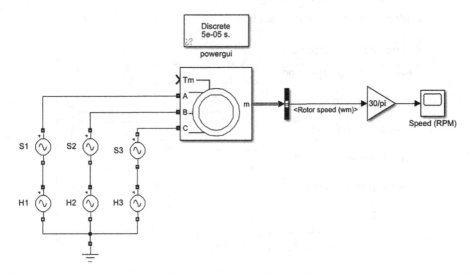

Figure 8-26. *Simulink model of Example 4*

Settings of sources are shown in Figures 8-27 to 8-32.

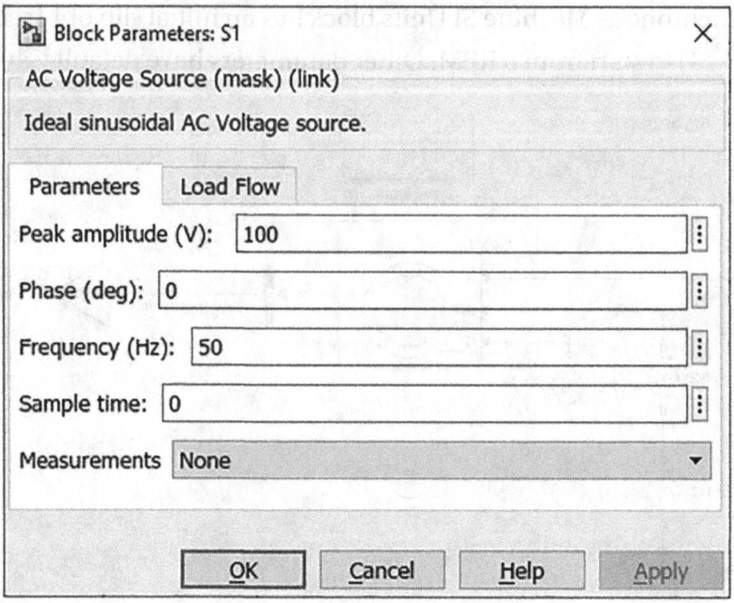

Figure 8-27. *Settings of S1*

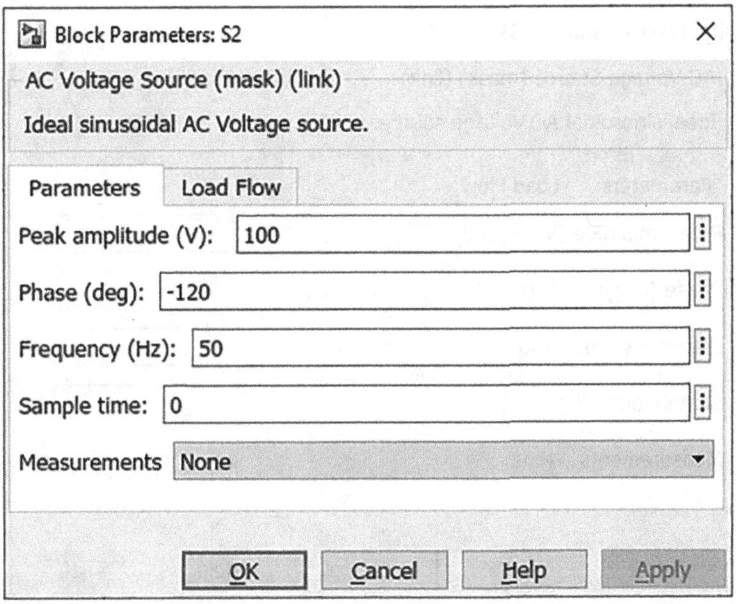

Block Parameters: S2 ✕

AC Voltage Source (mask) (link)

Ideal sinusoidal AC Voltage source.

Parameters | Load Flow

Peak amplitude (V): 100

Phase (deg): -120

Frequency (Hz): 50

Sample time: 0

Measurements None ▼

OK   Cancel   Help   Apply

Figure 8-28. *Settings of S2*

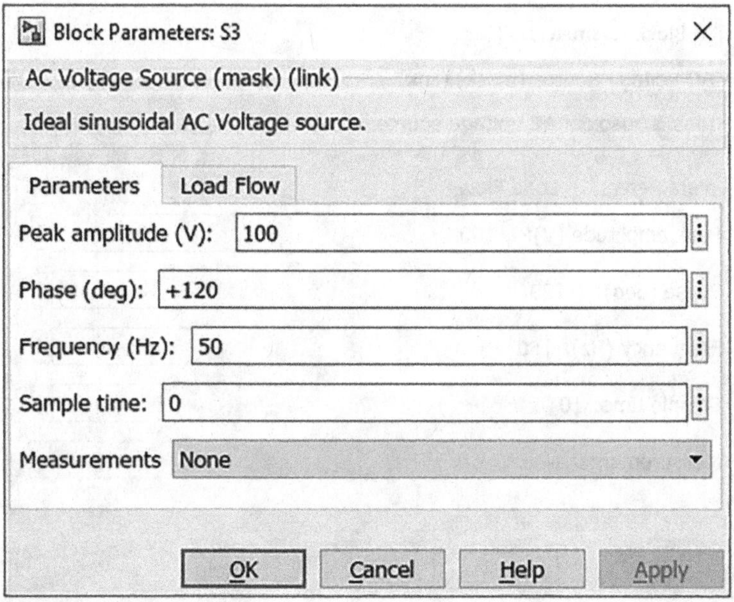

Figure 8-29. Settings of S3

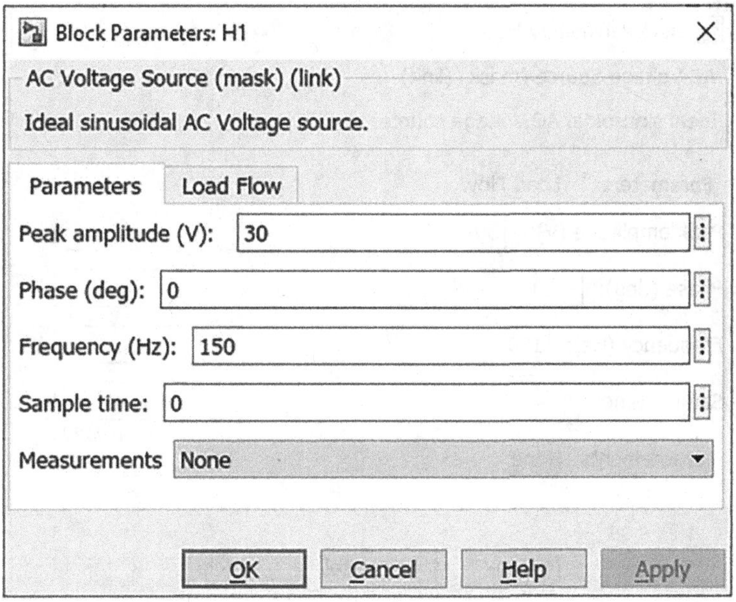

Block Parameters: H1 ✕

AC Voltage Source (mask) (link)

Ideal sinusoidal AC Voltage source.

Parameters	Load Flow

Peak amplitude (V): 30

Phase (deg): 0

Frequency (Hz): 150

Sample time: 0

Measurements None ▼

OK   Cancel   Help   Apply

Figure 8-30. *Settings of H1*

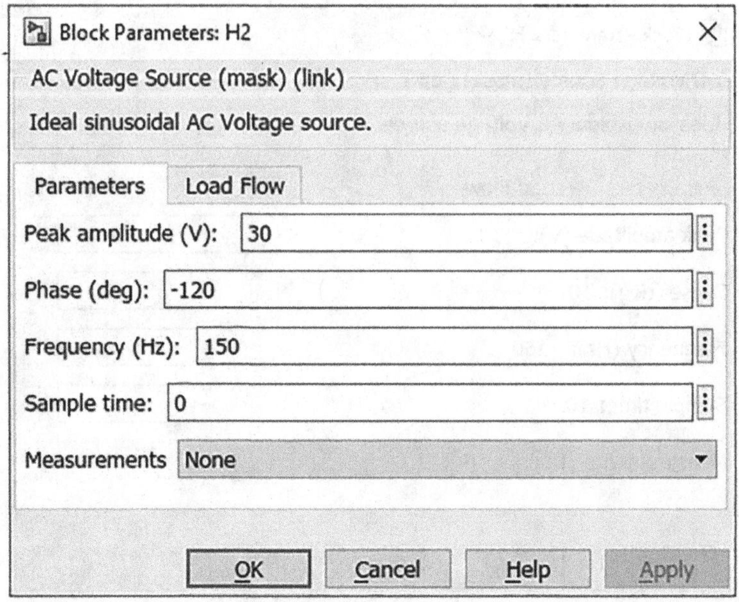

Figure 8-31. *Settings of H2*

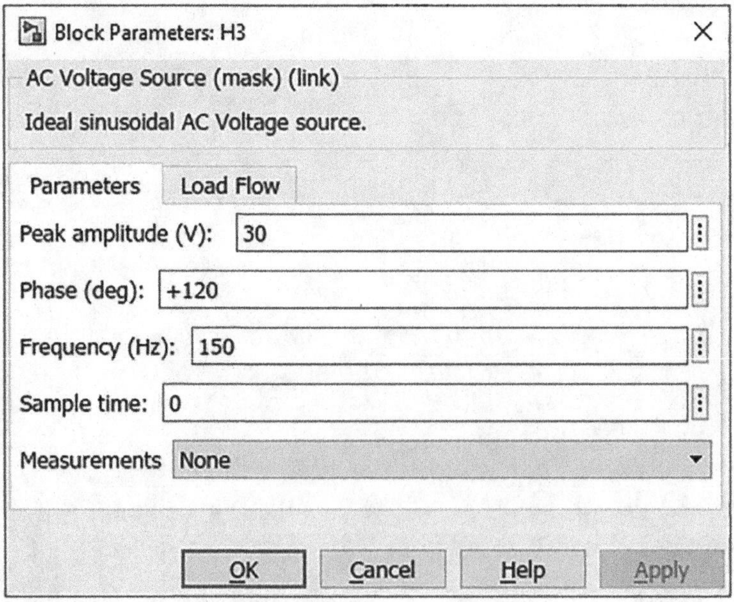

Figure 8-32. *Settings of H3*

Run the simulation. The result is shown in Figure 8-33. Zoom in the steady-state region (see Figure 8-34). The speed has some fluctuations.

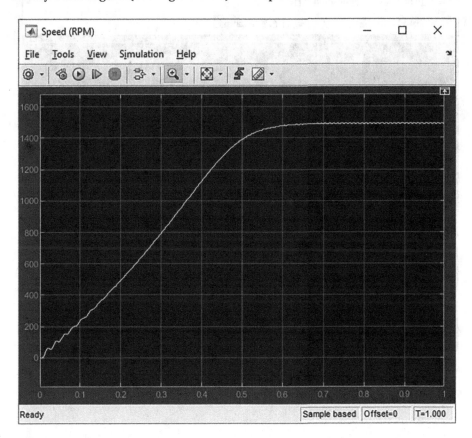

Figure 8-33. *Simulation result*

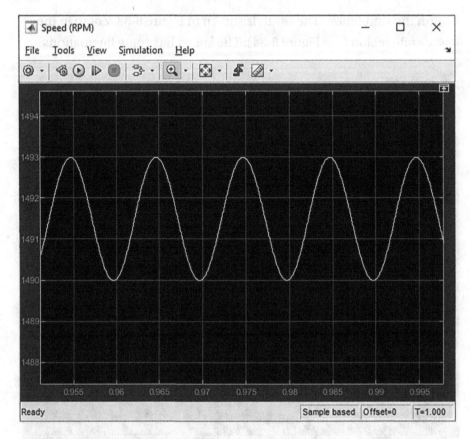

Figure 8-34. *Simulation result*

Summary

In this chapter we learned the simulation of DC motors, DC generators, and induction motors. We learned how to measure the speed and torque of the machine, as well.

In the next chapter, we will learn state space averaging (SSA), which is an important tool to extract the small-signal transfer functions of DC-DC converters.

CHAPTER 9

State Space Averaging

In this chapter we will extract a linear time invariant (LTI) model for DC-DC converters. DC-DC converters are nonlinear dynamic systems. So an LTI model is only an approximation for it. Although the obtained model is an approximation, it is well enough to start the controller design process.

This chapter introduces state space averaging (SSA), which is one of the most important tools to model DC-DC converters that operate in Continuous Current Mode (CCM). You will learn how to use SSA to extract the small-signal transfer function (control-to-output) of a DC-DC converter.

State Space Averaging (SSA)

Assume we want to compare two students. Student marks are given in Table 9-1.

Table 9-1. *Student marks*

Student	Math (4 credits)	Physics (4 credits)	Biology (2 credits)
A	75	70	55
B	80	65	60

© Farzin Asadi 2022
F. Asadi, *Simulation of Power Electronics Circuits with MATLAB®/Simulink®*,
Maker Innovations Series, https://doi.org/10.1007/978-1-4842-8220-5_9

Average of marks can be a good tool to compare the students: average

of student A is $\dfrac{75 \times 4 + 70 \times 3 + 55 \times 2}{4 + 3 + 2} = 68.89,$ and average of student B is

$\dfrac{80 \times 4 + 65 \times 3 + 60 \times 2}{4 + 3 + 2} = 70.55$. So the second student is more successful

since they have a higher average. Note each mark is multiplied by the
credits, so importance of the courses is entered into the averaging process.

The logic behind SSA is similar to the logic behind averaging of marks.
In SSA, we average circuits instead of marks. Let's study a simple example.
Consider the Buck converter shown in Figure 9-1.

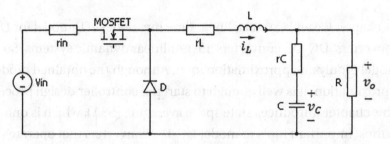

Figure 9-1. *Buck converter*

Based on the MOSFET status (on or off), two equivalent circuits can
be drawn.

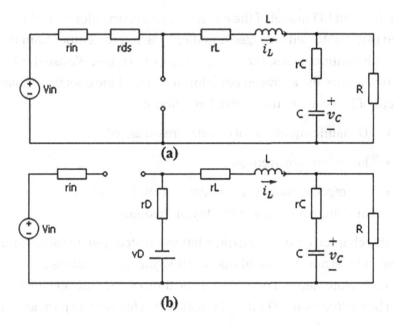

Figure 9-2. *a) Equivalent circuit for a closed MOSFET. b) Equivalent circuit for an open MOSFET*

We want to find a model for the Buck converter, but we have two circuits. Each circuit has its own dynamic equation. We need to find a way to average these two sets of equations.

Assume that the Buck converter of Figure 9-1 spends 80% of the switching period in the MOSFET on state (see Figure 9-2-(a)) and only 20% of the switching period in the MOSFET off state (see Figure 9-2-(b)). In this case, the Buck converter spends most of its time in the MOSFET on state. So it is a good idea to give a higher weight to the equations for the on MOSFET.

SSA uses the percentage of switching time as the weights. For instance, if the Buck converter spends 80% of switching time in the MOSFET on state, then the equation set for the on MOSFET is multiplied by 0.8, and the equation set for the off MOSFET is multiplied by 0.2.

We need an LTI model of the converter. So linearization must be applied to the obtained averaged equations. As you remember from the basic mathematic courses, $f(x_0 + \Delta x) \approx f(x_0) + f'(x_0)\Delta x$. We use the Taylor series to linearize the averaged equation set around the operating point.

Steps of SSA can be summarized as follows:

- Dynamic equations of circuits are extracted.

- Equations are averaged.

- Averaged equations are linearized around the operating point using the Taylor theorem.

In this chapter, we use the capital letters for steady-state values and the tilde for small-signal perturbations. Small-signal perturbations are smaller than steady-state values. For example, the duty cycle of the MOSFET (d) can be written as $d = D + \tilde{d}$. D indicates the steady-state part, and $\tilde{d}$ indicates the small-signal part. Note that $\tilde{d} \ll D$.

Dynamic Equations of a Buck Converter

Consider the Buck converter shown in Figure 9-3. rin, rL, and rC indicate the internal resistance of input source, series resistance of inductor, and series resistance of capacitor, respectively. We assume that the converter is operated in Continuous Current Mode (CCM).

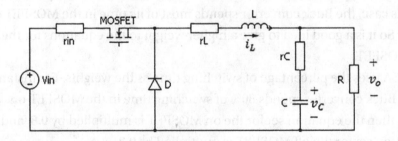

Figure 9-3. *Buck converter circuit*

MOSFET is closed and opened with the aid of pulses shown in Figure 9-4. When the pulse is high (i.e., high logic level), MOSFET is closed. According to Figure 9-4, MOSFET is closed for $d \times T$ seconds and is opened for $T - d \times T = (1 - d) \times T$ seconds. T and d indicate the switching period and duty cycle, respectively.

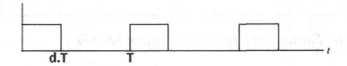

Figure 9-4. *MOSFET gate pulses*

Figure 9-5 shows the equivalent circuit for the closed MOSFET. rds indicates the resistance between drain and source.

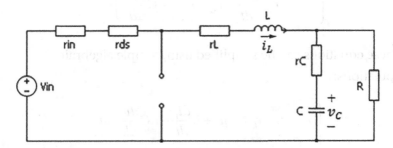

Figure 9-5. *Equivalent circuit for the closed MOSFET*

Figure 9-6 shows the equivalent circuit for the opened MOSFET. rD indicates the diode resistance, and vD indicates the forward voltage drop of the diode.

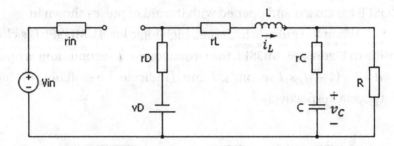

Figure 9-6. *Equivalent circuit for the open MOSFET*

When the MOSFET is closed, circuit equations can be written as

$$\begin{cases} (r_{in}+r_{ds}+r_L)i_L+L\dfrac{di_L}{dt}+R\left(i_L-C\dfrac{dv_C}{dt}\right)=v_{in} \\[4mm] r_C C\dfrac{dv_C}{dt}+v_C=R\left(i_L-C\dfrac{dv_C}{dt}\right) \end{cases} \qquad (9.1)$$

These equations can be simplified using simple algebraic manipulations:

$$\begin{cases} (r_{in}+r_{ds}+r_L+R)i_L+L\dfrac{di_L}{dt}-RC\dfrac{dv_C}{dt}=v_{in} \\[4mm] (r_C+R)C\dfrac{dv_C}{dt}+v_C=Ri_L \end{cases} \qquad (9.2)$$

$$\begin{cases} (r_{in}+r_{ds}+r_L+R)i_L+L\dfrac{di_L}{dt}-\dfrac{R}{R+r_C}(Ri_L-v_C)=v_{in} \\[4mm] C\dfrac{dv_C}{dt}=\dfrac{1}{R+r_C}(Ri_L-v_C) \end{cases} \qquad (9.3)$$

$$\begin{cases} L\dfrac{di_L}{dt}=-(r_{in}+r_{ds}+r_L+R)i_L+\dfrac{R^2}{R+r_C}i_L-\dfrac{R}{R+r_C}v_C+v_{in} \\[4mm] C\dfrac{dv_C}{dt}=\dfrac{1}{R+r_C}(Ri_L-v_C) \end{cases} \qquad (9.4)$$

Load voltage can be written as

$$v_o = R\left(i_L - C\frac{dv_C}{dt}\right) = R\left(\frac{r_C}{r_C + R}i_L + \frac{1}{R + r_C}v_C\right) \tag{9.5}$$

When the MOSFET is opened, circuit equations can be written as

$$\begin{cases} V_D + (r_D + r_L)i_L + L\dfrac{di_L(t)}{dt} + r_C C\dfrac{dv_C}{dt} + v_C = 0 \\[3mm] r_C C\dfrac{dv_C}{dt} + v_C = R\left(i_L - C\dfrac{dv_C}{dt}\right) \end{cases} \tag{9.6}$$

Equations can be simplified using simple algebraic manipulations:

$$\begin{cases} V_D + (r_D + r_L)i_L + L\dfrac{di_L(t)}{dt} + \dfrac{R.r_C}{R + r_C}i_L + \dfrac{R}{R + r_C}v_C = 0 \\[3mm] C\dfrac{dv_C}{dt} = \dfrac{R}{R + r_C}i_L - \dfrac{1}{R + r_C}v_C \end{cases} \tag{9.7}$$

$$\begin{cases} L\dfrac{di_L}{dt} = -\left(r_D + r_L + \dfrac{R.r_C}{R + r_C}\right)i_L - \dfrac{R}{R + r_C}v_C - V_D \\[3mm] C\dfrac{dv_C}{dt} = \dfrac{R}{R + r_C}i_L - \dfrac{1}{R + r_C}v_C \end{cases} \tag{9.8}$$

Output equation can be written as

$$v_o = R\left(i_L - C\frac{dv_C}{dt}\right) = R\left(\frac{r_C}{r_C + R}i_L + \frac{1}{R + r_C}v_C\right) \tag{9.9}$$

Averaging the Dynamic Equations of a Buck Converter

Inductor current equations are obtained as

$$\begin{cases} L\dfrac{di_L}{dt} = -\left(r_{in}+r_{ds}+r_L+R-\dfrac{R^2}{R+r_C}\right)i_L -\dfrac{R}{R+r_C}v_C+v_{in}, n.T<t<n.T+d.T \\[4mm] L\dfrac{di_L}{dt} = -\left(r_D+r_L+\dfrac{R.r_C}{R+r_C}\right)i_L -\dfrac{R}{R+r_C}v_C-V_D, \quad n.T+d.T<t<(n+1)T \quad (9.10) \end{cases}$$

where n is a natural number. Equations are multiplied by the length of time interval during which the equation is valid:

$$\begin{cases} L\dfrac{di_L}{dt}\times d.T = \left(-(r_{in}+r_{ds}+r_L+R)i_L +\dfrac{R^2}{R+r_C}i_L -\dfrac{R}{R+r_C}v_C+v_{in}\right)\times d.T \\[4mm] L\dfrac{di_L}{dt}\times(1-d).T = \left(-\left(r_D+r_L+\dfrac{R.r_C}{R+r_C}\right)i_L -\dfrac{R}{R+r_C}v_C-V_D\right)\times(1-d).T \quad (9.11) \end{cases}$$

Corresponding sides are added together:

$$d.T\times L\dfrac{di_L}{dt}+(1-d).T\times L\dfrac{di_L}{dt}$$

$$= d.T\times\left(-(r_{in}+r_{ds}+r_L+R)i_L +\dfrac{R^2}{R+r_C}i_L -\dfrac{R}{R+r_C}v_C+v_{in}\right)+(1-d).T$$

$$\times\left(-\left(r_D+r_L+\dfrac{R.r_C}{R+r_C}\right)i_L -\dfrac{R}{R+r_C}v_C-V_D\right) \quad (9.12)$$

Both sides are multiplied with $\dfrac{1}{d.T+(1-d)T}=\dfrac{1}{T}$:

$$d\times L\dfrac{di_L}{dt}+(1-d)\times L\dfrac{di_L}{dt}$$

$$=d\times\left(-\left(r_{in}+r_{ds}+r_L+R\right)i_L+\dfrac{R^2}{R+r_C}i_L-\dfrac{R}{R+r_C}v_C+v_{in}\right)$$

$$+(1-d)$$

$$\times\left(-\left(r_D+r_L+\dfrac{R.r_C}{R+r_C}\right)i_L-\dfrac{R}{R+r_C}v_C-V_D\right) \tag{9.13}$$

After some simple algebraic manipulations

$$L\dfrac{di_L}{dt}=-d\times\left(r_{in}+r_{ds}+r_L+R-\dfrac{R^2}{R+r_C}\right)i_L-(1-d)$$

$$\times\left(r_D+r_L+\dfrac{R.r_C}{R+r_C}\right)i_L-\dfrac{R}{R+r_C}v_C-(1-d)V_D+dv_{in}$$

or

$$L\dfrac{di_L}{dt}=-d\times R_1i_L-(1-d)\times R_2i_L-\dfrac{R}{R+r_C}v_C-(1-d)V_D+dv_{in} \tag{9.14}$$

where

$$R_1=r_{in}+r_{ds}+r_L+R-\dfrac{R^2}{R+r_C} \tag{9.15}$$

and

$$R_2=r_D+r_L+\dfrac{R.r_C}{R+r_C} \tag{9.16}$$

445

The same procedure can be applied to the capacitor voltage equations

$$\begin{cases} C\dfrac{dv_C}{dt} = \dfrac{R}{R+r_C}i_L - \dfrac{1}{R+r_C}v_C & n.T < t < n.T + d.T \\[3mm] C\dfrac{dv_C}{dt} = \dfrac{R}{R+r_C}i_L - \dfrac{1}{R+r_C}v_C & n.T + d.T < t < (n+1)T \end{cases} \tag{9.17}$$

where n is a natural number. Equations are multiplied by the length of time interval during which the equation is valid:

$$d \times C\dfrac{dv_C}{dt} + (1-d) \times C\dfrac{dv_C}{dt} = d \times \left(\dfrac{R}{R+r_C}i_L - \dfrac{1}{R+r_C}v_C \right)$$
$$+ (1-d)\left(\dfrac{R}{R+r_C}i_L - \dfrac{1}{R+r_C}v_C \right)$$

or

$$C\dfrac{dv_C}{dt} = \left(\dfrac{R}{R+r_C}i_L - \dfrac{1}{R+r_C}v_C \right) \tag{9.18}$$

So the averaged system can be written as

$$\begin{cases} L\dfrac{di_L}{dt} = -d \times R_1 i_L - (1-d) \times R_2 i_L - \dfrac{R}{R+r_C}v_C - (1-d)V_D + dv_{in} \\[3mm] C\dfrac{dv_C}{dt} = \dfrac{R}{R+r_C}i_L - \dfrac{1}{R+r_C}v_C \end{cases} \tag{9.19}$$

where

$$R_1 = r_{in} + r_{ds} + r_L + R - \dfrac{R^2}{R+r_C}$$

$$R_2 = r_D + r_L + \dfrac{R.r_C}{R+r_C}$$

This averaged system can be used to obtain the steady-state values of inductor current and capacitor voltage. Steady-state values can be obtained by replacing the left-hand side with zero and solving the obtained equations. Capital letters indicate the steady-state values. For instance, I_L indicates the steady-state inductor current.

$$\begin{cases} 0 = -D \times R_1 I_L - (1-D) \times R_2 I_L + \dfrac{R}{R + r_C} V_C - (1-D)V_D + DV_{IN} \\[4mm] 0 = \dfrac{R}{R + r_C} I_L - \dfrac{1}{R + r_C} V_C \end{cases} \tag{9.20}$$

Steady-state values are

$$\begin{cases} I_L = \dfrac{((R + r_C)(DV_{IN} - (1-D)V_D}{(R + r_C)R_2 + R^2 + D(R + r_C)(R_1 - R_2)} \\[4mm] V_C = \dfrac{((R + r_C)(DV_{IN} - (1-D)V_D}{(R + r_C)R_2 + (1-2D)R^2 + D(R + r_C)(R_1 - R_2)} \times R \end{cases} \tag{9.21}$$

The preceding result is obtained with the aid of the following MATLAB code. Figure 9-7 shows the output of this code:

```
clc
clear all

syms R1 R2 R D IL VC rC rL VD vIN

eq1=-D*R1*IL-(1-D)*R2*IL-R/(R+rC)*VC-(1-D)*VD+D*vIN;
eq2=R/(R+rC)*IL-1/(R+rC)*VC;

DC_operatingPoint=solve(eq1,eq2,[IL VC]);

disp('IL=')
pretty(simplify(DC_operatingPoint.IL))

disp('VC=')
pretty(simplify(DC_operatingPoint.VC))
```

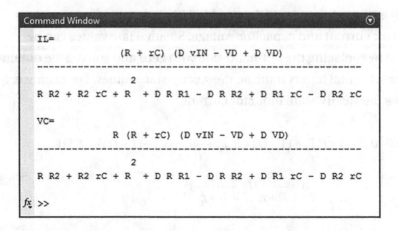

Figure 9-7. *Steady-state values of inductor current and capacitor voltage*

When rin= rds= rD= VD= 0, steady-state values are

$$\begin{cases} I_L = \dfrac{D \times V_{IN}}{R} \\ V_C = D \times V_{IN} \end{cases} \tag{9.22}$$

These are the familiar equations of an ideal (i.e., efficiency is 100%) Buck converter operating in CCM.

The averaging procedure must be applied to the output equation as well:

$$dT \times v_o + (1-d)T \times v_o = dT \times R\left(\frac{r_C}{r_C + R} i_L + \frac{1}{R + r_C} v_C \right)$$

$$+ (1-d)T \times R\left(\frac{r_C}{r_C + R} i_L + \frac{1}{R + r_C} v_C \right) \tag{9.23}$$

If we multiply both sides by $\dfrac{1}{T}$, we will obtain the following equation:

$$v_o = R\left(\frac{r_C}{r_C + R} i_L + \frac{1}{R + r_C} v_C \right) \tag{9.24}$$

Linearization of Averaged Equations

Averaged equations are obtained as

$$\begin{cases} L\dfrac{di_L}{dt} = -d \times R_1 i_L - (1-d) \times R_2 i_L - \dfrac{R}{R+r_C} v_C - (1-d)V_D + dv_{in} \\[3mm] C\dfrac{dv_C}{dt} = \dfrac{R}{R+r_C} i_L - \dfrac{1}{R+r_C} v_C \end{cases} \qquad (9.25)$$

where

$$R_1 = r_{in} + r_{ds} + r_L + R - \frac{R^2}{R+r_C}$$

$$R_2 = r_D + r_L + \frac{R \times r_C}{R+r_C}$$

Let's linearize these equations with the Taylor series. Assume that

$$i_L = I_L + \tilde{i}_L \qquad (9.26)$$

$$v_C = V_C + \tilde{v}_C \qquad (9.27)$$

$$d = D + \tilde{d} \qquad (9.28)$$

where $\tilde{i}_L \ll I_L$, $\tilde{v}_C \ll V_C$, and $\tilde{d} \ll D$. Diode forward voltage drop is assumed to be constant. These equations show that each variable has a steady-state value (I_L, V_C, and D) and a small perturbation ($\tilde{i}_L, \tilde{v}_C$, and $\tilde{d}$). Steady-state values are obtained by solving the average system equation with the left-hand side equal to zero (see equations 20 and 21). Averaged equations can be written as

$$L\frac{d\left(I_L+\tilde{i}_L\right)}{dt}=-\left(D+\tilde{d}\right)\times R_1\left(I_L+\tilde{i}_L\right)-\left(1-\left(D+\tilde{d}\right)\right)\times R_2\left(I_L+\tilde{i}_L\right)$$
$$-\frac{R}{R+r_C}\left(V_C+\tilde{v}_C\right)-\left(1-\left(D+\tilde{d}\right)\right)V_D+\left(D+\tilde{d}\right)\left(V_{IN}+\tilde{v}_{in}\right)\quad(9.29)$$

$$C\frac{d\left(V_C+\tilde{v}_C\right)}{dt}=\frac{R}{R+r_C}\left(I_L+\tilde{i}_L\right)-\frac{1}{R+r_C}\left(V_C+\tilde{v}_C\right)\qquad(9.30)$$

After simple algebraic manipulations

$$L\frac{d\left(I_L+\tilde{i}_L\right)}{dt}=-\left(D+\tilde{d}\right)\times R_1\left(I_L+\tilde{i}_L\right)-\left(1-\left(D+\tilde{d}\right)\right)\times R_2\left(I_L+\tilde{i}_L\right)$$
$$-\frac{R}{R+r_C}\left(V_C+\tilde{v}_C\right)-\left(1-\left(D+\tilde{d}\right)\right)V_D+\left(D+\tilde{d}\right)\left(V_{IN}+\tilde{v}_{in}\right)\Rightarrow$$

$$L\frac{d\left(I_L+\tilde{i}_L\right)}{dt}=-R_1DI_L-R_1D\tilde{i}_L-R_1I_L\tilde{d}-R_1\tilde{i}_L\tilde{d}+R_2\left(D-1\right)I_L$$
$$+R_2\left(D-1\right)\tilde{i}_L+R_2I_L\tilde{d}+R_2\tilde{i}_L\tilde{d}-\frac{R}{R+r_C}V_C-\frac{R}{R+r_C}\tilde{v}_c+\left(D-1\right)V_D$$
$$+V_D\tilde{d}+DV_{IN}+D\tilde{v}_{in}+V_{IN}\tilde{d}+\tilde{v}_{in}\tilde{d}\Rightarrow$$

$$L\frac{d\left(I_L+\tilde{i}_L\right)}{dt}=-R_1DI_L+R_2\left(D-1\right)I_L+\left(D-1\right)V_D-\frac{R}{R+r_C}V_C$$
$$+DV_{IN}+\tilde{v}_{in}\tilde{d}+R_2\tilde{i}_L\tilde{d}-R_1\tilde{i}_L\tilde{d}+\left(R_2\left(D-1\right)-R_1D\right)\tilde{i}_L$$
$$-\frac{R}{R+r_C}\tilde{v}_c+\left(V_{IN}+V_D+\left(R_2-R_1\right)I_L\right)\tilde{d}+D\tilde{v}_{in}\qquad(9.31)$$

is obtained. Note that $L\dfrac{d\left(I_L+\tilde{i}_L\right)}{dt}=L\dfrac{d\left(\tilde{i}_L\right)}{dt}$ since the derivative of a constant term is zero. Right-hand-side terms can be divided into three groups:

- $-R_1DI_L+R_2(D-1)I_L+(D-1)V_D-\dfrac{R}{R+r_C}V_C+DV_{IN}$

- $\tilde{v}_{in}\tilde{d}+R_2\tilde{i}_L\tilde{d}-R_1\tilde{i}_L\tilde{d}$

- $+\left(R_2(D-1)-R_1D\right)\tilde{i}_L-\dfrac{R}{R+r_C}\tilde{v}_c+\left(V_{IN}+V_D+(R_2-R_1)I_L\right)\tilde{d}+D\tilde{v}_{in}$

If we put the steady-state values into the

$-R_1DI_L+R_2(D-1)I_L+(D-1)V_D-\dfrac{R}{R+r_C}V_C+DV_{IN}$, the result will be 0. The

second group can be vanished as well. Note that the product of two small numbers is a small number around zero. That is why we ignore the second group terms. So we need to consider the third group only:

$$L\frac{d\left(\tilde{i}_L\right)}{dt}\approx+\left(R_2(D-1)-R_1D\right)\tilde{i}_L-\frac{R}{R+r_C}\tilde{v}_c+\left(V_{IN}+V_D+(R_2-R_1)I_L\right)\tilde{d}+D\tilde{v}_{in} \qquad (9.32)$$

The same procedure can be applied to the capacitor voltage equation (eq. (9.30)):

$$C\frac{d\left(V_C+\tilde{v}_C\right)}{dt}=\frac{R}{R+r_C}\left(I_L+\tilde{i}_L\right)-\frac{1}{R+r_C}\left(V_C+\tilde{v}_C\right)\Rightarrow$$

$$C\frac{d\left(V_C+\tilde{v}_C\right)}{dt}=\frac{R}{R+r_C}I_L-\frac{1}{R+r_C}V_C+\frac{R}{R+r_C}\tilde{i}_L-\frac{1}{R+r_C}\tilde{v}_C \qquad (9.33)$$

V_C is constant, and its derivative is zero. So we can write

$$C\frac{d(\tilde{v}_C)}{dt} = \frac{R}{R+r_C}I_L - \frac{1}{R+r_C}V_C + \frac{R}{R+r_C}\tilde{i}_L - \frac{1}{R+r_C}\tilde{v}_C \qquad (9.34)$$

Right-hand-side terms can be divided into two groups:

- $\dfrac{R}{R+r_C}I_L - \dfrac{1}{R+r_C}V_C$

- $\dfrac{R}{R+r_C}\tilde{i}_L - \dfrac{1}{R+r_C}\tilde{v}_C$

If we put the steady-state values into the $\dfrac{R}{R+r_C}I_L - \dfrac{1}{R+r_C}V_C$, the result will be 0. So we need to consider the second group only:

$$C\frac{d(\tilde{v}_C)}{dt} \approx \frac{R}{R+r_C}\tilde{i}_L - \frac{1}{R+r_C}\tilde{v}_C \qquad (9.35)$$

The output equation is linearized in the same way. V_o and $\tilde{v}_o$ indicate the large signal component of output voltage and small-signal component of output voltage, respectively:

$$v_o = R\left(\frac{r_C}{r_C+R}i_L + \frac{1}{R+r_C}v_C\right) \Rightarrow$$

$$V_o + \tilde{v}_o = R\left(\frac{r_C}{r_C+R}(I_L+\tilde{i}_L) + \frac{1}{R+r_C}(V_C+\tilde{v}_C)\right) \Rightarrow$$

$$V_o + \tilde{v}_o = \frac{R.r_C}{r_C+R}I_L + \frac{R}{R+r_C}V_C + \frac{R.r_C}{r_C+R}\tilde{i}_L + \frac{R}{R+r_C}\tilde{v}_C \qquad (9.36)$$

Output's large signal part can be obtained as

$$V_o = \frac{R.r_C}{r_C + R}I_L + \frac{R}{R + r_C}V_C \qquad (9.37)$$

If we put the steady-state values of I_L and V_C into the preceding equation, we will obtain the steady-state value of output voltage.

The linearized small-signal equation of output voltage is

$$\tilde{v}_o = \frac{R.r_C}{r_C + R}\tilde{i}_L + \frac{R}{R + r_C}\tilde{v}_C \qquad (9.38)$$

So the linearized small-signal model of the Buck converter can be written as

$$\begin{cases} \dfrac{d(\tilde{i}_L)}{dt} \approx \dfrac{1}{L}\left[\left(R_2(D-1)-R_1D\right)\tilde{i}_L - \dfrac{R}{R+r_C}\tilde{v}_c + \left(V_{IN}+V_D+(R_2-R_1)I_L\right)\tilde{d} + D\tilde{v}_{in} \right] \\[4mm] \dfrac{d(\tilde{v}_C)}{dt} \approx \dfrac{1}{C}\left[\dfrac{R}{R+r_C}\tilde{i}_L - \dfrac{1}{R+r_C}\tilde{v}_C \right] \\[4mm] \tilde{v}_o = \dfrac{R.r_C}{r_C+R}\tilde{i}_L + \dfrac{R}{R+r_C}\tilde{v}_C \end{cases}$$

where

$$R_1 = r_{in} + r_{ds} + r_L + R - \frac{R^2}{R+r_C}$$

$$R_2 = r_D + r_L + \frac{R \times r_C}{R+r_C} \qquad (9.39)$$

It can be written in the form of a linear time invariant state space model:

$$\begin{cases} \dot{x} = Ax + Bu \\ \quad y = \mathbb{C}x \end{cases} \tag{9.40}$$

where

$$x = \begin{bmatrix} \tilde{i}_L \\ \tilde{v}_c \end{bmatrix},$$

$$u = \begin{bmatrix} \tilde{d} \\ \tilde{v}_{in} \end{bmatrix},$$

$$y = v_o,$$

$$A = \begin{bmatrix} \dfrac{R_2(D-1) - R_1 D}{L} & -\dfrac{R}{(R+r_C)L} \\[3mm] \dfrac{R}{(R+r_C)C} & -\dfrac{1}{(R+r_C)C} \end{bmatrix},$$

$$B = \begin{bmatrix} \dfrac{\left(V_{IN} + V_D + (R_2 - R_1)I_L\right)}{L} & \dfrac{D}{L} \\[3mm] \dfrac{0}{C} & \dfrac{0}{C} \end{bmatrix},$$

and

$$\mathbb{C} = \begin{bmatrix} \dfrac{R.r_C}{r_C + R} & \dfrac{R}{r_C + R} \end{bmatrix}. \tag{9.41}$$

$\mathbb{C}$ is a matrix, and it must not be confused with capacitor value C.

Let's study a numeric example. Assume a Buck converter with R= 5 Ω, Vin=50 V, rin=0.1 Ω, L=400 μH, rL=0.1 Ω, C=100 μF, rC=0.05 Ω, D=0.41, rds=0.1 Ω, rD=0.1 Ω, and VD=0.7 V.

The following program calculates the small-signal transfer functions for the given values. After running the program,

$$\frac{\tilde{v}_o(s)}{\tilde{d}(s)} = \frac{6184s + 1.237 \times 10^9}{s^2 + 2574s + 2.568 \times 10^7} \text{ and } \frac{\tilde{v}_o(s)}{\tilde{v}_{in}(s)} = \frac{50.74s + 1.015 \times 10^7}{s^2 + 2574s + 2.568 \times 10^7} \text{ are}$$

obtained. Bode plots of these transfer functions are shown in Figures 9-8 and 9-9:

```
%This program calculates the small signal transfer
%functions for Buck converter
R=5;

VIN=50;
rin=.1;

L=400e-6;
rL=.1;

C=100e-6;
rC=.05;

rD=.01;
VD=.7;

rds=.1;

D=.41;

R1=rin+rds+rL+R*rC/(R+rC);
R2=rD+rL+R*rC/(R+rC);

IL=(R+rC)*(D*VIN-(1-D)*VD)/((R+rC)*R2+R^2+D*(R+rC)*(R1-R2));

A=[(R2*(D-1)-R1*D)/L -R/(R+rC)/L;R/(R+rC)/C -1/(R+rC)/C];
B=[(VIN+VD+(R2-R1)*IL)/L D/L;0 0];
CC=[R*rC/(rC+R) R/(R+rC)]; %C shows the capacitance so CC is
used for matrix
H=tf(ss(A,B,CC,0));
```

```
vO_d=H(1)% transfer function between output voltage and
duty ratio
vO_vin=H(2) %transfer function between output voltage and
input source
figure(1)
bode(vO_d), grid on
figure(2)
bode(vO_vin), grid on
```

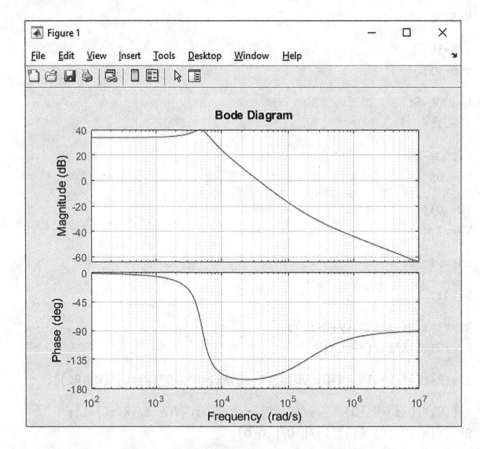

Figure 9-8. *Bode plot of $\frac{\tilde{v}_o(s)}{\tilde{d}(s)}$ (variable vO_d in the code)*

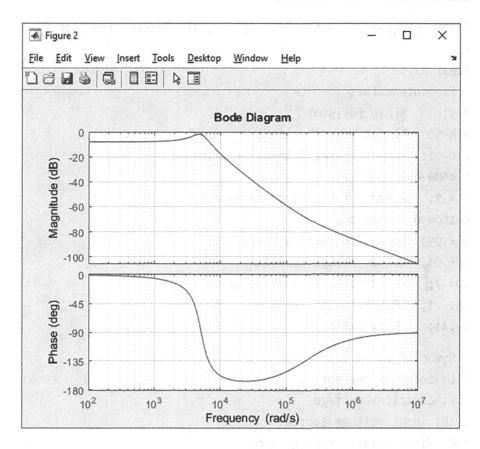

Figure 9-9. *Bode plot of $\dfrac{\tilde{v}_o(s)}{\tilde{v}_{in}(s)}$ (variable vO_vin in the code)*

Obtaining the Small-Signal Transfer Functions of the Buck Converter Using MATLAB

MATLAB can do the mathematical machinery of SSA easily without any error. The following program can extract the small-signal transfer function for the Buck converter. Output of this code is shown in Figure 9-10. The obtained result is the same as the previous analysis:

```
% This program extracts the small signal transfer function
clc
clear all;
% Elements values
R=5;       %Load resistor
VIN=50;    %Input source voltage
rin=.1;    %Input source internal resistance
L=400e-6;  %inductor
rL=.1;     %inductor series resistance
C=100e-6;  %capacitor
rC=.05;    %capacitor series resistance
rD=.01;    %Diode series resistance
VD=.7;     %Diode forward voltage drop
rds=.1;    %MOSFET on resistance
D=.41;     %Duty ratio

% Symbolic variables
%iL: inductor current
%vC: capacitor voltage
%vin: input voltage source
%vD: diode forward voltage drop
%d: duty cycle
syms iL vC vin vD d

%CLOSED MOSFET EQUATIONS
M1=(-(rin+rds+rL+(R*rC/(R+rC)))*iL-R/(R+rC)*vC+vin)/L;%d(iL)/dt
                                          for closed MOSFET
M2=(R/(R+rC)*iL-1/(R+rC)*vC)/C;               %d(vC)/dt for
                                          closed MOSFET
vO1=R*(rC/(rC+R)*iL+1/(R+rC)*vC);
%OPENED MOSFET EQUATIONS
M3=(-(rD+rL+R*rC/(R+rC))*iL-R/(R+rC)*vC-vD)/L;     %d(iL)/dt for
                                          opened MOSFET
```

```
M4=(R/(R+rC)*iL-1/(R+rC)*vC)/C;      %%d(vC)/dt for
                                      opened MOSFET
vO2=R*(rC/(rC+R)*iL+1/(R+rC)*vC);
%AVERAGING
MA1= simplify(d*M1+(1-d)*M3);
MA2= simplify(d*M2+(1-d)*M4);
vO= simplify(d*vO1+(1-d)*vO2);
% DC OPERATING POINT CALCULATION
MA_DC_1=subs(MA1,[vin vD d],[VIN VD D]);
MA_DC_2=subs(MA2,[vin vD d],[VIN VD D]);

DC_SOL= solve(MA_DC_1==0,MA_DC_2==0,iL,vC);

IL=eval(DC_SOL.iL);    %IL is the inductor current steady
                        state value
VC=eval(DC_SOL.vC);    %VC is the capacitor current steady
                        state value

%LINEARIZATION
% .
% x=Ax+Bu
%vector x=[iL;vC] is assumed. vector x is states.
%u=[vin;d] where vin=input voltage source and d=duty. vector u
is system inputs.
%
A11=subs(simplify(diff(MA1,iL)),[iL vC d vD],[IL VC D VD]);
A12=subs(simplify(diff(MA1,vC)),[iL vC d vD],[IL VC D VD]);

A21=subs(simplify(diff(MA2,iL)),[iL vC d vD],[IL VC D VD]);
A22=subs(simplify(diff(MA2,vC)),[iL vC d vD],[IL VC D VD]);

A=eval([A11 A12;
        A21 A22]);     %variable A is matrix A in state space
                        equation
```

```
B11=subs(simplify(diff(MA1,vin)),[iL vC d vD vin],
[IL VC D VD VIN]);
B12=subs(simplify(diff(MA1,d)),[iL vC d vD vin],
[IL VC D VD VIN]);

B21=subs(simplify(diff(MA2,vin)),[iL vC d vD vin],
[IL VC D VD VIN]);
B22=subs(simplify(diff(MA2,d)),[iL vC d vD vin],
[IL VC D VD VIN]);

B=eval([B11 B12;
        B21 B22]);      % variable B is matrix B in state space
                        equation

CC1=subs(simplify(diff(vO,iL)),[iL vC d vD],[IL VC D VD]);
CC2=subs(simplify(diff(vO,vC)),[iL vC d vD],[IL VC D VD]);
CC=eval([CC1 CC2]);     %variable CC is matrix C in state space
                        equation
                        % variable D shows duty so DD is used.
DD11=subs(simplify(diff(vO,vin)),[iL vC d vD vin],[IL VC D VD VIN]);
DD12=subs(simplify(diff(vO,d)),[iL vC d vD vin],[IL VC D
VD VIN]);

DD=eval([DD11 DD12]); % variable DD is matrix D in state space
                        equation
                        % variable D shows duty so DD is used.
H=tf(ss(A,B,CC,DD));

                        %transfer function between input source and load
                        resistor voltage
                        % ~
```

```
vR_vin=H(1,1)    % vR(s)
                 % ----
                 % ~
                 % vin(s)

                 %transfer function between duty ratio and load
                 resistor voltage
                 %~
vR_d=H(1,2)      %vR(s)
                 %----
                 %~
                 %d(s)
```

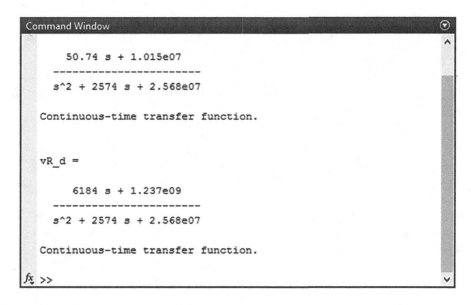

Figure 9-10. Calculated transfer functions

Summary

This chapter introduced state space averaging and its MATLAB implementation. State space averaging is an important tool to extract the small-signal transfer functions of DC-DC converters. Extraction of the small-signal transfer function permits us to design a controller for the converter.

In the next chapter, we will learn how to obtain the input/output impedance of a DC-DC converter.

CHAPTER 10

Input/Output Impedance of DC-DC Converters

In the previous chapter, we learned how to extract the dynamic model of a DC-DC converter operating in CCM mode. In this chapter we will learn how to extract the input/output impedance of a DC-DC converter operating in CCM mode. In this chapter our case studies are Buck-boost and boost converters. Input/output impedance of other types of converters can be extracted in a similar way.

Input and Output Impedances of a Buck-Boost converter

The input impedance of a DC-DC converter is the impedance seen from the input DC source ($Z_{in}(s) = \dfrac{v_G(s)}{i_G(s)}$). The output impedance is defined as the output voltage response of the converter for the excitation of current i_Z at constant input voltage v_G and duty cycle D. In some descriptions, the output impedance includes the load (Z_{o_2} in Figure 10-1); in others, it does

© Farzin Asadi 2022

F. Asadi, *Simulation of Power Electronics Circuits with MATLAB®/Simulink®*,
Maker Innovations Series, https://doi.org/10.1007/978-1-4842-8220-5_10

not (Z_{o_1} in Figure 10-1). According to Figure 10-1, $Z_{o_2}(s) = Z_{o_1}(s) \| R$ and $Z_{o_2}(s) = \dfrac{v_o(s)}{i_z(s)}$. In this book we use the $Z_{o_2}(s)$ definition to calculate the output impedance.

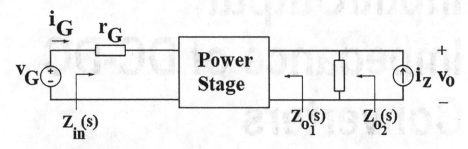

Figure 10-1. *Input impedance and two variants of output impedance of the converter*

Let's calculate the input and output impedances of a Buck-boost converter. Schematic of the Buck-boost converter is shown in Figure 10-2. Values of components are given in Table 10-1.

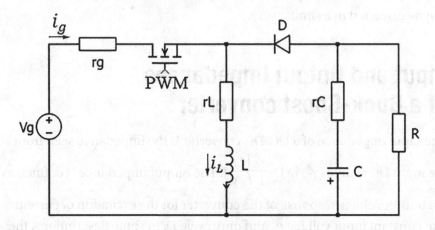

Figure 10-2. *Schematic of the PWM Buck-boost converter*

Table 10-1. *The Buck-boost converter parameters*

	Value
Output voltage, vo	−16 V
Duty ratio, D	0.4
Input DC source voltage, Vg	24 V
Input DC source internal resistance, rg	0.1 Ω
MOSFET drain-source resistance, rds	40 mΩ
Capacitor, C	80 μF
Capacitor ESR, rC	0.05 Ω
Inductor, L	20 μH
Inductor ESR, rL	10 mΩ
Diode voltage drop, vD	0.7 V
Diode forward resistance, rD	10 mΩ
Load resistor, R	5 Ω
Switching frequency, Fsw	100 KHz

When the MOSFET is closed, the diode is reverse biased. Figure 10-3 shows the equivalent circuit of this case.

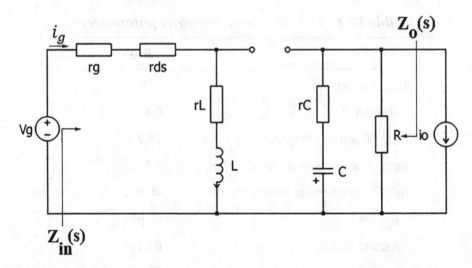

Figure 10-3. *Equivalent circuit of the Buck-boost converter for a closed MOSFET*

The differential equations of Figure 10-3 are

$$\frac{di_L(t)}{dt} = \frac{1}{L}\left(-\left(r_g + r_{ds} + r_L\right)i_L + v_g\right)$$

$$\frac{dv_C(t)}{dt} = \frac{1}{C}\left(\frac{R}{R+r_C}i_o - \frac{1}{R+r_C}v_C\right)$$

$$i_g = i_L$$

$$v_o = \frac{R}{R+r_C}v_C + \frac{R\times r_C}{R+r_C}i_o \qquad (10.1)$$

When the MOSFET is opened, the diode becomes forward biased. Figure 10-4 shows the equivalent circuit of this case.

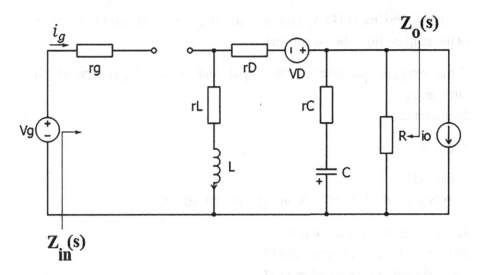

Figure 10-4. *Equivalent circuit of the Buck-boost converter for an open MOSFET*

The differential equations of Figure 10-4 are

$$\frac{di_L(t)}{dt} = \frac{1}{L}\left(-\left(r_D + r_L + \frac{R \times r_C}{R+r_C}\right)i_L - \frac{R}{R+r_C}v_C - \frac{R \times r_C}{R+r_C}i_o - v_D\right)$$

$$\frac{dv_C(t)}{dt} = \frac{1}{C}\left(\frac{R}{R+r_C}i_L - \frac{1}{R+r_C}v_C + \frac{R}{R+r_C}i_o\right)$$

$$i_g = 0$$

$$v_o = \frac{R \times r_C}{R+r_C}i_L + \frac{R}{R+r_C}v_C + \frac{R \times r_C}{R+r_C}i_o + V_D \qquad (10.2)$$

The following MATLAB code extracts the input and output impedances of the studied Buck-boost converter:

```
%This program calculates the input and output impedance of the
Buck-Boost
%converter.

clc

clear all
syms vg rg d rL L rC C R vC iL rds rD vD io

%Converter Dynamical equations
%M1: diL/dt for closed MOSFET.
%M2: dvC/dt for closed MOSFET.
%M3: current of input DC source for closed MOSFET.
%M4: output voltage of converter for closed MOSFET.

%M5: diL/dt for open MOSFET.
%M6: dvC/dt for open MOSFET.
%M7: current of input DC source for open MOSFET.
%M8: output voltage of converter for open MOSFET.

M1=(-(rg+rds+rL)*iL+vg)/L;
M2=(R/(R+rC)*io-vC/(R+rC))/C;
M3=iL;
M4=R*rC/(R+rC)*io+R/(R+rC)*vC;

M5=(-(rL+rD+rC*R/(R+rC))*iL-R/(R+rC)*vC-R*rC/(R+rC)*io-vD)/L;
M6=(R/(R+rC)*iL-1/(R+rC)*vC+R/(R+rC)*io)/C;
M7=0;
M8=rC*R/(rC+R)*iL+R/(R+rC)*vC+R*rC/(R+rC)*io+vD;

%Averaged Equations
diL_dt_ave=simplify(M1*d+M5*(1-d));
dvC_dt_ave=simplify(M2*d+M6*(1-d));
```

```
ig_ave=simplify(M3*d+M7*(1-d));
vo_ave=simplify(M4*d+M8*(1-d));

%DC Operating Point
DC=solve(diL_dt_ave==0,dvC_dt_ave==0,iL,vC);
IL=DC.iL;
VC=DC.vC;

%Linearization
A11=simplify(subs(diff(diL_dt_ave,iL),[iL vC io],[IL VC 0]));
A12=simplify(subs(diff(diL_dt_ave,vC),[iL vC io],[IL VC 0]));
A21=simplify(subs(diff(dvC_dt_ave,iL),[iL vC io],[IL VC 0]));
A22=simplify(subs(diff(dvC_dt_ave,vC),[iL vC io],[IL VC 0]));
AA=[A11 A12;A21 A22];

B11=simplify(subs(diff(diL_dt_ave,io),[iL vC io],[IL VC 0]));
B12=simplify(subs(diff(diL_dt_ave,vg),[iL vC io],[IL VC 0]));
B13=simplify(subs(diff(diL_dt_ave,d),[iL vC io],[IL VC 0]));

B21=simplify(subs(diff(dvC_dt_ave,io),[iL vC io],[IL VC 0]));
B22=simplify(subs(diff(dvC_dt_ave,vg),[iL vC io],[IL VC 0]));
B23=simplify(subs(diff(dvC_dt_ave,d),[iL vC io],[IL VC 0]));

BB=[B11 B12 B13;B21 B22 B23];


C11=simplify(subs(diff(ig_ave,iL),[iL vC io],[IL VC 0]));
C12=simplify(subs(diff(ig_ave,vC),[iL vC io],[IL VC 0]));

C21=simplify(subs(diff(vo_ave,iL),[iL vC io],[IL VC 0]));
C22=simplify(subs(diff(vo_ave,vC),[iL vC io],[IL VC 0]));
CC=[C11 C12; C21 C22];

D11=simplify(subs(diff(ig_ave,io),[iL vC io],[IL VC 0 ]));
D12=simplify(subs(diff(ig_ave,vg),[iL vC io],[IL VC 0]));
D13=simplify(subs(diff(ig_ave,d),[iL vC io],[IL VC 0]));
```

```
D21=simplify(subs(diff(vo_ave,io),[iL vC io],[IL VC 0 ]));
D22=simplify(subs(diff(vo_ave,vg),[iL vC io],[IL VC 0]));
D23=simplify(subs(diff(vo_ave,d),[iL vC io],[IL VC 0]));
DD=[D11 D12 D13;D21 D22 D23];

%Components Values
%Variables have underline are used to store the numeric values
of components
%Variables without underline are symbolic variables.
%for example:
%L: symbolic vvariable shows the inductor inductance
%L_: numeric variable  shows the inductor inductance value.
L_=20e-6;
rL_=.01;
C_=80e-6;
rC_=.05;
rds_=.04;
rD_=.01;
VD_=.7;
D_=.4;
VG_=24;
rg_=.1;
R_=5;

AA_=eval(subs(AA,[vg rg rds rD vD rL L rC C R d io],[VG_ rg_
rds_ rD_ VD_ rL_ L_ rC_ C_ R_ D_ 0]));
BB_=eval(subs(BB,[vg rg rds rD vD rL L rC C R d io],[VG_ rg_
rds_ rD_ VD_ rL_ L_ rC_ C_ R_ D_ 0]));
CC_=eval(subs(CC,[vg rg rds rD vD rL L rC C R d io],[VG_ rg_
rds_ rD_ VD_ rL_ L_ rC_ C_ R_ D_ 0]));
DD_=eval(subs(DD,[vg rg rds rD vD rL L rC C R d io],[VG_ rg_
rds_ rD_ VD_ rL_ L_ rC_ C_ R_ D_ 0]));
```

470

```
sys=ss(AA_,BB_,CC_,DD_);
sys.stateName={'iL','vC'};
sys.inputname={'io','vg','d'};
sys.outputname={'ig','vo'};

ig_io=sys(1,1);
ig_vg=sys(1,2);
ig_d=sys(1,3);

vo_io=sys(2,1);
vo_vg=sys(2,2);
vo_d=sys(2,3);

Zin=1/ig_vg; %input impedance
Zout=vo_io;  %output impedance

%Draws the bode diagram of input/output impedance
figure(1)
bode(Zin), grid minor

figure(2)
bode(Zout), grid minor

%Display the DC operating point of converter
disp('steady state operating point of converter')
disp('IL')
disp(eval(subs(IL,[vg rg rds rD vD rL L rC C R d io],[VG_ rg_
rds_ rD_ VD_ rL_ L_ rC_ C_ R_ D_ 0])));
disp('VC')
disp(eval(subs(VC,[vg rg rds rD vD rL L rC C R d io],[VG_ rg_
rds_ rD_ VD_ rL_ L_ rC_ C_ R_ D_ 0])));
```

The program gives the following results:

$$\frac{v_o(s)}{d(s)} = -0.94123 \frac{\left(s + 1.267 \times 10^5\right)\left(s - 1.168 \times 10^5\right)}{s^2 + 7560s + 2.332 \times 10^8}$$

$$Z_{in}(s) = \frac{v_g(s)}{i_g(s)} = 0.000125 \frac{s^2 + 7560s + 2.332 \times 10^8}{s + 2475}$$

$$Z_o(s) = \frac{v_o(s)}{i_o(s)} = 0.049505 \frac{\left(s + 2.5 \times 10^5\right)\left(s + 4194\right)}{s^2 + 7560s + 2.332 \times 10^8} \tag{10.3}$$

Bode diagrams of open-loop input impedance and open-loop output impedance are shown in Figures 10-5 and 10-6, respectively. Note that we calculated the open-loop impedances. Negative feedback can decrease the output impedance of the converter. The relation between the open-loop output impedance ($Z_{O,\,OL}$) and closed-loop output impedance ($Z_{O,\,CL}$) is

$$Z_{O,CL} = \frac{Z_{O,OL}}{1 + K_L}$$ where K_L is the loop gain.

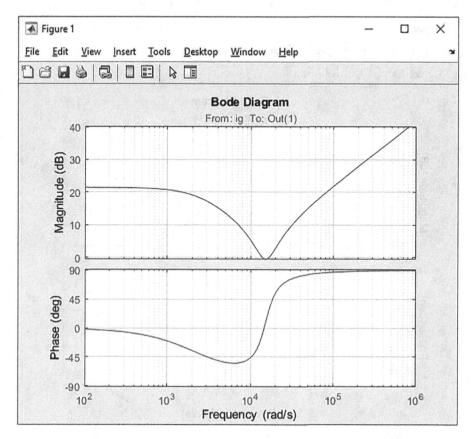

Figure 10-5. *Open-loop input impedance of the Buck-boost converter*

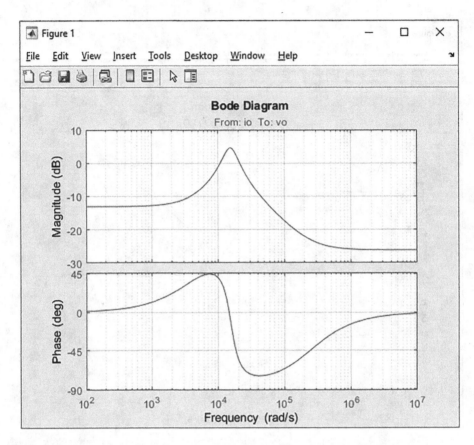

Figure 10-6. *Open-loop output impedance of the Buck-boost converter*

Input and Output Impedances of the Boost Converter

Let's study the open-loop input/output impedance of the boost converter. Schematic of the boost converter is shown in Figure 10-7. Values of components are given in Table 10-2.

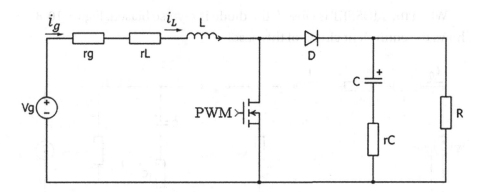

Figure 10-7. *Schematic of the PWM boost converter*

Table 10-2. *The boost converter parameters*

	Value
Output voltage, vo	30 V
Duty ratio, D	0.6
Input DC source voltage, Vg	12 V
Input DC source internal resistance, rg	0.1 Ω
MOSFET drain-source resistance, rds	40 mΩ
Capacitor, C	100 µF
Capacitor ESR, rC	0.05 Ω
Inductor, L	120 µH
Inductor ESR, rL	10 mΩ
Diode voltage drop, vD	0.7 V
Diode forward resistance, rD	10 mΩ
Load resistor, R	50 Ω
Switching frequency, Fsw	25 KHz

When the MOSFET is closed, the diode is reverse biased. Figure 10-8 shows the equivalent circuit of this case.

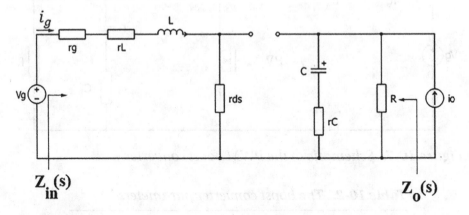

Figure 10-8. *Equivalent circuit of the boost converter for a closed MOSFET*

The differential equations of Figure 10-8 are

$$\frac{di_L(t)}{dt} = \frac{1}{L}\left(-\left(r_g + r_{ds} + r_L\right)i_L + v_g\right)$$

$$\frac{dv_C(t)}{dt} = \frac{1}{C}\left(-\frac{1}{R+r_C}v_C + \frac{R}{R+r_C}i_o\right)$$

$$i_g = i_L$$

$$v_o = \frac{R}{R+r_C}v_C + \frac{R \times r_C}{R+r_C}i_o \tag{10.4}$$

When the MOSFET is opened, the diode becomes forward biased. Figure 10-9 shows the equivalent circuit of this case.

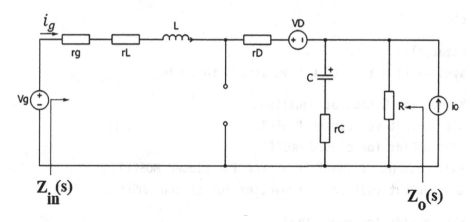

Figure 10-9. *Equivalent circuit of the boost converter for an open MOSFET*

The differential equations of Figure 10-9 are

$$\frac{di_L(t)}{dt} = \frac{1}{L}\left(-\left(r_g + r_L + r_D + \frac{R \times r_C}{R+r_C}\right)i_L - \frac{R}{R+r_C}v_C - \frac{R \times r_C}{R+r_C}i_o + v_g - v_D\right)$$

$$\frac{dv_C(t)}{dt} = \frac{1}{C}\left(\frac{R}{R+r_C}i_L - \frac{1}{R+r_C}v_C + \frac{R}{R+r_C}i_o\right)$$

$$i_g = i_L$$

$$v_o = \frac{R \times r_C}{R+r_C}i_L + \frac{R}{R+r_C}v_C + \frac{R \times r_C}{R+r_C}i_o \qquad (10.5)$$

The following MATLAB code extracts the input and output impedances of the studied boost converter:

```
%This program calculates the input and output impedance of
the Boost
%converter.
```

```
clc

clear all
syms vg rg d rL L rC C R vC iL rds rD vD io

%Converter Dynamical equations
%M1: diL/dt for closed MOSFET.
%M2: dvC/dt for closed MOSFET.
%M3: current of input DC source for closed MOSFET.
%M4: output voltage of converter for closed MOSFET.

%M5: diL/dt for open MOSFET.
%M6: dvC/dt for open MOSFET.
%M7: current of input DC source for open MOSFET.
%M8: output voltage of converter for open MOSFET.

M1=(-(rg+rL+rds)*iL+vg)/L;
M2=(-vC/(R+rC)+R/(R+rC)*io)/C;
M3=iL;
M4=R/(R+rC)*vC+R*rC/(R+rC)*io;

M5=(-(rg+rL+rD+R*rC/(R+rC))*iL-R/(R+rC)*vC-R*rC/
(R+rC)*io+vg-vD)/L;
M6=((R/(R+rC))*iL-vC/(R+rC)+R/(R+rC)*io)/C;
M7=iL;
M8=R*rC/(R+rC)*iL-R/(R+rC)*vC+R*rC/(R+rC)*io;

%Averaged Equations
diL_dt_ave=simplify(M1*d+M5*(1-d));
dvC_dt_ave=simplify(M2*d+M6*(1-d));
ig_ave=simplify(M3*d+M7*(1-d));
vo_ave=simplify(M4*d+M8*(1-d));

%DC Operating Point
DC=solve(diL_dt_ave==0,dvC_dt_ave==0,iL,vC);
```

```
IL=DC.iL;
VC=DC.vC;

%Linearization
A11=simplify(subs(diff(diL_dt_ave,iL),[iL vC io],[IL VC 0]));
A12=simplify(subs(diff(diL_dt_ave,vC),[iL vC io],[IL VC 0]));
A21=simplify(subs(diff(dvC_dt_ave,iL),[iL vC io],[IL VC 0]));
A22=simplify(subs(diff(dvC_dt_ave,vC),[iL vC io],[IL VC 0]));
AA=[A11 A12;A21 A22];

B11=simplify(subs(diff(diL_dt_ave,io),[iL vC io],[IL VC 0]));
B12=simplify(subs(diff(diL_dt_ave,vg),[iL vC io],[IL VC 0]));
B13=simplify(subs(diff(diL_dt_ave,d),[iL vC io],[IL VC 0]));

B21=simplify(subs(diff(dvC_dt_ave,io),[iL vC io],[IL VC 0]));
B22=simplify(subs(diff(dvC_dt_ave,vg),[iL vC io],[IL VC 0]));
B23=simplify(subs(diff(dvC_dt_ave,d),[iL vC io],[IL VC 0]));

BB=[B11 B12 B13;B21 B22 B23];

C11=simplify(subs(diff(ig_ave,iL),[iL vC io],[IL VC 0]));
C12=simplify(subs(diff(ig_ave,vC),[iL vC io],[IL VC 0]));

C21=simplify(subs(diff(vo_ave,iL),[iL vC io],[IL VC 0]));
C22=simplify(subs(diff(vo_ave,vC),[iL vC io],[IL VC 0]));
CC=[C11 C12; C21 C22];

D11=simplify(subs(diff(ig_ave,io),[iL vC io],[IL VC 0 ]));
D12=simplify(subs(diff(ig_ave,vg),[iL vC io],[IL VC 0]));
D13=simplify(subs(diff(ig_ave,d),[iL vC io],[IL VC 0]));

D21=simplify(subs(diff(vo_ave,io),[iL vC io],[IL VC 0 ]));
D22=simplify(subs(diff(vo_ave,vg),[iL vC io],[IL VC 0]));
D23=simplify(subs(diff(vo_ave,d),[iL vC io],[IL VC 0]));
DD=[D11 D12 D13;D21 D22 D23];
```

```
%Components Values
%Variables have underline are used to store the numeric values
of components
%Variables without underline are symbolic variables.
%for example:
%L: symbolic vvariable shows the inductor inductance
%L_: numeric variable  shows the inductor inductance value.
L_=120e-6;
rL_=.01;
C_=100e-6;
rC_=.05;
rds_=.04;
rD_=.01;
VD_=.7;
D_=.6;
VG_=12;
rg_=.1;
R_=50;

AA_=eval(subs(AA,[vg rg rds rD vD rL L rC C R d io],
[VG_ rg_ rds_ rD_ VD_ rL_ L_ rC_ C_ R_ D_ 0]));
BB_=eval(subs(BB,[vg rg rds rD vD rL L rC C R d io],
[VG_ rg_ rds_ rD_ VD_ rL_ L_ rC_ C_ R_ D_ 0]));
CC_=eval(subs(CC,[vg rg rds rD vD rL L rC C R d io],
[VG_ rg_ rds_ rD_ VD_ rL_ L_ rC_ C_ R_ D_ 0]));
DD_=eval(subs(DD,[vg rg rds rD vD rL L rC C R d io],
[VG_ rg_ rds_ rD_ VD_ rL_ L_ rC_ C_ R_ D_ 0]));

sys=ss(AA_,BB_,CC_,DD_);
sys.stateName={'iL','vC'};
sys.inputname={'io','vg','d'};
sys.outputname={'ig','vo'};
```

```
ig_io=sys(1,1);
ig_vg=sys(1,2);
ig_d=sys(1,3);

vo_io=sys(2,1);
vo_vg=sys(2,2);
vo_d=sys(2,3);

Zin=1/ig_vg; %input impedance
Zout=vo_io;  %output impedance

%Draws the bode diagram of input/output impedance
figure(1)
bode(Zin), grid minor

figure(2)
bode(Zout), grid minor

%Display the DC operating point of converter
disp('steady state operating point of converter')
disp('IL')
disp(eval(subs(IL,[vg rg rds rD vD rL L rC C R d io],
[VG_ rg_ rds_ rD_ VD_ rL_ L_ rC_ C_ R_ D_ 0])));
disp('VC')
disp(eval(subs(VC,[vg rg rds rD vD rL L rC C R d io],
[VG_ rg_ rds_ rD_ VD_ rL_ L_ rC_ C_ R_ D_ 0])));
```

The program gives the following results:

$$\frac{v_o(s)}{d(s)} = -0.007199 \frac{\left(s + 2 \times 10^6\right)\left(s - 6.703 \times 10^4\right)}{s^2 + 1367s + 1.356 \times 10^7}$$

$$Z_{in}(s) = \frac{v_g(s)}{i_g(s)} = 0.00012 \frac{s^2 + 1367s + 1.356 \times 10^7}{s + 200}$$

$$Z_o(s) = \frac{v_o(s)}{i_o(s)} = 0.049995 \frac{(s + 2 \times 10^6)(s + 1160)}{s^2 + 1367s + 1.356 \times 10^7} \tag{10.6}$$

Bode diagrams for open-loop input impedance and open-loop output impedance are shown in Figures 10-10 and 10-11, respectively.

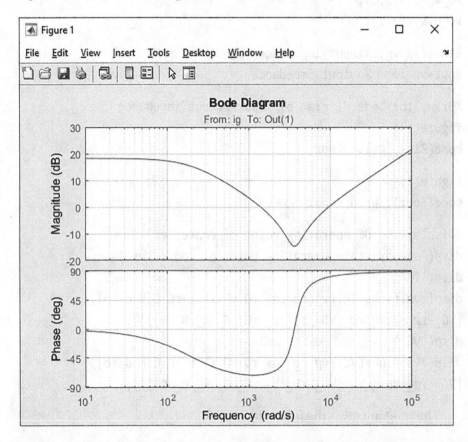

Figure 10-10. *Open-loop input impedance of the boost converter*

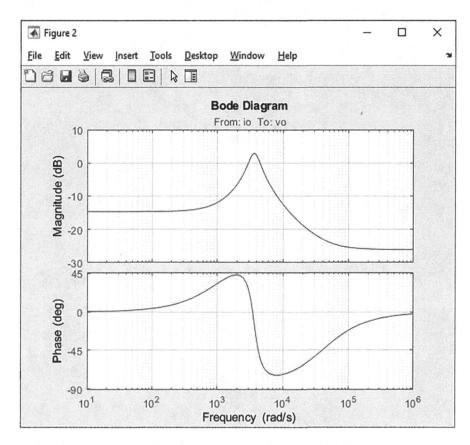

Figure 10-11. *Open-loop output impedance of the boost converter*

Summary

Input and output impedances of DC-DC converters are important especially when you want to cascade two or more converters. In this chapter we learned how to extract the input/output impedance of DC-DC converters with the aid of SSA.

The next chapter reviews some of the important theoretical concepts used in the previous chapters.

CHAPTER 11

Review of Some of the Important Theoretical Concepts

In the previous chapters, we learned how to simulate a power electronic circuit in the MATLAB/Simulink environment. In this chapter we will review some of the important theoretical concepts used in the book.

Instantaneous Power

The instantaneous power of a device ($p(t)$) is defined as

$$p(t) = v(t) \times i(t) \tag{11.1}$$

where $v(t)$ is the voltage across the device and $i(t)$ is the current through the device. The instantaneous power is generally a time-varying quantity. If the passive sign convention illustrated in Figure 11-1 is observed, the device is absorbing power if $p(t)$ is positive at a specified value of time t. The device is supplying power if $p(t)$ is negative.

© Farzin Asadi 2022
F. Asadi, *Simulation of Power Electronics Circuits with MATLAB®/Simulink®*,
Maker Innovations Series, https://doi.org/10.1007/978-1-4842-8220-5_11

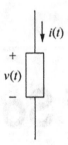

Figure 11-1. *Passive sign convention: p(t) > 0 indicates power is being absorbed*

For instance, consider the simple circuit shown in Figure 11-2. In this circuit, $v_{in}(t) = 311\,sin\,(377t)$ and $R = 50\,\Omega$.

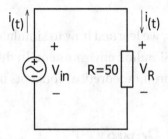

Figure 11-2. *A simple resistive circuit*

According to Ohm's law, $i(t) = \dfrac{v_{in}(t)}{R} = 6.22sin(377t)$, and instantaneous power for resistor R is

$$p_R(t) = 311sin(377t) \times 6.22sin(377t) = 2345sin(377t)^2. \qquad (11.2)$$

The obtained result is positive for all the times, that is, $\forall t,\ sin\,(377t)^2 > 0$. This is expected since the resistor dissipates power.

The instantaneous power of an AC source can be calculated with the aid of Figure 11-3.

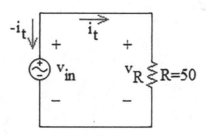

Figure 11-3. *Calculation of instantaneous power of input AC source*

The instantaneous power of an AC source is

$$p_{V_{in}}(t) = 311sin(377t) \times -6.22sin(377t) = -2345\,sin(377t)^2 \qquad (11.3)$$

The obtained result is negative for all the time instants. This is expected since the AC source supplies the power into the load. For instance, at $t = 12\ ms$, $p_{V_{in}}(t) = -2.263\ kW$ and $p_R(t) = +2.263\ kW$. This means that at $t = 12\ ms$, the AC source supplies 2.263 kW and the resistor absorbs 2.263 kW. Figure 11-4 shows the instantaneous power waveforms on the same graph.

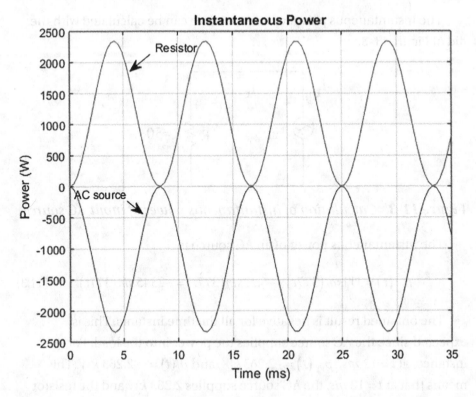

Figure 11-4. *Graph of instantaneous power for input AC source and load resistor*

Average Power

Function $f(t)$ is periodic if

$$\exists T > 0, \forall t \ f\left(t + T\right) = f\left(t\right) \tag{11.4}$$

T is called the period. For instance, $f(t) = sin\ (t)$ is periodic since $f(t + 2\pi) = f(t)$.

If device voltage ($v(t)$) and current ($i(t)$) are periodic, that is, $v(t) = v(t + T)$ and $i(t) = i(t + T)$, then the instantaneous power will be periodic since

488

$$p(t) = v(t) \times i(t)$$

$$p(t+T) = v(t+T) \times i(t+T) = v(t) \times i(t) = p(t) \qquad (11.5)$$

The average power for such a periodic waveform is defined as

$$P = \frac{1}{T} \int_{t_0}^{t_0+T} p(t) dt = \frac{1}{T} \int_{t_0}^{t_0+T} v(t) \times i(t) dt \qquad (11.6)$$

Assume that $v(t)$ is a constant function, that is, $v(t) = V_{dc}$. In this case the average power can be calculated by

$$P = \frac{1}{T} \int_{t_0}^{t_0+T} v(t) \times i(t) dt = \frac{1}{T} \int_{t_0}^{t_0+T} V_{dc} \times i(t) dt = V_{dc} \left[\frac{1}{T} \int_{t_0}^{t_0+T} i(t) dt \right] = V_{dc} I_{avg} \quad (11.7)$$

The average power for constant $i(t)$, that is, $i(t) = I_{dc}$, can be found in the same way:

$$P = \frac{1}{T} \int_{t_0}^{t_0+T} v(t) \times i(t) dt = \frac{1}{T} \int_{t_0}^{t_0+T} v(t) \times I_{dc} dt = I_{dc} \left[\frac{1}{T} \int_{t_0}^{t_0+T} v(t) dt \right] = I_{dc} V_{avg} \quad (11.8)$$

Effective Value of a Signal

Consider the simple circuit shown in Figure 11-5. The input source is a periodic voltage source, that is, $v(t + T) = v(t)$. The load is purely resistive.

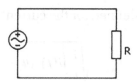

Figure 11-5. *A resistor is connected to a periodic voltage source*

The average power consumed by the resistor is

$$P = \frac{1}{T}\int_0^T p(t)\,dt = \frac{1}{T}\int_0^T v(t) \times i(t)\,dt = \frac{1}{T}\int_0^T \frac{v(t)^2}{R}\,dt = \frac{1}{R}\left[\frac{1}{T}\int_0^T v(t)^2\,dt\right] \quad (11.9)$$

Now consider the circuit shown in Figure 11-6. The input source is a constant DC voltage source, that is, $v(t) = V_{dc}$.

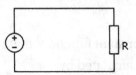

Figure 11-6. *The same resistor (as the one in Figure 11-5) is connected to a DC source*

In this case the power consumed by the resistor is $\dfrac{V_{dc}^{\ 2}}{R}$. Power

consumption of both circuits is the same when $V_{dc} = \sqrt{\dfrac{1}{T}\int_0^T v(t)^2\,dt}$. Since

$$\frac{1}{R}\left[\frac{1}{T}\int_0^T v(t)^2\,dt\right] = \frac{V_{dc}^{\ 2}}{R} \Rightarrow V_{dc} = \sqrt{\frac{1}{T}\int_0^T v(t)^2\,dt} \quad (11.10)$$

the $\sqrt{\dfrac{1}{T}\int_0^T v(t)^2\,dt}$ is called the Root Mean Square (RMS) or effective value of a signal $v(t)$. So the RMS value of a periodic signal $v(t)$ is a DC value, which produces the same amount of heat in the resistive load as the periodic signal $v(t)$.

The RMS value can be defined for the current waveforms as well:

$$I_{rms} = \sqrt{\frac{1}{T}\int_0^T i(t)^2\,dt} \quad (11.11)$$

Example 11.1

Determine the RMS value of the periodic pulse waveform shown in Figure 11-7.

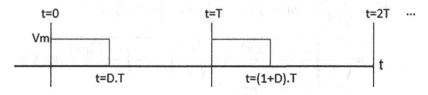

Figure 11-7. *Waveform of Example 11.1*

Solution

$$v(t) = \begin{cases} V_m & 0 < t < DT \\ 0 & DT < t < T \end{cases}$$

$$V_{rms} = \sqrt{\frac{1}{T} \int_0^T v(t)^2 \, dt} = \sqrt{\frac{1}{T} \left(\int_0^{DT} V_m^2 \, dt + \int_{DT}^T 0 \, dt \right)} = \sqrt{\frac{1}{T} \left(V_m^2 DT \right)} = V_m \sqrt{D}$$

Example 11.2

Determine the RMS values of the following waveforms $\left(\omega = \dfrac{2\pi}{T} \right)$:

a) $v(t) = V_m \sin(\omega t)$.

b) $v(t) = |V_m \sin(\omega t)|$.

c) $v(t) = \begin{cases} V_m \sin(\omega t) & 0 < t < \dfrac{T}{2} \\ 0 & \dfrac{T}{2} < t < T \end{cases}$

Solution

a)

$$V_{rms} = \sqrt{\frac{1}{T}\int_0^T \left(V_m sin\left(\omega t\right)\right)^2 dt} = \sqrt{\frac{1}{T}\times V_m^2 \int_0^T sin\left(\omega t\right)^2 dt}$$

$$= \sqrt{\frac{V_m^2}{T}\int_0^T \frac{1-cos\left(2\omega t\right)}{2}dt} = \sqrt{\frac{V_m^2}{T}\int_0^T \frac{1}{2}dt - \int_0^T \frac{cos\left(2\omega t\right)}{2}dt}$$

$$= \sqrt{\frac{V_m^2}{T}\times\frac{T}{2}-0} = \sqrt{\frac{V_m^2}{2}} = \frac{V_m}{\sqrt{2}}$$

b) The RMS value of $v(t) = |V_m\ sin\ (\omega t)|$ is the same as $v(t) = V_m\ sin\ (\omega t)$. Since $(|V_m sin\ (\omega t)\ |)^2 = (V_m sin\ (\omega t)\ )^2$, so the RMS value of $v(t) = |V_m\ sin\ (\omega t)|$ is $\frac{V_m}{\sqrt{2}}$. Graph of $v(t) = |V_m\ sin\ (\omega t)|$ is shown in Figure 11-8. Such a waveform is called full-wave rectified in power electronics.

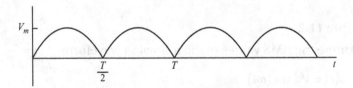

Figure 11-8. *Full-wave rectified sinusoidal waveform*

c) Graph of $v(t) = \begin{cases} V_m sin\left(\omega t\right) & 0<t<\dfrac{T}{2} \\ 0 & \dfrac{T}{2}<t<T \end{cases}$ is shown in Figure 11-9. Such a waveform is called half-wave rectified in power electronics.

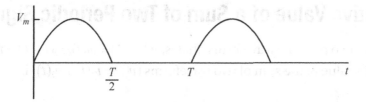

Figure 11-9. *Half-wave rectified sinusoidal waveform*

$$V_{rms} = \sqrt{\frac{1}{T}\left(\int_0^{\frac{T}{2}}\left(V_m sin\left(\omega t\right)\right)^2 dt + \int_{\frac{T}{2}}^{T} 0dt\right)} = \sqrt{\frac{1}{T}\times V_m^{\ 2}\int_0^{\frac{T}{2}}sin\left(\omega t\right)^2 dt}$$

$$= \sqrt{\frac{V_m^{\ 2}}{T}\int_0^{\frac{T}{2}}\frac{1-cos\left(2\omega t\right)}{2}dt} = \sqrt{\frac{V_m^{\ 2}}{T}\int_0^{\frac{T}{2}}\frac{1}{2}dt - \int_0^{\frac{T}{2}}\frac{cos\left(2\omega t\right)}{2}dt}$$

$$= \sqrt{\frac{V_m^{\ 2}}{T}\times\frac{T}{4}-0} = \sqrt{\frac{V_m^{\ 2}}{4}} = \frac{V_m}{2}$$

The RMS value of triangular wave shapes can be calculated using the formulas shown in Figure 11-10.

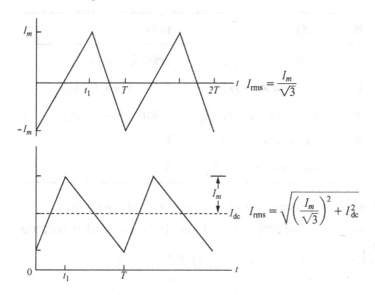

Figure 11-10. *RMS values of triangular waveforms*

Effective Value of a Sum of Two Periodic Signals

Consider two periodic waveforms, that is, $v_1(t + T) = v_1(t)$, $v_2(t + T) = v_2(t)$. The RMS value of the sum of two waveforms $(v(t) = v_1(t) + v_2(t))$ is

$$V_{rms}^{2} = \frac{1}{T}\int_0^T (v_1 + v_2)^2 \, dt = \frac{1}{T}\int_0^T (v_1^2 + 2v_1v_2 + v_2^2) \, dt$$

$$= \frac{1}{T}\int_0^T v_1^2 \, dt + \frac{1}{T}\int_0^T 2v_1v_2 \, dt + \frac{1}{T}\int_0^T v_2^2 \, dt \qquad (11.12)$$

Sometimes the $\frac{1}{T}\int_0^T v_1(t)v_2(t)\,dt$ term is zero. The $\frac{1}{T}\int_0^T v_1(t)v_2(t)\,dt$ is

the iner product of $v_1(t)$ and $v_2(t)$. When $\frac{1}{T}\int_0^T v_1(t)v_2(t)\,dt = 0$, the signals

$v_1(t)$ and $v_2(t)$ are called orthogonal. Table 11-1 shows some of the important orthogonal functions.

Table 11-1. *Some of the important orthogonal functions ($\omega = \frac{2\pi}{T}$, $n \neq m$, and k is a constant)*

No.	$v_1(t)$	$v_2(t)$
1	$sin(n \times \omega \times t + \varphi_1)$	$sin(m \times \omega \times t + \varphi_2)$
2	$sin(n \times \omega \times t + \varphi_1)$	$cos(m \times \omega \times t + \varphi_2)$
3	$cos(n \times \omega \times t + \varphi_1)$	$cos(m \times \omega \times t + \varphi_2)$
4	$sin(n \times \omega \times t + \varphi_1)$	k
5	$cos(m \times \omega \times t + \varphi_1)$	k

For instance, according to the second row of the table, $sin(n \times \omega \times t + \varphi_1)$ and $cos(m \times \omega \times t + \varphi_2)$ (when $n \neq m$) are orthogonal since $\frac{1}{T}\int_0^T sin(n\omega t + \varphi_1) \times cos(m\omega t + \varphi_2)\,dt = 0$.

The RMS value of two orthogonal functions $v_1(t)$ and $v_2(t)$ can be calculated with the aid of the following formula:

$$V_{rms}^2 = \frac{1}{T}\int_0^T (v_1 + v_2)^2\, dt = \frac{1}{T}\int_0^T (v_1^2 + 2v_1v_2 + v_2^2)\, dt$$

$$V_{rms}^2 = \frac{1}{T}\int_0^T v_1^2\, dt + \frac{1}{T}\int_0^T 2v_1v_2\, dt + \frac{1}{T}\int_0^T v_2^2\, dt$$

$$V_{rms}^2 = \frac{1}{T}\int_0^T v_1^2\, dt + \frac{1}{T}\int_0^T v_2^2\, dt$$

$$V_{rms} = \sqrt{V_{1,rms}^2 + V_{2,rms}^2} \qquad (11.13)$$

The RMS value of the sum of more than two orthogonal functions (each two terms are assumed to be orthogonal) can be calculated in the same way:

$$\left(v(t) = \sum_{n=1}^{N} v_n(t)\, \forall k, l\, 1 \le k \le N, 1 \le l \le N, k \ne l, \frac{1}{T}\int_0^T v_k(t)v_l(t)\, dt = 0 \right) \Rightarrow$$

$$V_{rms} = \sqrt{V_{1,rms}^2 + V_{2,rms}^2 + V_{3,rms}^2 + \dots} = \sqrt{\sum_{n=1}^{N} V_{n,rms}^2} \qquad (11.14)$$

Example 11.3

Determine the RMS value of $v(t) = 4 + 8\sin(\omega_1 t + 10°) + 5\sin(\omega_2 t + 50°)$ under the following conditions:

a) $\omega_2 = 2\omega_1$

b) $\omega_2 = \omega_1$

Solution:

a) When $\omega_2 = 2\omega_1$, the $v(t) = 4 + 8 \sin (\omega_1 t + 10°) + 5 \sin (2\omega_1 t + 50°)$. According to Table 11-1, all the functions are orthogonal to each other, so

$$V_{rms} = \sqrt{V_{1,rms}^2 + V_{2,rms}^2 + V_{3,rms}^2} = \sqrt{4^2 + \left(\frac{8}{\sqrt{2}}\right)^2 + \left(\frac{5}{\sqrt{2}}\right)^2} = 7.78\,V$$

b) When $\omega_2 = \omega_1$, the $v(t) = 4 + 8 \sin (\omega_1 t + 10°) + 5 \sin (\omega_1 t + 50°)$. $8 \sin (\omega_1 t + 10°)$ and $5 \sin (\omega_1 t + 50°)$ are not orthogonal to each other. So we can't use the previous formulas. Note

that $a \times sin(\omega t) + b \times cos(\omega t) = \sqrt{a^2 + b^2} \sin\left(\omega t + tan^{-1}\left(\frac{b}{a}\right)\right)$. So

$$v(t) = 4 + 8sin(\omega_1 t + 10°) + 5sin(\omega_1 t + 50°)$$

$$= 4 + 12.3sin(\omega_1 t + 25.2°)$$

The two terms of the last equation are orthogonal to each other (see Table 11-1). So the RMS value is

$$V_{rms} = \sqrt{4^2 + \left(\frac{12.3}{\sqrt{2}}\right)^2} = 9.57\,V$$

Example 11.4

In this example we show how RMS values can be calculated with the aid of MATLAB. Assume

$v(t) = 311 \sin (2\pi \times 60t) + 100 \sin (2\pi \times 2 \times 60t) + 20 \sin (2\pi \times 3 \times 60t)$ is given. The RMS value can be calculated easily:

$$V_{rms} = \sqrt{\left(\frac{311}{\sqrt{2}}\right)^2 + \left(\frac{100}{\sqrt{2}}\right)^2 + \left(\frac{20}{\sqrt{2}}\right)^2} = 231.43\,V$$

The commands shown in Figure 11-11 calculate the RMS value of a given signal. The first two lines sample a period of a given signal. The sampling time is $\dfrac{1}{6000} = 166.7\,\mu s$. The rms command is used to calculate the RMS value of a sampled signal.

```
Command Window                                                    ⊙
>> t=0:1/6000:1/60;
>> v=311*sin(2*pi*60*t)+100*sin(2*pi*2*60*t)+20*sin(2*pi*3*60*t);
>> rms(v)

ans =

 230.2829

fx >> |
```

Figure 11-11. *Calculation of the RMS value of*
v(t) = 311 sin (2π × 60t) + 100 sin (2π × 2 × 60t) + 20 sin (2π × 3 × 60t)
with $\dfrac{1}{6000}$ *steps*

The result is 230.283, which is a little bit lower than the expected value of 231.43. If you decrease the sampling time from 166.7μs to 16.67μs, you get a more accurate result (Figure 11-12).

```
Command Window                                                    ⊙
  >> t=0:1/60000:1/60;
  >> v=311*sin(2*pi*60*t)+100*sin(2*pi*2*60*t)+20*sin(2*pi*3*60*t);
  >> rms(v)

  ans =

     231.3158

fx >> |
```

Figure 11-12. *Calculation of the RMS value of*
$v(t) = 311 \sin (2\pi \times 60t) + 100 \sin (2\pi \times 2 \times 60t) + 20 \sin (2\pi \times 3 \times 60t)$
with $\dfrac{1}{60000}$ *steps*

Measurement of RMS Values of Signals

The cheap multimeters are not suitable devices to measure the RMS value
of signals inside power electronic converters. The cheap multimeters are
able to measure the RMS value of pure sinusoidal signals, that is, the one
shown in Figure 11-13.

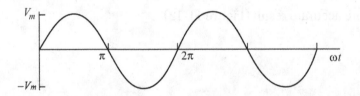

Figure 11-13. *Pure sinusoidal waveform*

Figure 11-14 shows one of the methods that the cheap multimeter
measures the RMS value of a signal. V_X is the signal under measurement.
Assume that V_X is a pure sinusoidal waveform, that is, a signal such as
the one shown in Figure 11-13. Then the capacitor is charged up to Vm
volts (voltage drop of diode is neglected) where Vm is the peak value of

voltage under measurement. So the analog-to-digital converter reads the maximum of input signal. The read value is simply multiplied by $\dfrac{1}{\sqrt{2}}$, and the result, that is, $\dfrac{Vm}{\sqrt{2}}$, is the RMS value of the input signal. This method only works for pure sinusoidal signals and doesn't produce a correct result if the input signal is not pure sinusoidal.

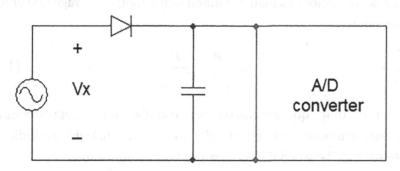

Figure 11-14. *A simple circuit for detection of input AC signal peak value*

The expensive multimeters sample the input waveform and use a processor to calculate the RMS value. So the wave shape of the input signal doesn't affect the measurements. Such a multimeter has "TRUE RMS" label on it. So ensure that your multimeter is TRUE RMS type if you want to measure the RMS value of a signal of a power electronic converter. Digital oscilloscopes can be used to measure the RMS value of signals as well.

Apparent Power and Power Factor

Apparent power (S) is the product of the RMS value of voltage and RMS value of current magnitudes:

$$S = V_{rms} \times I_{rms} \tag{11.15}$$

The power factor of a load is defined as the ratio of average power to apparent power:

$$pf = \frac{P}{S} = \frac{P}{V_{rms} I_{rms}} \tag{11.16}$$

The preceding equation can be used to analyze both linear circuits and nonlinear circuits. In the linear circuit case, $PF = cos(\alpha)$ where α indicates the phase angle between the voltage and current sinusoids.

Power Computations for Linear Circuits

The steady-state voltages and currents of a linear circuit that has sinusoidal AC sources are sinusoidal. Assume an element with the following voltage and current:

$$v(t) = V_m cos(\omega t + \theta)$$
$$i(t) = I_m cos(\omega t + \varphi) \tag{11.17}$$

Then the instantaneous power is

$$p(t) = v(t)i(t) = [V_m cos(\omega t + \theta)][I_m cos(\omega t + \varphi)] \tag{11.18}$$

According to basic trigonometric identities

$$(cos\,A)(cos\,B) = \frac{1}{2}[cos(A+B) + cos(A-B)] \tag{11.19}$$

So instantaneous power can be written as

$$p(t) = \left(\frac{V_m I_m}{2}\right)\left[\cos\left(2\omega t + \theta + \varphi\right) + \cos\left(\theta - \varphi\right)\right] \qquad (11.20)$$

The average power can be calculated easily:

$$p(t) = \frac{1}{T}\int_0^T p(t)\,dt = \left(\frac{V_m I_m}{2}\right)\int_0^T\left[\cos\left(2\omega t + \theta + \varphi\right) + \cos\left(\theta - \varphi\right)\right]dt$$

$$= \left(\frac{V_m I_m}{2}\right)\cos\left(\theta - \varphi\right)$$

$$= V_{rms}I_{rms}\cos\left(\theta - \varphi\right) \qquad (11.21)$$

So the power factor of the circuit is $\dfrac{V_{rms}I_{rms}\cos\left(\theta - \varphi\right)}{V_{rms}I_{rms}} = \cos\left(\theta - \varphi\right)$. The

average power (measured with units of Watts, W) is the part of the power that is consumed by the resistors in the circuit. In the steady state, no net power is absorbed by an inductor or a capacitor. The term *reactive power* (measured with units of Volt-Ampere Reactive, VAR) is commonly used in conjunction with voltages and currents for inductors and capacitors. Reactive power is characterized by energy storage during one-half of the cycle and energy retrieval during the other half. Reactive power (Q) is calculated as

$$Q = V_{rms}I_{rms}\sin\left(\theta - \varphi\right) \qquad (11.22)$$

By convention, inductors absorb positive reactive power, and capacitors absorb negative reactive power.

Complex power (measured with units of Volt-Ampere, VA) is defined as ($j = \sqrt{-1}$)

$$S = P + jQ \qquad (11.23)$$

Apparent power is the magnitude of complex power:

$$S = |S| = \sqrt{P^2 + Q^2} \tag{11.24}$$

Example 11.5

In the following circuit (Figure 11-15), $v_1(t) = 311 \sin(2 \times \pi \times 50 \times t)$, $L = 0.1\ H$, and $R = 40\ \Omega$. Determine the apparent power, average (active) power, reactive power, and power factor.

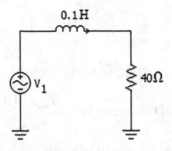

Figure 11-15. *Circuit of Example 11.5*

Solution:

$$Z = R + j \times L \times \omega = 40 + 31.415j$$

$$\varphi = \left(\frac{L\omega}{R}\right) = \left(\frac{31.415}{40}\right) = 38.14° = 0.666\ Rad$$

$$V = \frac{311}{\sqrt{2}} < 0° = 219.92 \angle 0°$$

$$I = \frac{V}{Z} = \frac{219.92e^{j0}}{40 + 31.42j} = 3.4 - 2.67j = 4.323e^{-0.666j}$$

$$S = |V \times I| = 950.824\ VA$$

$$P = V \times I \times \cos(\varphi) = 747.63\ W$$

$$Q = V \times I \times sin(\varphi) = 587.46 \, VAR$$

$$PF = cos(\varphi) = 0.786$$

Fourier Series

A periodic and non-sinusoidal signal $f(t)$ that satisfies certain conditions (Dirichlet conditions) can be written as the sum of sinusoids. The Fourier series of $f(t) = f(t + T)$ can be written as ($\omega_0 = \dfrac{2\pi}{T}$):

$$f(t) = a_0 + \sum_{n=1}^{\infty} \left[a_n cos(n\omega_0 t) + b_n sin(n\omega_0 t) \right] \qquad (11.25)$$

where a_0, a_n, and b_n are

$$a_0 = \frac{1}{T} \int_{-\frac{T}{2}}^{\frac{T}{2}} f(t) dt$$

$$a_n = \frac{2}{T} \int_{-\frac{T}{2}}^{\frac{T}{2}} f(t) cos(n\omega_0 t) dt$$

$$b_n = \frac{2}{T} \int_{-\frac{T}{2}}^{\frac{T}{2}} f(t) sin(n\omega_0 t) dt \qquad (11.26)$$

503

The $a_0 = \dfrac{1}{T} \displaystyle\int_{-\frac{T}{2}}^{\frac{T}{2}} f(t)\,dt$ is called the average value of $f(t)$. The preceding

equations can be written in the following forms as well (remember

that $a \times sin(\omega t) + b \times cos(\omega t) = \sqrt{a^2 + b^2}\, sin\left(\omega t + tan^{-1}\left(\dfrac{b}{a}\right)\right)$):

A)   Sum of sines

$$f(t) = a_0 + \sum_{n=1}^{\infty} C_n sin(n\omega_0 t + \theta_n)$$

$$C_n = \sqrt{a_n^2 + b_n^2} \text{ and } \theta_n = \left(\dfrac{a_n}{b_n}\right) \tag{11.27}$$

B)   Sum of cosines

$$f(t) = a_0 + \sum_{n=1}^{\infty} C_n cos(n\omega_0 t + \theta_n)$$

$$C_n = \sqrt{a_n^2 + b_n^2} \text{ and } \theta_n = \left(-\dfrac{b_n}{a_n}\right) \tag{11.28}$$

The following equation can be used to determine the RMS value of a
signal using its Fourier series coefficients:

$$F_{rms} = \sqrt{\sum_{n=0}^{\infty} F_{n,rms}^2} = \sqrt{a_0^2 + \sum_{n=1}^{\infty}\left(\dfrac{C_n}{\sqrt{2}}\right)^2} = \sqrt{a_0^2 + \sum_{n=1}^{\infty}\left(\dfrac{a_n^2 + b_n^2}{2}\right)} \tag{11.29}$$

Fourier Series of Important Wave Shapes

Fourier series of important wave shapes are shown in Figures 11-16 to 11-20.

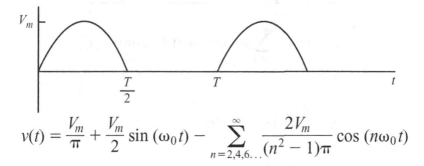

$$v(t) = \frac{V_m}{\pi} + \frac{V_m}{2} \sin(\omega_0 t) - \sum_{n=2,4,6...}^{\infty} \frac{2V_m}{(n^2 - 1)\pi} \cos(n\omega_0 t)$$

Figure 11-16. *Fourier series of a half-wave rectified waveform*

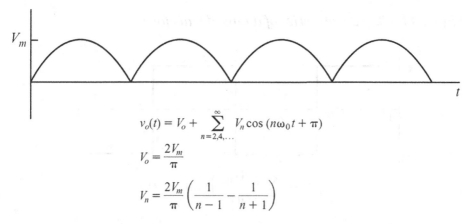

$$v_o(t) = V_o + \sum_{n=2,4,...}^{\infty} V_n \cos(n\omega_0 t + \pi)$$

$$V_o = \frac{2V_m}{\pi}$$

$$V_n = \frac{2V_m}{\pi}\left(\frac{1}{n-1} - \frac{1}{n+1}\right)$$

Figure 11-17. *Fourier series of a full-wave rectified waveform*

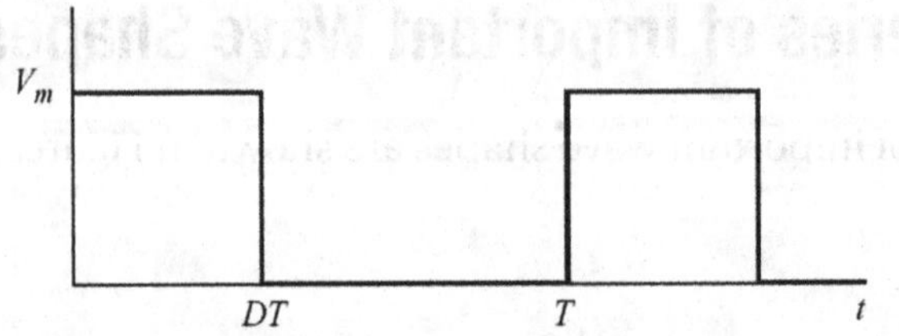

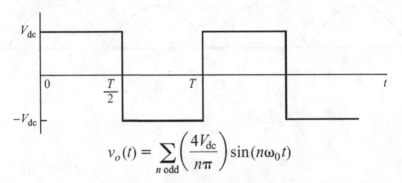

$$f(t) = a_0 + \sum_{n=1}^{\infty} [a_n \cos(n\omega_0 t) + b_n \sin(n\omega_0 t)]$$

$$a_0 = V_m D$$

$$a_n = \left(\frac{V_m}{n\pi}\right) \sin(n2\pi D)$$

$$b_n = \left(\frac{V_m}{n\pi}\right)[1 - \cos(n2\pi D)]$$

Figure 11-18. *Fourier series of a pulsed waveform*

$$v_o(t) = \sum_{n \text{ odd}} \left(\frac{4V_{dc}}{n\pi}\right) \sin(n\omega_0 t)$$

Figure 11-19. *Fourier series of a square wave*

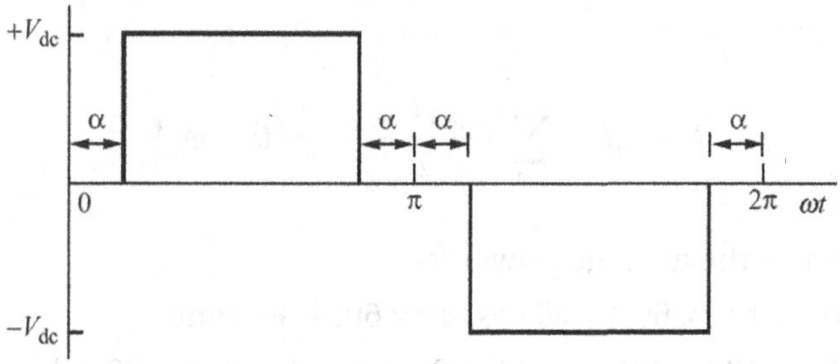

$$v_o(t) = \sum_{n\ odd} V_n \sin(n\omega_0 t)$$

$$V_n = \left(\frac{4V_{dc}}{n\pi}\right)\cos(n\alpha)$$

Figure 11-20. *Fourier series of a modified square wave*

Calculation of Average Power Using the Fourier Series

Assume that the Fourier series of voltage and current of an element is given as follows:

$$v(t) = V_0 + \sum_{n=1}^{\infty} V_n \cos(n\omega_0 t + \theta_n)$$

$$i(t) = I_0 + \sum_{n=1}^{\infty} I_n \cos(n\omega_0 t + \varphi_n) \qquad (11.30)$$

Then the average power(i.e., $\dfrac{1}{T}\displaystyle\int_0^T v(t)i(t)\,dt$) can be calculated as

$$P = \sum_{n=0}^{\infty} P_n = V_0 I_0 + \sum_{n=1}^{\infty} V_{n,rms} I_{n,rms} \cos(\theta_n - \varphi_n) \qquad (11.31)$$

507

or

$$P = V_0 I_0 + \sum_{n=1}^{\infty} \frac{V_{n,max} I_{n,max}}{2} cos\left(\theta_n - \varphi_n\right) \qquad (11.32)$$

For instance, the average power for
$v(t) = 10 + 20\ cos\ (2\pi \times 60t) + 30\ cos\ (4\pi \times 60t + 30°)$ and
$i(t) = 2 + 2.65\ cos\ (2\pi \times 60t - 48.5°) + 2.43\ cos\ (4\pi \times 60t - 36.2°)$ is 52.2 W.

Total Harmonic Distortion (THD)

THD quantifies the non-sinusoidal property of a waveform. THD is often applied in situations where the dc term is zero. Assume that the Fourier series of the signal is given ($f(t)$ can be either a voltage or current waveform):

$$f(t) = \sum_{n=1}^{\infty} \left[a_n cos\left(n\omega_0 t\right) + b_n sin\left(n\omega_0 t\right) \right] \qquad (11.33)$$

Then the THD of the signal is defined as

$$THD = \sqrt{\frac{F_{rms}^2 - F_{1,rms}^2}{F_{1,rms}^2}} \qquad (11.34)$$

where F_{rms} and $F_{1,rms}$ indicate the RMS value of signal $f(t)$ and RMS value of the fundamental harmonic of $f(t)$ (note that $F_{rms} = \sqrt{\sum_{n=1}^{\infty} \frac{\left(a_n^2 + b_n^2\right)}{2}}$

and $F_{1,rms} = \sqrt{\frac{\left(a_1^2 + b_1^2\right)}{2}}$). For instance, for a current waveform of $i(t) = 4 \sin(\omega_0 t) + 1.5 \sin(3\omega_0 t) + 0.64 \sin(5\omega_0 t)$, the THD is

$\sqrt{\dfrac{3.0545^2 - 2.829^2}{2.829^2}} = 0.408$. It is quite common to express the THD in

percentage, so the THD for the aforementioned current waveform is 40.8%.

Example 11.6

Determine the THD of

$v(t) = 311 \sin(2\pi \times 60t) + 100 \sin(2\pi \times 2 \times 60t) + 20 \sin(2\pi \times 3 \times 60t)$.

Solution

The RMS value of given waveforms is

$V_{rms} = \sqrt{\left(\dfrac{311}{\sqrt{2}}\right)^2 + \left(\dfrac{100}{\sqrt{2}}\right)^2 + \left(\dfrac{20}{\sqrt{2}}\right)^2} = 231.43\,V$. The peak value of the

fundamental harmonic is 311 V. So the RMS value of the fundamental

harmonic is $V_{1,rms} = \dfrac{311}{\sqrt{2}} = 219.91\,V$. Finally, the THD is

$$THD = \sqrt{\dfrac{V_{rms}^2 - V_{1,rms}^2}{V_{1,rms}^2}} = \sqrt{\dfrac{231.43^2 - 219.91^2}{219.91^2}} = 0.33 \text{ or } 33\%$$

Example 11.7

Determine the THD for the given voltage waveform:

$$v(t) = \begin{cases} -100 & -1ms < t < 0 \\ +100 & 0 < t < 1ms \end{cases}$$

Solution

The graph of one period of the given waveform is shown in
Figure 11-21.

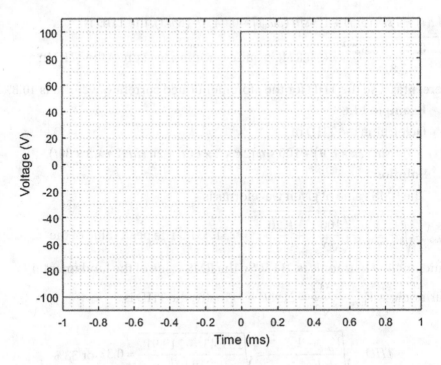

Figure 11-21. *Graph of given v(t)*

The Fourier series of $v(t)$ is

$$v(t) = \sum_{n=1,3,5}^{\infty} \frac{2 \times 200}{n\pi} sin(n\omega_0 t) \tag{11.35}$$

The RMS value of $v(t)$ is

$$V_{rms} = \sqrt{\frac{1}{T}\int_0^T v(t)^2\, dt} = \sqrt{\frac{1}{2m}\int_{-1m}^0 (-100)^2\, dt + \frac{1}{2m}\int_0^{1m} (100)^2\, dt} = 100\,V \tag{11.36}$$

The fundamental harmonic (first harmonic) of $v(t)$ has the peak value

of $V_1 = \dfrac{2 \times 200}{\pi} = 127.324\,V$. So the RMS value of the fundamental harmonic

is $V_{1,rms} = \dfrac{V_1}{\sqrt{2}} = \dfrac{127.324}{\sqrt{2}} = 90.0325\,V$. Finally, the THD is

$$THD = \sqrt{\frac{V_{rms}^{\,2} - V_{1,rms}^{\,2}}{V_{1,rms}^{\,2}}} = \sqrt{\frac{100^2 - 90.0325^2}{90.0325^2}} = 0.4834 \text{ or } 48.34\% \qquad (11.37)$$

Summary

This chapter reviewed some of the theoretical concepts that were used throughout the book. Concepts like instantaneous power, average power, RMS value of a signal, apparent power and power factor, Fourier series, and THD were reviewed with some numerical examples.

Correction to: Simulation of Power Electronics Circuits with MATLAB®/ Simulink®

Correction to:

Farzin Asadi, *Simulation of Power Electronics Circuits with MATLAB®/Simulink®*
https://doi.org/10.1007/978-1-4842-8220-5

This book was published without Series ID, Print ISSN number &
Electronic ISSN Number. This has now been updated in the book with the
Series ID - 17311, Print ISSN: 2948-2542 & Electronic ISSN: 2948-2550.

The updated version of this book can be found at
https://doi.org/10.1007/978-1-4842-8220-5

© Farzin Asadi 2023
F. Asadi, *Simulation of Power Electronics Circuits with MATLAB®/Simulink®*,
Maker Innovations Series, https://doi.org/10.1007/978-1-4842-8220-5_12

Exercises

Exercises for Chapters 1 and 2

1. A DC motor is a rotary machine that converts DC currents into mechanical energy. The electric equivalent circuit of the armature and free body diagram of the rotor is shown in Figure 1.

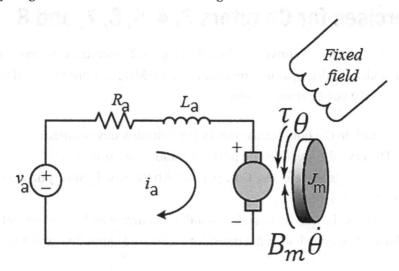

Figure 1. *Schematic representation of a DC motor system*

Using Newton's second law and Kirchhoff's Voltage Law (KVL)

$$\begin{cases} J_m \dfrac{d^2\theta(t)}{dt^2} = K_t i_a(t) - B_m \dfrac{d\theta(t)}{dt} \\ L_a \dfrac{di_a}{dt} = v_a(t) - R_a i_a(t) - K_b \dfrac{d\theta(t)}{dt} \end{cases} \tag{1}$$

© Farzin Asadi 2022
F. Asadi, *Simulation of Power Electronics Circuits with MATLAB®/Simulink®*,
Maker Innovations Series, https://doi.org/10.1007/978-1-4842-8220-5

where J_m, θ, τ, B_m, L_a, R_a, i_a, v_a, K_t, and K_b indicate moment of inertia, angle of motor's shaft, developed torque ($\tau = K_t i_a(t)$), friction coefficient, armature inductance, armature resistance, armature current, input voltage, torque constant, and back EMF constant, respectively. Draw the Simulink model of the DC motor and simulate it to see the armature current $i_a(t)$ and shaft position $\theta(t)$. Assume that

$$J_m = 0.000052 \ kg.m^2, B_m = 0.01 \ N.m.s, L_a = 0.23 \ H, R_a = 2 \ \Omega, \ K_t = 0.235 \frac{N.m}{A},$$

and $K_b = 0.235 \ V.s.$

Exercises for Chapters 3, 4, 5, 6, 7, and 8

1. Consider the boost converter shown in Figure 2. Forward voltage drop of the diode and drain-source resistance of the MOSFET are assumed to be 0.001 V and 0.001 Ω, respectively.

    a) Simulate the boost converter in the Simulink environment.

    b) Observe the steady-state portion of inductor current and capacitor voltage waveforms. Compare it with the steady-state portion of Figures 2-65 and 2-66.

    c) Observe the transient section of inductor current and capacitor voltage waveforms. Compare it with the transient section of Figures 2-65 and 2-66.

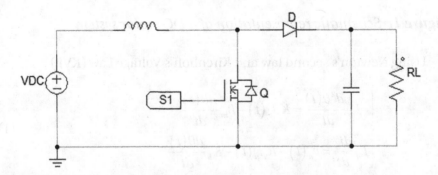

Figure 2. *Schematic of Exercise 1. VDC= 12 V, L=150 μH, and C= 68 μF. Switching frequency and duty cycle are 25 kHz and 0.6, respectively*

2. Simulate the boost converter shown in Figure 2 and measure the output power and efficiency of the converter. Forward voltage drop of the diode and drain-source resistance of the MOSFET are assumed to be 0.8 V and 0.01 Ω, respectively.

3. a) Simulate the boost converter shown in Figure 2 with the aid of the Boost Converter block shown in Figure 3. Use Simulink Help to learn the details of the Boost Converter block.

b) Simulate the Buck converter of Example 1 in Chapter 5 with the aid of the Buck Converter block shown in Figure 3. Use Simulink Help to learn the details of the Buck Converter block.

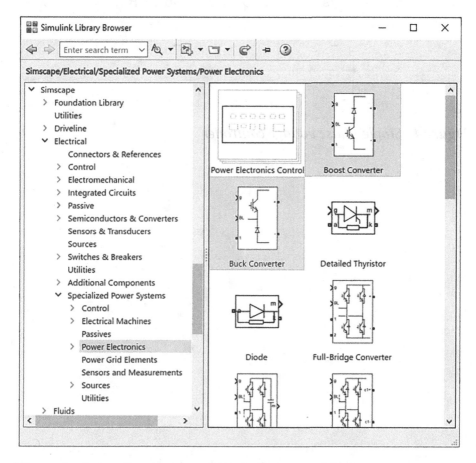

Figure 3. *Boost Converter and Buck Converter blocks*

4. A single-phase voltage controller is shown in Figure 4. SCR S1 is triggered at $2k\pi + \alpha$, and SCR S2 is triggered at $(2k + 1)\pi + \alpha$ angles (k= 0, 1, 2, ...). The load voltage and current waveforms are shown in Figure 5. Use Simulink to simulate the circuit for $\alpha = 30°$, $60°$, and $90°$.

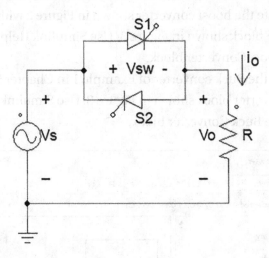

Figure 4. *Single-phase voltage controller*

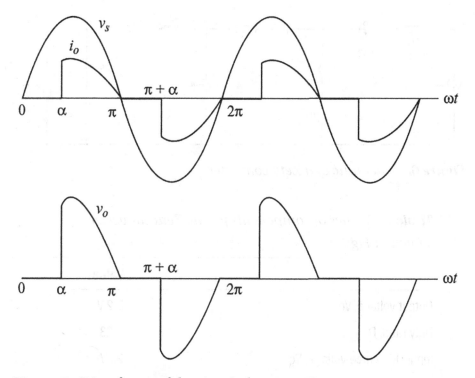

Figure 5. *Waveforms of the circuit shown in Figure 4*

5. Connect a three-phase squirrel-cage AC motor to the output of a three-phase inverter and study the effect of the frequency of output voltage on the motor speed.

Exercises for Chapters 9 and 10

1. Calculate the input/output impedance of a Buck converter with R= 5 Ω, Vin=50 V, rin=0.1 Ω, L=400 μH, rL=0.1 Ω, C=100 μF, rC=0.05 Ω, D=0.41, rds=0.1 Ω, rD=0.1 Ω, and VD=0.7 V (see Figures 8-5 and 8-6).

2. Schematic of a Zeta converter is shown in Figure 6. Values of the components are given in Table 1. The converter operates in CCM for values given in Table 1.

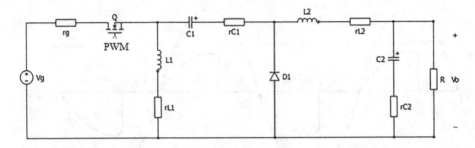

Figure 6. Schematic of a Zeta converter

Table 1. Values of components for the Zeta converter shown in Figure 6

	Value
Output voltage, Vo	5.2 V
Duty ratio, D	0.23
Input DC source voltage, Vg	20 V
Input DC source internal resistance, rg	0.0 Ω
MOSFET drain-source resistance, rds	10 mΩ
Capacitor, C1	100 µF
Capacitor Equivalent Series Resistance (ESR), rC1	0.19 Ω
Capacitor, C2	220 µF
Capacitor Equivalent Series Resistance (ESR), rC2	0.095 Ω
Inductor, L1	100 µH
Inductor ESR, rL1	1 mΩ
Inductor, L2	55 µH
Inductor ESR, rL2	0.55 mΩ
	(continued)

Table 1. (*continued*)

	Value
Diode voltage drop, vD	0.7 V
Diode forward resistance, rD	10 mΩ
Load resistor, R	6 Ω
Switching frequency, Fsw	100 kHz

The Zeta converter is composed of two switches: a MOSFET switch and a diode. The MOSFET is closed for $D.T$ seconds. D and T indicate duty cycle and switching period, respectively. When the MOSFET is closed, the diode is opened. The equivalent circuit of this case is shown in Figure 7.

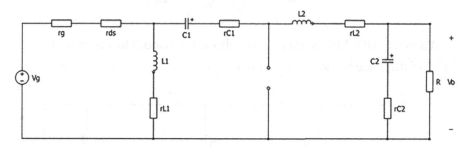

Figure 7. *Equivalent circuit of the Zeta converter for a closed MOSFET*

The differential equations of Figure 7 can be written as

$$
\begin{cases}
L_1 \dfrac{di_{L_1}}{dt} = -\left(r_{L_1} + r_g + r_{ds}\right)i_{L_1} - \left(r_g + r_{ds}\right)i_{L_2} + v_g \\[2mm]
L_2 \dfrac{di_{L_2}}{dt} = -\left(r_g + r_{ds}\right)i_{L_1} - \left(r_g + r_{ds} + r_{C_1} + r_{L_2} + \dfrac{R \times r_{C_2}}{R + r_{C_2}}\right)i_{L_2} + v_{C_1} - \dfrac{R}{R + r_{C_2}}v_{C_2} + v_g \\[2mm]
C_1 \dfrac{dv_{C_1}}{dt} = -i_{L_2} \\[2mm]
C_2 \dfrac{dv_{C_2}}{dt} = \dfrac{R}{R + r_{C_2}}i_{L_2} - \dfrac{1}{R + r_{C_2}}v_{C_2}
\end{cases}
$$

$$
v_o = r_{C_2} C_2 \frac{dv_{C_2}}{dt} + v_{C_2} = \frac{R \times r_{C_2}}{R + r_{C_2}}i_{L_2} + \frac{R}{R + r_{C_2}}v_{C_2} \tag{2}
$$

When the MOSFET is opened, the diode is closed. The equivalent circuit of this case is shown in Figure 8.

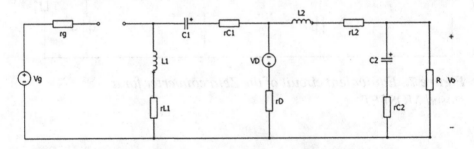

Figure 8. *Equivalent circuit of the Zeta converter for an open MOSFET*

The differential equations of Figure 8 can be written as

$$
\begin{cases}
L_1 \dfrac{di_{L_1}}{dt} = -\left(r_{L_1} + r_{C_1} + r_D\right)i_{L_1} - r_D i_{L_2} - v_{C_1} - v_D \\[2ex]
L_2 \dfrac{di_{L_2}}{dt} = -r_D i_{L_1} - \left(r_D + r_{L_2} + \dfrac{R \times r_{C_2}}{R + r_{C_2}}\right)i_{L_2} - \dfrac{R}{R + r_{C_2}}v_{C_2} - v_D \\[2ex]
C_1 \dfrac{dv_{C_1}}{dt} = i_{L_1} \\[2ex]
C_2 \dfrac{dv_{C_2}}{dt} = \dfrac{R}{R + r_{C_2}}i_{L_2} - \dfrac{1}{R + r_{C_2}}v_{C_2}
\end{cases}
$$

$$
v_o = r_{C_2} C_2 \dfrac{dv_{C_2}}{dt} + v_{C_2} = \dfrac{R \times r_{C_2}}{R + r_{C_2}}i_{L_2} + \dfrac{R}{R + r_{C_2}}v_{C_2} \tag{3}
$$

Use MATLAB to calculate the $\dfrac{\tilde{v}_o(s)}{\tilde{d}(s)}$ and $\dfrac{\tilde{v}_o(s)}{\tilde{v}_{in}(s)}$ transfer functions.

3. Use MATLAB to calculate the input/output impedance of the Zeta converter of Exercise 2. Required differential equations are given in the following.

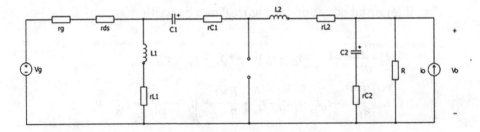

Figure 9. *Equivalent circuit of the Zeta converter for a closed MOSFET*

The differential equations of Figure 9 are

$$
\begin{cases}
L_1 \dfrac{di_{L_1}}{dt} = -\left(r_{L_1} + r_g + r_{ds}\right)i_{L_1} - \left(r_g + r_{ds}\right)i_{L_2} + v_g \\[2mm]
L_2 \dfrac{di_{L_2}}{dt} = -\left(r_g + r_{ds}\right)i_{L_1} - \left(r_g + r_{ds} + r_{C_1} + r_{L_2} + \dfrac{R \times r_{C_2}}{R + r_{C_2}}\right)i_{L_2} \\[2mm]
\qquad\qquad + v_{C_1} - \dfrac{R}{R + r_{C_2}}v_{C_2} - \dfrac{R \times r_{C_2}}{R + r_{C_2}}i_o + v_g \\[2mm]
C_1 \dfrac{dv_{C_1}}{dt} = -i_{L_2} \\[2mm]
C_2 \dfrac{dv_{C_2}}{dt} = \dfrac{R}{R + r_{C_2}}i_{L_2} - \dfrac{1}{R + r_{C_2}}v_{C_2} + \dfrac{R}{R + r_{C_2}}i_o
\end{cases}
$$

$$
v_o = r_{C_2} C_2 \dfrac{dv_{C_2}}{dt} + v_{C_2} = \dfrac{R \times r_{C_2}}{R + r_{C_2}}i_{L_2} + \dfrac{R}{R + r_{C_2}}v_{C_2} + \dfrac{R \times r_{C_2}}{R + r_{C_2}}i_o \tag{4}
$$

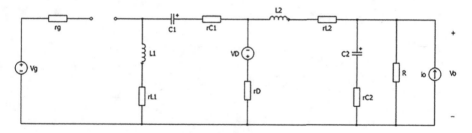

Figure 10. *Equivalent circuit of the Zeta converter for an open MOSFET*

The differential equations of Figure 10 are

$$
\begin{cases}
L_1 \dfrac{di_{L_1}}{dt} = -\left(r_{L_1} + r_{C_1} + r_D\right)i_{L_1} - r_D i_{L_2} - v_{C_1} - v_D \\[2ex]
L_2 \dfrac{di_{L_2}}{dt} = -r_D i_{L_1} - \left(r_D + r_{L_2} + \dfrac{R \times r_{C_2}}{R + r_{C_2}}\right)i_{L_2} - \dfrac{R}{R + r_{C_2}}v_{C_2} - \dfrac{R \times r_{C_2}}{R + r_{C_2}}i_o - v_D \\[2ex]
C_1 \dfrac{dv_{C_1}}{dt} = i_{L_1} \\[2ex]
C_2 \dfrac{dv_{C_2}}{dt} = \dfrac{R}{R + r_{C_2}}i_{L_2} - \dfrac{1}{R + r_{C_2}}v_{C_2} + \dfrac{R}{R + r_{C_2}}i_o
\end{cases}
$$

$$
v_o = r_{C_2} C_2 \frac{dv_{C_2}}{dt} + v_{C_2} = \frac{R \times r_{C_2}}{R + r_{C_2}}i_{L_2} + \frac{R}{R + r_{C_2}}v_{C_2} + \frac{R \times r_{C_2}}{R + r_{C_2}}i_o \tag{5}
$$

Index

Printed in the United States
by Baker & Taylor Publisher Services